Family Circle

Favorite

Recipes

COOKBOOK

BY THE EDITORS OF FAMILY CIRCLE
EDITED BY RALPH GENOVESE

All Recipes Tested in Family Circle's Test Kitchens

Published by
Paramount Publishing, Inc.

Published by Paramount Publishing, Inc., Suite 413, Building B
800 Roosevelt Road, Glen Ellyn, Illinois 60137
Copyright © 1977 by The Family Circle, Inc.
No part of this book may be reproduced, for any
reason, by any means, including any method of
photographic reproduction, without the written permission of the
publisher.

Printed in the U.S.A.

Library of Congress Catalog Card Number: 77-14713

ISBN: 0-918668-03-4

Twenty Fourth Printing—July 1984
    All correspondence and inquiries should be directed to:
            Paramount Publishing, Inc.
            Suite 413, Building B
            800 Roosevelt Road
            Glen Ellyn, Illinois 60137

CONTENTS

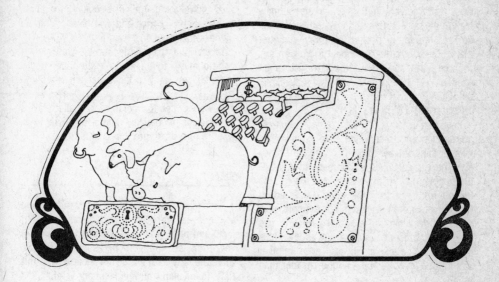

1

DOLLAR-SAVING
MEAT DISHES

There are no two ways about it—Americans love meat. So much so that most of us include this basic food in at least one meal a day. However, cost fluctuations and shortages can sometimes daunt the staunchest meat fan. But there's no real reason to be discouraged when you realize that with planning and some knowledge of the meat department in your supermarket, you can trim the fat off your meat bill and still satisfy family appetites. For example, there are ways, as outlined on pages 4 and 5, to turn one roast into three separate, freshly-cooked meals. There are other ways to stretch a tiny bit of meat a long way, as demonstrated in our casserole, pasta and soup chapters. Further, on the next 17 pages you'll find a good selection of recipes and ideas for using budget cuts of meat in ways that will please the most discerning palate.

• Use every bit of meat you buy. Melt down fat trimmings for drippings, and simmer bones and lean cuttings for soup stock or gravy. Time-saver tip: Shop for a week's supply of meat at once, trim it all before storing, then take care of the trimmings in one swoop.

• In general, it isn't thrifty to buy on sales to stock your freezer. Why? Supermarkets routinely feature the same cuts, and there's no need to tie up meat money in freezer inventory. A better plan: Buy extra cuts that appeal to you on any shopping trip and freeze them to use when needed. Veal, for example, isn't always available, but when it is, that's the time to buy enough for several meals and freeze it.

• Buy meat in terms of meals; leftovers that are not enough for a second meal are expensive.

• Meat sales are one of the first steps to economy. The United States Department of Agriculture reports that the more expensive the cut, the less often it is featured. But when it does go on sale, the price drop is greater. For example, porterhouse steak may be advertised once in five weeks, but the price is then cut about 30¢ a pound. As a weekend special, even popular ground beef may be 10¢ a pound cheaper than usual.

• Always buy well-trimmed meat with an even fat covering and lean flecked with fat—that's all you need for flavor. Remember that a roast at $1.29 a pound costs 8¢ an ounce, and any excess fat you trim away costs the same amount.

• Save on meat by buying larger cuts and slicing your own steaks and chops. For example, one large loin of pork will give you enough meat for a pork roast, pork chops and barbecued backbones

• But don't become your own butcher unless you have to. Check the price of the cut-up meat. Sometimes it's the same price per pound as the big piece you would have to cut up yourself.

• Remember that grades in meat indicate appearance only. The highest grade "U.S. Prime" (sold mainly to restaurants) has no more food value than the lowest grade, "Standard." "Choice," the second grade, is the grade available in most supermarkets. Choose the grade that offers you the best price.

• Chill canned meats such as chopped ham, beef, pork luncheon meat or corned beef before you slice them. They'll cut more neatly and in thinner, more uniform slices, giving you more servings for your money.

• If shopping for one meal, never buy more meat than you need. When you repeatedly throw away little bits of leftovers, you are throwing away real money. Approximately 63¢ goes into the garbage when you discard 1 cup (5 ounces) of leftover beef roast that cost 99¢ a pound as purchased. Such meat could be slivered and reheated with crisp-cooked mixed vegetables. Serve on rice and you have a Chinese dinner—for about $1.

• Invest in a sharp little boning knife and a good-quality carving knife. Keep them razor-sharp. If you want to cut a bargain roast into steaks, you're all set.

• Buy a wooden (or metal) meat mallet. This is the original "tenderizer," and a must when you want to turn slices into thin cutlets.

BEEF

• Generally, beef is in the greatest supply and at the lowest prices from mid-winter to spring; lamb and pork, from mid-winter to late spring; veal from late spring to mid-summer. It may, therefore, pay to stock up on meat during this time (particularly during February, March and April).

• Watch for savings on large packages of ground beef. Those weighing more than five pounds often cost 3¢ to 5¢ a pound less than smaller sizes. If you have a freezer, make up several meat loaves and freeze part. Or shape a supply of patties and freeze for sandwiches.

• Don't get hung up on ground beef. Ground lamb or veal patties are usually priced about the same as ground beef and give menus a new lift.

• For steak on a budget, choose chuck, bottom round or shoulder steak. Marinate or tenderize the meat first, then broil or grill to medium-rare for maximum tenderness.

• Chuck roast on sale? Buy a thick one; then, at home, cut it into pieces for a Swiss-steak dinner. Savings will be 20¢ to 30¢ a pound over the store-cut meat tagged SWISS STEAK.

• When porterhouse and T-bone steaks are the same price, pick porterhouse—it has a larger tenderloin.

• Flank steak, sometimes marked LONDON BROIL, is usually not an economical cut. One reason is supply;

there are only two on each animal. For your money, the tender broiling steaks—porterhouse, T-bone, sirloin or top round—offer more enjoyable eating.

• Which is thriftier—a thick family-size steak or thinner individual steaks for each serving? Surprising as it may seem, the family-size one. For example, a three-pound boneless sirloin cut 1¼ inches thick will make six servings. You'll need at least five pounds of T-bone steaks to serve six. At $1.59 a pound, the sirloin costs $4.77; at $1.49 a pound, the T-bones cost $7.45. The difference: $2.68.

• Attractively priced alternates for a rib roast: Sirloin tip or rump roast. Prime or choice grades may be oven-roasted and have little waste.

• The smaller muscle of a blade-bone chuck steak can be broiled if you use tenderizer on it. Cook to desired doneness and top with buttery crumbs that have been tossed with grated lemon and orange rind. The larger muscle can be pot-roasted in a sauce flavored with leftover wine or beer. Both meals serve 4 if you start with a 3-pound steak.

• A small eye of round roast goes a long way if you make it into sukiyaki. Freeze the meat until barely firm, then cut into paper-thin slices and pound with a meat mallet. Stir-fry slices in a bit of oil; add fresh spinach, slivered celery and onions, and soy-flavored beef broth. Cook briefly. Serve with rice.

• You can feed all the party guests lavishly with teriyaki hors d'oeuvres made from one 1½- to 2-pound flank steak. It's solid meat, but needs to be tenderized by scoring with a knife on both sides. Freeze until just firm, then cut on the diagonal into very thin slices. Thread accordion-fashion on a skewer; marinate in a pungent baste; broil; serve hot.

• If beef shank is really a bargain, buy it to cube for stew or braise whole for individual roasts.

• Nutritionally, liver packs a wallop. Slice thin, and broil to rare. Or, put through the food chopper and add to meat loaf. The price is right.

• Ever try beef heart? The flavor is excellent. Cut out the fat, veins and arteries; wash thoroughly. Cut into strips. Braise with onions and herbs until fork tender.

• Rediscover canned corned beef, beef stew, chopped beef, meat in barbecue sauce. For a couple, or a small family, the cost per serving is sometimes cheaper than starting from scratch, because there is no waste.

• Beef-shank crosscuts, at least 1½ inches thick, make perfect individual pot roasts at penny-pinching prices.

• Most meat counters carry ready-cubed beef for stewing. But because store labor and meat trimmings cost money, you'll rate a double dividend if you buy beef chuck and cut it up yourself, then simmer the bone and trimmings for broth for soup.

• All kidneys—beef, pork, lamb and veal—are good buys, with no waste. Prices remain fairly steady, and because all kinds work equally well in recipes, you can depend on what's available.

VEAL AND LAMB

• Veal and lamb for stewing often cost less than the same cut of beef, and if your market is having a sale, you'll find these stew meats a delectable way to stretch your budget.

• For keeping your budget and yourself fit, lamb breast really measures up.

PORK & HAM

• When you want fresh pork, compare the price of pork shoulder with a leg cut (fresh ham). The shoulder may cost so much less that you can add on an extra pound or two of meat for the same total price.

• Fresh pork hocks are a bargain when your budget's in a squeeze, even though it takes a pound for each serving.

• Consider all ham prices and buy what fits your purse and purpose. Whole or half smoked hams are usually the same price per pound. And though a butt portion may be a few cents higher per pound than a shank end, it's a better choice because you get more meat. Center steaks are the most expensive.

• Count on pork sausage for dinner as well as for breakfast—it makes an easy hearty meal. Your best buy: Bulk sausage. Because of fixing time and labor, patties are priced about 10¢ higher; links, about 20¢ higher.

• Fancy-quality bacon may not be your most frugal buy. Use the regular sliced kinds for showy platters, but for sandwiches or recipe ingredients, ends and pieces, cuts or slab bacon net big flavor at substantial savings.

HOW TO GET THREE MEALS FROM A PORK LOIN ROAST

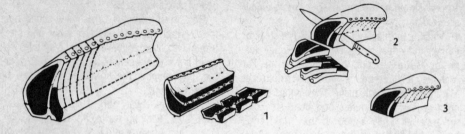

Start by selecting a good-size rib cut of pork loin. (1) Have the butcher saw through the ribs, high enough to leave an inch-thick layer of meat on the backbones. Have him chop the backbones into serving-size pieces. Cook as you would spareribs. (2) Cut chops for another meal from the remaining roast by slicing between the ribs. (3) Cook the remaining piece of meat as a pork roast for your third fresh-cooked dinner.

HOW TO MAKE FOUR MEALS FROM HALF A HAM

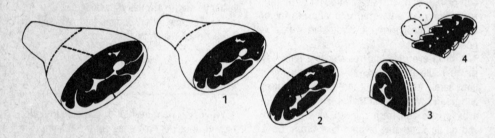

Choose a full-cut shank half of ham. (1) Have the butcher saw off a generous end for making a "boiled" dinner with carrots, onions, potatoes and cabbage. (2) Divide the center part of the ham into two portions. Bake the piece with the bone. (3) Cut the large end of the boneless piece into thick slices for frying or broiling. (4) Cut the smaller end into thin slices for use in making a dish of scalloped ham and potatoes.

HOW TO MAKE THREE MEALS FROM ONE PORK BUTT

For three economy meals, buy a five- to seven-pound fresh pork shoulder. (1) Cut as shown to divide into two pieces. Use the piece with the bone for a one-meal roast. (2) Cut steaks from the large end of the boneless piece, about a half-inch thick. Braise the steaks as you would pork chops. (3) Cut the small end of the boneless piece into half-inch cubes. Use the diced pork for chop suey or a casserole of corn and pork.

HOW TO MAKE TWO MEALS FROM A RIB ROAST

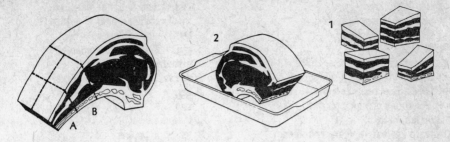

While not an economy cut in itself, beef rib roast can be budget-minded if you plan two meals from one roast. Have your butcher saw through the bones at A and B. (1) Then cut between the ribs to make individual servings of short ribs. (2) Now, for your roast, you have the tenderest "heart" of the piece you bought. To get more servings—and to make it juicier—keep oven heat at 325° to cut shrinkage to a minimum.

HOW TO GET THREE MEALS FROM ONE POT ROAST

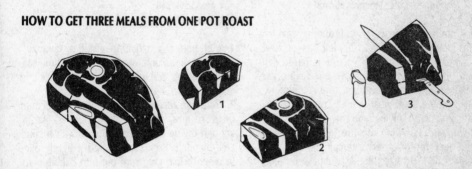

With a simple bit of cutting in your kichen, you can get three meals from a thick round-bone pot roast like the one above. (1) From the round end of the roast, cut a piece to use in a beef-and-vegetable stew. Cut this boneless piece into cubes. (2) Then from the center, cut a thick piece for a chunky pot roast. (3) With a sharp knife and a saucer under your hand for safety, split the remaining piece for two Swiss steaks.

HOW TO GET THREE MEALS FROM ONE LEG OF LAMB

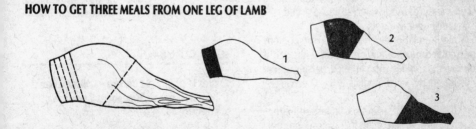

Buy a full-cut leg of lamb. Ask your butcher to cut off a few lamb steaks and to cut through the shank, leaving about a pound of meat on the bone. (1) Broil the lamb steaks as you would loin chops. (2) Use the easy-to-carve center portion of the leg for a roast. (3) Later, cut the meat from the shank into cubes for another freshly cooked meal. Use these tender, boneless pieces in an Irish stew, lamb curry or shish kebab.

5

BURGUNDY BEEF LOAF

1 cup Burgundy
¼ cup finely chopped celery
1 clove garlic
1 bay leaf
2½ pounds ground round or chuck
2½ cups soft bread crumbs (5 slices)
1 large onion, finely chopped (1 cup)
1 tablespoon chopped parsley
2 teaspoons salt
¼ teaspoon leaf rosemary, crumbled
¼ teaspoon leaf thyme, crumbled
¼ teaspoon pepper
2 eggs
1 can condensed beef broth
1 teaspoon Worcestershire sauce
¼ cup water
Burgundy Sauce (recipe follows)

1. Combine wine, celery, garlic and bay leaf in a small saucepan; bring to boiling; lower heat; simmer, uncovered, until volume is reduced to half, about 10 minutes. Remove and discard garlic and bay leaf; cool wine mixture completely.
2. Combine beef, bread crumbs, onion, parsley, salt, rosemary, thyme and pepper in a large bowl; add the wine mixture, eggs, ½ cup of the beef broth (reserve remaining broth for sauce) and Worcestershire. Mix until well-blended. Shape into an oval loaf on a lightly oiled shallow baking pan.
3. Bake in moderate oven (350°) 1 hour and 10 minutes, until loaf is a rich brown. Remove with 2 wide spatulas to a heated serving platter; keep warm. Add reserved broth and ¼ cup water to drippings in the pan; bring to boiling, stirring constantly to loosen browned bits. Strain into a 1-cup measure. (Add water, to make 1 cup.)
4. Make Burgundy Sauce.
5. Arrange small buttered whole carrots, onions and sautéed mushrooms on platter with loaf, if you wish; sprinkle with chopped parsley. Serve with Burgundy Sauce. Makes 8 to 10 servings.

BURGUNDY SAUCE—Sauté 1 tablespoon chopped shallots or green onion in 2 tablespoons butter or margarine in a medium-size saucepan about 5 minutes; stir in 3 tablespoons flour; gradually add the reserved broth and ½ cup Burgundy. Cook, stirring constantly, until sauce thickens and bubbles 3 minutes. Stir in 1 teaspoon chopped parsley. Makes about 1½ cups.

VEGETABLE-BEEF LOAF

2 tablespoons butter or margarine
1 small zucchini squash, shredded (1 cup)
1 small onion, chopped (¼ cup)
1 can (1 pound) Italian tomatoes
2 pounds meat-loaf mixture
1 cup soft bread crumbs (2 slices)
2 eggs
½ cup milk
2 teaspoons salt
¼ teaspoon pepper
¼ teaspoon leaf marjoram, crumbled
¼ teaspoon leaf thyme, crumbled
Sauce:
2 tablespoons chopped onion
1 envelope or teaspoon instant beef broth
½ cup boiling water
¼ teaspoon salt
⅛ teaspoon pepper

1. Melt butter or margarine in skillet; sauté zucchini and onion until tender. Chop 2 of the canned tomatoes; add to zucchini mixture. Cool the entire mixture slightly.
2. Combine zucchini mixture, meat-loaf mixture, bread crumbs, eggs, milk, salt, pepper, marjoram and thyme in a large mixing bowl. Mix until well-blended. Pack mixture into a lightly oiled 9x5x3-inch loaf pan; turn out into baking pan.
3. Bake in moderate oven (350°) 1 hour and 10 minutes. Remove to serving platter; keep warm.
4. Make sauce: Sauté onion in pan drippings in baking pan. Dissolve beef broth in boiling water. Chop remaining tomatoes; add with beef broth to onion. Cook, stirring constantly, until sauce thickens, about 3 minutes. Add salt and pepper. Spoon over meat loaf. Garnish with sliced, stuffed olives, if you wish. Makes 8 servings.

CHOUCROUTE GARNI

2 cans (1 pound, 11 ounces each) sauerkraut
6 ham hocks, weighing about 3 pounds
2 cups dry white wine
1 bay leaf
6 whole cloves
1 medium-size onion, peeled
1½ pounds knockwurst
1 red apple, quartered, cored and sliced
12 new potatoes (about 1¼ pounds)

1. Soak sauerkraut 5 minutes in cold water in a large bowl; drain well.
2. Place ham hocks in a Dutch oven or a large heat-proof casserole. Add drained sauerkraut, wine and bay leaf. Press cloves into onion; press onion down into sauerkraut. Heat to boiling; reduce heat; cover. Simmer very slowly 1½ hours, tossing with a fork once or twice, or until ham hocks are almost tender.
3. Score knockwurst with a sharp knife; place on sauerkraut; simmer 20 minutes longer. Add apple slices, pushing them down into sauerkraut; cook 10 minutes longer.
4. Scrub potatoes well; cook in boiling salted water to cover in a medium-size saucepan 20 minutes, or until done.
5. Arrange choucroute with potatoes on a large deep platter. Serve with wholewheat bread and individual servings of mustard, if you wish. Makes 6 servings.

BEER-BRAISED LOIN OF PORK

    1 pork loin roast, about 5 pounds
    3 large onions, chopped (3 cups)
    1 pound carrots, peeled and diced
    1 bottle or can (12 ounces) dark beer
    2 teaspoons salt
    ¼ teapsoon pepper
    1 bay leaf
    5 whole cloves

1. Brown pork loin well on all sides in a kettle or Dutch oven; remove from pan. (Or brown in a large heavy roasting pan on surface burners.)
2. Sauté onions and carrots until soft in pork drippings. Stir in beer, salt, pepper, bay leaf and whole cloves. Return pork to kettle and cover. (If using roasting pan, cover tightly with aluminum foil.)
3. Braise in moderate oven (350°) 2 hours, or until pork is tender when pierced with a two-tined fork. Place pork on platter and keep warm.
4. Pour cooking liquid from kettle into a large bowl. Skim off fat; remove bay leaf. Place liquid and solids in container of electric blender and whirl at low speed until smooth (or press through sieve). Pour sauce into saucepan. Heat to boiling, stirring often. Stir in a little gravy coloring, if you wish. Generously spoon the sauce over the pork after it has been sliced. Makes 8 servings.

DOUBLE PEPPER BEEF

    2 medium-size green peppers, halved, seeded and thinly sliced
    2 medium-size sweet red peppers, halved, seeded and thinly sliced
    2 tablespoons olive oil or vegetable oil
    1 chuck steak fillet (about 1½ pounds)
    1 cup water
    1 teaspoon Italian seasoning, crumbled
    1 teaspoon salt
    ¼ teaspoon pepper

1. Sauté peppers in oil until soft in large skillet; remove to hot platter; keep warm.
2. Cook steak in oil remaining in skillet, turning once, 5 minutes on each side or until steak is as done as you like it. Slice steak and arrange with peppers on hot platter.
3. Stir water, Italian seasoning, salt and pepper into skillet. Cook, stirring constantly, scraping to loosen cooked-on juices in skillet. Boil 3 minutes to reduce volume by one-third. Pour over sliced beef and peppers. Serve with hot cooked rice, if you wish. Makes 6 servings.

SUKIYAKI

    1 chuck steak fillet (about 1½ pounds)
    ¼ cup vegetable oil
    2 medium-size sweet potatoes, pared and thinly sliced
    ½ pound green beans, tipped and cut in 1-inch pieces
    1 small green pepper, halved, seeded and cut into thin strips
    1 small sweet red pepper, halved, seeded and cut into thin strips
    1 cup thinly sliced celery
    ½ cup soy sauce
    1 cup water
    1 small head Chinese cabbage, shredded
    1 bunch green onions, trimmed and cut into 2-inch pieces
    4 large mushrooms, trimmed and sliced

1. Trim all fat from steak; cut meat into very thin strips. (For easier cutting of raw beef, partially freeze steak 1 hour to firm meat.)
2. Heat oil in a large skillet with a cover. Add steak strips and sauté, stirring occasionally, 2 to 3 minutes, or until brown; remove with a slotted

spoon and keep strips warm. Reserve for Step 5.

3. Add potatoes, green beans, green and red pepper, and celery; sauté 2 to 3 minutes, or until vegetables start to soften.

4. Combine soy sauce and water in a cup; pour over vegetables; cover. Simmer 5 minutes. Stir in shredded cabbage, green onions and mushrooms; cover. Cook 5 minutes longer, or until cabbage wilts and vegetables are crisply tender.

5. Return cooked steak strips to pan and heat until piping-hot. Serve with hot cooked rice and more soy sauce, if you wish. Makes 6 servings.

KÖNIGSBERG MEATBALLS

- 4 slices bread
- ½ cup milk
- 2 pounds meat-loaf mixture
- 1 can (2 ounces) anchovy fillets, drained and chopped
- 3 eggs
- 1 small onion, grated
- 2 tablespoons grated lemon rind
- 1 teaspoon salt
- ¼ teaspoon pepper
- 2 envelopes instant beef broth or 1 teaspoon granulated beef bouillon
- 4 cups water
- ¼ cup (½ stick) butter or margarine
- ¼ cup flour
- 1 teaspoon sugar
- ½ cup dry white wine
- 2 tablespoons well-drained capers
- 1 tablespoon lemon juice

1. Place bread slices in single layer in a shallow dish; pour milk over; let stand until absorbed (about 10 minutes); break apart with fork into small pieces.

2. Combine meat-loaf mixture, half the anchovies, eggs, onion, lemon rind, salt, pepper and bread in a large bowl, mixing lightly. Shape into 32 balls.

3. Combine beef broth and water in a large skillet; heat to boiling; add meatballs, lowering into boiling broth with a slotted spoon. Simmer, uncovered, 15 minutes, or until no longer pink in center (break one open to test). Remove with slotted spoon to a deep platter. Reserve cooking liquid.

4. Make sauce: Melt butter or margarine in a medium-size saucepan; stir in flour and sugar;

cook until bubbly, stirring constantly. Gradually add wine and 2 cups of the cooking liquid, continuing to stir until mixture is thickened and bubbles 1 minute. Stir in capers, lemon juice and remaining half of anchovies, stirring until anchovies are blended into sauce. Spoon over meatballs. Serve with a side portion of sauerkraut and mashed or boiled potatoes, if you wish. Makes 8 servings.

PARSLIED STEAKS

- 6 frozen chopped beef steaks (from a 2-pound package)
- 4 tablespoons butter or margarine
- 4 green onions, trimmed and chopped
- ½ cup chopped parsley
- ½ teaspoon salt
- ½ teaspoon leaf marjoram, crumbled
- ¼ teaspoon cracked or coarse grind pepper

1. Sauté steaks on both sides, following label directions, in butter or margarine in a large skillet; remove to hot platter, overlapping steaks; keep warm while making sauce.

2. Sauté green onions in drippings in skillet until soft; stir in parsley, salt, marjoram and pepper; heat just until bubbling. Pour down center of steaks. Frame with broccoli spears and pan-browned or mashed potatoes, if you wish. Makes 6 servings.

DEVILED CHUCK BROIL

- 1 bone-in chuck steak (about 2 pounds)
- ⅔ cup wine vinegar
- 2 tablespoons vegetable oil
- 1 small onion, chopped (¼ cup)
- 2 tablespoons prepared mustard
- ½ teaspoon cracked or coarse grind pepper
- 2 cups soft white bread crumbs (4 slices)
- 2 tablespoons melted butter or margarine

1. Trim any excess fat from steak and score remaining fat edge every inch. (Reserve a few pieces of fat.) Place steak in a shallow dish.

2. Mix vinegar, oil, onion, mustard and pepper in a bowl; pour over steak. Marinate in refrigerator, turning once, at least 2 hours.

3. Remove steak from marinade and pat dry

with paper toweling.

4. Rub broiler rack with a few fat trimmings to prevent sticking. Broil steak 4 inches from heat, 5 minutes; turn steak; broil 5 minutes longer, or until it is as done as you like it.

5. While steak broils, toss bread crumbs with melted butter or margarine in a small bowl.

6. Remove broiler pan from heat; top steak evenly with prepared crumbs. Return steak to broiler and broil 2 minutes longer, or until crumbs are golden. Remove to serving platter; slice and serve. Makes 6 servings.

LAMB RIBLET STEW

    4 pounds lamb riblets or breast of lamb, cut into serving-size pieces
    ½ pound medium-size onions, peeled and quartered
    2 cups water
    3 teaspoons salt
    1 teaspoon Worcestershire sauce
    ½ teaspoon leaf rosemary, crumbled
    ¼ teaspoon pepper
    6 medium-size potatoes, pared and cut into 1-inch pieces (about 2 pounds)
    1 large sweet potato, pared and cut into 1-inch pieces (about 10 ounces)
    1 leek, washed and sliced ¼ inch thick
    1 tablespoon butter or margarine
    ¼ cup flour
    ⅓ cup water

1. Heat a kettle or Dutch oven over medium heat. Brown lamb, a few pieces at a time, removing pieces as they brown. (No need to add extra fat for browning.) Saute onions in drippings in kettle 10 minutes, or until nicely browned. Remove; reserve.

2. Return meat to kettle; add water, salt, Worcestershire, rosemary and pepper. Heat to boiling; lower heat; cover; simmer 30 minutes. Add potatoes, sweet potatoes and onions, pushing them down under liquid. Simmer 40 minutes longer, or until meat and potatoes are tender. Meanwhile sauté leek in butter or margarine in small skillet, 10 minutes, or just until tender. (Do not brown.)

3. Lift out meat and vegetables and arrange on a shallow heated serving dish along with leek; cover and keep warm.

4. Let fat rise to top of meat-vegetable broth;

skim off all possible fat; heat broth to boiling.

5. Blend flour and water in a small cup; stir into boiling broth. Cook and stir until gravy thickens and bubbles 1 minute. Pour over lamb. Sprinkle with chopped parsley, if you wish. Makes 6 servings.

MAKE-EASY LAMB STEW

    3 pounds lean shoulder of lamb, cubed
    2 teaspoons salt
    2 bay leaves
    4 cups water
    1 can (1 pound) whole onions, drained
    1 can (1 pound) whole potatoes, drained
    1 can (1 pound) lima beans, drained
    4 tablespoons flour
    ⅓ cup cold water
    3 tablespoons chopped parsley

1. Combine lamb, salt, bay leaves and water in a kettle or Dutch oven. Heat to boiling; reduce heat; cover; simmer 1 hour, or until meat almost falls off bones.

2. Lift out meat with a slotted spoon; let cool until easy to handle, then take meat from bones and trim off fat.

3. Let fat rise to top of broth and skim off; remove bay leaves. Return lamb to broth; add onions, potatoes, lima beans; cover; heat 15 minutes.

4. Blend flour and water in a small cup; stir into stew. Cook and stir until gravy thickens and bubbles 1 minute. Serve in soup plates or shallow bowls. Sprinkle with chopped parsley. Makes 8 servings.

OVEN-GRILLED CHEDDAR STEAK

    1 chuck beef steak, weighing about 3½ pounds
      Instant unseasoned meat tenderizer
    3 tablespoons bottled steak sauce
    ¼ cup chopped pecans
    ½ cup grated Cheddar cheese

1. Remove steak from refrigerator 1 hour before cooking. When ready to cook, sprinkle with meat tenderizer, following the label directions; brush both sides with steak sauce; place on rack

in broiler pan placed close to the heat source.
2. Bake in very hot oven (450°) 25 minutes for rare, or until done as you like steak; remove from oven; turn off heat.
3. Sprinkle pecans, then cheese over steak; return to heated oven just until cheese melts.
4. Carve into ¼-inch-thick slices; spoon juices over. Makes 6 servings.

BRAISED LAMB WITH MARJORAM GRAVY

    1 boned lamb shoulder, rolled and tied (about 3 pounds)
    2 tablespoons vegetable oil
    ½ cup water
    1 medium-size onion, quartered
 1½ teaspoons salt
    ½ teaspoon celery seed
    ⅛ teaspoon pepper
    3 large potatoes, pared and cut into 2-inch cubes
    3 large carrots, pared and cut into thin strips
    3 large stalks of celery, cut into thin strips
    1 tablespoon flour
    ¼ teaspoon leaf marjoram, crumbled
    2 anchovy fillets, chopped

1. Brown meat on all sides in vegetable oil in a kettle or Dutch oven. Add water, onion, salt, celery seed and pepper; heat to boiling; lower heat; cover. Simmer 45 minutes.
2. Add potatoes and carrots, pushing them down into the broth; simmer 30 minutes. Stir in celery; simmer 30 minutes longer, or until the meat is tender.
3. Place lamb on a carving board; keep warm. Remove vegetables from kettle with a slotted spoon to a heated serving platter; keep warm while making gravy.
4. To prepare Marjoram Gravy: Pour cooking liquid into a 2-cup measure; let stand until fat rises to top. Skim off all fat; return 2 tablespoons fat to kettle. Add water to liquid to measure 1 cup.
5. Blend flour into fat in kettle; heat, stirring constantly, just until bubbly. Stir in the 1 cup liquid, marjoram and anchovies; cook, stirring constantly, until the gravy thickens and bubbles for about 1 minute.
6. Carve meat and place slices on platter with vegetables; spoon the Marjoram Gravy over the meat. Makes 6 servings.

BEEF GOULASH BUDAPEST

    1 bone-in chuck roast (about 3 pounds)
    4 tablespoons (½ stick) butter or margarine
    2 large onions, chopped (2 cups)
    1 small clove of garlic, crushed
    1 tablespoon paprika
    2 teaspoons salt
    ½ teaspoon caraway seeds
    4 ripe medium-size tomatoes, peeled and chopped
    ½ cup dry red wine
    3 tablespoons flour
      Water
      Cooked noodles

1. Trim bone and fat from beef; cut beef into 1-inch cubes; brown, part at a time, in butter or margarine in a kettle or Dutch oven; remove beef cubes as they brown; reserve.
2. Sauté onions and garlic in drippings in kettle until soft. Stir in paprika, salt and caraway seeds; cook 1 minute. Stir in tomatoes, wine and reserved beef cubes. Heat to boiling; reduce heat; cover. Simmer 1 hour and 15 minutes, or until beef is tender.
3. Blend flour with a little water in a cup to make a smooth paste; stir into bubbling goulash; cook, stirring constantly, until mixture thickens and bubbles 1 minute. Serve with cooked noodles. Makes 8 servings.

BRAISED STUFFED BREAST OF VEAL

    1 boned breast of veal (about 2¼ pounds)
    ¾ teaspoon salt
    ⅛ teaspoon pepper
    2 tablespoons chopped parsley
    ½ teaspoon leaf basil, crumbled
    ½ pound sausage meat (from a 1 pound package)
    1 cup grated carrots (about 3 large carrots)
    1 tablespoon butter or margarine
    ½ cup sliced celery
    1 medium-size onion, sliced
    1 can (about 14 ounces) chicken broth
      Water
    3 tablespoons flour

1. Spread breast of veal flat on a cutting board. (It should measure about 8"x15".

Sprinkle with salt, pepper, parsley and basil. Combine sausage meat with grated carrots in a small bowl; spread evenly over surface of veal, pressing firmly. Roll up veal from short end, jelly-roll fashion. Tie crosswise with heavy string at 1½-inch intervals.

2. Brown meat in butter or margarine in Dutch oven; add celery and onion; sauté 5 minutes longer. Add chicken broth; simmer, covered, 2 hours, or until meat is tender. Remove meat to a carving board.

3. Strain pan juices through a sieve; press vegetables through; pour into a 2-cup measure; add water if necessary to make 1¾ cups. Return to Dutch oven.

4. Combine flour and 6 tablespoons water in a 1-cup measure; blend until smooth. Pour into juices in Dutch oven. Cook, stirring constantly, until sauce thickens and bubbles 3 minutes.

5. Remove string from veal; cut into thin slices; serve with vegetable sauce. Makes 8 servings.

DUCHESS SAUTÉED BEEF LIVER

- 1 egg yolk
- 2 cups mashed potatoes (about 4 medium-size potatoes)
- ¼ cup flour
- 1½ teaspoons salt
- ¼ teaspoon pepper
- 1½ pounds sliced beef liver
- 2 tablespoons vegetable oil
- 2 medium onions, sliced
- 1 green pepper, cut lengthwise into strips
- 1 tomato, cut into wedges
- 1½ cups water
- 1 envelope or teaspoon instant beef broth

1. Beat egg yolk into mashed potatoes; spoon into pastry bag fitted with a star tip. Pipe potatoes in a border around edge of a 10-inch, round ovenproof platter or board.

2. Bake in hot oven (400°) 15 minutes, or until potatoes are golden-brown.

3. Meanwhile mix flour, salt and pepper on wax paper. Cut liver into serving-size pieces, if needed; coat with flour mixture.

4. Sauté liver in hot oil in a large skillet 4 minutes on each side, or until brown and done as you like liver. Arrange slices, overlapping, inside border of potatoes. Keep hot at lowest oven temperature.

5. Sauté onions and pepper strips in same skillet, adding more oil if needed, 10 minutes, or until soft and golden. Stir in tomato; sauté 2 minutes longer. Arrange on top of liver.

6. Add water and instant beef broth to skillet. Bring to boiling, stirring and scraping to dissolve browned bits. Simmer, uncovered, 2 minutes. Pour over liver. Sprinkle with chopped parsley, if you wish. Serve at once. Makes 6 servings.

SPICY GLAZED HAM

- 1 fully cooked bone-in ham, weighing about 10 pounds
- 1 cup dark corn syrup
- ⅔ cup firmly packed brown sugar
- 2 tablespoons prepared mustard

1. Place ham, fat side up, on a rack in a shallow roasting pan. Insert meat thermometer into the thickest part of meat without touching bone.

2. Bake in slow oven (325°) 2¼ hours; remove from oven; cut away the rind and score the fat.

3. Mix corn syrup, brown sugar and mustard in a small bowl; brush part over ham.

4. Continue baking, brushing several times with glaze, 30 minutes, or until richly glazed and thermometer registers 140°.

5. Remove to a heated serving platter. Let stand 20 minutes before slicing. Makes 16 servings.

HAM AND SAUSAGE LOAF

- 1 cup corn bread stuffing mix (from an 8-ounce package)
- ¾ cup boiling water
- 1 can (8 ounces) cream-style corn
- 1 egg
- ½ cup chopped parsley
- 1 pound cooked ham, ground (4 cups)
- 1 pound bulk sausage
- ¼ cup dark corn syrup

1. Combine corn bread stuffing mix with boiling water in a large bowl. Blend in corn, egg and parsley. Add ham and sausage; mix lightly until well-blended.

2. Moisten a 6-cup melon mold or bowl and pack meat mixture firmly into mold: invert loaf onto shallow baking pan

3. Bake in moderate oven (350°) 1 hour and 15 minutes. Brush loaf with syrup and bake 15 minutes longer, or until loaf is well-glazed. Serve on platter garnished with glazed sweet potato slices and buttered asparagus, if you wish. Makes 6 servings.

VEAL MARENGO

    1 package (8 ounces) medium egg noodles
    1 tablespoon butter or margarine
    1 tablespoon vegetable oil
    6 frozen breaded veal patties (about 1½ pounds)
    1 can (1 pound) whole boiled onions, drained
    1 can (4 ounces) whole mushrooms, drained
    1 envelope (1½ ounces) spaghetti sauce mix
    1 can (1 pound) tomatoes
    1 can (1 pound) tomato wedges
    ½ cup garlic croutons
    2 tablespoons chopped parsley

1. Cook noodles following label directions; drain. Spread in shallow 8-cup baking dish.
2. Heat butter or margarine with oil in large skillet; sauté veal patties about 3 minutes on each side. Overlap browned patties down center of noodles. Keep warm.
3. Toss onions and mushrooms in same skillet to brown lightly. Arrange around patties.
4. Add spaghetti sauce mix to same skillet with tomatoes and juice from the can of tomato wedges. Stir over low heat until sauce bubbles.
5. Tuck the tomato wedges around the veal patties. Pour the sauce over all. Sprinkle with croutons.
6. Bake in a hot oven (400°) 20 minutes, or until sauce is bubbly. Sprinkle with chopped parsley. Makes 6 servings.

SCANDINAVIAN PORK POT

    1 rib-end pork loin, about 7 ribs, backbone cracked (about 3 pounds)
    2 tablespoons vegetable oil
    2 teaspoons salt
    ½ teaspoon ground ginger
    ¼ teaspoon pepper
    ¼ teaspoon dry mustard
    1 large orange

    1 lemon
    Water
    2 tablespoons dark corn syrup
    1 pound small white onions, peeled
    1 cup dried apricots
    1 cup pitted prunes
    1 tablespoon cornstarch

1. Trim excess fat from pork; brown on all sides in vegetable oil in a kettle or Dutch oven. Sprinkle with salt, ginger, pepper and mustard.
2. Meanwhile, remove the thin bright-colored rind from the orange and lemon with a sharp knife; reserve. Squeeze juice from orange and lemon into a 1-cup measure; add water to make 1 cup liquid. Stir into kettle with corn syrup and rinds. Heat to boiling; reduce heat; cover. Simmer 1½ hours.
3. Add onions, apricots and prunes; simmer 1 hour longer, or until pork is tender. Place pork on a heated serving platter. Remove onions, apricots and prunes from kettle with a slotted spoon and arrange on meat platter. Discard orange and lemon rinds. Skim fat from liquid.
4. To make gravy: Combine cornstarch with small amount of water in a cup; stir into cooking liquid in kettle; cook, stirring constantly, until sauce thickens and bubbles 3 minutes. Serve with pork. Makes 4 servings.

BOEUF SAUTÉ BORDELAISE

    1½ pounds ground chuck
    1 envelope ground-beef seasoning mix
    1 tablespoon dry red wine
    ¼ pound mushrooms, quartered
    ½ cup dry red wine
    1 can (15 ounces) beef gravy

1. Combine ground chuck, ground-beef seasoning mix and 1 tablespoon dry red wine. Shape into 4 oval patties.
2. Heat a large skillet over medium heat. Sauté patties 4 minutes on each side; remove from the skillet.
3. Sauté quartered mushrooms briefly in the same skillet. Stir in ½ cup dry red wine; simmer for about 1 minute.
4. Add canned beef gravy; heat to boiling. Return beef patties to skillet for 1 minute. Garnish with a watercress cluster and a tomato rose, if you wish. Makes 4 servings.

2

PENNY-WISE POULTRY

It's simple common sense. When food prices are high, it pays to look for items that offer a great deal for your money. Fortunately, poultry is one food you don't have to search for. It's always available and comes inexpensively packaged in ways to suit every budget, taste and family size. And for menu variety, it's hard to beat. It can be fried, roasted, broiled, boiled or braised, and comes to you invitingly in casseroles, soups and stews. In this chapter we explore some of these ideas using chicken and turkey. Also, since it pays to buy chicken whole and do your own cutting and boning, we've included a page of illustrations to show you how to go about it, plus a list of ideas on other ways to save even more. Add chicken to your weekly menu—you'll be called penny-wise, but no one will ever say you're being pound foolish.

WHEN YOU SHOP FOR CHICKEN

• Chicken may come to you packed in over 30 different ways; there's a pack for every cooking purpose and family preference.

Here are some of your chicken choices:

• Whole chicken with heart, liver, gizzard (called giblets) often packed inside. The meat yield for a whole broiler-type is 51.2 percent of the bird by weight. You will need approximately ¾ pound chicken per serving. A three-pound bird yields four servings; a two-pound bird yields two servings.

• Packaged chicken pieces include drumstick, thighs, breasts and wings. One serving is one-half breast, or a thigh and drumstick, or a combination of the smaller pieces.

• Chicken halves cook faster than the whole chicken. They come packed in 1½- to 2½-pound weights. Allow one chicken half to a portion.

• Chicken quarters are convenient and easy to cook. The quarters usually come in 2½-pound packages. Allow one-quarter per person.

• Drumsticks are great finger foods. They weigh four to five ounces each. Two make one serving.

• Thighs are delicious dark meat in convenient form. Use "as is" or bone them for a real treat. They average four ounces each.

• Breasts have the greatest amount of meat of the chicken pieces. They're a good value for the money and so low in calories. A three-ounce portion has only 185 calories or 115 without the skin. Allow one-half breast per serving. Breasts range from 12 to 15 ounces each.

• Wings are great party nibblers. Two wings usually make one serving. Each wing is approximately two ounces.

• Chicken livers are really delicious and reasonable. Allow ¼ pound per serving.

• Choose the kind—whole or cut-up—and weight best suited to the way you want to cook it. Choosiness pays off, too, when your family prefers either light or dark meat, or when you want special parts for a special dish.

• When buying chicken whole, remember these points: Broiler-fryers (one to three pounds) are the youngest, most tender chickens, but they yield the least meat. Roasting chickens, at between four and six pounds are older and less tender, but meatier. Stewing chickens, the oldest and least tender, are the meatiest and most economical. Keep in mind, also, that poultry is graded only on the basis of "U.S. Grade A" or "U.S. Grade B." There's no such thing as "Prime" chicken. And when it comes to brands, a Grade A turkey is a Grade A turkey. Same for chickens.

• Save chicken livers in a container in the freezer until you've accumulated enough to make a whole meal.

• Watch for specials on chicken, then buy some for today's dinner, some for the freezer. And remember—it takes little extra work to fry a big batch of parts, put a second bird in to roast, or stew an extra one for another day's treat.

• When you get the chicken home, loosen the supermarket wrapping and store in the coldest part of the refrigerator, depending upon its design, up to two days.

TURKEY-BUYING TIPS

• Shall it be a tom or a hen? Both are equally tender, equally fine eating. And there is no difference in the cooking or length of roasting time. Most labels simply say TURKEY, but, in some areas, large toms weighing 20 pounds and over are often advertised as such and are usually priced a few cents a pound less than smaller birds. For a large family or a big holiday feast, you couldn't find a better buy.

• What size should you buy? Giblets and neck are included in the weight of each wrapped bird, so consider this when figuring the size turkey you'll need. Good rules of thumb are: Allow 1 pound per serving when buying a turkey weighing less than 12 pounds, or ½ to ¼ pound per serving for one over 12 pounds. Remember, too, that, since it takes so little additional time and fuel to roast a larger bird, it's smart shopping to buy a big one that'll give you generous first-day slices plus extra for snacks and a second-day dinner treat. If you count on about 1½ pounds of turkey per person, you'll have enough.

• When preparing turkey or chicken, take the wing tips, back, heart, neck and gizzard—any parts your family may not care to eat, and freeze them. Save them until the turkey is carved bare or additional parts accumulate. (You need about four pounds). Defrost parts, cut up a carrot, celery stalk, onion, and add these to four quarts of water in a large pot. Bring to a boil, reduce heat and simmer for about two hours. The result: Delicious, concentrated, versatile stock.

How to Cut and Bone a Chicken

1. Place chicken breast side up. Using a sharp knife, make lengthwise slit through skin and flesh from neck to cavity. Turn bird over and repeat cut.

A

B

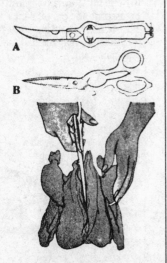

2. Using poultry shears (**A**) or kitchen shears (**B**), cut right through bones (ribs). Cutting to one side of breastbone is easier than cutting through it.

3. Turn chicken over. Cut through bones, cutting to one side of the backbone. You may remove backbone. A small bird is cut this way for serving.

4. For quartering chicken, continue using shears. Cut across half the bird, following the natural division just below the rib cage and the breastbone.

5. Thigh may be left attached to leg for broiling; but for frying, bend leg joint. Cut through joint with a sharp knife, separating leg from the thigh.

6. To separate wing from the breast, bend joint. Cut through joint with a sharp knife. The chicken will now be in eight pieces and ready for frying.

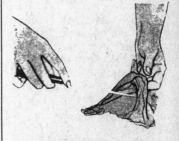

7. If your recipe calls for skinned chicken breasts, use a sharp, small paring knife to start, then slip fingers between skin and flesh and peel skin.

8. To bone chicken breast, use a small paring knife. Cut meat away from rib bones with quick little strokes, feeling your way along with your fingers.

How to Stuff and Truss a Chicken

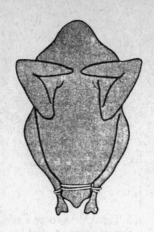

First rinse chicken clean with cold running water inside and out. Pat dry. Rub lightly with salt.

1. Spoon stuffing lightly into neck (do not pack, for stuffing expands when cooking). Pull neck skin over the opening and fasten to back with a skewer or toothpick.

2. Stuff body cavity lightly. Close the opening by running skewers or toothpicks through the skin from one side of the opening to the other; then lace securely with string in a criss-cross fashion.

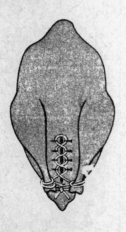

3. Loop the same string around the drumstick ends and tie them together, then fasten them to the tailpiece.

4. Fold wings up and over the back; this will help brace the chicken in the roasting pan.

Brush chicken lightly with melted butter or margarine and place, breast up, in a roasting pan.

Or, if barbecuing on a spit:

Press wings close to breast and run a string around under the chicken to completely encircle it, securing the wings snugly against the breast. The chicken should be tied so it makes a compact bundle.

How to Carve a Chicken

1. Use a sharp, thin-bladed knife and long-tined fork. Remove all trussing equipment from the chicken—skewers, toothpicks, cord or thread. Then, place the chicken breast-up on a serving platter or carving board in front of you. The legs should be toward your right. Grasp end of leg nearest you and bend it down

toward the platter while you cut through thigh joint to separate whole leg from body. Separate drumstick and thigh by cutting through joint.

2. Stick fork into breast near breastbone and cut off wing close to body. Slanting knife inward slightly may make it easier to hit the joint.

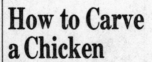

3. Slice white meat starting at tip of breastbone and cutting down toward wing joint. Repeat with other side of chicken, turning platter if necessary.

Menu Ideas

Put these menus into action the very next time you have guests for dinner. They're designed to put you at ease during important entertaining moments and they illustrate chicken's ability to blend with seasonings, side dishes and other courses. Try the menus and then create your own to go with all our chicken recipes.

EASYGOING BUFFET

Pineapple Juice
Cheese Bread
★Chicken a la Orange
★Chive Risotto   Creamed Peas
Salad Bowl
Raspberry Sherbet
Coffee

CHICKEN A LA ORANGE

Bake at 350° for 1 hour.
Makes 8 servings.

8 boneless chicken breasts (about 10 ounces each)

⅓ cup flour
1½ teaspoons salt
1 teaspoon garlic powder
½ teaspoon paprika
⅓ cup sliced almonds
5 tablespoons butter or margarine
1 can (6 ounces) frozen concentrated orange juice
1½ cups water
1 teaspoon leaf rosemary, crumbled
¼ teaspoon leaf thyme, crumbled
2 tablespoons cornstarch
Chive Risotto

1. Coat chicken with a mixture of flour, 1 teaspoon salt, garlic powder and paprika.
2. Sauté almonds in butter or margarine until golden in a large frying pan; remove from pan. Brown chicken breasts in drippings in same pan; place in a single layer in a baking pan, 13x9x2. Pour all drippings from pan.
3. Stir orange-juice concentrate, water, rosemary, thyme and ½ teaspoon salt into pan. Heat to boiling; pour over chicken; cover.
4. Bake in moderate oven (350°) 1 hour, or until chicken is tender. Remove to another pan; keep warm. Reheat liquid in baking pan to boiling; thicken with cornstarch.
5. Spoon Chive Risotto onto a large serving platter; arrange chicken over rice; sprinkle with almonds. Serve sauce separately to spoon over chicken.

CHIVE RISOTTO: Sauté 2½ cups packaged enriched precooked rice in 3 tablespoons butter or margarine, stirring constantly, until golden in a large frying pan. Drain liquid from 2 cans (3 or 4 ounces each) chopped mushrooms into a 4-cup measure; add water to make 2½ cups. Stir into rice with mushrooms, 3 envelopes instant chicken broth and ¼ cup cut chives. Heat to boiling; cover; remove from heat. Let stand 10 minutes. Makes 8 servings.

HOLIDAY SPECIAL

Bouillon Soup
★Cornish Hens Indienne

★Parsley Rice   Buttered Carrots
Salad
Cloverleaf Rolls

CORNISH HENS INDIENNE

Roast at 375° for 1 hour and 20 minutes.
Makes 6 servings.

6 frozen Rock Cornish game hens (about 1
  pound each), thawed
Salt
¼ teaspoon pepper
¼ teaspoon leaf thyme, crumbled
½ cup (1 stick) butter or margarine, melted
4 slices bacon, diced
1 medium-size onion, chopped (½ cup)
1 tablespoon flour
1 tablespoon sugar
2 teaspoons curry powder
2 teaspoons instant chicken bouillon
1 cup apricot nectar
1 tablespoon lemon juice
Parsley Rice
Buttered carrots

1. Remove giblets from body cavities of hens
   and save to simmer for soup. Rinse hens
   inside and out; pat dry with paper toweling.
2. Mix 1 teaspoon salt with pepper and thyme
   in a cup; sprinkle ¼ teaspoonful inside
   each hen; tie legs together. Place hens,
   breast side up, in a jellyroll pan. Brush
   with part of the melted butter or margarine.
3. Roast in moderate oven (375°), brushing
   once or twice with remaining melted butter
   or margarine and drippings in pan, 1 hour.
   Cut away strings with scissors; spoon all
   drippings from pan.
4. While hens roast, sauté bacon until almost
   crisp in a medium-size saucepan; remove
   with a slotted spoon and drain on paper
   toweling. Stir onion into drippings; sauté
   until soft.
5. Blend in flour, sugar, curry powder, chicken
   bouillon and ½ teaspoon salt; cook, stirring constantly, until bubbly. Stir in apricot nectar and lemon juice. Heat, stirring
   constantly, to boiling; simmer 5 minutes, or
   until mixture thickens slightly; spoon about
   half over hens.
6. Roast 10 minutes; spoon remaining curry
   mixture over top to make a thick coating.
   Continue roasting 10 minutes, or until hens
   are tender and richly glazed.
7. Spread rice on a large deep serving platter;
   arrange hens on top. Spoon carrots at each
   end.

PARSLEY RICE: Combine 1 cup uncooked
rice, 2 tablespoons butter or margarine, 2 teaspoons instant chicken bouillon and 2¼ cups
boiling water in a 6-cup baking dish; cover.
Bake along with hens in moderate oven
(375°) 1 hour, or until rice is tender and
liquid is absorbed. Fluff rice with a fork; stir
in ¼ cup chopped parsley. Makes 6 servings.

SUNDAY, SUNDAY

Deviled Eggs
★Parisian Chicken Roasts
Fried Apple Slices
Potatoes and Peas in Cream
Green Beans
Salad
Crescent Rolls

PARISIAN CHICKEN ROASTS

Roast at 400° for 1 hour and 15 minutes.
Makes 6 servings.

3 broiler-fryers (about 2½ pounds each)
¾ cup (1½ sticks) butter or margarine
1 teaspoon salt
¼ teaspoon pepper
⅔ cup lemon marmalade

1. Remove giblets from body cavities of chickens; save to simmer for soup. Rinse chickens inside and out; pat dry. Tie legs together. Place, breast side up, on a rack in
   a roasting pan.
2. Melt butter or margarine in a small saucepan; stir in salt and pepper; brush part
   over chickens.
3. Roast in hot oven (400°), brushing once
   with more butter mixture, 45 minutes.
4. While chickens cook, stir lemon marmalade
   into remaining butter mixture; heat slowly,
   stirring constantly, until marmalade melts.
   Brush half over chickens.
5. Roast 15 minutes; brush with remaining
   marmalade mixture. Roast 15 minutes
   longer, or until chickens are tender and
   richly glazed.
6. Place on a large serving platter; cut away
   strings. Overlap fried apple slices around
   edge of platter. Carve chickens into serving-size pieces.

Appetizers, Pâtés and Dips

Some like them hot, some like them cold. Regardless of the preference, we're sure you'll agree appetizers are one of the biggest assets a hostess can have. They allow you time to visit with guests before disappearing into the kitchen for last-minute dinner preparations, and they help stimulate appetites for that glorious meal you've been working on. Since chicken is easy to prepare and has the ability to blend well with so many foods and seasonings, it becomes an extremely good choice for the appetizer tray. Our recipes show how to combine it with eggs, mushrooms, ham, shrimp, cheese, sour cream and just about all the herbs and spices you can think of. The combinations range from finger chicken served with sauces to molds and chafing dish specials. All add up to a delightful way to begin an evening.

FINGER DRUMSTICKS

Pick-me-ups, garnished with lemon slices and served hot from a chafing dish.

Bake at 400° for 1 hour and 10 minutes.
Makes 12 servings.

3 pounds small chicken wings (about 15)
½ cup sugar
3 tablespoons cornstarch
1 teaspoon salt
½ teaspoon ground ginger
¼ teaspoon pepper
¾ cup water
⅓ cup lemon juice
¼ cup soy sauce

1. Singe chicken wings, if needed. Cut off tips and discard. Divide each wing in half by cutting through joint with a sharp knife. Place in a single layer on broiler pan rack.
2. Bake in hot oven (400°), turning once, 30 minutes.
3. Mix sugar, cornstarch, salt, ginger and pepper in a small saucepan; stir in water, lemon juice and soy sauce. Cook, stirring constantly, until mixture thickens and boils 3 minutes. Brush part over chicken wings.
4. Continue baking, turning and brushing several times with remaining lemon mixture, 40 minutes, or until richly glazed.
5. When ready to serve, place in a chafing dish or keep-hot server. Frame with a ring of thin lemon slices, if you wish. Serve hot.

GOLDEN CHICKEN NUGGETS

These make-aheads will disappear fast at your next get-together.

Bake at 400° for 10 minutes.
Makes 4 to 5 dozen nuggets.

4 whole chicken breasts
½ cup unseasoned fine dry bread crumbs
¼ cup grated Parmesan cheese
2 teaspoons monosodium glutamate
1 teaspoon salt
1 teaspoon dried leaf thyme
1 teaspoon dried leaf basil
½ cup butter or margarine, melted

1. Bone chicken breasts; remove skin. Cut each breast half into 6 to 8 nuggets, about 1½ inches square.

2. Combine bread crumbs, cheese, monosodium glutamate, salt and herbs.
3. Dip chicken nuggets in melted butter, then in crumb mixture. Place in single layer on foil-lined baking sheets. Bake in hot oven (400°) 10 minutes. Chill until ready to use.

CHICKEN AND SHRIMPS MARENGO

For favorite guests—here's a festive appetizer, served in a chafing dish, warmer or scallop shells.

Makes 8 servings.

1 chicken breast (about 12 ounces)
4 tablespoons vegetable oil
½ teaspoon monosodium glutamate
1 large onion, chopped (1 cup)
1 clove garlic, minced
2 tablespoons flour
1 can (2¼ ounces) deviled ham
1 can (8 ounces) stewed tomatoes
1 can (3 or 4 ounces) whole mushrooms
1 teaspoon Worcestershire sauce
1 pound fresh shrimps, shelled and deveined
Chopped parsley

1. Pull skin from chicken breast; cut meat from bones in two large pieces, then cut into 1-inch pieces.
2. Brown in 2 tablespoons of the vegetable oil in a medium-size frying pan; sprinkle with monosodium glutamate; cover. Cook slowly 15 minutes, or until tender.
3. While chicken cooks, sauté onion and garlic until soft in remaining 2 tablespoons vegetable oil in a second medium-size frying pan; blend in flour; cook, stirring constantly, until bubbly.
4. Blend in deviled ham, then stir in tomatoes, mushrooms and their liquid, and Worcestershire sauce. Cook, stirring constantly, until mixture thickens and boils 1 minute; remove chicken from its frying pan with a slotted spoon and stir into sauce.
5. Stir shrimps into chicken drippings in frying pan; cook slowly, turning once, 10 minutes, or until tender. Stir into sauce mixture.
6. Spoon into scallop shells, a chafing dish or a keep-hot server; sprinkle with chopped parsley. Serve with small triangles of crisp toast, if you wish.

PÂTÉ CONTINENTAL

It's a lot of work and must be made well ahead, but the result is a beautiful pâté loaf to grace a party table.

Bake at 350° for 1½ hours.
Makes 8 servings.

1 pound beef liver
½ pound chicken livers
1 medium-size onion, chopped (½ cup)
2 tablespoons butter or margarine
¼ cup water
1 envelope instant chicken broth OR
   1 chicken bouillon cube
2 eggs, beaten
¼ teaspoon ground allspice
¼ teaspoon leaf thyme, crumbled
5 slices bacon
Beef Aspic
1 hard-cooked egg, shelled

1. Snip out any large tubelike membranes from beef liver; cut into chunks. Halve chicken livers; snip out veiny parts or skin.
2. Put both meats through a food chopper, using a fine blade; place in a medium-size bowl.
3. Sauté onion in butter or margarine until soft in a small frying pan; stir in water and chicken broth or bouillon cube; heat to boiling, crushing bouillon cube, if used, with a spoon; stir into liver mixture with eggs, allspice and thyme.
4. Place 3 slices of the bacon in a loaf pan, 5x3x2; spoon in liver mixture; top with remaining bacon. Cover pan tightly with foil.
5. Set in baking pan on oven shelf; pour boiling water into pan to depth of about 1 inch.
6. Bake in moderate oven (350°) 1½ hours, or until loaf starts to pull away from sides of pan; remove from pan of water; take off foil. Cool loaf, then chill overnight.
7. Make Beef Aspic.
8. Peel bacon from top of loaf; loosen loaf around edges with a knife; invert onto a plate; peel off remaining bacon. Wash pan and dry well.
9. Pour ¼ cup of the aspic into loaf pan; place in a pan of ice and water to speed setting; chill just until sticky-firm.
10. While layer chills, halve hard-cooked egg lengthwise, cutting just through the white. Slice yolk carefully; cut white into 8 or 10 tiny flower shapes with a truffle cutter.
11. Arrange two of the yolk slices and white cut-outs in a pretty pattern on sticky-firm aspic in pan; carefully pour in another ½ cup aspic; let set until sticky-firm.
12. Place pâté loaf over aspic layer in pan; pour in enough of the remaining aspic to fill pan to rim. Remove from ice and water; chill in refrigerator at least 4 hours, or until aspic is firm. Pour remaining aspic into a pan, 8x8x2; chill.
13. Just before serving, run a sharp-tip thin-blade knife around top of loaf, then dip pan *very quickly* in and out of hot water. Cover pan with a chilled serving plate; turn upside down; gently lift off pan.
14. Cut remaining aspic layer into tiny cubes; spoon around pâté loaf. Garnish with radish flowers and snips of radish leaves.

To make radish flowers, trim large radishes. Holding each, tip end up, cut lengthwise into 10 or 12 sections, not quite to stem. Place in ice and water until "petals" open up.

BEEF ASPIC: Soften 1 envelope unflavored gelatin in ¾ cup cold water in a small saucepan; heat, stirring constantly, just until gelatin dissolves; remove from heat. Stir in 1 can condensed beef consommé and 2 tablespoons lemon juice. Cool.

ORANGE CHICKEN D'OEUVRE

A glamorous appetizer served with a zesty orange sauce.

Bake at 400° for 15 minutes.
Makes 6 appetizer servings (24 to 30 balls).

2 cups ground cooked chicken
½ cup fine soft bread crumbs
1 teaspoon salt
¼ teaspoon pepper
1 teaspoon minced onion
1 egg
1 tablespoon chicken broth

1. Combine all ingredients in medium bowl. Form into balls ¾ to 1 inch in diameter.
2. Place on greased baking sheet. Bake in hot oven (400°) for 15 minutes.
3. Place in small chafing dish; add Orange Sauce (see page 20) and keep warm; serve with cocktail picks. Or serve on cocktail picks, with Orange Sauce as a dip.

ORANGE SAUCE

½ cup currant jelly
½ teaspoon minced onion
¼ teaspoon red-pepper sauce
¾ teaspoon salt
½ teaspoon dry mustard
¼ teaspoon ginger
1 tablespoon chopped dill OR 1 teaspoon
    dried dill weed
1½ cups orange juice
2 tablespoons cornstarch
2 tablespoons cold water

1. In small saucepan heat currant jelly, onion, red-pepper sauce, salt, dry mustard, ginger, dill and orange juice until boiling.
2. Blend cornstarch with cold water and stir into mixture in saucepan. Cook until thickened, stirring constantly.

CHICKEN CANAPES

Flavory salad is heaped into tiny pastry shells and topped with a miniature tomato slice.

Makes 5 dozen, or about 25 servings.

Canapé Shells
1 can (6 ounces) chopped broiled mushrooms
2 cans (5 to 6 ounces each) boned chicken,
    very finely chopped OR 2 cups very finely
    chopped cooked chicken
½ cup very finely diced celery
⅔ cup dairy sour cream
1 teaspoon grated onion
½ teaspoon curry powder
½ teaspoon salt
Cherry tomatoes, sliced
Parsley

1. Make, bake and cool Canapé Shells.
2. Drain and chop mushrooms very fine. Combine with chicken and celery in a bowl.
3. Mix sour cream, onion, curry powder and salt in a 1-cup measure; spoon over chicken mixture; toss well to mix; chill.
4. Just before serving, spoon into Canapé Shells, using 1 rounded teaspoonful for each. Garnish with a slice of cherry tomato and a sprig of parsley.

CANAPÉ SHELLS: Prepare 1 package piecrust mix, following label directions, or make pastry from your own favorite two-crust recipe. Roll out, half at a time to a 12-inch round on lightly floured pastry cloth or board; cut into small rounds with a 1¾-inch scalloped cutter. Fit into tiny muffin-pan cups; prick shells with a fork. Reroll and cut out all trimmings. Bake in hot oven (425°) 7 minutes, or until delicately golden. Remove from cups; cool completely on wire racks. Makes about 5 dozen.

MAKE-AHEAD NOTE: Canapé Shells may be made a day ahead, if you like, then stacked and stored in a container with a tight-fitting cover. For 100 servings, make 3 times the recipe. For variety, fill with your favorite seafood or ham salad.

CHICKEN TANGO DIP

The secret ingredient (instant coffee) makes this a delicious, mellow dip.

Makes 2 cups.

1 can (5 ounces) chicken spread
1 cup (8-ounce carton) dairy sour cream
¼ cup mayonnaise or salad dressing
¼ cup finely chopped walnuts
2 teaspoons instant coffee
¼ teaspoon salt
Dash of pepper
1 teaspoon lemon juice

1. Combine all ingredients in a medium-size bowl; stir lightly until well blended. Chill several hours to season.
2. Spoon into small bowls; sprinkle with paprika, if you wish. Serve with crisp greenpepper squares, carrot sticks, potato chips, pretzels or your favorite crackers.

CHICKEN-SESAME BITES

Your guests will think you're a genius because most of the preparation for these appetizers is done ahead of time.

Makes about 4 dozen appetizers.

2 whole chicken breasts
3 tablespoons lemon juice
2 tablespoons soy sauce
1 tablespoon sugar
1 tablespoon sherry
¼ cup butter or margarine
Toasted sesame seeds

1. Bone chicken breasts; remove skin. Cut meat in 1-inch pieces; place in shallow dish.
2. Combine lemon juice, soy sauce, sugar and sherry; pour over chicken, let stand ½ hour or more.
3. Sauté chicken in butter 5 minutes. Dip in sesame seeds. Serve with wooden picks.

CHICKEN ROLLS

A first-rate first course, or party fare: Crisp gingery rolls of white meat and ham.

Makes 6 servings (3 rolls each).

1 whole chicken breast (about 12 ounces)
2 slices boiled ham, each cut into 9 pieces
18 small thin strips crystallized ginger
1 egg
¼ cup milk
½ cup sifted regular flour
½ teaspon salt
½ teaspoon sugar
Shortening or vegetable oil for frying

1. Pull skin from chicken breast; halve breast and cut meat in 1 piece from bone, then cut each half into 9 even pieces. Place, 2 or 3 at a time, between waxed paper and pound very thin with mallet or rolling pin until about 2 inches wide.
2. Top each with a piece of ham and ginger; roll up. Place, seam side down, in a single layer on a large platter; cover; chill.
3. When ready to cook, beat egg with milk in a medium-size bowl; beat in flour, salt and sugar until smooth. (Batter will be medium-thin.)
4. Melt enough shortening or pour in enough vegetable oil to make a 4-inch depth in an electric deep-fat fryer or large saucepan; heat to 380°.
5. Dip chicken rolls, 2 at a time, into batter; hold over bowl to let excess drip back.
6. Fry in hot shortening, turning once, 3 minutes, or until golden; lift out with a slotted spoon; drain on paper toweling. Serve hot with dips of prepared horseradish-mustard and Plum Sauce (see chapter on SAUCES).

MAKE-AHEAD TIP: Rolls may be fried several hours ahead and chilled. To reheat, arrange, not touching, in a shallow baking pan and heat in very hot oven (450°) 10 minutes.

CHICKEN LIVER BROIL

Serve as an appetizer or as a main dish.

Makes 6 to 8 appetizer servings.

1 pound chicken livers
¼ cup bottled chili sauce
2 tablespoons vegetable oil
2 tablespoons Worcestershire sauce
1 teaspoon monosodium glutamate

1. Halve livers; snip out any veiny parts.
2. Mix remainder of ingredients in large bowl. Add livers and toss; let stand an hour.
3. Remove livers from marinade; thread onto long skewers; place on rack in broiler pan. Broil, 5 to 6 inches from the heat, turning several times, 5 minutes.
4. While livers cook, heat marinade to boiling in small saucepan. Remove livers from skewers and arrange on a serving plate; serve sauce in a small bowl as a dip.

PÂTÉ MIMOSA

A pearly chicken-flavored mold.

Makes 12 servings.

1 envelope unflavored gelatin
1 envelope instant chicken broth
1½ cups water
½ cup mayonnaise or salad dressing
2 teaspoons cider vinegar
1 teaspoon grated onion
1 teaspoon prepared horseradish
1 teaspoon salt
⅛ teaspoon cayenne pepper
6 slices crisp bacon, crumbled
4 hard-cooked eggs, shelled and sieved

1. Combine gelatin, chicken broth and water in a small saucepan; heat, stirring constantly, until gelatin dissolves.
2. Beat in mayonnaise or salad dressing, vinegar, onion, horseradish, salt and cayenne pepper. Pour into a shallow pan; chill in freezer 20 minutes, or until firm at edges.
3. Spoon into a bowl; beat until fluffy. Fold in bacon and eggs; spoon into a 3-cup mold. Chill until firm.
4. Unmold onto a serving plate. Garnish with sieved hard-cooked egg yolk.

PATE-CHEESE MOLD

Stuffed olives crown a pretty double-molded spread of meat and cheese.

Makes 25 servings.

MEAT LAYER

1 envelope unflavored gelatin
1 envelope instant chicken broth OR
   1 chicken bouillon cube
1 cup water
1 tablespoon lemon juice
3 large stuffed green olives, sliced
½ pound bologna
¼ cup mayonnaise or salad dressing
¼ cup sweet mustard relish (from a
   9-ounce jar)

CHEESE LAYER

1 envelope unflavored gelatin
¼ cup water
2 wedges (1⅓ ounces each) Camembert
   cheese
¼ pound blue cheese
¼ teaspoon curry powder
1 egg, separated
1 cup (8-ounce carton) dairy sour cream
Green food coloring

1. Make meat layer: Soften gelatin with chicken broth or bouillon cube in water in a small saucepan. Heat, stirring constantly and crushing cube, if using, with a spoon, just until gelatin dissolves. Measure ¼ cup into a 6-cup mold; stir in lemon juice. (Keep remaining gelatin mixture at room temperature.)
2. Set mold in a pan of ice and water to speed setting; chill just until syrupy-thick. Arrange stuffed olive slices in gelatin to make a pretty pattern. Chill until sticky-firm.
3. While mold chills, remove skin from bologna; put meat through a food chopper, using a fine blade. Mix with remaining gelatin mixture, mayonnaise or salad dressing and relish in a medium-size bowl; spoon over sticky-firm olive layer in mold. Continue chilling in same pan of ice and water until sticky-firm while making cheese layer.
4. Make cheese layer: Soften gelatin in water in a small saucepan; heat slowly just until gelatin dissolves.

5. Beat Camembert and blue cheeses until well-blended in a medium-size bowl; beat in curry powder, egg yolk and the dissolved gelatin.
6. Beat egg white until it stands in firm peaks in a small bowl. Fold into cheese mixture, then fold in sour cream. Tint mixture light green with a drop or two of food coloring.
7. Spoon over sticky-firm meat layer in mold; cover with waxed paper, foil or transparent wrap. Chill in refrigerator several hours, or until firm. (Overnight is best.)
8. When ready to unmold, run a sharp-tip, thin-blade knife around top of mold, then dip mold *very quickly* in and out of a pan of hot water. Cover mold with a serving plate; turn upside down; gently lift off mold. Surround with your choice of crisp crackers.

PÂTÉ MAISON

Prepare the chicken livers, add the seasonings and cream and you're ready to bring out the appetizer tray.

Makes 1⅓ cups Pâté.

¼ cup butter or margarine
1 pound chicken livers
½ cup finely chopped onion
1 teaspoon salt
¼ teaspoon each dry mustard, freshly
   ground black pepper and powdered thyme
⅛ teaspoon mace
¼ cup cream

1. Heat butter in skillet. Add chicken livers and onion; cook over medium heat, stirring frequently, for 5 to 8 minutes or until livers are done and onion is tender but not brown.
2. Force livers with onion through strainer or food mill. Blend in seasonings and cream. Turn into serving container or mold. Serve with thinly sliced French bread, crackers or toast rounds.

HAM AND CHICKEN PINWHEELS

These pretty little appetizers, with their fresh parsley edging, are sliced dainty-thin just before serving.

Makes about 5 dozen.

1 can (4½ ounces) deviled ham
1 teaspoon prepared mustard
2½ teaspoons grated onion
Dash liquid red-pepper seasoning
1 can (4¾ ounces) chicken spread
½ teaspoon anchovy paste
½ teaspoon Worcestershire sauce
1 loaf unsliced bread (white or whole wheat)
1 cup (2 sticks) butter or margarine, softened
5 ripe olives, chopped
1 whole pimiento, chopped
3 cups finely chopped parsley (about 2 large bunches)

1. Combine ham, mustard, teaspoon of the grated onion and red-pepper seasoning in a small bowl.
2. Combine chicken spread, anchovy paste, the remaining grated onion and Worcestershire in a second small bowl.
3. Trim crusts from top and sides of unsliced loaf, leaving bottom crust intact. Cut lengthwise into eight ¼-inch-thick slices; cover with dampened paper toweling to prevent drying.
4. Roll bread slices lightly with rolling pin. Spread with softened butter or margarine. Spread deviled-ham filling on 4 slices and chicken filling on remaining 4 slices.
5. Taking 1 slice of deviled ham at a time, sprinkle chopped olives along the near long edge and roll up tightly, jelly-roll fashion. Spread outer surface with butter or margarine and roll in chopped parsley. Wrap tightly in plastic wrap, twisting ends well.
6. Repeat with remaining deviled-ham slices and chopped olives. Sprinkle chopped pimiento on chicken slices and repeat rolling, coating and wrapping.
7. Do-ahead note: Place wrapped rolls in foil or plastic boxes; cover firmly; label and freeze.
8. Party day: Slice each frozen roll into 8 thin sandwiches with a sharp knife. Arrange on serving plates (they will thaw quickly).

NOTE: If you do not wish to freeze sandwiches, they should be chilled for at least 8 hours in plastic wrap before slicing.

If unsliced bread is not available, sandwiches may be prepared using sliced bread. Trim the crusts from 2 slices of bread; roll lightly. Place slices side by side; butter joining edges. Press edges together; proceed as above, rolling from long edge so joining is in the center of roll.

CORN-CRISPED DRUMSTICKS

They look like fried chicken, but these drumsticks are actually baked . . . with no messy clean-up.

Bake at 350° for 1 hour.
Makes 8 servings.

2 cups packaged corn flake crumbs
2 teaspoons monosodium glutamate
2 teaspoons salt
¼ teaspoon pepper
16 drumsticks
¾ cup evaporated milk

1. Combine corn flake crumbs with monosodium glutamate, salt and pepper in shallow dish.
2. Line 2 shallow baking sheets or pans with aluminum foil.
3. Dip drumsticks in evaporated milk, then roll immediately in seasoned corn flake crumbs. Place the drumsticks in foil-lined pans; do not crowd.
4. Bake in moderate oven (350°) 1 hour, or until tender. At the end of ½ hour, exchange place of pans on the shelves; continue to bake. No need to cover or turn chicken while cooking. Serve with Deviled Dunking Sauce.

DEVILED DUNKING SAUCE: Combine ⅓ cup prepared mustard, ⅓ cup pickle relish, 1 can (8 ounces) tomato sauce, 1 tablespoon horseradish, 1 tablespoon of Worcestershire sauce and ⅛ teaspoon cayenne; mix thoroughly. Makes 1⅔ cups sauce.

Memories are made of moments that surpass the ordinary. The child better remembers cold winter days that included hot, homemade soup for lunch than days that were just cold. The adult thinks back with more pleasure to evenings that offered a hearty broth in front of the fire than to an evening just in front of the fire.

Soup sets the mood for relaxed, enjoyable moments; when it includes chicken, the moments become truly memorable. As our recipes prove, hot or cold, creamy or clear, thin or hearty, chicken soup is easy and fun to make. You can start from scratch or use canned soup as a base. Whatever your choice, make some soup now. The day will be worth remembering.

Soups for Every Season

BASIC CHICKEN BROTH

It is well worthwhile to make homemade chicken broth. This recipe gives you enough broth and meat to make 2 soups and even extra meat for a salad or casserole, if you wish.

Makes 12 cups.

2 broiler-fryers, 3 to 3½ pounds each
Chicken giblets
2 medium carrots, pared
1 large parsnip, pared
1 large onion, chopped (1 cup)
2 stalks celery
2 celery tops
3 sprigs parsley
1 leek, washed well
Water
2 tablespoons salt
12 peppercorns

1. Combine chicken, chicken giblets, carrots, parsnip, onion and celery in a large kettle; tie celery tops, parsley and leek together with a string; add to kettle. Add enough cold water to cover chicken and vegetables, about 12 cups.
2. Heat slowly to boiling; skim; add salt and peppercorns; reduce heat. Simmer very slowly 1 to 1½ hours, or until meat falls off the bones. Remove meat and vegetables from broth, discard the bundle of greens.
3. Strain broth through cheesecloth into a large bowl. (There should be about 12 cups.) Use this delicious broth in the following soup recipes or in any of our recipes calling for chicken broth.
4. When cool enough to handle, remove and discard skin and bones from chicken; cut meat into bite-size pieces; use as called for in following recipes, or use in salads, casseroles, etc. To store in refrigerator, up to 3 to 4 days, keep in covered container. To freeze, pack in small portions, 1 or 2 cups, in plastic bags or freezer containers, to use as needed.
5. To store in refrigerator, up to 4 days, leave fat layer on surface of broth until ready to use, then lift fat off and discard, or use in other cooking. To freeze, transfer broth to freezer containers, allowing space on top for expansion. Freeze until ready to use (3 to 4 months maximum).

CHICKEN SOUP WITH DUMPLINGS

A creamy-thick soup with tender little chicken balls and vegetables to munch.

Makes 6 servings.

CHICKEN DUMPLINGS

1 cup diced cooked chicken (from Basic Chicken Broth)
1 cooked chicken liver
1 egg
⅓ cup flour
¼ cup milk
1 teaspoon salt
Dash of pepper
Dash of nutmeg
1 tablespoon chopped parsley
1 cup water
6 cups Basic Chicken Broth

SOUP

¼ cup chopped green onion
¼ cup chicken fat, butter or margarine
¼ cup flour
1 package (10 ounces) frozen mixed vegetables
½ teaspoon salt
1½ cups diced cooked chicken (from Basic Chicken Broth)

1. Combine chicken, liver, egg, flour, milk, salt, pepper and nutmeg in blender; blend at high speed until smooth. Turn into small bowl, stir in parsley; cover.
2. Bring water and 1 cup of the CHICKEN BROTH to boiling in large saucepan. Shape chicken mixture, one-half at a time, into ¾-inch balls with a teaspoon. Drop one by one into boiling broth. Simmer gently, uncovered, 8 to 10 minutes; remove with a slotted spoon; keep warm. Repeat with second half.
3. Sauté onion in chicken fat, or butter or margarine in kettle or Dutch oven, until soft but not brown, 3 to 4 minutes; stir in flour; gradually add remaining chicken broth; stirring constantly; bring to boiling; add vegetables and salt; cover. Cook 10 minutes, or until vegetables are tender.
4. Add chicken dumplings, cooking broth and chicken; heat 5 minutes. Ladle into soup bowls; serve with crusty bread.

CHICKEN IN THE POT

Eat this country-style soup with your spoon plus a knife and fork.

Makes 6 servings.

1 broiler-fryer (3 pounds)
1 pound small new potatoes, washed
4 carrots, pared and diced
2 turnips, pared and diced
2 stalks celery with tops, diced
1 leek, trimmed and washed well
1 tablespoon salt
2 sprigs of parsley
6 peppercorns
1 bay leaf
5 to 6 cups water

1. Cut chicken into serving-size pieces: 2 legs, 2 thighs and 2 wings. Cut each side of breast crosswise into 3 pieces. Layer chicken, potatoes, carrots, turnips, celery and leek in a 3-quart flameproof casserole or Dutch oven; sprinkle salt between layers. Add water almost to cover.
2. Tie tops from celery, parsley, peppercorns and bay leaf in a piece of cheesecloth. Push under liquid.
3. Bring to boiling; reduce heat; cover. Simmer 45 minutes to 1 hour, or until meat and vegetables are tender. Discard herb bag.
4. Ladle into soup bowls, spooning 2 pieces of chicken into each bowl. Serve with crusty bread.

CHICKEN-LEMON SOUP

Here's a cool and tangy opener for a warm-weather supper.

Makes 4 to 6 servings.

1 envelope chicken-noodle soup mix
1 cup thinly sliced celery
4 teaspoons lemon juice
2 hard-cooked eggs, finely diced

1. Prepare soup mix, following label directions; cook 5 minutes; add celery and cook 2 minutes longer.
2. Remove from heat; stir in lemon juice; pour into bowl; cover; chill.
3. Serve in cups or small bowls, with diced hard-cooked eggs sprinkled over.

CHUNKY CHICKEN-BEEF SOUP

An entire broiler-fryer and plenty of beef go into this made-from-scratch soup.

Makes 8 servings.

1½ pounds chuck beefsteak, cut into
   ½-inch cubes
1 large onion, chopped (1 cup)
1 broiler-fryer (about 2½ to 3 pounds),
   quartered
1 cup chopped celery
2 teaspoons salt
1 teaspoon seasoned salt
½ teaspoon pepper
½ teaspoon leaf rosemary, crumbled
½ teaspoon leaf thyme, crumbled
1 bay leaf
10 cups water
2 cups uncooked medium noodles

1. Brown beef in its own fat in a kettle or Dutch oven; stir in onion and sauté lightly.
2. Add chicken, celery, salt, seasoned salt, pepper, rosemary, thyme, bay leaf and water to kettle; heat to boiling; cover. Simmer 1 hour, or until chicken is tender; remove from kettle. Continue cooking beef 20 minutes, or until tender; remove bay leaf.
3. While beef finishes cooking, pull skin from chicken and take meat from bones; cut meat into cubes. Return to kettle; heat to boiling.
4. Stir in noodles. Cook 10 minutes, or until noodles are tender.
5. Ladle into soup plates. Sprinkle with chopped parsley and serve with your favorite crisp crackers, if you wish.

WHAT IS BROTH?

Broth is a stock or clear soup made of water in which meat, fowl or fish and vegetables have been simmered. It's used as a base for soups, sauces and gravies, as the liquid for cooking vegetables, rice, noodles or pasta and as a baste for roasted poultry as it cooks.

Broth is also referred to as stock, bouillon and consommé.

CHICKEN AND HAM BURGOO

A meal to come home for: Robust stew, perfect for an after-the-game or after-skating crowd of hungry dynamos.

Makes 12 servings.

1 roasting chicken (about 3 pounds)
4 smoked ham hocks, (about 1 pound each)
Water
3 teaspoons salt
½ teaspoon cayenne pepper
2 cups diced pared potatoes
2 cups diced pared carrots
2 large onions, chopped (2 cups)
1 package (10 ounces) frozen Fordhook lima
   beans
2 cups shredded cabbage
2 cups fresh corn kernels
2 cups thinly sliced celery
2 cups diced tomatoes
1 package (10 ounces) frozen whole okra
2 tablespoons Worcestershire sauce
1 cup diced green pepper
½ cup chopped parsley

1. Combine chicken and ham hocks in a kettle or roasting pan; add just enough water to cover. Heat to boiling; cover. Simmer 1½ hours, or until chicken is tender; remove from kettle. Continue cooking ham hocks 1 hour, or until tender; remove from kettle.
2. Let broth stand until fat rises to top, then skim off. Measure broth and return 12 cups to kettle. Stir in salt, cayenne, potatoes, carrots, onions and lima beans. Heat to boiling; simmer 15 minutes.
3. While vegetables cook, remove skin from chicken and ham hocks; take meat from bones, discarding fat; dice meat.
4. Stir cabbage, corn, celery, tomatoes, okra and Worcestershire sauce into kettle; simmer 15 minutes, or until all vegetables are crisply tender. Stir in green pepper, parsley and diced meats; heat just to boiling.
5. Ladle into soup plates or bowls. Serve with corn bread or crusty hard rolls, if you wish.

CHOWDER DIAMOND HEAD

Ginger, pineapple and coconut make this an enchanting South Seas soup.

Makes 6 servings.

1 cup sliced celery
1 small onion, chopped (¼ cup)
2 tablespoons butter or margarine
½ teaspoon ground ginger
2 cans condensed cream of chicken soup
1⅓ cups water
1⅓ cups milk
1 can (5 ounces) boned chicken, diced
1 can (about 9 ounces) pineapple tidbits,
   drained
Shredded coconut

1. Sauté celery and onion in butter or margarine until soft in a large heavy saucepan or Dutch oven; add ginger, blending thoroughly.
2. Stir in soup, water and milk. Add chicken and pineapple. Heat, stirring frequently, until bubbly-hot.
3. Ladle into soup bowls. Sprinkle with coconut. Serve with hot buttered rolls, if you wish.

CHICKEN CHOWDER

Canned soups are just the beginning!

Makes 6 servings.

3 cups water
1 can or 1 envelope chicken noodle soup mix
1 can or 1 envelope cream of mushroom soup
   mix
½ cup sliced pared carrots
¼ cup sliced celery
¼ cup chopped green pepper
1 can (5 or 6 ounces) boned chicken, diced
3 cups light or table cream

1. Heat water to boiling in a large saucepan; stir in soup mixes until blended, then carrots, celery and green pepper.
2. Heat to boiling; simmer 10 minutes.
3. Stir in chicken and cream; heat very slowly just until bubbly.
4. Ladle into heated soup plates or bowls. Serve with your favorite crisp crackers.

CHICKEN-CORN CHOWDER

Canned chicken soup, canned corn, canned milk—by the time the kids wash up, soup's on!

Makes 6 servings.

1 medium-size onion, chopped (½ cup)
2 tablespoons butter or margarine
2 cans condensed chicken noodle soup
1 soup can water
1 can (about 1 pound) cream-style corn
1 small can evaporated milk (⅔ cup)
¼ teaspoon pepper
2 tablespoons chopped parsley

1. Sauté onion in butter or margarine just until soft in medium-size saucepan.
2. Stir in remaining ingredients, except parsley. Heat just to boiling.
3. Pour into heated soup bowls or mugs; sprinkle with parsley.

CUCUMBER-CHICKEN CUP

Float a spoonful of sour cream on top.

Makes 6 servings.

2 cans condensed chicken broth
2 soup cans of water
1 large cucumber, pared and shredded
⅓ cup dairy sour cream
Dillweed

1. Combine chicken broth and water in a medium-size saucepan; heat to boiling. Stir in cucumber and salt to taste, if needed. Heat again until bubbly.
2. Ladle into soup cups or small bowls. Float a spoonful of sour cream on each; sprinkle dillweed over cream. Serve with small wheat crackers, if you wish.

BASIC BROTH SOUP COOKERY

A savory, richly flavored stock is essential for good soup. It can be the base for cream soups, stews, chowders and appetizer soups. Whenever your soup recipe calls for stock, use canned broth if you don't plan to make one from scratch.

COLD CURRIED CHICKEN SOUP

This is one of the most delicious of all iced soups.

Makes 6 servings.

3 tart apples, pared, cored and sliced (apples must be tart)
1 large onion, peeled and sliced
1 tablespoon butter or margarine
2 teaspoons curry powder
Salt to taste
Freshly ground pepper to taste
3 drops red-pepper seasoning
3 cups chicken consommé or broth
1 cup dry white wine
1 cup light cream
¼ to ½ cup very finely diced cooked chicken
Paprika

1. Cook apples and onion in butter or margarine over low heat, stirring often, until soft. Do not let them brown.
2. Stir in curry powder and cook 3 minutes longer. Add salt, pepper, red-pepper seasoning, chicken consommé or broth and wine. Simmer, covered, 10 minutes, stirring frequently.
3. Puree in blender or press through a fine sieve. Chill thoroughly.
4. Just before serving, stir in cream and chicken; sprinkle with paprika. Serve icy cold.

HOT SENEGALESE SOUP

This creamy soup is an exotic but very easy version of an honored specialty.

Makes 8 servings.

2 cans condensed cream of chicken soup
3 cups milk
½ teaspoon curry powder
2 tablespoons toasted coconut

1. Combine soup, milk and curry powder in medium-size saucepan; heat just until bubbly-hot, then beat with rotary beater until creamy smooth.
2. Pour into 8 small bowls or cups, dividing evenly; sprinkle with coconut.

CHICKEN N' VEGETABLES

An easy-to-make soup that's ready to serve in about 30 minutes.

Makes 6 hearty servings.

1 medium-size onion, chopped
2 medium-size potatoes, peeled and chopped
1 can (1 pound) whole kernel corn, drained
1 package (10 ounces) frozen lima beans, cooked and drained
2 cans (13¾ ounces each) chicken broth
1 can (1 pt. 10 oz.) tomato juice
1 cup cooked chicken
1½ teaspoons salt
¼ teaspoon pepper
1 tablespoon butter or margarine
1 tablespoon Worcestershire sauce

Combine all ingredients in a large kettle or Dutch oven; simmer about 30 minutes or until vegetables are done.

COMPANY SOUP

Garnish this tasty soup with bacon, scallions and cucumbers.

Makes 4 to 6 servings.

3 cans (13¾ ounces each) chicken broth
¼ cup dry white wine (optional)
1½ teaspoons salt
⅛ teaspoon pepper
1 teaspoon leaf tarragon, crumbled
1½ cups cooked chicken, chopped
1 package (10 ounces) frozen green peas, cooked and drained
1 can (7½ ounces) water chestnuts, sliced
⅓ cup sliced ripe olives
Chopped cooked bacon
Diced hard-boiled chopped scallions
Cucumber slices

Combine soup ingredients in a large kettle or Dutch oven; cook over a low flame for 15 minutes. Serve with garnishes (bacon, scallions and cucumber slices) in individual bowls or on one serving tray.

MULLIGATAWNY SOUP

A classic soup with origins in India, is richly flavored with exotic curry.

Makes 6 servings.

3 medium carrots, pared and sliced
2 stalks of celery, sliced
6 cups Basic Chicken Broth (see page 26)
3 cups cooked diced chicken (from Basic Chicken Broth)
1 large onion, chopped (1 cup)
4 tablespoons (½ stick) butter or margarine
1 apple, pared, quartered, cored and chopped
5 teaspoons curry powder
1 teaspoon salt
¼ cup flour
1 tablespoon lemon juice
2 cups hot cooked rice
¼ cup chopped parsley
6 lemon slices (optional)

1. Cook carrots and celery in 1 cup broth in a medium-size saucepan 20 minutes, or until tender. Add chicken; heat just until hot; cover; keep warm.
2. Sauté onion until soft in butter or margarine in Dutch oven; stir in apple, curry powder and salt; sauté 5 minutes longer, or until apple is soft; add flour. Gradually stir in remaining chicken broth; heat to boiling, stirring constantly; reduce heat; cover; simmer 15 minutes.
3. Add vegetables and chicken with the broth they were cooked in; bring just to boiling. Stir in lemon juice.
4. Ladle into soup plates or bowls; pass hot cooked rice and chopped parsley and lemon slices, if you wish, for each to add his own garnish. Good with crusty French bread.

CHILLED CHICKEN CREAM

Celery seeds give canned cream soup an exceptional flavor.

Makes 6 servings.

1 can condensed cream of chicken soup
1 cup light or table cream
½ cup milk
1 teaspoon lemon juice
½ teaspoon celery seeds

1. Combine all ingredients in an electric-blender container; cover. Blend 1 minute, or until creamy smooth: (Or beat slightly longer with an electric beater.) Chill.
2. Pour into mugs or cups. Garnish each with a celery-stick stirrer and serve with tiny croutons to sprinkle over, or a dash of paprika, if you wish.

CHICKEN QUEBEC

Serve this spoon-up main dish in soup plates to enjoy with thick slices of crusty bread.

Makes 6 servings.

1 stewing chicken, cut into serving-size pieces
6 slices back bacon
1 medium-size onion, chopped (½ cup)
1 teaspoon salt
3 or 4 peppercorns
6 cups water
1 package (8 ounces) elbow macaroni
1 tablespoon parsley flakes

1. Trim fat from chicken; melt fat in large heavy kettle or Dutch oven. Brown chicken, a few serving-size pieces at a time; drain on paper toweling.
2. Fry bacon lightly in same kettle; remove and set aside; pour off all fat. Return browned chicken and bacon to kettle; add onion, salt, peppercorns and water.
3. Cover tightly; heat to boiling, then simmer 2 hours, or until chicken is tender. (If much fat has cooked out, remove the kettle from heat; let stand 5 to 10 minutes; then skim off all fat.)
4. Reheat to boiling; stir in macaroni and parsley flakes. (Add 1 cup water, if needed.) Cook, uncovered, stirring occasionally, 15 to 20 minutes, or until macaroni is tender. Season to taste with salt, if needed.

NOTE: If little new potatoes are in season, use in place of macaroni. Leave jackets on and cook in stew, covered, until tender.

BRUNSWICK CHOWDER

Chicken, canned soup and vegetables add up to this satisfying meal in a bowl.

Makes 8 servings.

1 broiler-fryer (about 2 ¼ pounds), quartered
5 teaspoons seasoned salt
Water
1 large onion, chopped (1 cup)
2 tablespoons butter or margarine
2 packages (10 ounces each) frozen Fordhook lima beans
2 cans condensed tomato-rice soup
2 cups thinly sliced celery
2 cans (1 pound each) cream-style corn

1. Combine chicken, 3 teaspoons of the salt and 4 cups water in a kettle; cover. Simmer 45 minutes, or until chicken is tender. Take meat from bones; dice. Strain broth into a 4-cup measure; add water, if needed, to make 4 cups.
2. Sauté onion in butter or margarine until soft in same kettle; add lima beans, soup, two soup cans of water and celery; cover. Simmer 15 minutes, or until beans are tender. Stir in chicken, broth, corn and remaining 2 teaspoons seasoned salt.
3. Heat slowly just to boiling. Ladle into heated soup bowls.

COLD SENEGALESE SOUP

Midsummer's dream: A cold and simple gourmet dish.

Makes 6 servings.

1 can condensed cream of chicken soup
1 tall can evaporated milk
1 tablespoon lemon juice
1 teaspoon curry powder

1. Combine all ingredients in large bowl; beat (or blend in an electric blender) until creamy-smooth; chill.
2. Serve in cups or bowls. If you like, sprinkle with chopped toasted almonds or flaked coconut.

Chicken in a Hurry

To the casual observer, a table set with delightfully prepared food means one thing: Dinner is going to be great. Unfortunately, the chef of the house often views this scene with a sigh of relief. Hours of kitchen time have gone into making dinner happen.

Happily, you don't have to be in the martyr's seat when it comes to chicken dinner. It's naturally easy to prepare and when joined with recipes specifically designed to save you time, it adds up to a meal everyone will enjoy.

Our short-time recipes include make-ahead dishes that are especially practical for working wives; and those in the Fast and Simple section are geared for new cooks and mothers-on-the go.

Since some of the recipes can be prepared well ahead of time, they're also great for a day when you've been out just enjoying yourself.

Fast and Simple

3. Return onion to pan; add remaining ingredients; cover tightly. Simmer 40 minutes, or until chicken is tender.

CHICKEN CREOLE

this recipe will have dinner on the table in half an hour.

Makes 4 servings.

1 broiler-fryer, cut in serving-size pieces
2 teaspoons salt, divided
½ teaspoon paprika
2 tablespoons butter or margarine
1 medium onion, sliced
1 medium green pepper, cut in strips
½ cup chopped celery
1 can (1 pound) tomatoes
½ teaspoon dried leaf thyme
1 can (3 or 4 ounces) mushrooms

1. Sprinkle chicken pieces with 1 teaspoon salt and paprika. Melt butter in large skillet; add chicken and brown on all sides.
2. Add onion, green pepper, celery, tomatoes, remaining 1 teaspoon salt and thyme.
3. Bring to a boil, reduce heat, cover and simmer 20 minutes. Add mushrooms and liquid. Simmer 5 to 10 minutes longer.

QUICK CACCIATORE

An easy way to make the Italian favorite.

Makes 4 servings.

1 medium-size onion, chopped (½ cup)
3 tablespoons salad oil
1 broiler-fryer (about 3 pounds) cut in serving-size pieces
½ teaspoon salt
⅛ teaspoon pepper
1 clove garlic, minced
1 can (about 1 pound) tomatoes
1 tablespoon vinegar
½ teaspoon rosemary
½ teaspoon sugar

1. Sauté onion in 1 tablespoon salad oil in large frying pan about 5 minutes; remove and save for Step 3.
2. Sprinkle chicken with salt and pepper; brown in same frying pan with remaining 2 tablespoons oil and garlic.

CHICKEN-TOMATO SKILLET

The chicken pieces are browned and cooked with fresh rosy tomatoes and dill.

Makes 4 servings.

1 broiler-fryer, cut in serving-size pieces
1½ teaspoons salt, divided
¼ teaspoon pepper
2 tablespoons butter or margarine
¼ cup chopped onion
½ cup chopped celery with leaves
4 medium tomatoes, peeled and chopped
¼ cup snipped fresh dill or 1 tablespoon dried dill weed
Grated Parmesan cheese

1. Sprinkle chicken with 1 teaspoon of the salt and pepper. Heat butter in a large skillet. Add chicken and brown on all sides. Remove from skillet.
2. Add onion and celery; cook until tender. Add tomatoes and dill; sprinkle with remaining ½ teaspoon salt. Add chicken; spoon some of the tomato mixture over chicken
3. Cover; simmer 30 minutes, until chicken is tender. Serve sprinkled light with grated Parmesan cheese.

CHICKEN BAKED WITH BARBECUE SAUCE

Whip the sauce together in no time, spoon it over chicken, pop the dish in the oven, and forget it while it cooks to savory tenderness.

Bake at 400° about 1 hour.
Makes 6 servings.

2 broiler-fryers (about 2 pounds each), cut in serving-size pieces
Butter or margarine
Barbecue Sauce

1. Wash chicken pieces; pat dry; remove skin if you wish.
2. Arrange chicken pieces in a single layer in a well-buttered large shallow baking pan.

3. Spoon Barbecue Sauce over chicken so pieces are well coated. (If you have any leftover sauce, it will keep in a covered jar in the refrigerator.)
4. Bake, uncovered, in hot oven (400°) about 1 hour, or until chicken is tender.

BARBECUE SAUCE

Makes 2½ cups.

2 cans (8 ounces each) tomato sauce
1 medium-size onion, chopped (½ cup)
1 clove garlic, minced
¼ cup soy sauce
2 tablespoons sugar
1 teaspoon dry mustard
⅛ teaspoon cayenne

Mix all ingredients in a medium-size bowl.

MEDITERRANEAN CHICKEN

A savory skillet dish that's quickly prepared.

Makes 4 servings.

1 broiler-fryer, quartered
1½ teaspoons salt, divided
¼ teaspoon pepper
3 tablespoons butter or margarine
1 medium onion, chopped
½ cup chicken broth
1 medium eggplant, pared and cubed
2 medium tomatoes, peeled and chopped
¼ teaspoon each, dried leaf basil, thyme and oregano
¼ cup grated Parmesan or Romano cheese

1. Sprinkle chicken with 1 teaspoon salt and pepper. Heat butter in a large skillet; add chicken and brown on both sides. Remove from skillet.
2. Add onion and cook until tender.. Add broth, scraping brown particles from bottom of skillet. Add eggplant and tomatoes; sprinkle with herbs and remaining ½ teaspoon salt. Add chicken; spoon some of the vegetable mixture over chicken.
3. Cover; simmer 30 minutes, until chicken is tender. Serve sprinkled with grated Parmesan or Romano cheese.

CHINESE CHICKEN WITH RICE

When you've got less than 30 minutes to prepare dinner, this is the dish to choose.

Makes 6 servings.

3 boneless chicken breasts (chicken cutlets), weighing about 1¼ pounds
½ pound mushrooms
1 can (5 ounces) bamboo shoots
3 green onions
1 small stalk celery
1 small sweet red pepper OR 1 can or jar (4 ounces) pimientos
4 tablespoons vegetable oil
¼ cup dry sherry
2 tablespoons soy sauce
2 tablespoons cornstarch
1 cup chicken broth (from an about-14-ounce can)
2 cups precooked rice (from a 14-ounce package)
Boiling Water
Salt

1. Pull skin from chicken breasts; slice meat thin. Trim mushrooms and slice. Drain bamboo shoots and slice, if needed; trim green onions and celery; slice both thin. Halve red pepper, seed, and dice. (If using pimientos, drain and cut into strips.)
2. Sauté chicken quickly in vegetable oil in a large frying pan 3 minutes, or until chicken turns white.
3. Stir in mushrooms, bamboo shoots, green onions, celery and red pepper; sauté 2 minutes. Stir in sherry and soy sauce; cover. Cook 2 minutes, or until vegetables are crisply tender.
4. Blend cornstarch into chicken broth until smooth in a small bowl; stir into frying pan. Cook, stirring constantly, until sauce thickens and boils for 3 minutes.
5. While chicken mixture cooks, prepare rice with boiling water and salt, following label directions. Spoon around edge on a large serving platter; spoon chicken mixture on top. Garnish with a half mushroom and serve with additional soy sauce, if you wish.

CHICKEN CORDON BLEU

A party aristocrat, and easy to make in spite of its fancy French name.

Bake at 400° for 40 minutes.
Makes 4 servings.

2 whole chicken breasts (about 12 ounces each)
4 thin slices boiled ham, about 3 inches square
2 triangles (1 ounce each) process Gruyere cheese, sliced
4 tablespoons (½ stick) butter or margarine
½ cup fine dry bread crumbs
½ teaspoon salt
⅛ teaspoon paprika

1. Halve chicken breasts; remove skin, if you wish, then cut meat in one piece from bones. Pull each half breast open in the middle to make a deep pocket.
2. Fold ham around cheese slices, dividing evenly; tuck one into each pocket.
3. Melt butter or margarine in a pie plate; mix bread crumbs, salt and paprika in a second pie plate.
4. Roll stuffed chicken breasts first in butter or margarine, then in crumb mixture to coat well. Place in a single layer in buttered baking dish.
5. Bake in hot oven (400°) 40 minutes, or until chicken is golden brown.

SPANISH RICE CHICKEN BAKE

A packaged mix is your short cut to a fine Castilian dish.

Bake at 350° for 1 hour.
Makes 8 servings.

2 broiler-fryers (about 3 pounds each), quartered
¼ cup flour
¼ cup salad oil
1½ cups raw rice
3 cups water
1 envelope Spanish rice seasoning mix
1 large green pepper, cut in 8 rings
1 cup sliced stuffed green olives

1. Shake chicken with flour in paper bag to coat well. Brown, a few pieces at a time, in salad oil in large frying pan; drain on paper toweling.
2. Place rice in a 10-cup shallow baking dish; arrange browned chicken on top.
3. Stir water into chicken drippings in frying pan; blend in Spanish rice seasoning mix; heat to boiling. Pour over chicken and rice; cover.
4. Bake in moderate oven (350°) 30 minutes; uncover and lay green pepper rings and sliced olives on top. Cover and bake 30 minutes longer, or until chicken and rice are tender, and liquid is absorbed.

Make-Aheads

CHICKEN TETRAZZINI

This excellent chicken-spaghetti-cheese dish is an all-time party favorite—especially with hostesses, who can make it ahead of time.

Bake at 450° for 20 minutes.
Makes 6 servings.

1 package (8 ounces) thin spaghetti
1 small onion, chopped (¼ cup)
2 tablespoons butter or margarine
2 tablespoons flour
1 envelope instant chicken broth OR 1 chicken bouillon cube
1 teaspoon salt
1 teaspoon dry mustard
½ teaspoon pepper
1 large can evaporated milk
1 can (3 or 4 ounces) sliced mushrooms
2 pimientos, diced
3 cups diced cooked chicken
1 cup (¼ pound) grated sharp Cheddar cheese
¼ cup grated Parmesan cheese

1. Cook spaghetti, following label directions; drain; place in buttered 8-cup shallow baking dish.
2. While spaghetti cooks, sauté onion in butter or margarine until soft in large saucepan. Remove from heat; blend in flour, instant broth or bouillon cube, salt, dry mustard

and pepper. Slowly stir in evaporated milk, then liquid from mushrooms plus water to make 1½ cups. Cook, stirring constantly, until sauce thickens and boils 1 minute; stir in mushrooms and pimientos.

3. Mix 2 cups sauce with drained spaghetti in baking dish, making a well in center to hold the chicken mixture.

4. Combine chicken with remaining sauce; spoon into dish with spaghetti; sprinkle cheeses on top.

5. Bake in hot oven (450°) 20 minutes, or until bubbly and golden. (If made ahead, cover lightly, cool, then chill until 30 minutes before baking. If put into oven cold, allow an additional 15 to 20 minutes' baking time.)

AHEAD OF TIME CHICKEN CASSEROLE

This meal-in-one dish understands a busy household and caters to its cook.

Bake at 350° for 1 hour.
Makes 4 servings.

1 cup creamed cottage cheese
1½ cups sour cream
6 tablespoons grated Parmesan cheese
1½ teaspoons salt
¼ teaspoon red-pepper sauce
¼ cup sliced pitted ripe olives
3 cups spinach or regular medium egg noodles, cooked
2½ cups cooked cut-up chicken (from Simmered Chicken)

1. In large bowl mix cottage cheese, sour cream, 4 tablespoons Parmesan cheese, salt and red-pepper sauce. Stir in olives, noodles and chicken.

2. Turn into a greased 2-quart casserole. Sprinkle with remaining 2 tablespoons Parmesan cheese. Cover and refrigerate.

3. One hour before serving, place in moderate oven (350°); bake, covered, for 35 minutes. Uncover and bake 25 minutes more.

FREEZER TIP

Slightly undercook dishes which must be cooked again. Those that require an hour of reheating can be undercooked by 30 minutes.

SIMMERED CHICKEN

Makes about 2½ cups diced cooked chicken.

1 broiler-fryer (about 3 pounds), whole or cut in serving-size pieces
2 cups water
1 small onion, sliced
2 celery tops
2 bay leaves
1 teaspoon monosodium glutamate
1 teaspoon salt
¼ teaspoon pepper

1. Put chicken in kettle; add water and remaining ingredients. Bring to a boil, cover tightly. Reduce heat and simmer 1 hour.

2. Remove from heat; strain broth. Refrigerate chicken and broth. When chicken is cool, remove meat from bones; dice.

QUICK CHICKEN CASSEROLE

Built-in cream sauce makes this easy-do casserole a dinner winner.

Bake at 375° for 15 minutes.
Makes 4 servings.

2 packages (10 ounces each) frozen corn, carrots and pearl onions with cream sauce
2 cans (5 ounces each) boned chicken
¼ cup chopped parsley
1 package refrigerated butterflake dinner rolls
Sesame seeds

1. Cook vegetables in a large saucepan, following label directions; drain. Dice chicken and add to saucepan with chopped parsley. Stir; pour into a 6-cup baking dish.

2. Separate rolls to make 24 even pieces. Arrange, buttery-side up, on top of hot mixture; sprinkle with sesame seeds.

3. Bake in moderate oven (375°) 15 minutes, or until biscuits are golden.

CHICKEN WITH MUSHROOMS AND SOUR CREAM

A little mixing makes it all happen.

Makes 4 servings.

2 whole chicken breasts
3 tablespoons butter or margarine
2 tablespoons finely chopped scallions
½ teaspoon salt
1 can (10½ ounces) condensed cream of
    mushroom soup
1 can (3 or 4 ounces) sliced mushrooms
¼ cup water
½ cup dairy sour cream
Hot cooked rice

1. Bone chicken breasts; remove skin. Cut each breast half into 10 or 12 strips. Assemble remaining ingredients.
2. Melt butter or margarine in a large skillet over high heat. Add chicken and scallions; sprinkle with salt. Cook 6 minutes.
3. Add undiluted mushroom soup, sliced mushrooms with liquid and water. Heat to boiling, stirring until mixture is smooth. Reduce heat; blend in sour cream. Do not boil. Serve over hot cooked rice.

CHICKEN IN ORANGE SAUCE

This luscious dish can be made the day before.

Makes 4 servings.

1 broiler-fryer, cut in serving-size pieces
½ cup (1 stick) butter or margarine
¼ cup flour
2 tablespoons brown sugar
1 teaspoon salt
½ teaspoon ground ginger
⅛ teaspoon pepper
1½ cups orange juice
½ cup water
2 oranges, pared and sectioned

1. Wash chicken pieces; pat dry. Brown slowly in butter or margarine in large frying pan; remove from pan; set aside.
2. Blend flour, brown sugar, salt, ginger and pepper into drippings in pan; cook, stirring all the time, just until mixture bubbles. Stir in orange juice and water slowly; continue cooking and stirring until sauce thickens; boil 1 minute; remove from heat.

3. Return chicken to pan; cool. Cover and chill (this much can be done the day before).
4. About 45 minutes before serving time, reheat chicken and sauce just to boiling, then simmer, covered, 30 minutes. Lay orange sections around chicken; continue cooking 15 minutes longer, or until chicken is tender. Serve with fluffy hot rice.

CHICKEN AND HAM SEVILLE

Slices of chicken and stuffed rolls of ham bake with a spicy fruit glaze.

Bake at 350° about 1 hour.
Makes 12 servings.

6 whole chicken breasts, split
1 bottle (8 ounces) Italian salad dressing
2 tablespoons minced onion
1 cup diced celery
4 tablespoons (½ stick) butter or margarine
1¼ cups water
1 can (6 ounces) frozen concentrated orange
    juice
1 package (8 ounces) ready-mix bread
    stuffing (4 cups)
¼ cup chopped celery leaves
12 large slices boiled ham, cut not more than
    ⅛-inch thick (about 2 pounds)
½ cup orange marmalade
2 teaspoons ground ginger

1. Remove skin and snip off small rib bones from chicken breasts. Arrange in a single layer in large shallow baking pan, 13x9x2; pour salad dressing over; turn to coat all sides; cover lightly; let stand at room temperature, turning occasionally, 2 to 3 hours, or overnight in refrigerator.
2. Sauté onion and celery in butter or margarine 2 to 3 minutes in medium-size frying pan. Stir in water and ¼ cup orange juice; heat to boiling. Pour over stuffing and celery leaves in a bowl; stir to moisten.
3. Spoon a scant ½ cup stuffing into each slice of ham; roll up; fasten with a wooden pick if needed; place, folded side down, in single layer in greased large baking pan; cover lightly. (This much can be done a day ahead and kept chilled.)
4. About 1 hour before serving, take chicken and ham rolls from refrigerator. Drain marinade off chicken into a small bowl; stir in saved concentrated orange juice, marmalade and ginger. Brush over meats.

5. Place chicken, uncovered, in moderate oven (350°). Bake, basting often with marmalade mixture, about 1 hour, or until tender.
6. Bake ham, uncovered, in same oven, also basting with marmalade mixture, about 40 minutes, or until heated and glazed.
7. Arrange meats in separate piles on a heated platter; garnish with watercress and preserved kumquats stuck with fancy picks, if you wish.

CHICKEN AND PINEAPPLE CASSEROLE

The chicken is glazed with a gleaming fruit sauce.

Bake at 375° for 1 hour and 5 minutes.
Makes 8 servings.

2 broiler-fryers, quartered
2 tablespoons salt, divided
1 tablespoon melted butter or margarine
1 can (1 pound, 4 ounces) sliced pineapple in syrup
2 cans (1 pound, 1 ounce each) yams in syrup
3 tablespoons cornstarch
¼ cup lemon juice
½ teaspoon dry mustard
½ teaspoon ginger
2 teaspoons instant minced onion
½ cup currant jelly
8 maraschino cherries with stems

1. Sprinkle chicken quarters with 1½ teaspoons salt. Place skin side up in shallow 3-quart casserole. Brush with melted butter or margarine. Bake in moderate oven (375°) for 45 minutes.
2. While chicken is baking, prepare sauce. Drain syrup from pineapple and yams into saucepan. Add cornstarch, lemon juice, remaining ½ teaspoon salt, dry mustard, ginger and instant minced onion. Stir until cornstarch is well blended. Add currant jelly. Cook, stirring constantly, until mixture thickens and comes to a boil. Remove from heat.
3. When chicken has baked for 45 minutes, remove from oven. Add drained pineapple slices and yams. Pour sauce over all. Return to oven and bake 20 minutes longer, until chicken is tender. Serve garnished with maraschino cherries.

CORN-FLAKE CHICKEN

You can give this chicken its corn-flake coating ahead of time and refrigerate it, oven-ready, till you're ready.

Bake at 425° about 45 minutes.
Makes 4 servings, 2 pieces each.

1 broiler-fryer (about 3 pounds), cut into 8 serving-size pieces
½ cup buttermilk
½ cup packaged corn-flake crumbs
½ cup flour
1 teaspoon salt
1 teaspoon poultry seasoning
4 tablespoons (½ stick) melted butter or margarine

1. Remove chicken skin, if you wish; then dip chicken pieces in buttermilk in shallow pan; coat with mixture of corn-flake crumbs, flour, salt and poultry seasoning combined in second shallow pan; arrange chicken pieces in single layer in well-buttered baking pan; pour melted butter or margarine over. (This much may be done ahead.)
2. Bake in hot oven (425°) 45 minutes, or until tender.

KING MIDAS CHICKEN

An obliging casserole that minds itself in the oven.

Bake at 350° for 1¼ hours.
Makes 4 servings.

1 broiler-fryer, cut in serving-size pieces
1 teaspoon salt
1 can (8¼ ounces) crushed pineapple in syrup
¼ cup prepared mustard
½ cup chopped chutney
½ cup coarsely chopped pecans

1. Sprinkle chicken pieces on both sides with salt. Place skin side up in single layer in shallow 2-quart casserole.
2. Mix together pineapple and remaining ingredients; spoon over chicken. Bake uncovered in moderate oven (350°) for 1 hour and 15 minutes.

When chicken takes to the oven, the result is delightful–whether it's baked or broiled to a tender golden-brown or roasted whole with its own stuffing.
Oven chicken is also easy. Once you've finished the basic preparations and the chicken is popped in the oven, your work is done (except for a peek now and then or a quick basting with a buttery sauce).
If it's stuffed, the flavor possibilities are almost endless. For instance, the stuffing recipes in this chapter range from a simple bread-crumb mixture to an elaborate blending of fruits and nuts.
Added to your own repertoire of recipes, they'll guarantee mouth-watering diversity for many meals to come

Chicken: Baked, Broiled, Roasted and Fried Favorites

Baked Chicken

CREAMY BAKED CHICKEN

Two cream soups make the rich gravy; one also adds flavor to fluffy corn biscuits on top.

Bake at 350° about 1 hour, then at 450° about 15 minutes.
Makes 4 servings.

1 broiler-fryer (2½ to 3½ pounds), cut in
　serving-size pieces
1 can condensed cream-of-mushroom soup
1 can condensed cream-of-chicken soup
½ cup plus 3 tablespoons milk
½ teaspoon ground ginger
1 cup biscuit mix
¼ cup yellow cornmeal
½ tablespoon finely chopped crystallized
　ginger

1. Cut away small bones from chicken breasts; remove all skin if you prefer chicken cooked without it.
2. Arrange chicken pieces in buttered 12-cup casserole; combine the cream-of-mushroom soup, ½ can (½ cup plus 2 tablespoons) cream-of-chicken soup (save the rest for Step 4), ½ cup milk and ground ginger in small bowl; mix well; pour over chicken pieces in casserole; cover.
3. Bake in moderate oven (350°) 30 minutes; remove cover; stir to mix sauce and juices from chicken; cover again; bake 30 minutes longer, or until chicken is tender. Reset oven to hot (450°).
4. Combine biscuit mix, cornmeal and crystallized ginger in small bowl; mix 3 tablespoons milk with saved chicken soup; stir into biscuit mixture, mixing lightly.
5. Remove casserole from oven; uncover casserole and drop dough by spoonfuls to make 8 mounds in a ring on top of chicken.
6. Bake in hot oven (450°) about 15 minutes longer, or until biscuits are puffed and golden-brown.

HERB IDEA

For oven chicken: Mix a pinch of marjoram into melted butter or margarine for coating the chicken before you put it in the oven, or when you baste while cooking.

CURRY GLAZED CHICKEN

The happy blend of curry and marmalade makes this a special-occasion dish.

Bake at 400° for 1 hour.
Makes 8 servings.

2 broiler-fryers, quartered
6 tablespoons (¾ stick) butter or margarine
1 large onion, chopped (1 cup)
8 slices raw bacon, finely diced
2 tablespoons flour
1 tablespoon curry powder
1 can condensed beef broth
¼ cup marmalade (ginger or orange)
2 tablespoons catsup
2 tablespoons lemon juice

1. Wash chicken quarters; pat dry; remove skin, if you wish.
2. Melt butter or margarine in a large shallow baking pan. Dip chicken in butter to coat both sides; then arrange, meaty side up, in a single layer in same pan.
3. Bake in hot oven (400°) 20 minutes, or until starting to turn golden.
4. While chicken bakes, combine remaining ingredients in a medium-size saucepan; heat, stirring constantly, to boiling, then simmer, stirring often, 15 minutes, or until thick. Spoon about half over chicken to make a thick coating.
5. Continue baking 20 minutes; spoon on rest of glaze. Bake 20 minutes longer, or until chicken is tender and richly glazed.

SMOTHERED CHICKEN

Baked in liquid under cover, chicken makes its own delicious gravy.

Bakes at 350° for 1 hour.
Makes 6 servings.

3 broiler-fryers (about 2 pounds each), split
⅔ cup flour
2 teaspoons salt
¼ teaspoon pepper
6 tablespoons (¾ stick) butter or margarine
1 medium-size onion, chopped (½ cup)
2½ cups water

1. Wash chicken halves; pat dry. Shake with mixture of ⅓ cup flour, 1½ teaspoons salt and pepper in a paper bag to coat evenly.

2. Brown pieces, several at a time, in butter or margarine in a large frying pan; place in a single layer in a roasting pan.
3. Sauté onion until soft in drippings in frying pan; stir in 1½ cups of the water and remaining ½ teaspoon salt. Heat, stirring constantly, to boiling; pour over chicken; cover.
4. Bake in moderate oven (350°) for 1 hour or until chicken is tender. Remove to a heated serving platter and keep warm in slow oven while making gravy.
5. Blend remaining ⅓ cup flour and 1 cup water until smooth in a 2-cup measure. Heat liquid in roasting pan to boiling; slowly stir in flour mixture. Cook, stirring constantly, until gravy thickens and boils 1 minute. Darken with a few drops bottled gravy coloring, if you wish. Serve separately to spoon over chicken.

CHICKEN CORIANDER

This unusual chicken dish has a delightfully spicy flavor.

Bake at 350° for 1 hour.
Makes 6 servings.

3 chicken breasts (about 12 ounces each)
4 tablespoons (½ stick) butter or margarine
1 small onion, grated
1 tablespoon ground coriander
1½ teaspoons salt
½ teaspoon chili powder
1 tablespoon lemon juice
Pan Gravy

1. Halve chicken breasts; remove skin, if you wish; then cut meat in one piece from bones.
2. Melt butter or margarine in a shallow baking pan; stir in seasonings.
3. Roll chicken in mixture to coat well, then arrange in a single layer in same pan. Bake in moderate oven (350°) 30 minutes; turn.
4. Continue baking, basting several times with buttery liquid in pan, 30 minutes longer, or until chicken is tender. Serve with Pan Gravy (for recipe, turn to chapter on GRAVIES).

ONION DIP CHICKEN

Sharp onion-soup mix gives this crumb-coated chicken a zesty flavor.

Bake at 350° for 1 hour.
Makes 8 servings.

2 broiler-fryers (about 2 pounds each), cut up
1 envelope (1⅜ ounces) onion-soup mix
1 cup soft bread crumbs (2 slices)
1 teaspoon salt
⅛ teaspoon pepper

1. Remove skin from chicken, if you wish; cut away small bones from breast pieces.
2. Combine soup mix, bread crumbs, salt and pepper in a paper bag. Shake chicken pieces, a few at a time, in mixture to coat well. Place, not touching, in a single layer in a buttered large shallow baking pan.
3. Bake in moderate oven (350°) 1 hour, or until chicken is tender and richly browned.

CHICKEN DIABLE

The flavor secret: Honey, mustard and curry powder, an oddly delectable blend.

Bake at 375° for 1 hour.
Makes 4 servings.

1 broiler-fryer (about 3 pounds), cut up
4 tablespoons (½ stick) butter or margarine
½ cup honey
¼ cup prepared mustard
1 teaspoon salt
1 teaspoon curry powder

1. Wash chicken pieces; pat dry; remove skin, if you wish.
2. Melt the butter or margarine in a shallow baking pan; stir in remaining ingredients. Roll chicken in butter mixture to coat both sides; then arrange, meaty side up, in a single layer in same pan.
3. Bake in moderate oven (375°) 1 hour, or until chicken is tender and richly glazed.

BAKED CHICKEN ORIENTALE

This chicken has a rich honey-and-soy glaze, at once sweet and sour.

Bake at 350° for 1 hour.
Makes 4 servings.

1 broiler-fryer (about 3 pounds), cut in serving-size pieces
½ cup flour
1 teaspoon salt
¼ teaspoon pepper
8 tablespoons (1 stick) butter or margarine
¼ cup honey
¼ cup lemon juice
1 tablespoon soy sauce

1. Wash chicken pieces; drain. Shake in mixture of flour, salt and pepper in paper bag to coat well.
2. Melt 4 tablespoons of the butter or margarine in a baking dish, 13x9x2; roll the chicken pieces, one at a time, in melted butter to coat all over. Place, skin side down, in single layer in baking dish.
3. Place baking dish in moderate oven (350°); bake for 30 minutes.
4. Melt remaining 4 tablespoons butter or margarine in small saucepan; stir in honey, lemon juice and soy sauce until well mixed.
5. Turn chicken; pour honey mixture over. Bake, basting several times with syrup and drippings in pan, 30 minutes longer, or until tender and richly glazed.

SAN FERNANDO PEPPER CHICKEN

Seasoned pepper—a spunky blend—flavors this Southwest chicken dish.

Bake at 350° for 1 hour.
Makes 6 servings.

½ cup (1 stick) butter or margarine
2 broiler-fryers (about 2 pounds each), cut in serving-size pieces
1½ tablespoons seasoned pepper
2 teaspoons salt
Savory Mushroom Gravy

1. Melt butter or margarine in large shallow baking pan. Roll chicken pieces one at a time in butter to coat well; then arrange, skin side down, in single layer in pan.

2. Combine seasoned pepper and salt in a small cup; sprinkle half evenly over the chicken.
3. Bake in moderate oven (350°) 30 minutes; turn; sprinkle remaining seasoning mixture over. Bake 30 minutes longer, or until chicken is tender and lightly browned.
4. Arrange on heated serving platter; keep warm in a slow oven while making gravy. Serve gravy in separate bowl to spoon over chicken.

SAVORY MUSHROOM GRAVY: Pour off all chicken drippings from pan; return ¼ cupful. Stir in 1 can condensed cream-of-mushroom soup mix. Blend in ½ cup water. Cook slowly, stirring constantly, 8 to 10 minutes, until thickened. Makes 2 cups.

BAKED LEMON CHICKEN

Lemon baste is the secret ingredient here.

Bake at 375° for 1 hour.
Makes 4 servings.

1 broiler-fryer (about 2½ pounds)
½ cup flour
1¼ teaspoons salt
1 teaspoon leaf tarragon, crumbled
½ cup (1 stick) butter or margarine
⅓ cup lemon juice
1 tablespoon instant minced onion
1 clove of garlic, mashed
⅛ teaspoon pepper

1. Cut broiler-fryer into serving-size pieces.
2. Combine flour, 1 teaspoon of the salt and tarragon in a plastic bag. Shake chicken in flour to coat; tap off excess.
3. Melt butter or margarine in a 13x9x2-inch baking pan. Coat chicken on all sides in melted butter or margarine, then turn the pieces skin-side up.
4. Bake in moderate oven (375°), brushing often with pan drippings, 30 minutes.
5. Meanwhile, make Lemon Baste: Mix lemon juice, instant minced onion, garlic, remaining ¼ teaspoon salt and pepper in a small bowl. Brush chicken pieces with part of the Lemon Baste.
6. Bake, brushing occasionally with remaining Lemon Baste, 30 minutes longer, or until chicken is tender.

POTATO-FLAKE CHICKEN

Mashed potato flakes make the coating for oven-crisped chicken.

Bake at 350° for 1½ hours.
Makes 6 servings.

⅔ cup evaporated milk (from a tall can)
1 teaspoon salt
1 teaspoon mixed Italian herbs
⅛ teaspoon pepper
1 envelope (1½ cups) instant mashed
    potato flakes
2 broiler-fryers (about 2 pounds each), cut up
Quick Cream Gravy

1. Pour evaporated milk into a pie plate; stir in salt, Italian herbs and pepper. Empty mashed potato flakes into a second pie plate.
2. Dip chicken pieces into evaporated milk mixture, then into potato flakes to coat well. Place in single layer on ungreased cooky sheet.
3. Bake in moderate oven (350°) 1½ hours, or until tender and golden brown.
4. Serve with Quick Cream Gravy (for recipe, turn to chapter on GRAVIES).

BUTTER BAKED WINGS AND DRUMSTICKS

Finger food with a poultry seasoning flavor.

Bake at 375° for 45-60 minutes.
Makes 12 servings.

12 drumsticks (3 pounds)
12 wings (2 pounds)
2 teaspoons salt
¼ teaspoon pepper
2 cups saltine cracker crumbs
1 teaspoon poultry seasoning
1 cup (2 sticks) butter, melted

1. Sprinkle chicken with the salt and pepper. Combine crumbs and poultry seasoning. Dip chicken in butter, then roll in crumbs to coat well.
2. Place on two foil-lined 15½x10½x1-inch baking pans. Drizzle remaining butter over chicken. Bake in moderate oven (375°) 45 to 60 minutes, until tender.

RUBY CHICKEN

A freezer-to-oven chicken with a tangy fruit sauce.

Bake at 350° for 2 hours.
Makes 12 servings, or 6 servings for 2 meals.

3 broiler-fryers (2½ pounds each), quartered
1 tablespoon salt
¼ cup vegetable oil
3 medium-size onions, chopped (1½ cups)
1½ teaspoons ground cinnamon
1½ teaspoons ground ginger
1 tablespoon grated orange rind
2 cups orange juice
3 tablespoons lemon juice
2 cans (1 pound each) whole-berry cranberry
    sauce

1. Sprinkle chicken pieces with salt. Brown chicken on one side in hot oil, using two skillets; turn, add onions; brown on second side.
2. Sprinkle on the cinnamon and ginger. Add orange rind and juice and lemon juice. Cover; simmer 20 minutes. Add cranberry sauce. Simmer, covered, 15 minutes longer, or until almost tender. Cool quickly.
3. Line two 10-cup freezer-to-table baking dishes with heavy foil. Remove chicken to foil-lined dishes.
4. Measure cooking liquid and thicken, if you wish. Allow 1 tablespoon of flour mixed with 2 tablespoons water for each cup of liquid. Bring to boiling, cook 3 minutes, cool, pour over chicken.
5. Freeze chicken and sauce. When frozen, remove foil-wrapped food from baking dishes; return to freezer.
6. To serve: Remove foil, place food in same baking dish. Heat, covered, in moderate oven (350°), turning pieces once, 2 hours, or until bubbly-hot.

PINEAPPLE-STUFFED CHICKEN BREASTS

An elegant chicken served with a sweet-sour sauce.

Bake at 350° for 40-45 minutes.
Makes 8 servings.

8 whole small chicken breasts, boned
1¼ teaspoons salt, divided
1 can (8¼ ounces) crushed pineapple
6 tablespoons butter or margarine, divided
½ cup chopped green pepper
½ cup chopped celery
¼ cup chopped onion
½ teaspoon dried leaf tarragon
½ cup fine dry bread crumbs
1 tablespoon chopped pimiento
Sweet-Sour Pineapple Sauce

1. Place boned chicken breasts skin side down on board. Sprinkle with ¾ teaspoon salt.
2. Drain pineapple and reserve the syrup for Sweet-Sour Pineapple Sauce.
3. Heat 4 tablespoons butter or margarine in skillet; add green pepper, celery, onion and remaining ½ teaspoon salt. Cook until vegetables are tender. Remove from heat; add tarragon, bread crumbs, pimiento and drained pineapple; mix well.
4. Place about ¼ cup stuffing mixture in center of each chicken breast; fold the sides over and fasten with skewers or string.
5. Heat remaining 2 tablespoons butter in large skillet. Add chicken breasts, four at a time, and brown lightly on all sides. Remove to shallow baking pan. Bake in 350° oven 40 to 45 minutes, until tender. Serve with Sweet-Sour Pineapple Sauce.

SWEET-SOUR PINEAPPLE SAUCE

1 tablespoon vegetable oil
½ cup chopped green pepper
2 tablespoons chopped onion
1 can (8¼ ounces) pineapple slices in syrup
Syrup reserved from crushed pineapple
4 teaspoons cornstarch
¾ cup water
1 chicken bouillon cube
1 tablespoon brown sugar
¼ teaspoon dried leaf tarragon
2 tablespoons vinegar
1 tablespoon soy sauce
2 tablespoons diced pimiento

1. Heat vegetable oil in saucepan. Add green pepper and onion; cook 2 minutes.
2. Drain syrup from pineapple slices and add to saucepan with syrup reserved from the crushed pineapple in stuffing.
3. Blend cornstarch with water; add to saucepan.
4. Add bouillon cube, brown sugar, tarragon, vinegar and soy sauce. Cook, stirring constantly, until mixture thickens and comes to a boil.
5. Cut pineapple slices in half; add to sauce with pimiento. Heat and serve over chicken breasts.

ITALIAN CHICKEN BAKE

Perfect for a large buffet dinner you want to enjoy.

Bake at 350° for 30 minutes.
Makes 16 servings.

3 broiler-fryers (about 3 pounds each), cut up
1 medium-size onion, peeled and sliced
2½ teaspoons salt
½ teaspoon peppercorns
1 pound mushrooms, trimmed and sliced
1 cup (2 sticks) butter or margarine
1 cup fine soft bread crumbs
½ cup regular flour
¼ teaspoon pepper
¼ teaspoon ground nutmeg
2 cups light cream or table cream
½ cup dry sherry
1 package (1 pound) thin spaghetti, broken
    in 2-inch lengths
1 cup grated Parmesan cheese

1. Combine chicken, onion, 1 teaspoon of the salt, peppercorns and enough water to cover in a kettle. Heat to boiling; cover. Cook 40 minutes, or until chicken is tender. Remove from broth and cool until easy to handle. Strain broth into a 4-cup measure and set aside for making sauce.
2. Pull skin from chicken and take meat from bones; cube meat; place in a large bowl.
3. Sauté mushrooms in ¼ cup of the butter or margarine until soft in a large frying pan; combine with chicken.
4. Melt remaining butter or margarine in a saucepan. Measure out ¼ cup and toss with bread crumbs in a bowl; set aside.

5. Stir flour, the remaining 1½ teaspoons salt, pepper and nutmeg into remaining butter or margarine in saucepan; cook, stirring constantly, until bubbly. Stir in 3½ cups of the chicken broth and cream. Continue cooking and stirring until sauce thickens and boils 1 minute; remove from heat. Stir in sherry.

6. While sauce cooks, cook spaghetti, following label directions; drain well. Spoon into two baking dishes, 13x9x2. Spoon chicken mixture over spaghetti; spoon sauce over all.

7. Add Parmesan cheese to bread-crumb mixture and toss lightly to mix. Sprinkle over mixture in baking dishes.

8. Bake in moderate oven (350°) 30 minutes, or until bubbly and crumb topping is toasted. Garnish with bouquets of watercress, sliced mushrooms and pimiento strips, if you wish.

DAY-BEFORE NOTE: Fix the 2 casseroles through Step 7; cover and chill. About an hour before serving, remove from refrigerator and uncover. Bake in moderate oven (350°) 40 minutes, or until bubbly. If casseroles must stand a bit before serving, leave in oven with heat turned off.

BISCUIT-CHICKEN ROLLS

Cheese, chicken and biscuits combined for an old-fashioned kind of treat.

Bake chicken at 450° for 15 minutes; then bake biscuit and chicken at 450° for 10 minutes.

Makes 10 snack servings, or 5 meal servings.

5 chicken thighs, boned
½ teaspoon salt
¼ teaspoon pepper
1 teaspoon instant minced onion
¼ teaspoon each, dried leaf basil and oregano
1 can (8 ounces) refrigerated country-style or buttermilk biscuits
Swiss cheese slices

1. To bone chicken thighs, cut along thinner side of thigh to the bone, slashing thigh the length of the bone. Holding one end of the bone, scrape the meat away until bone is free. Cut off rounded piece of cartilage. Remove skin and cut each boned thigh in half lengthwise.

2. Sprinkle on both sides with salt, pepper, instant minced onion, basil and oregano. Place in shallow baking pan and bake in hot oven (450°) 15 minutes.

3. Stretch each biscuit into oval. Cut strips of cheese slightly smaller than biscuit ovals; place on biscuits. Place pieces of cooked chicken across each biscuit. Fold cheese and biscuit over chicken and place, seam side down, on foil-lined baking sheet. Bake in hot oven (450°) 10 minutes, or until biscuit is browned.

Broiled Chicken

KEY LIME CHICKEN BROIL

A zesty splash of lime and tarragon seasons tender broiled chicken.

Makes 6 servings.

3 broiler-fryers (about 2 pounds each), split
½ cup lime juice
½ cup vegetable oil
1 tablespoon grated onion
2 teaspoons tarragon, crushed
1 teaspoon seasoned salt
¼ teaspoon seasoned pepper

1. Wash chickens; pat dry. Place, skin side down, on rack in broiler pan.

2. Mix lime juice, vegetable oil, onion, tarragon, and seasoned salt and pepper in a small bowl. Brush generously over chickens.

3. Broil, turning every 10 minutes and brushing with more lime mixture, 40 minutes, or until the chickens are tender and richly browned. Remove to a heated large serving platter.

BROILED CHICKEN BING

Elegant sweet-sour cherry sauce dresses up crisply broiled chicken.

Makes 6 servings.

3 broiler-fryers (about 2 pounds each), split
2 cups Dark Cherry Sauce

1. Wash chickens; pat dry. Place, skin side down, on rack in broiler pan.
2. Broil, turning every 10 minutes, until the chickens are tender and brown—about 40 minutes. Remove to heated serving platter.
3. Spoon hot Dark Cherry Sauce over all and serve immediately.

DARK CHERRY SAUCE

Makes about 2 cups.

1 can (1 pound) pitted dark sweet cherries
2 tablespoons cornstarch
1 tablespoon prepared mustard
1 tablespoon molasses
Few drops red-pepper seasoning
Dash of salt
3 tablespoons lemon juice

1. Drain syrup from cherries into a 2-cup measure; add water to make 1½ cups. (Save cherries for Step 3.)
2. Blend a few tablespoons syrup into cornstarch until smooth in a small saucepan; stir in remaining syrup, mustard, molasses, red-pepper seasoning and salt. Cook over low heat, stirring constantly, until mixture thickens and boils 3 minutes.
3. Stir in cherries and lemon juice; heat slowly just until bubbly. Serve hot.

CALORIE- AND FAT-SAVER

Because of the fat in chicken skin, broiler-fryers can be broiled without additional fat. Simply sprinkle with salt, pepper, monosodium glutamate, lemon juice and an herb such as tarragon, thyme or basil. Broiled chicken may also be basted with a barbecue sauce near the end of cooking time.

Roasted Chicken

LITTLE CHICKEN ROASTS

When you plan to make this delicious recipe, remember that everyone rates a half chicken and a portion of stuffing.

Roast at 400° for 1½ hours.
Makes 6 servings.

3 whole broiler-fryers (1½ pounds each)
Salt
½ cup (1 stick) butter or margarine
1 can (about 9 ounces) crushed pineapple
3 cups soft bread crumbs (6 slices)
½ cup flaked coconut
½ cup chopped celery
½ teaspoon salt
¼ teaspoon poultry seasoning
2 tablespoons bottled steak sauce
Sweet-and-Sour Sauce

1. Rinse chickens inside and out with cold water; drain, then pat dry. Sprinkle inside with salt.
2. Melt butter or margarine in a small saucepan. Drain syrup from pineapple into a cup and set aside for Step 6.
3. Combine pineapple with bread crumbs, coconut and celery in a medium-size bowl; drizzle 4 tablespoons of the melted butter or margarine over; toss with a fork until crumbs are lightly coated. (Save remaining butter or margarine for Step 5.)
4. Stuff neck and body cavities of chickens lightly with the pineapple-bread mixture. Smooth neck skin over stuffing and skewer to back; close body cavity and tie legs to tail. Place chickens in a roasting pan.
5. Stir salt and poultry seasoning into saved 4 tablespoons butter or margarine in saucepan; brush part over chickens.
6. Roast for 1 hour in a hot oven (400°), basting several times with butter mixture. Stir saved pineapple syrup and steak sauce into any remaining butter in saucepan; brush generously over chickens.
7. Continue roasting, basting once or twice more, 30 minutes longer, or until drumsticks move easily and meaty part of thigh feels soft.
8. Remove chickens to heated serving platter; keep warm while making sauce.

9. When ready to serve, cut away strings from chickens. Garnish platter with watercress and preserved mixed fruits, if you wish. Pass sauce in a separate bowl.

SWEET-AND-SOUR SAUCE: Blend 2 tablespoons cornstarch into drippings in roasting pan; stir in 1 cup water. Cook, stirring all the time, just until mixture thickens and boils 3 minutes. Stir in 2 tablespoons brown sugar and 1 tablespoon of lemon juice. Strain into heated serving bowl. Makes about 1¼ cups.

ROAST CAPON

This elegant fowl should be simply prepared so as not to detract from its own fine flavor.

Roast at 325° about 2½ hours.
Makes 6 servings.

1 ready-to-cook capon (about 7 pounds)
Salt
Pepper
6 cups stuffing
Melted butter or margarine

1. Sprinkle the chicken inside with salt and pepper.
2. Pack stuffing lightly into neck cavity. (Bread-and-Butter Stuffing is good with capon; for recipe, see section on STUFFINGS.) Smooth neck skin over stuffing and fasten with wooden picks or skewers to back of bird; twist wing tips until they rest flat against fastened neck skin.
3. Stuff body cavity lightly; fasten opening, and tie legs together and fasten to tailpiece.
4. Place capon, breast side up, on rack in a large open roasting pan; brush well with melted butter or margarine; cover breast with double-thick cheesecloth moistened with additional fat.
5. Roast in slow oven (325°) 2½ hours, or until meaty part of drumstick is tender when pierced with a 2-tine fork; baste frequently during roasting.
6. Place capon on heated serving platter and serve while hot.

COUNTRY ROAST CHICKEN

Corn bread stuffing makes this an extra special roast.

Bake at 375° for 1½ hours.
Makes 8 servings.

2 broiler-fryers (about 3 pounds each)
1 cup water
½ teaspoon salt
1 package (8 ounces) corn bread-stuffing mix
1 medium-size onion, chopped (½ cup)
½ cup sliced celery
½ cup (1 stick) butter or margarine
¼ cup bacon drippings OR ¼ cup (½ stick) butter or margarine, melted

1. Remove giblets and necks from chicken packages and place (except livers) with water and salt in a small saucepan; cover. Simmer 45 minutes. Add livers; cover; simmer 15 minutes longer; cool.
2. Remove giblets and necks from broth; reserve broth. Chop giblets and the meat from necks; place in a large bowl; stir in stuffing mix.
3. Simmer reserved broth until reduced to ½ cup; reserve.
4. Sauté onion and celery in the ½ cup butter or margarine for 5 minutes in a medium-size skillet. Add with reserved broth to stuffing mixture in bowl; toss until evenly moistened.
5. Stuff neck and body cavities lightly with stuffing. Skewer neck skin to back; close body cavity and tie legs to tail. Place chickens on rack in roasting pan. Brush with part of bacon drippings or butter or margarine.
6. Roast in moderate oven (375°) basting every 30 minutes with bacon drippings or butter or margarine, 1½ hours, or until tender.
7. To serve: Place on heated serving platter. Cut chickens into quarters with poultry shears.

SAVORY ROAST CHICKEN

Attention beginners: You almost can't muff this one. Look for the good-buy young roasters, heavy with meat on their frames.

Roast at 375° about 2 hours.
Makes 4 servings.

1 roasting chicken (about 4 pounds)
½ teaspoon salt
2 cups Savory Stuffing
1 to 2 tablespoons butter or margarine

1. Wash chicken and pat dry. Sprinkle inside with salt.
2. Stuff neck and body cavities lightly with Savory Stuffing. Skewer neck skin to body, secure body closed, tie legs to tailpiece.
3. Place chicken on rack in shallow roasting pan; rub with butter or margarine. Roast at (375°) about 2 hours (figure time at 30 minutes per pound), or until drumstick moves easily at joint.

GLAZED CHICKEN WITH PEACHES

A mouth-watering masterpiece of glossy little roasters on a bed of rice with golden peaches.

Roast at 375° for 1½ to 2 hours.
Makes 6 servings.

2 roasting chickens (about 3½ pounds each)
1 teaspoon salt
2 cups stuffing
2 tablespoons melted butter or margarine
Golden Glaze and Golden Peaches

1. Wash and dry chickens; sprinkle the inside with salt; stuff neck and body cavities lightly with stuffing. (Savory Stuffing is good with this chicken.) Skewer neck skin to body, close body cavity and tie legs to tailpiece; place on rack in shallow roasting pan; brush with butter or margarine.
2. Roast in moderate oven (375°) 1½ to 2 hours (figure roasting time at 30 minutes per pound for one bird), or until drumstick moves easily at joint.
3. About 20 minutes before chickens are done, brush with Golden Glaze; continue roasting (brush once more after 10 minutes) until chickens are done.
4. Serve on a bed of rice on a heated platter, garnished with Golden Peaches.

GOLDEN GLAZE AND GOLDEN PEACHES

Bake at 375° for 20 minutes.

1 can (about 1 pound) peach halves
2 tablespoons bottled meat sauce

1. Drain peach halves, saving syrup in small bowl; arrange peaches, cut side up, in shallow baking dish.
2. Blend meat sauce into syrup for Golden Glaze and brush over chickens; brush peach halves with rest of glaze for Golden Peaches; bake peaches in oven along with chicken during last 20 minutes of roasting time.

Stuffings

HAWAIIAN STUFFING

Makes about 2½ cups.

1½ cups soft bread crumbs
⅓ cup flaked coconut
¼ cup finely chopped celery
¼ cup drained, crushed pineapple
1 tablespoon grated orange peel
2 tablespoons melted butter or margarine

Combine all ingredients in a bowl and toss lightly to blend.

FRUIT STUFFING

Makes 7 cups.

1 can (pound) sliced apples
Water
½ cup (1 stick) butter or margarine
1 package (2 cups) ready-mix bread stuffing
1 cup chopped peanuts
½ cup seedless raisins

1. Drain apples and add water to apple liquid to make 1 cup. Heat to boiling in large saucepan.
2. Stir in butter or margarine until melted.
3. Add ready-mix stuffing, apples, peanuts and raisins, tossing lightly to mix.

SAVORY STUFFING

Makes 2 cups.

½ cup chopped celery leaves
2 tablespoons chopped onion
4 tablespoons (½ stick) butter or margarine
½ cup water
2 cups ready-mix bread stuffing (½ of an
   8-ounce package)

1. Sauté celery leaves and onion in butter or
   margarine in medium-size saucepan. Add
   water; heat to boiling.
2. Stir in bread stuffing; toss with fork just
   until moistened.

BREAD-AND-BUTTER STUFFING

Makes about 3 cups.

3 cups (about 6 slices) small dry bread cubes.
   To make dry bread cubes: Spread cubes
   out on baking sheet; bake in a very slow
   oven (300°) 15 minutes, or until
   cubes are dry but not brown
1 small onion, finely chopped (¼ cup)
2 tablespoons chopped parsley
1½ teaspoons crumbled basil
¼ teaspoon salt
⅛ teaspoon pepper
1 egg
¼ cup (½ stick) melted butter or margarine

1. Combine bread cubes, onion, parsley, basil,
   salt, pepper and egg in medium-size bowl.
2. Sprinkle melted butter or margarine over
   bread mixture; toss with fork until
   blended.

GOURMET STUFFING

Makes 2 cups.

3 chicken livers
4 tablespoons (½ stick) butter or margarine
2 cups soft bread crumbs (4 slices)
2 tablespoons chopped onion
1 tablespoon water
1 teaspoon Worcestershire sauce
½ teaspoon salt

1. Sauté livers in butter or margarine, stirring often, in frying pan 5 minutes, or until
   livers lost their pink color.

2. Remove livers and chop, then add to bread
   crumbs in medium-sized bowl. Sauté onion
   just until soft in same frying pan.
3. Stir water, Worcestershire sauce and salt
   into onions in the frying pan; pour over
   crumb mixture. Toss lightly to mix well.
   (Mixture will be crumbly, not wet.)

APRICOT-WALNUT STUFFING

Makes 4 cups.

1 medium-size onion, chopped (½ cup)
4 tablespoons (½ stick) butter or margarine
½ cup chopped dry apricots
1 envelope instant chicken broth OR
   1 chicken bouillon cube
⅓ cup water
6 slices white bread, cubed (about 3 cups)
½ cup chopped walnuts

1. In a large frying pan, sauté onion in butter
   or margarine until soft; stir in apricots,
   chicken broth or bouillon cube and water.
   Heat to boiling, crushing bouillon cube if
   used; remove from heat.
2. Add cubed bread and walnuts; toss until
   evenly moist.

HILO STUFFING

Makes 4 cups.

1 cup uncooked white rice
4 tablespoons (½ stick) butter or margarine
1 medium-size onion, chopped (½ cup)
2 envelopes instant chicken broth OR
   2 chicken bouillon cubes
2½ cups water
½ cup chopped macadamia nuts
   (from a 6-ounce jar)
½ cup flaked coconut

1. In a large saucepan, sauté rice in butter or
   margarine, stirring often, just until golden.
2. Stir in onion, chicken broth or bouillon
   cubes and water; heat to boiling, crushing
   cubes, if using, with a spoon; cover. Simmer 20 minutes, or until rice is tender and
   liquid is absorbed.
3. Sprinkle with nuts and coconut; toss lightly
   to mix.

BASIC FRIED CHICKEN

Essential to any good cook's repertoire, this chicken can't be hurried—but it is certainly worth waiting for.

Makes 4 servings.

1 broiler-fryer (about 3 pounds)
½ cup flour
1 teaspoon salt
⅛ teaspoon pepper
1 cup bacon drippings or part drippings and
    shortening

1. Cut chicken into 8 serving-size pieces—2 breasts, 2 wings, 2 thighs, 2 drumsticks. (Simmer bony back pieces to make broth for gravy, if you wish.) Wash chicken, but do not dry. This is important so skin will take on a thick flour coating.
2. Mix flour, salt and pepper in a bag. Shake pieces, a few at a time, to coat evenly.
3. Heat bacon drippings ¼-inch deep in a large heavy frying pan on medium heat, or in an electric skillet to 360°. Arrange chicken in a single layer in hot fat.
4. Brown slowly for 15 minutes. When pink juices start to show on top, turn and brown the other side 15 minutes. Slow cooking, plus turning just once, gives the chicken its crisp coating.
5. When pieces are browned, pile all back into pan or skillet and cover. Lower range heat to simmer or reset control at 260°. Let chicken cook 20 minutes longer, or until it's richly golden and fork-tender.

VARIATIONS: For added flavor, mix ½ teaspoon dried leaf thyme, tarragon, basil or poultry seasoning, or 1 teaspoon curry powder to the flour.

COATINGS THAT STICK

Chicken coated with seasoned flour before frying has a very thin crust. For a crisp, heavier crust, lightly dust chicken with flour and dip pieces in buttermilk or in a mixture of 1 egg beaten with ⅓ cup milk and 2 tablespoons lemon juice. Then roll in seasoned flour and place on wire racks. Let the chicken stand for 30 minutes for the coating to dry; roll in flour again if the coating is still moist. Proceed as usual for skillet-fried or oven-fried chicken.

IOWA FRIED CHICKEN

A convenient chicken that requires only 5 easy-to-get ingredients.

Makes 8 servings.

1½ cups yellow cornmeal
1 envelope Italian salad dressing mix
½ cup cream for whipping
2 broiler-fryers (about 2 pounds each), cut up
Vegetable oil

1. Combine cornmeal and salad dressing mix on a sheet of waxed paper; pour cream into a pie plate.
2. Dip chicken pieces into cream, then roll in cornmeal mixture to coat well; let stand on wire racks about 5 minutes.
3. Pour vegetable oil to a depth of 1 inch into each of 2 large frying pans; heat until a few drops of water sprinkled into oil sizzle. Add chicken and brown slowly, turning several times; cover. Cook 20 minutes longer, or until chicken is tender. Drain on paper toweling. Serve hot.

GOLDEN-COATED FRIED CHICKEN

Bread the chicken pieces and chill them, then fry very slowly—this gives the crusty golden coat.

Makes 6 servings.

2 broiler-fryers (about 2 pounds each), cut in
    serving-size pieces
1 cup (8-ounce carton) dairy sour cream
2 tablespoons lemon juice
1 teaspoon salt
1 teaspoon garlic salt
1 teaspoon Worcestershire sauce
1¼ cups fine dry bread crumbs
Shortening or vegetable oil for frying
1 package chicken gravy mix

1. Wash chicken pieces; pat dry.
2. Mix sour cream, lemon juice, salt, garlic salt and Worcestershire sauce in a small bowl; place bread crumbs in a pie plate. Brush chicken pieces with sour cream mixture, then roll in crumbs to coat well.
3. Place in a single layer on a cooky sheet. Chill at least 1 hour. Chill remaining sour cream mixture for Step 6.

4. Melt enough shortening or pour in enough vegetable oil to make ½-inch depth in a large frying pan.

5. Brown chicken, a few pieces at a time, very slowly in hot fat; return all pieces to pan; cover. Cook over *very low* heat 30 minutes or until chicken is tender.

6. Prepare chicken gravy mix, following label directions. Stir ¼ cup of the hot gravy into remaining sour cream mixture; stir back into remaining gravy in pan; heat slowly just until hot. Serve separately to spoon over chicken.

COUNTRY FRIED CHICKEN

Chicken the way it was served down on the farm in Grandma's day (if you were lucky). It's crisp and flavory, with gravy.

Makes 6 to 8 servings.

2 broiler-fryers (about 2 pounds each), cut into serving-size pieces
⅔ cup flour
2 teaspoons salt
1 teaspoon paprika
¼ teaspoon pepper
1 cup bacon drippings
2 cloves garlic
1 bay leaf
2 cups Milk Gravy

1. Wash and dry chicken pieces. Shake, a few at a time, in mixture of flour, salt, paprika and pepper in a paper bag to coat well.

2. Heat bacon drippings with whole cloves of garlic and bay leaf in large frying pan.

3. Place chicken in single layer in hot drippings. (Do not crowd as pieces should have enough room to brown without touching each other.) Cook slowly, turning once or twice to brown both sides. (It will take about 30 minutes.)

4. Return all chicken to frying pan; cover; cook slowly 20 minutes, or until tender. Uncover; cook 5 minutes longer to crisp coating. Remove chicken to heated platter; keep hot in slow oven long enough to make Milk Gravy.

MILK GRAVY: Tip pan and pour off all drippings into a cup, leaving crusty brown bits in pan. (Be sure to remove garlic cloves and bay leaf.) Return 3 tablespoons drippings to pan; blend in 3 tablespoons flour; cook, stirring all the time, just until mixture bubbles. Stir in 1 cup water and 1 cup milk slowly; continue cooking and stirring, scraping brown bits from bottom and sides of pan, until gravy thickens and boils 1 minute. Season to taste with salt. Makes about 2 cups.

FRIED CHICKEN DIVINE

The chicken strips are served with a milk gravy over rice.

Makes 8 servings.

4 large breasts, boned
1 cup flour
2 teaspoons salt
2 teaspoons paprika
¼ teaspoon pepper
1 cup buttermilk
Shortening or vegetable oil for frying
5 cups hot cooked rice

1. Cut chicken breasts into ½-inch strips. Combine flour, salt, paprika and pepper. Dip chicken strips into buttermilk, then roll in seasoned flour.

2. Heat oil ½-inch deep in skillet until drop of water added to fat sizzles.

3. Add chicken strips and fry until golden brown. To serve, mound rice on platter. Pour over Sauce Divine and top with fried chicken strips.

SAUCE DIVINE

5 tablespoons butter or margarine
5 tablespoons flour
1 teaspoon salt
¼ teaspoon cayenne
2 chicken bouillon cubes
3 cups milk

Melt butter or margarine in saucepan. Blend in flour, salt, cayenne and bouillon cubes. Gradually add milk and cook, stirring constantly, until mixture thickens and comes to a boil.

GINGER CRISP CHICKEN

Secret of this favorite is double cooking: First baking, then frying. The ginger in the golden crust gives it a slightly spicy flavor.

Bake at 350° for 1 hour.
Makes 6 servings.

2 broiler-fryers (about 2 pounds each), cut in serving-size pieces
2 teaspoons salt
1 teaspoon rosemary
½ cup water
1½ cups Ginger Batter
Shortening or salad oil for frying

1. Wash chicken pieces; pat dry. Place in a single layer in a large shallow baking pan; sprinkle with the salt and rosemary; add water; cover.
2. Bake in moderate oven (350°) for 1 hour.
3. While chicken cooks, make Ginger Batter.
4. Remove chicken from pan; pull off skin and remove small rib bones, if you wish; drain chicken thoroughly on paper toweling.
5. Melt enough shortening or pour in enough salad oil to make a depth of 2 inches in a large frying pan or electric deep-fat fryer. Heat until hot (350° in electric fryer).
6. Dip chicken pieces, 2 or 3 at a time, into Ginger Batter; hold over bowl to let excess drip back.
7. Fry in hot shortening 3 minutes, or until golden-brown. Lift out with a slotted spoon; drain well. Keep warm on a hot platter, covered with foil, until all pieces are cooked.

GINGER BATTER

Makes about 1½ cups.

1¼ cups sifted regular flour
1 teaspoon baking powder
1 teaspoon salt
½ teaspoon ground ginger
1 egg
1 cup milk
¼ cup salad oil

1. Sift flour, baking powder, salt and ginger into a medium-size bowl.
2. Add remaining ingredients all at once; beat with a rotary beater until smooth.

BATTER-FRIED CHICKEN

A Deep South style of fried chicken you'll want to try regardless where you live.

Bake at 375° for 45 minutes.
Makes 12 servings.

3 broiler-fryers, cut in serving-size pieces
¼ cup water
2 teaspoons salt
1 quart salad oil
Batter

1. Place chicken pieces in baking pan; add water and sprinkle with salt. Cover with foil; bake in moderate oven (375°) 45 minutes. Remove chicken pieces from liquid; dry well. If desired, remove skin.
2. Heat salad oil to 350° in a heavy 3-quart saucepan.
3. Dip chicken pieces in Batter; drain off excess. Fry, 2 or 3 pieces at a time, until golden brown, about 3 minutes. Drain on paper towels.

BATTER

1¼ cups sifted all-purpose flour
1 teaspoon baking powder
½ teaspoon salt
1 egg
1 cup milk
¼ cup salad oil

Sift flour, baking powder and salt into mixing bowl. Add remaining ingredients; beat with rotary beater until smooth.

SOUTHERN FRIED CHICKEN

Time-honored, trusty, crusty chicken with cream gravy.

Makes 6 servings.

2 broiler-fryers (about 2 pounds each), cut up
3 cups light cream or table cream
2 cups plus 1 tablespoon sifted flour
2½ teaspoons salt
½ teaspoon pepper
Shortening or vegetable oil

1. Wash chicken pieces; pat dry. Place in a single layer in a large shallow dish; pour 1 cup of the cream over top; chill at least 20 minutes.

2. Shake chicken pieces, a few at a time, in a mixture of the 2 cups flour, 2 teaspoons salt and ¼ teaspoon pepper in a paper bag to coat well. Dip each again in remaining cream in dish; shake again in flour mixture.
3. Melt enough shortening or pour enough vegetable oil into each of two large heavy frying pans to make a depth of 1½ inches; heat. Add chicken pieces, skin side down. Brown slowly, turning once, then continue cooking 30 minutes, or until tender. Remove; keep warm while making gravy.
4. Pour all drippings from frying pans into a small bowl; measure 2 tablespoonfuls and return to one pan. Stir in 1 tablespoon of flour, remaining ½ teaspoon salt and ¼ teaspoon pepper. Cook, stirring constantly, until bubbly. Stir in remaining 2 cups cream; continue cooking and stirring, until gravy thickens and boils 1 minute. Serve separately.

TEMPURA FRIED CHICKEN

This tender golden-brown chicken is covered with a crispy coat that will make your family shout "More!"

Bake at 325° for 15 minutes.
Makes 8 servings.

2 broiler-fryers (about 2½ pounds each)
Salt and pepper
1 egg
1 cup cold water
1¼ cups sifted all-purpose flour
1 teaspoon salt
½ teaspoon ground ginger
½ teaspoon ground cloves
Oil or shortening for frying

1. Cut chickens into serving-size pieces. Sprinkle with salt and pepper. Refrigerate while preparing batter.
2. Beat egg until foamy in a medium-size bowl. Stir in cold water. Sift flour, salt, ginger and cloves into same bowl and beat until smooth. Chill at least 1 hour.
3. Add enough oil or shortening to a large heavy skillet to make a 2-inch depth when heated. Heat to 360° on a deep fat thermometer, or until a cube of bread turns golden in 15 seconds.
4. Dip chilled chicken pieces into batter with tongs. Hold over bowl several seconds to allow excess batter to run off.

5. Fry chicken, a few pieces at a time, turning often, until rich golden brown. Transfer browned chicken to a shallow baking pan. (Do not stack in pan, keep in one layer.)
6. Bake in slow oven (325°) 15 minutes, or until chicken is tender when pierced with a fork. Serve with duck sauce or spicy preserves, if you wish.

BUTTERMILK FRIED CHICKEN

A crunchy chicken topped with a creamy buttermilk gravy.

Makes 4 servings.

1 broiler-fryer (about 2½ pounds)
2½ cups buttermilk
1 cup flour
1½ teaspoons salt
½ teaspoon leaf rosemary, crumbled
¼ teaspoon pepper
Shortening or vegetable oil

1. Cut chicken into serving-size pieces.
2. Pour ½ cup of the buttermilk into a shallow dish. Combine flour, salt, rosemary and pepper in a plastic bag.
3. Dip chicken pieces in buttermilk; shake in flour mixture to coat well. Dip again in buttermilk and flour mixture to build a thick coating. Place chicken pieces on wire rack for 15 minutes to allow coating to set. Reserve remaining flour mixture.
4. Melt enough shortening, or pour enough oil, into a large heavy skillet with a cover to ½-inch depth. Place over medium heat. When a few drops of water sizzle when flicked into the hot fat, add the chicken pieces skin-side down. Cook slowly, turning once, 20 minutes, or until chicken is golden.
5. Reduce heat; cover skillet. Cook 30 minutes longer, or until chicken is tender. Remove cover for last 5 minutes for a crunchy crust. Place chicken on platter; keep hot.
6. Pour off all fat into a cup. Return 2 tablespoons to skillet; blend in 3 tablespoons of the reserved flour mixture; cook, stirring constantly just until bubbly. Gradually add remaining 2 cups buttermilk; continue cooking and stirring, scraping to loosen brown bits in pan, until gravy is thickened and bubbles 1 minute. Taste; season with additional salt and pepper, if you wish. Spoon over chicken.

Chicken in Parts

Someone once noted that it's the little things in life that mean a lot. Chicken is no exception. It doesn't take a whole bird to make dinner a success. Chicken parts, which include the breasts, thighs, drumsticks, wings and livers, can be used in a great number of imaginative ways.

For white meat fans, breasts offer the most meat for the money. The thighs, drumsticks and wings offer less meat but no less flavor.

And chicken livers are a delicately-flavored part that finds many uses on your menu.

Buying chicken in parts is an economy move, too, particularly for a small family, or for one whose preference is for only white or dark meat.

And for those who generally prepare a whole chicken, the parts are a nice change of pace.

These little things can mean a great big delicious meal.

Breasts

CHICKEN BREASTS MORNAY

A nippy cheese sauce sparks bland and deli-cate white meat.

Bake at 350° for 55 to 60 minutes.
Makes 4 servings.

4 chicken breasts
¼ cup flour seasoned with
   ½ teaspoon salt and dash of pepper
¼ cup (½ stick) melted butter or margarine
Mornay Sauce

1. Dust chicken breasts with seasoned flour.
2. Place in small, shallow baking dish, skin side down; pour melted butter or marga-rine over and around chicken.
3. Bake in moderate oven (350°) 30 minutes; turn chicken breasts; bake 25 to 30 minutes longer, basting 2 or 3 times during baking, until chicken is golden-brown and tender when pierced with a fork.
4. Place on heated serving platter; serve with Mornay Sauce.

MORNAY SAUCE

Makes about 1¼ cups.

2 teaspoons butter or margarine
2 tablespoons flour
½ teaspoon salt
⅛ teaspoon pepper
½ cup milk
½ cup chicken stock
¾ cup grated sharp Cheddar cheese
½ teaspoon prepared mustard
½ teaspoon Worcestershire sauce
1 tablespoon chopped parsley

1. Melt butter or margarine in small sauce-pan; remove from heat.
2. Blend in flour, salt and pepper; stir in milk and chicken stock.
3. Cook over low heat, stirring constantly, until sauce thickens and boils 1 minute.
4. Add cheese, mustard and Worcestershire sauce; continue cooking, stirring occasion-ally, until cheese melts; remove from heat.
5. Stir in parsley; serve hot.

GOURMET CHICKEN BREASTS

Rich creamed chicken breasts are sparked with water chestnuts and pimientos for a fancy touch.

Makes enough for 2 meals, 4 servings each.

4 chicken breasts (about 12 ounces each)
1 small onion, quartered
Few celery tops
2 teaspoons salt
6 peppercorns
1½ cups water
½ cup (1 stick) butter or margarine
½ cup flour
¼ teaspoon nutmeg
Dash of pepper
1 tablespoon lemon juice
2 pimientos, chopped
1 can (5 ounces) water chestnuts, drained
   and sliced
1 cup cream

1. Simmer chicken with onion, celery tops, 1 teaspoon of the salt, peppercorns and water in a large saucepan 30 minutes, or until tender. Remove chicken from broth; cool until easy to handle. Strain broth into a 2-cup measure; add water, if needed, to make 2 cups; set aside for making the sauce in Step 3.
2. Remove skin from chickens, then pull chicken from bones; dice meat. (There should be about 4 cups.)
3. Melt butter or margarine in a large sauce-pan; blend in flour, remaining 1 teaspoon salt, nutmeg and pepper; cook, stirring constantly, just until bubbly. Stir in the 2 cups chicken broth; continue cooking and stirring until sauce thickens and boils 1 minute. (It will be very thick.) Remove from heat.
4. Stir in lemon juice, diced chicken, pimien-tos and water chestnuts.
5. Spoon half of mixture into a 6-cup freezer container then cool, cover, label, date and freeze.
6. Stir cream very slowly into remaining mix-ture in saucepan. Heat, stirring often, just until hot. (If you prefer mixture thinner, stir in about ½ cup milk.) Spoon into patty shells, or over your choice of buttered toast, rice or mashed potato.

NOTE: To heat frozen chicken, set container in a pan of hot water, replacing water as it cools, just until mixture is thawed enough to slide into top of a large double boiler. Add 2 tablespoons butter or margarine and 1 cup cream; heat, stirring several times, over simmering water, until hot. (Thin slightly with milk as above, if you wish.)

CHICKEN BREASTS SUPREME

An easygoing concoction of creamed white meat baked over rice with a crust of buttery crumbs topping it all.

Bake at 400° for 20 minutes.
Makes 6 servings.

3 whole chicken breasts (about 2½ pounds)
3 cups water
1 teaspoon salt
4 peppercorns
Handful of celery tops
2 cups precooked rice
1 can (about 11 ounces) chicken gravy
1 tablespoon butter or margarine
½ cup ready-mix bread stuffing (from an 8-ounce package)

1. Combine chicken breasts with water, salt, peppercorns and celery tops in a medium-size saucepan; cover. Cook 20 minutes, or until tender. Strain broth into a 4-cup measure; pour in water, if necessary, to make 2½ cups.
2. Let chicken stand until cool enough to handle, then remove skin and bones; cut meat into serving-size pieces.
3. Cook rice in 2 cups of the broth in same saucepan, following label directions. Stir remaining ½ cup broth into chicken gravy in small saucepan; heat slowly just until bubbly.
4. Spoon rice into 8-cup baking dish; top with chicken pieces; pour gravy over. Melt butter or margarine in small saucepan; stir in bread stuffing. Sprinkle on top.
5. Bake in a hot oven (400°) 20 minutes, or until bubbly-hot.

MANDARIN CHICKEN BREASTS

these chicken breasts are completely gourmet.

Makes 6 servings.

6 chicken breasts (about 12 ounces each), boned
Salt
1½ cups hot cooked rice
3 tablespoons butter or margarine
1 tablespoon chopped parsley
¼ teaspoon leaf rosemary, crumbled
¼ teaspoon leaf basil, crumbled
¼ cup flour
½ teaspoon paprika
2 envelopes instant chicken broth or 2 teaspoons granulated chicken bouillon
1¾ cups water
1 tablespoon instant minced onion
2 tablespoons lemon juice
1 bay leaf
1 tablespoon cornstarch
1 can (about 11 ounces) mandarin-orange segments, drained
1 cup seedless green grapes

1. Sprinkle insides of chicken breasts lightly with salt.
2. Combine rice, 1 tablespoon of the butter or margarine, ¼ teaspoon salt, parsley, rosemary and basil in a large bowl; toss lightly to mix; spoon into hollows in chicken breasts. Fold edges over stuffing to cover completely; fasten with wooden picks.
3. Mix flour, paprika and ½ teaspoon salt in a pie plate; dip chicken breasts into mixture to coat well. Brown slowly in remaining 2 tablespoons butter or margarine in a large frying pan.
4. Stir in chicken broth, water, onion, lemon juice and bay leaf; heat to boiling; cover.
5. Simmer 25 minutes, or until chicken is tender; remove bay leaf. Place chicken on a heated deep serving platter; keep warm. Reheat liquid to boiling.
6. Smooth cornstarch with a little water to a paste in a cup; stir into liquid in frying pan. Cook, stirring constantly, until sauce thickens and boils 3 minutes. Stir in mandarin-orange segments and grapes; heat until bubbly. Spoon over chicken. Garnish with additional grapes and mandarin-orange segments, if you wish.

CURRIED CHICKEN AND VEGETABLES

A different curry—tender, boneless chicken breasts in an aromatic curried vegetable sauce, served over steaming rice.

Makes 8 servings.

4 whole chicken breasts, split (about 12 ounces each)
¼ cup flour (for chicken)
½ teaspoon salt (for chicken)
⅛ teaspoon pepper (for chicken)
¼ cup (½ stick) butter or margarine
1 large onion, chopped (1 cup)
1 green pepper, halved, seeded and diced
1 tablespoon flour (for sauce)
1 teaspoon salt (for sauce)
⅛ teaspoon pepper (for sauce)
2 tablespoons curry powder
1 can (8 ounces) tomatoes
2 envelopes or teaspoons instant chicken broth
2¼ cups water
6 cups hot cooked rice

1. Pull skin from split chicken breasts; bone. Flatten each half by placing between 2 pieces of wax paper and pounding with the back of a heavy knife or mallet. Cut each half into 2 pieces (fillets).
2. Combine ¼ cup flour, ½ teaspoon salt and ⅛ teaspoon pepper in a plastic bag. Add chicken fillets; shake well to coat.
3. Melt butter or margarine in a large skillet; sauté chicken fillets until brown on both sides. Remove from skillet.
4. Sauté onion and green pepper until almost tender in same skillet. Stir in the 1 tablespoon flour, 1 teaspoon salt, ⅛ teaspoon pepper and curry powder. Add tomatoes, instant chicken broth and water; bring to boiling.
5. Lower heat; simmer, covered, 20 minutes. Remove the cover and simmer 5 minutes longer, or until sauce thickens.
6. Return chicken fillets to sauce and cover. Simmer 15 minutes longer, or until chicken is tender.
7. Do-ahead note: Line a 10-cup shallow freezer-to-table baking dish with heavy foil. Arrange chicken in dish and spoon sauce over; wrap; label and freeze. When frozen, remove foil-wrapped food from dish; return to freezer.
8. Party day: Remove food from freezer and peel off foil. Place in same dish. Bake, covered, in moderate oven (350°) 1 hour, or until bubbly-hot. Serve with hot rice.

BROILED CHICKEN WITH CREAM SAUCE

Broiled chicken breasts are served on crisp bacon and blanketed with creamy sauce.

Makes 6 servings.

3 large whole chicken breasts, split (about 2 pounds)
¼ cup (½ stick) butter or margarine, melted
1 can (about 11 ounces) chicken gravy
¼ cup light or table cream
1 teaspoon lemon juice
2 or 3 drops red-pepper seasoning
12 slices Canadian-style bacon (about ½ pound)

1. Remove skin from chicken and cut away meat from bones in one piece. (Use a sharp thin-bladed knife, cutting close to bones, and meat will pull away easily; simmer bones in water for a broth for another day, if you wish.)
2. Place chicken, rounded side down, on greased broiler rack; brush with half the melted butter or margarine; broil about 10 minutes; turn; brush again with remaining butter or margarine; broil 10 to 12 minutes longer, or until golden-brown and tender when pierced with a fork.
3. While chicken cooks, combine chicken gravy, cream, lemon juice and red-pepper seasoning in small saucepan; heat, stirring often, just to boiling.
4. Arrange bacon slices in single layer in shallow pan; 2 to 3 minutes before chicken is done, slide pan into hot oven (from broiling chicken) to cook bacon and crisp any fat edges.
5. Put 2 slices bacon on each dinner plate; top with half a chicken breast; spoon about ¼ cup heated sauce over.

SOUTH PACIFIC CHICKEN BREASTS

Fruity, spicy—a glorious example of Island cuisine.

Makes 6 servings.

6 whole chicken breasts (about 12 ounces each)
1 tablespoon cinnamon
1½ teaspoons curry powder
1½ teaspoons garlic salt
½ cup honey
¾ cup grapefruit juice
1 can (about 8 ounces) crushed pineapple

1. Place chicken breasts in a large frying pan or kettle. Blend cinnamon, curry powder, garlic salt and honey in a 2-cup measure; stir in grapefruit juice; pour over chicken; cover.
2. Simmer, stirring liquid in bottom of pan often so honey won't scorch, 20 minutes, or until chicken is tender.
3. Remove from liquid, letting any excess drip back into pan; slip off skin, if you wish. Place chicken on broiler rack.
4. Stir pineapple and syrup into liquid in pan; brush over chicken.
5. Broil, 4 to 6 inches from heat, 5 minutes, or until lightly glazed.

CHICKEN AND MUSHROOM DUET

Tender chicken breasts with mushrooms and noodles in a creamy gravy.

Makes 6 servings.

3 whole chicken breasts (2½ to 3 pounds), split
2 cups water
1 slice onion
Handful of celery tops
1 teaspoon salt
4 peppercorns
1 package (8 ounces) noodles
½ pound fresh mushrooms, sliced
2 tablespoons butter or margarine
1 can (about 11 ounces) chicken gravy

1. Combine chicken breasts, water, onion, celery tops, salt and peppercorns in large saucepan. Simmer, covered, 20 minutes, or until chicken is tender.

2. While chicken simmers, cook noodles in large amount boiling salted water, following label directions; drain; place in greased shallow 8-cup casserole.
3. Sauté mushrooms in butter or margarine in large frying pan; arrange in clusters on top of noodles. (Keep casserole warm in heated oven while browning the chicken and heating the gravy.)
4. Drain chicken breasts (strain broth and save for soup). Brown chicken quickly in same frying pan, adding more butter or margarine, if needed; place on noodles.
5. Stir chicken gravy into frying pan; heat to boiling; pour over and around chicken.

CHICKEN BREASTS MANDALAY

This delectable chicken has a light curry-and-fruit-flavored sauce.

Bake at 350° for 2 hours.
Makes 8 servings.

4 chicken breasts (about 12 ounces each)
3 tablespoons flour
1 tablespoon curry powder
2 teaspoons salt
4 tablespoons vegetable oil
1 tablespoon sugar
2 envelopes instant beef broth or 2 beef bouillon cubes
1 large onion, chopped (1 cup)
1 cup water
1 jar (about 5 ounces) baby-pack apricots
2 tablespoons lemon juice
2 teaspoons soy sauce

1. Pull skin from chicken breasts; halve each.
2. Shake with mixture of flour, curry powder and salt in a paper bag to coat lightly and evenly.
3. Brown pieces in vegetable oil in a large frying pan; place in a 10-cup baking dish.
4. Stir sugar, beef broth or bouillon cubes, onion, water, apricots, lemon juice and soy sauce into drippings in frying pan; heat to boiling, crushing bouillon cubes, if used, with a spoon. Pour over chicken.
5. Bake, covered, in moderate oven (350°) 1 hour, or until chicken is tender and sauce is bubbly hot. Serve over hot fluffy rice or noodles, if you wish.

Drumsticks

DRUMSTICK FRICASSEE

Meaty chicken legs, sweet potato and peas in rich gravy are topped with lemon-flecked dumplings.

Makes 2 servings.

4 drumsticks (about 1 pound)
½ small onion, sliced
¼ cup chopped celery tops
1 teaspoon salt
⅛ teaspoon pepper
1½ cups water
2 teaspoons flour
1 large sweet potato, pared and sliced ½ inch thick
1 cup frozen peas (from a 1½-pound bag)
Lemon Dumplings

1. Cook chicken with onions, celery tops, salt and pepper in 1 cup water 30 minutes, or until tender.
2. Blend flour into ½ cup water; stir into broth; cook, stirring constantly, until gravy thickens and boils 1 minute.
3. Add potato and peas; heat to boiling, then simmer 10 minutes while making Lemon Dumplings.
4. Drop batter in 4 mounds on top of hot chicken and vegetables; cover tightly. Cook 20 minutes, or until dumplings are fluffy-light.
5. Lift off dumplings; spoon chicken, vegetables and gravy into serving dishes; top with dumplings. Garnish with grated lemon rind, if you wish.

LEMON DUMPLINGS: Combine ⅔ cup sifted flour, 1 teaspoon baking powder, ½ teaspoon grated lemon rind and ¼ teaspoon salt. Stir 1 teaspoon lemon juice into ⅓ cup milk. (No need to fuss if mixture curdles.) Add all at once to dry ingredients; stir just until flour mixture is moistened completely.

STUFFED DRUMSTICKS NAPOLI

Each golden leg contains a zippy salami stuffing.

Makes 8 servings.

8 chicken drumsticks with thighs (about 5 pounds)
1 piece (4 ounces) salami
½ cup flour
2 teaspoons salt
1 teaspoon paprika
1 teaspoon leaf oregano, crumbled
⅛ teaspoon pepper
½ cup vegetable oil

1. Cut through chicken legs at joints to separate drumsticks and thighs, then cut an opening along bone of each drumstick and in meaty part of each thigh to make a pocket for a salami slice.
2. Cut salami into 16 strips; stuff 1 strip into each piece of chicken.
3. Shake pieces, a few at a time, in mixture of flour, salt, paprika, oregano and pepper in a paper bag to coat evenly.
4. Cook pieces slowly in vegetable oil in a large frying pan 20 minutes; turn; cover loosely. Cook 20 minutes longer, or until tender and crisply golden. Serve warm or cold.

DRUMSTICK BAKE

Convenience foods serve as a base for this oven treat.

Bake at 425° for 50 minutes.
Makes 6 servings.

½ cup (1 stick) butter or margarine
1 package (5 ounces) barbecue-flavor potato chips
⅓ cup undiluted evaporated milk
12 chicken drumsticks
2 cans (15 ounces each) macaroni with cheese sauce
1 can (about 15 ounces) spaghetti with tomato sauce
1 tablespoon instant minced onion
1 large tomato, cut in 6 wedges

1. Melt butter or margarine in a jelly-roll pan.
2. Crush potato chips coarsely. (Tip: Leave chips in bag and simply squeeze it with your hands.) Slit bag; spread open.

3. Pour milk into a shallow dish. Dip drumsticks, 1 at a time, into milk, then roll in potato chips to coat well all over; place in a single layer in butter in pan.
4. Bake in hot oven (425°) 25 minutes; spoon drippings in pan over chicken. Bake 25 minutes longer, or until tender.
5. While chicken bakes, mix macaroni, spaghetti and onion in a 12-cup baking dish; cover. Heat in oven with chicken 20 minutes, or until bubbly.
6. To serve, arrange drumsticks, spoke fashion, over macaroni mixture in dish; place tomato wedges in a circle in center. Garnish with parsley, if you wish.

DRUMSTICKS PIERRE

Not for timid palates, this highly seasoned dish.

Makes 4 servings.

8 drumsticks (about 2 pounds)
¼ cup flour seasoned with ½ teaspoon salt and a dash of pepper
3 tablespoons butter or margarine
1 can (about 1 pound) tomatoes
½ cup water
2 tablespoons brown sugar
2 tablespoons vinegar
2 tablespoons Worcestershire sauce
1 teaspoon salt
1 teaspoon chili powder
1 teaspoon dry mustard
½ teaspoon celery seeds
1 clove garlic, minced
Few drops hot-pepper sauce

1. Dust drumsticks with the seasoned flour.
2. Melt butter or margarine in large heavy frying pan with tight-fitting cover; brown chicken over medium heat on all sides; drain on absorbent paper.
3. Combine all remaining ingredients in same pan.
4. Bring to boil; reduce heat; return chicken to pan; cover.
5. Simmer chicken 40 to 45 minutes, or until tender.
6. Serve with pan sauce.

SKILLET CHICKEN AND VEGETABLES

You can start this meal-in-one well beforehand and refrigerate it, then finish cooking it just before dinnertime.

Makes 6 servings.

6 drumsticks with thighs (about 3 pounds)
6 slices bacon, halved
⅓ cup flour
1 teaspoon salt
¼ teaspoon pepper
2 cans (12 ounces each) Mexican-style corn
¾ cup milk
2 packages (10 ounces each) frozen Fordhook lima beans
1 cup thinly sliced celery

1. Cut through chicken legs at joints to separate drumsticks and thighs; wash pieces and dry.
2. Sauté bacon until crisp in a large heavy frying pan; remove and drain on paper toweling. Wrap and chill until just before serving time.
3. Brown chicken pieces in bacon drippings in same pan; remove and set aside.
4. Stir flour, salt and pepper into drippings; cook, stirring constantly, until bubbly. Drain liquid from corn into a small bowl; stir milk into corn liquid, then stir into flour mixture in frying pan. Continue cooking and stirring until gravy thickens and boils 1 minute. Return chicken, arranging pieces in a single layer; cover. Chill, along with corn.
5. An hour before serving, heat chicken and gravy very slowly to boiling; simmer 45 minutes; pile chicken in center of pan.
6. Pour boiling water to cover over limas and celery in a medium-size bowl; let stand 3 minutes, breaking up limas as they thaw; drain. Place at one side of chicken in pan; place corn at other side; cover. Simmer 10 minutes. Arrange bacon over chicken; continue cooking 5 minutes, or until beans are tender and bacon is heated through. Just before serving, garnish with parsley, if you wish.

Thighs

CHICKEN SCALLOPINE

Garnish with lemon and serve on toast points.

Makes 4 servings.

8 chicken thighs, boned
1 teaspoon salt
2 tablespoons butter or margarine
1 tablespoon lemon juice
2 tablespoons chopped parsley
1 tablespoon chopped chives
¼ teaspoon dried leaf marjoram

1. Place boned thighs between 2 pieces of foil; pound with side of cleaver or rolling pin to flatten. Sprinkle with salt.
2. Melt butter over medium heat in a large skillet. Add chicken, skin side down. Cook about 10 minutes, until lightly browned. Turn; sprinkle with lemon juice and herbs. Cook about 10 minutes, until tender.
3. Serve on buttered toast points; garnish with thin lemon slice.

PIZZA CHICKS

Use 12 small skewers or stuffing pins to secure these delicious chicken-cheese rolls.

Bake at 400° for 40 minutes.
Makes 4 servings.

8 chicken thighs, boned
½ teaspoon salt
1 teaspoon instant minced onion
1 teaspoon parsley flakes
4 ounces Mozzarella cheese
8 ounces spaghetti or linguini
2 cans (8 ounces each) tomato sauce
½ teaspoon dried leaf basil
½ teaspoon dried leaf oregano
Grated Parmesan cheese

1. Place boned thighs skin side down on cutting board. Sprinkle with the salt, instant minced onion and parsley flakes.
2. Cut Mozzarella cheese into 8 pieces, about 2½"x½"x¾". Place a piece of cheese on each boned thigh; fold sides over cheese and fasten with skewer.
3. Place skewered side down in foil-lined pan. Bake in hot oven (400°) 40 minutes.

4. While mini-rolls are baking, cook spaghetti according to package directions. Combine tomato sauce with basil and oregano in a small saucepan; heat.
5. Place mini-rolls on cooked spaghetti on serving platter. Pour tomato sauce over all. Serve sprinkled with the grated Parmesan cheese.

Wings

KENTUCKY BURGOO

A delicious soup-stew for cold days.

Makes 6 servings.

1½ pounds chicken wings (about 12)
1 medium-size onion, chopped (½ cup)
5 cups water
1 can (1 pound) stewed tomatoes
2 tablespoons bottled steak sauce
⅛ teaspoon cayenne
3½ teaspoons salt
½ pound ground beef
2 cans (1 pound each) mixed vegetables
1 small head cabbage (about 1 pound), shredded
2 cups instant mashed potato flakes
¼ cup chopped parsley

1. Cut apart chicken wings at joints with a sharp knife. Combine with onion, water, tomatoes, steak sauce, cayenne and 3 teaspoons of the salt in a large heavy kettle or Dutch oven. Heat to boiling; reduce heat; cover. Simmer 30 minutes.
2. Mix ground beef lightly with remaining ½ teaspoon salt; shape into 18 little meatballs.
3. Add mixed vegetables and cabbage to chicken mixture; bring to a boil; add meatballs; reduce heat; cover. Simmer 10 minutes. Stir in potato flakes. Remove from heat.
4. Sprinkle with parsley. Spoon into soup bowls. Serve with hot corn bread, if you wish.

BREADED CHICKEN WINGS

A batch of tasty tidbits for nibblers.

Bake at 350° for 1 hour.
Makes 50 pieces.

3 pounds chicken wings (about 25)
½ cup vegetable oil
1 teaspoon seasoned salt
1½ cups corn-flake crumbs or bread crumbs

1. Trim tips from chicken wings. (Save for soup kettle.) Divide wings in half by cutting through remaining joints with a knife.
2. Mix vegetable oil and seasoned salt in a pie plate; place corn-flake or bread crumbs in a second pie plate. Roll chicken pieces in oil mixture, then in crumbs to coat evenly. Place, not touching, in a large shallow pan.
3. Bake in moderate oven (350°) 1 hour, or until golden. Serve hot.

CRUSTY CHICKEN WINGS

Crusty wing drumsticks, hot and savory from the oven, great with frosty drinks.

Bake at 375° for 40 minutes.
Makes 30 pieces.

3 pounds chicken wings (about 15)
1 small can evaporated milk (⅔ cup)
1 tablespoon prepared mustard
1 clove of garlic, minced
1 cup fine dry bread crumbs
1 teaspoon instant minced onion
1 teaspoon seasoned salt
¼ teaspoon seasoned pepper
1 envelope or teaspoon instant chicken broth

1. Trim tips from chicken wings. (Save for soup kettle.) Divide each wing in half by cutting through joint.
2. Blend milk, mustard and garlic in a shallow dish. Combine bread crumbs, onion, salt, pepper and broth in another dish.
3. Dip chicken pieces into milk mixture, then into crumbs to coat well.
4. To freeze: Place chicken wings in a single layer in buttered foil pans. Cover with foil or transparent wrap; freeze.
5. Bake in moderate oven (375°) 40 minutes, turning once, until chicken is tender.

PICKUP CHICKEN STICKS

Luscious finger-food to serve at an open house, buffet lunch or cocktail party.

Bake at 350° for 1 hour.
Makes 50 pieces.

3 pounds chicken wings (about 25)
1 cup (2 sticks) butter or margarine
1½ cups sifted flour
⅓ cup finely crushed toasted almonds
1 tablespoon salt
½ teaspoon ground ginger

1. Singe chicken wings, if necessary; cut off tips. (Save for soup kettle.) Divide each wing in half by cutting through joint. Wash and drain on paper toweling.
2. Melt butter or margarine in large shallow baking pan. Mix flour, crushed almonds, salt and ginger in pie plate.
3. Roll chicken pieces, one at a time, in butter or margarine in pan, letting any excess drip back. Roll in flour to coat. Arrange, not touching, in single layer in same pan.
4. Bake in moderate oven (350°) 1 hour, or until tender and richly golden on bottom. Brown in broiler for 3 to 5 minutes.

Livers

HERBED CHICKEN LIVERS

Sautéed with a delightful blend of herbs, these livers will take only minutes to prepare.

Makes 4 servings.

1 pound chicken livers, cut in half
¾ teaspoon salt
⅛ teaspoon pepper
1 tablespoon minced onion
1 tablespoon minced parsley
½ teaspoon dried leaf tarragon
Flour
2 tablespoons butter or margarine

1. Sprinkle livers with salt, pepper, onion, parsley, tarragon. Dust lightly with flour.
2. Melt butter or margarine in skillet over medium heat; add livers and cook about 5 minutes, turning occasionally.

CHICKEN LIVERS AND EGGS

A perfect dish to whip up for brunch, light supper or midnight snack.

Makes 4 servings.

6 eggs
6 tablespoons milk
¾ teaspoon salt
Dash of pepper
½ pound chicken livers OR 1 package
    (8 ounces) frozen chicken livers, thawed
Salt and pepper
2 teaspoons butter or margarine

1. Combine eggs, milk, salt and pepper in medium-size bowl; beat until foamy; save.
2. Cut chicken livers into small pieces; sprinkle with salt and pepper.
3. Melt butter or margarine in medium-size frying pan; fry livers over medium heat, stirring several times, 3 to 4 minutes, or until lightly browned.
4. Add milk-egg mixture; cook over low heat, stirring several times, 3 to 4 minutes, or until eggs are set.

CHICKEN-LIVER-MUSHROOM KEBABS

An interesting variation on the popular kebab theme.

Makes 4 servings.

4 bacon strips, cut in quarters
12 small mushroom caps
12 chicken livers (about 1 pound)
2 tablespoons melted butter or margarine
Salt and pepper

1. On a 7-inch skewer, string a folded-over piece of bacon, a mushroom cap and a chicken liver; repeat 2 more times, ending with bacon; repeat to fill 4 skewers.
2. Place in shallow baking pan; brush with melted butter or margarine.
3. Place in broiler with top of food 4 inches from unit or tip of flame, and broil 10 minutes, or until livers are cooked through and bacon is crisp, turning once and basting once or twice with drippings. Sprinkle with salt and pepper to taste.
4. Remove food from each skewer onto a hot plate and serve.

CHICKEN LIVERS WITH BACON CRISPS

Harmonious morsels, oven baked and served on toast.

Bake at 400° for 30 minutes.
Makes 6 servings.

12 slices (about ½ pound) bacon
1 pound chicken livers
4 tablespoons flour
1 teaspoon salt
½ teaspoon paprika
6 slices hot toast
Pepper

1. Lay bacon slices in single layer on rack of broiler pan. (If slices don't separate easily, heat in oven for a few minutes.) Bake in hot oven (400°) 10 minutes, or until crisp. (No need to turn.) Remove rack with bacon on it; keep warm. (Leave oven heat on.)
2. Shake chicken livers in mixture of flour, salt and paprika in paper bag to coat well; lay in hot drippings in broiler pan.
3. Bake in hot oven (400°) 10 minutes, or until browned on underside; turn; bake 10 minutes longer, or until browned on other side. Drain on paper toweling.
4. Arrange toast slices in single layer on heated large serving platter; brush very lightly with bacon drippings from broiler pan. Arrange livers on top; sprinkle with pepper; top with criss-crossed bacon slices.

CHICKEN LIVERS STROGANOFF

Sour cream sauce turns these delicacies into a Continental dish.

Makes 6 servings.

1 pound chicken livers
2 tablespoons butter or margarine
½ teaspoon oregano
½ teaspoon Worcestershire sauce
1 medium-size onion, chopped (½ cup)
2 tablespoons flour
½ teaspoon salt
Dash of pepper
1 can (6 ounces) sliced mushrooms
¼ cup dairy sour cream

1. Halve chicken livers; snip out any veiny parts or skin with scissors.

2. Brown livers slowly in butter or margarine seasoned with oregano and Worcestershire sauce; remove from pan. Add onion to pan; sauté until soft.
3. Blend in flour, salt and pepper; stir in mushrooms and liquid. Heat, stirring constantly, to boiling; return livers; cover. Simmer 3 minutes, or just until livers lose their pink color.
4. Stir about ¼ cup liver mixture into sour cream, then stir back into remaining in pan. Heat very slowly just until hot. Serve over fluffy rice and garnish with crisp bacon slices, if you wish.

CHICKEN LIVERS GREEK STYLE

Specially flavored chicken livers combine with tender eggplant for a different dinner idea.

Makes 6 servings.

1 eggplant (about 1 pound), sliced ½ inch thick
5 tablespoons flour
1 teaspoon salt
2 tablespoons vegetable oil
4 tablespoons (½ stick) butter or margarine
1½ pounds chicken livers, washed and cut in half
1 medium-size onion, sliced
½ teaspoon leaf basil, crumbled
1 can condensed chicken broth
2 tomatoes, peeled and cut in eighths
2 tablespoons chopped parsley

1. Dip eggplant slices in mixture of 3 tablespoons of the flour and salt. Sauté in oil and 2 tablespoons of butter or margarine about 3 minutes on each side, or until soft in a large skillet. Arrange, overlapping, around edge of serving dish. Keep warm.
2. Sauté chicken livers and onion in remaining butter or margarine in same skillet 6 minutes, or until browned. Stir in remaining 2 tablespoons flour and basil. Gradually stir in broth.
3. Heat, stirring constantly, until mixture thickens and bubbles 1 minute. Add tomatoes; cover; reduce heat; simmer 5 minutes. Spoon into center of serving dish with eggplant border. Sprinkle with parsley and serve with hot cooked rice, if you wish.

CHICKEN-LIVER-TOMATO KEBABS

A light and pretty dish bound to boost a hostess' reputation.

Makes 4 servings.

12 chicken livers (about 1 pound)
4 slices bacon, halved
16 cherry tomatoes
2 tablespoons Worcestershire sauce

1. Halve chicken livers; snip out any veiny parts or skin with scissors.
2. Sauté bacon slices until partly cooked in a medium-size frying pan; remove and drain well on paper toweling. Wrap slices around 8 of the liver halves; hold in place with wooden picks, if needed.
3. Thread each of 8 long thin skewers this way: Cherry tomato, plain chicken liver half, bacon-wrapped liver, plain liver half and cherry tomato, allowing about ¼ inch between each. Place on rack in broiler pan; brush with part of the Worcestershire sauce.
4. Broil, 6 inches from heat, 7 minutes; turn. Brush with remaining Worcestershire sauce, then continue broiling 7 minutes, or until bacon is crisp. Remove wooden picks before serving.

LITTLE LIVERS SPECIALTY

Don't overcook these delicious tidbits.

Makes 4 servings.

1 pound chicken livers
¼ cup sifted flour
½ teaspoon salt
⅛ teaspoon pepper
2 tablespoons butter or margarine
1 can (3 or 4 ounces) sliced mushrooms
1½ teaspoons Worcestershire sauce

1. Shake chicken livers, a few at a time, in mixture of flour, salt and pepper in paper bag to coat evenly.
2. Brown in butter or margarine in large frying pan over low heat. Stir in mushrooms and liquid and Worcestershire sauce.
3. Cover loosely; cook slowly 10 minutes, or just until liquid is absorbed.

A chicken in every pot? Hardly. The theme of this chapter is a chicken in one pot–an idea that makes dinner child's play for even the busiest cook. Casseroles, one of the housewife's dreams come true, are joined here by chicken pies and stews. All are cooked in one pot, be it a Dutch oven, large kettle or oven-proof dish. And all provide a complete meal-in-one dinner (add salad and rolls if the spirit moves you).

The casseroles and pies can be made with leftover chicken, or from scratch; the stews provide the basis for leftovers. They'll keep after the first serving, to be frozen or refrigerated, and then reheated on another night. As you can see, this is not only one-pot, meal-in-one cooking–it's more than anyone could ask for.

Meal-In-One Chicken

Casseroles

MOCK COQ AU VIN

Long slow cooking gives this aristocrat a mellow flavor. Its seasoning secrets: Apple cider, mixed vegetable juices.

Bake at 350° for 2 hours and 15 minutes.
Makes 4 servings.

1 stewing chicken (about 4 pounds), cut
   in serving-size pieces
⅓ cup flour
1½ teaspoons salt
3 tablespoons butter or margarine
½ cup diced cooked ham
12 small white onions, peeled
1 can (12 ounces) mixed vegetable juices
   (1½ cups)
1½ cups apple cider
1 can (3 or 4 ounces) mushroom caps
1 clove garlic, minced
6 peppercorns
6 whole cloves
1 bay leaf

1. Wash chicken pieces; pat dry. Shake with the flour and salt in a paper bag to coat thoroughly.
2. Brown pieces, a few at a time, in butter or margarine in a large frying pan; place in a 12-cup baking dish; sprinkle with ham and top with onions.
3. Stir the vegetable juices, cider, mushrooms and their liquid and garlic into drippings in pan; heat to boiling, scraping brown bits from bottom of pan. Pour over chicken.
4. Tie seasonings in a tiny cheesecloth bag; add to casserole; cover.
5. Bake in moderate oven (350°) 2 hours and 15 minutes, or until chicken is very tender.
6. Uncover; remove spice bag and let chicken stand for 5 to 10 minutes, or until fat rises to top, then skim off. Garnish chicken with parsley, if you wish.

DIXIE CHICKEN DINNER

A lively dish with layers of chicken, beans, olives and tomatoes.

Bake at 350° for 1 hour.
Makes 8 servings.

2 broiler-fryers (about 2 pounds each)
¾ cup flour
2 teaspoons salt
1 teaspoon leaf basil, crumbled
4 tablespoons vegetable oil
2 cans (1 pound each) cooked dried
   lima beans
1 can (1 pound) cut green beans, drained
½ cup sliced stuffed green olives
½ cup sliced pitted ripe olives
4 medium-size firm ripe tomatoes, sliced
   ½-inch thick
1 clove garlic, minced
½ cup apple juice or water

1. Cut chicken into serving-size pieces. Shake pieces with a mixture of ½ cup flour, salt and basil in a paper bag to coat evenly.
2. Brown slowly in vegetable oil in a large frying pan 10 minutes on each side; remove and set aside.
3. While chicken browns, drain liquid from lima beans into a 2-cup measure; combine limas with green beans, and green and ripe olives in a greased 12-cup shallow baking dish. Place tomato slices in a single layer over vegetables.
4. Pour all drippings from frying pan, then measure 4 tablespoonfuls and return to pan; stir in remaining ¼ cup flour and garlic; cook, stirring constantly, just until bubbly.
5. Combine apple juice with saved bean liquid and additional water to make 2 cups; stir into flour mixture in frying pan. Continue cooking and stirring until sauce thickens and boils 1 minute; pour over vegetables in baking dish. Arrange browned chicken in a single layer on top, then press pieces down into vegetables slightly.
6. Bake in moderate oven (350°) 1 hour, or until chicken is tender and sauce bubbles up. Sprinkle with chopped parsley, if you wish.

CHICKEN MARENGO

This dish originated in the Italian town of Marengo; they say it was invented to serve to Napoleon.

Bake at 350° for 1½ hours.
Makes 8 servings.

6 slices bacon, cut in 1-inch pieces
2 broiler-fryers (about 2 pounds each), cut up
½ cup flour
2 teaspoons salt
¼ teaspoon pepper
2 medium-size onions, chopped (1 cup)
1 clove garlic, minced
1 can (3 or 4 ounces) whole mushrooms
2 cans (1 pound each) tomatoes
¼ cup chopped parsley
Few drops bottled red-pepper seasoning
1 cup Golden Croutons

1. Fry bacon until almost crisp in large frying pan. Lift out with slotted spoon; drain on paper toweling and set aside for Step 6. Leave drippings in pan.
2. Wash and dry chicken pieces well. Snip off small rib bones with kitchen scissors, if you wish. Shake chicken in mixture of flour, salt and pepper in paper bag to coat well. (Save any leftover flour mixture for Step 4.)
3. Brown chicken, a few pieces at a time, in bacon drippings; place in a 12-cup shallow baking dish.
4. Sauté onion and garlic until soft in same frying pan; stir in saved flour mixture. Drain liquid from mushrooms. (Save mushrooms for Step 6.) Stir liquid, tomatoes, parsley and the red-pepper seasoning into frying pan; heat to boiling, stirring constantly.
5. Spoon over chicken in baking dish; cover. (Casserole can be put together up to this point, then chilled. Remove from refrigerator and let stand at room temperature 30 minutes before baking.)
6. Bake in moderate oven (350°) 1 hour and 20 minutes, or until chicken is tender. Uncover; sprinkle with saved bacon pieces and mushrooms. Bake 10 minutes longer, or until bacon is crisp.
7. Just before serving, sprinkle Golden Croutons over top; garnish with more chopped parsley, if you wish.

GOLDEN CROUTONS: Trim crusts from 2 slices of white bread; cut into 1½-inch cubes. Spread in single layer in shallow baking pan. Toast in moderate oven (350°) 10 minutes, or until golden. Makes 1 cup.

NEOPOLITAN CHICKEN

Families that love spaghetti will welcome this chicken-and-potatoes with spaghetti-sauce flavor.

Bake at 350° for 1½ hours.
Makes 6 servings.

2 broiler-fryers (about 2 pounds each), cut up
¼ cup flour
1 teaspoon salt
⅛ teaspoon pepper
2 tablespoons olive or salad oil
1 medium-size onion, chopped (½ cup)
1 clove garlic, minced
1 cup water
1 envelope spaghetti-sauce mix
3 medium-size tomatoes, chopped
¼ cup chopped parsley
6 medium-size potatoes, pared and cut in 1-inch cubes
1 large green pepper, seeded and cut into wide strips

1. Shake chicken with flour, salt and pepper in a paper bag to coat well. Brown, a few pieces at a time, in olive oil or salad oil in frying pan; place in an 8-cup baking dish.
2. Sauté onion and garlic until softened in same frying pan; stir in water, then spaghetti-sauce mix; heat to boiling. Stir in tomatoes and parsley. Simmer, uncovered, 15 minutes.
3. Pour over chicken in baking dish; top with potato cubes and pepper strips; cover.
4. Bake in moderate oven (350°) 1½ hours, or until chicken is tender.

THE DISAPPEARING CASSEROLE TRICK

Line a freezer-to-oven baking dish with foil, add the ingredients and freeze. When frozen, remove the food wrapped in the foil, relieving the dish for duty. To serve, remove food from foil, return to the same baking dish and bake.

CHICKEN TIJUANA

A casserole with a saucy seasoning of olives, green pepper, tomatoes and herbs.

Bake at 350° for 50 minutes.
Makes 4 servings.

1 broiler-fryer (about 2½ pounds)
2 cups water
¼ teaspoon salt
½ cup flour
2 tablespoons butter or margarine
3 tablespoons vegetable oil
3 medium-size tomatoes, peeled and
    quartered
¼ cup pimiento-stuffed olives, sliced
1 large onion, chopped (1 cup)
1 large green pepper, halved, seeded and
    chopped
1 teaspoon leaf basil, crumbled
1 teaspoon seasoned salt
1 teaspoon paprika
⅓ cup grated Parmesan cheese

1. Cut wings from chicken. Remove giblets and neck from chicken package and place (except liver) with wings, water, and the ¼ teaspoon salt in a small saucepan; cover. Simmer 45 minutes. Add liver; cover; cook 15 minutes longer. Strain broth into a small bowl; reserve for Step 4. Chop giblets and the meat from wings and neck; reserve.
2. Cut chicken into serving-size pieces. Shake chicken, a few pieces at a time, in a plastic bag with flour to coat; tap off excess. Reserve 1 tablespoon of the flour for Step 4.
3. Sauté chicken in butter or margarine and oil, turning once, about 15 minutes, or until golden brown, in a large skillet. Place chicken in a 10-cup baking dish. Add tomatoes and olives.
4. Add onion and green pepper to drippings in skillet; sauté until tender. Stir in basil, the 1 tablespoon reserved flour, seasoned salt and paprika. Cook 1 minute, stirring constantly. Stir in 1 cup of the reserved broth; cook and stir until sauce thickens and bubbles 1 minute. Stir in chopped chicken and giblets, and cheese. Pour over chicken and vegetables; cover.
5. Bake in moderate oven (350°) 50 minutes, or until chicken is tender.

CHICKEN AND ONIONS AU CASSEROLE

White meat and onions in a creamy sauce, with green peas mixed in like little gems.

Bake at 350° for 1½ hours.
Makes 8 servings.

1 package (8 ounces) medium noodles
1 package (9 ounces) frozen onions in
    cream sauce
2 cans condensed golden mushroom soup
1 package (10 ounces) frozen green peas
4 chicken breasts (about 12 ounces each)
Chopped pistachio nuts (optional)

1. Cook noodles, following the label directions; drain. Combine with onions and 1 can of the mushroom soup in a greased shallow 12-cup baking dish; sprinkle with peas.
2. While noodles cook, pull skin from chicken breasts; cut each in half. Arrange in a single layer over peas; spread with remaining can of soup; cover.
3. Bake in moderate oven (350°) 1½ hours, or until chicken is tender and sauce is bubbly. Garnish with chopped pistachio nuts, if you wish.

BRUNSWICK CHICKEN

This chicken dish includes corn, lima beans, a peppy tomato sauce.

Bake at 350° for 1½ hours.
Makes 8 servings.

2 broiler-fryers (about 2 pounds each), cut up
½ cup flour
1 envelope herb-salad-dressing mix
¼ cup shortening
1 large onion, chopped (1 cup)
1 tablespoon sugar
2 cans (about 1 pound each) tomatoes
1 package (10 ounces) frozen whole-kernel
    corn, cooked and drained
1 package (10 ounces) frozen Fordhook
    lima beans, cooked and drained

1. Shake chicken in mixture of flour and salad-dressing mix in paper bag to coat well. Brown, a few pieces at a time, in shortening in large frying pan; arrange in a 12-cup baking dish.

2. Sauté onion in same frying pan; blend in any remaining seasoned flour, and sugar; stir in tomatoes. Heat to boiling, stirring constantly.
3. Spoon corn and lima beans around chicken in baking dish; pour tomato sauce over; cover with lid or foil; chill. Remove from refrigerator and let stand at room temperature 30 minutes before baking.
4. Bake in moderate oven (350°) 1½ hours, or until chicken is tender.

CASSEROLE-ROASTED CHICKEN

Here's one potato lovers will really enjoy.

Bake at 325° for 1¼ hours.
Makes 4 servings.

1 broiler-fryer (about 3 pounds)
1½ teaspoons salt
¼ teaspoon pepper
16 small white onions, peeled
12 small red, new potatoes
3 tablespoons butter or margarine
3 tablespoons vegetable oil
½ cup boiling water
1 envelope instant chicken broth OR
    1 teaspoon granulated chicken bouillon
1 teaspoon leaf basil, crumbled
1 tablespoon chopped parsley

1. Sprinkle chicken cavities with ½ teaspoon of the salt and pepper. Peel onions. Scrub potatoes; pare a band around the center of each.
2. Melt butter or margarine with the vegetable oil in a large heavy flameproof casserole or Dutch oven. Add chicken; brown on all sides.
3. Combine boiling water and chicken broth in a 1-cup measure, stirring until dissolved; add to casserole with chicken.
4. Place onions and potatoes around chicken; sprinkle with basil and remaining 1 teaspoon salt; cover.
5. Bake in slow oven (325°), basting once or twice with juices, 1¼ hours, or until chicken and vegetables are tender. Sprinkle with parsley.

SENEGALESE CHICKEN CASSEROLE

Mildly spiced with curry, chicken and noodles baked in a custard-type sauce.

Bake at 325° for 1¼ hours.
Makes 8 servings.

1 broiler-fryer (about 3 pounds)
1 small onion, sliced
Few celery tops
1½ teaspoons curry powder
2 teaspoons salt
⅛ teaspoon pepper
1½ cups water
Milk
1 package (8 ounces) fine noodles
1 package (10 ounces) frozen peas
1 can (5 ounces) toasted slivered almonds
4 eggs
1 cup cream for whipping

1. Combine chicken with onion, celery tops, curry powder, salt, pepper and water in a large saucepan; cover. Simmer 45 minutes, or until tender.
2. Remove chicken from broth; cool until easy to handle. Strain broth into a 2-cup measure; skim any excess fat, then add milk, if needed, to make 2 cups; set aside for Step 5.
3. Pull skin from chicken and take meat from bones. Cut meat into bite-size pieces.
4. While fixing chicken, cook noodles and peas in separate saucepans, following label directions; drain. Combine with chicken and almonds in a buttered 10-cup baking dish.
5. Beat eggs slightly in a medium-size bowl; stir in the 2 cups chicken broth from Step 2 and cream. (This much can be done ahead.)
6. Pour custard mixture over chicken mixture, then stir lightly so liquid seeps to bottom. Bake in slow oven (325°) 1 hour and 15 minutes, or until custard sets. (Cover lightly with foil during last 15 minutes to keep top moist.) Garnish with diced red apple and coconut, if you wish.

MAKE-AHEAD NOTE: Cover chicken-noodle mixture in baking dish and custard mixture in bowl and chill. About 1¼ hours before serving combine both, following Step 6; place in a cold oven; set heat control at slow (325°). Bake 1 hour and 15 minutes.

CHICKEN AND NOODLE CASSEROLE

Comforting, old family friend—always good and dependable.

Bake at 350° for 2 hours.
Makes 4 to 6 servings.

1 stewing chicken (4 to 5 pounds), cut into serving-size pieces
2 medium-size onions, chopped (1 cup)
1 tablespoon Worcestershire sauce
1 can condensed cream of mushroom soup
Hot noodles

1. Trim any excess fat from chicken pieces; remove skin from legs and breast.
2. Spread onion in bottom of a 12-cup baking dish; arrange chicken in 2 layers on top.
3. Stir Worcestershire sauce into soup in can; spoon over chicken; cover.
4. Bake in moderate oven (350°) 1 hour; uncover and stir to mix soup and chicken juices; cover again.
5. Bake 1 hour longer, or until chicken is very tender. Let casserole stand about 1 minute, or until fat rises to the top; skim. Serve chicken with hot noodles, gravy.

CHICKEN IN THE GARDEN

Fresh asparagus, new potatoes and celery combine with chicken quarters in this meal-in-one dish.

Bake at 375° for 1 hour.
Makes 4 servings.

1 broiler-fryer, quartered
1½ teaspoons salt, divided
1 teaspoon dried leaf tarragon, divided
2 tablespoons butter or margarine
1 pound small new potatoes, pared
2 tablespoons snipped fresh chives
2 tablespoons chopped fresh parsley
2 cups diagonally cut celery pieces
1 pound asparagus (break off ends of stems where they snap easily)
1 tablespoon fresh lemon juice

1. Sprinkle chicken on both sides with ½ teaspoon salt and ½ teaspoon tarragon. Heat butter or margarine in large skillet; add chicken, skin side down, and brown slowly; turn, and brown other side. Transfer the

chicken to a shallow 3- or 4-quart casserole.
2. Add potatoes to the butter in skillet; cook slowly over low heat for about 5 minutes and add to casserole. Sprinkle chicken and potatoes with chives, parsley and drippings from skillet. Cover tightly with casserole lid or aluminum foil.
3. Bake in 375° oven 30 minutes. Remove from oven and remove cover.
4. Add celery pieces and asparagus. Sprinkle vegetables with remaining 1 teaspoon salt and ½ teaspoon tarragon; spoon juices in casserole over asparagus and celery. Drizzle with lemon juice.
5. Cover tightly and bake 30 minutes longer, or until chicken and vegetables are tender; baste occasionally with the juices in the casserole.

Stews

POT-ROASTED CHICKEN WITH CREAM GRAVY

A French way of simmering a large chicken to savory tenderness.

Makes 4 to 6 servings.

4 tablespoons (½ stick) butter or margarine
1 stewing chicken (4 to 5 pounds)
2 teaspoons leaf thyme
1 can condensed beef broth
3 tablespoons flour
1 small can evaporated milk (⅔ cup)

1. Melt butter or margarine in heavy kettle or Dutch oven; brush part on inside of chicken, then sprinkle chicken with 1 teaspoon thyme. Brown chicken lightly on all sides in remaining butter or margarine.
2. Turn chicken, breast side up; pour beef broth over; sprinkle with remaining 1 teaspoon thyme; cover tightly.
3. Simmer, basting a few times with pan juices, 1½ hours, or until tender. Remove to heated serving platter; keep hot while making gravy.
4. Pour broth from kettle into 4-cup measure. Let fat rise to top, then skim off. Add water to broth, if needed, to make 2½ cups.

5. Return 2 tablespoons fat to kettle; blend in flour; stir in broth. Cook, stirring constantly, until gravy thickens and boils 1 minute. Blend in evaporated milk; heat just to boiling.
6. Serve chicken with buttered noodles and spoon gravy over all.

BROWN CHICKEN FRICASSEE

Chicken browned with onions and topped off with cornmeal dumplings should please all grown men and little boys.

Makes 6 servings.

1 stewing chicken (about 5 pounds), cut up
¼ cup flour
2 teaspoons salt
1 teaspoon poultry seasoning
¼ teaspoon pepper
3 tablespoons salad oil
2 medium-size onions, sliced and separated into rings
1 bay leaf
4 cups water
Cornmeal Dumplings

1. Wash chicken; drain. Shake pieces, a few at a time, in mixture of flour, salt, poultry seasoning and pepper in a paper bag to coat well.
2. Brown slowly in salad oil in a large heavy frying pan; remove. Add onion rings, sauté until they are soft.
3. Return chicken to pan; add bay leaf and water; cover. Simmer 1½ hours or until chicken is tender.
4. Prepare Cornmeal Dumplings. Heat chicken until boiling rapidly; drop dough into 12 small mounds on top; cover.
5. Cook, covered, 20 minutes. (No peeking, or the dumplings won't puff properly.)
6. Remove chicken and dumplings to a heated serving platter; remove bay leaf; serve gravy in a separate bowl.

CORNMEAL DUMPLINGS: Sift 1½ cups sifted flour, ¼ cup yellow cornmeal, 3 teaspoons baking powder and 1 teaspoon salt into a medium-size bowl. Cut in 2 tablespoons shortening with a pastry blender until mixture is crumbly. Stir in 1 cup milk just until flour mixture is moistened. (Dough will be soft.)

DAPPLED DUMPLING FRICASSEE

Kettle chicken cooked tender, served with gravy and topped with parsley-sprigged dumplings.

Makes 6 servings.

1 stewing chicken (about 5 pounds), cut up
4 cups plus ½ cup cold water
1 large onion, sliced
1 cup chopped celery and leaves
1 medium-size carrot, scraped and sliced
2 teaspoons salt
¼ teaspoon pepper
6 tablespoons flour
Dappled Dumplings

1. Combine chicken, 4 cups water, onion, celery and leaves, carrot, salt and pepper in large kettle or Dutch oven with tight-fitting cover. Cover; heat to boiling, then simmer 1½ to 2 hours, or until chicken is tender.
2. Remove from broth; cool slightly; slip off skin, if you wish. Strain and measure broth; add water, if needed, to make 5 cups. Press vegetables through strainer into broth in kettle; heat to boiling.
3. Stir ½ cup cold water into flour in cup to make a smooth paste; stir into hot broth. Cook, stirring constantly, until gravy thickens and boils 1 minute. Season with salt and pepper to taste, if needed.
4. Return chicken to gravy in kettle; heat slowly to boiling while stirring up Dappled Dumplings.
5. Drop dough in 12 mounds on top of steaming chicken. Cook, covered, 20 minutes. (No peeking, or the dumplings won't puff properly.)
6. Arrange chicken and dumplings on a heated serving platter; pass gravy in separate bowl.

DAPPLED DUMPLINGS: Sift 2 cups sifted flour, 3 teaspoons baking powder and 1 teaspoon salt into medium-size bowl. Cut in 2 tablespoons shortening with pastry blender until mixture is crumbly. Stir in ¼ cup chopped parsley and 1 cup milk just until flour is moistened. (Dough will be soft.)

HERB IDEA

Add a touch of rosemary to broth when cooking chicken stew. Just be sure to strain the broth for gravy.

CHICKEN, HUNTER'S STYLE

This is an easy-to-prepare blend of chicken and vegetables.

Makes 4 servings.

1 broiler-fryer (about 3 pounds)
1 tablespoon vegetable oil
1 tablespoon butter or margarine
¼ pound mushrooms, trimmed and sliced
2 large tomatoes, peeled, seeded and chopped (2 cups)
¼ cup sliced green onions
1 small clove of garlic, crushed
¾ cup water
2 tablespoons lemon juice
1 teaspoon leaf chervil or thyme, crumbled
1 teaspoon salt
⅛ teaspoon pepper
1 tablespoon cornstarch

1. Cut chicken into serving-size pieces. Brown in oil and butter or margarine in a large skillet with a cover.
2. Add mushrooms, tomatoes, green onions, garlic, ½ cup of the water, lemon juice, chervil, salt and pepper; cover. Simmer 45 minutes, or until chicken is tender. Remove chicken to a heated serving platter; keep hot while making gravy.
3. Blend cornstarch with remaining water in a cup; stir into liquid in skillet. Cook, stirring constantly, until mixture thickens and bubbles 3 minutes. Pour over chicken.

COUNTRY CAPTAIN

A classic Southern dish with a touch of the Orient.

Makes 8 servings.

2 broiler-fryers (about 2½ pounds each)
¼ cup flour
2 teaspoons salt
½ teaspoon pepper
3 tablespoons vegetable oil
1 large onion, chopped (1 cup)
1 large green pepper, halved, seeded, and chopped
1 large clove of garlic, crushed
3 teaspoons curry powder
1 can (1 pound) tomatoes
½ cup raisins or currants
Hot cooked rice

1. Cut chicken into serving-size pieces.
2. Combine flour with 1 teaspoon of the salt and ¼ teaspoon of the pepper in a plastic bag. Shake chicken, a few pieces at a time, in flour mixture to coat; tap off excess.
3. Brown chicken, part at a time, in oil in a kettle. Remove chicken; keep warm.
4. Add onion, green pepper, garlic and curry powder to drippings remaining in kettle; sauté until soft. Add tomatoes (breaking with spoon), raisins and reserved chicken; cover. Simmer 1 hour, or until chicken is tender. Arrange chicken on a bed of rice. Spoon sauce over top.

PIMIENTO CHICKEN STEW

A hearty meal topped with peppy pimiento biscuits.

Makes 8 servings.

1 stewing chicken (4 to 5 pounds), cut in serving-size pieces
½ cup flour
1 envelope herb salad-dressing mix
1 large onion, chopped (1 cup)
2 cans (about 1 pound each) tomatoes
2 cups water
1 teaspoon sugar
2 cups diced celery
2 cups fresh lima beans OR 1 can (about 1 pound) lima beans and liquid (cut water to 1½ cups)
1½ cups fresh corn kernels or 1 can (12 or 16 ounces) whole-kernel corn
1 can (4 ounces) pimientos
¼ cup chopped parsley
Pimiento Biscuits

1. Remove all fat from chicken, and skin from breasts, thighs and drumsticks; melt fat in large heavy kettle or Dutch oven.
2. Shake chicken with flour and herb salad-dressing mix in paper bag to coat evenly; brown, a few pieces at a time, in fat in kettle. Remove chicken and set aside.
3. Sauté onion until soft in same kettle; stir in tomatoes, water and sugar; add celery, lima beans, corn and chicken; cover.
4. Simmer 1 hour, or until chicken is tender; let stand 5 to 10 minutes; skim excess fat.
5. Save 1 pimiento for Pimiento Biscuits; dice remaining; stir into stew with parsley; serve with Pimiento Biscuits.

PIMIENTO BISCUITS

Bake at 400° for 10 minutes.
Makes 12 biscuits.

1¾ cups biscuit mix
½ cup yellow cornmeal
2 tablespoons melted butter or margarine
1 pimiento, chopped
⅔ cup milk

1. Mix biscuit mix, cornmeal, melted butter or margarine and pimiento with a fork in a medium-size bowl; stir in milk just until no dry mix appears; spoon in 12 mounds onto ungreased cooky sheet.
2. Bake in hot oven (400°) 10 minutes, or until golden.

CHICKEN 'N MUSHROOMS

Serve this fricassee with homemade gravy over hot biscuits.

Makes 6 servings.

1 stewing chicken (about 5 pounds), cut up
½ cup sliced celery
1 large onion, sliced
2 medium-size carrots, pared and sliced (1 cup)
1 bay leaf
½ teaspoon peppercorns
3 teaspoons salt
Water
2 tablespoons butter or margarine
1 can (3 or 4 ounces) sliced mushrooms, drained
½ cup flour

1. Place chicken in a kettle or Dutch oven; add celery, onion, carrots, bay leaf, peppercorns, salt and water to cover. Heat to boiling; reduce heat; cover. Simmer 2½ hours, or until chicken is tender.
2. Remove chicken to heated deep serving dish; keep hot while making gravy.
3. Strain broth into a large bowl; let stand until fat rises to top. Skim off fat, then measure 3 tablespoonfuls back into kettle; reserve broth.
4. Heat the butter or margarine with the chicken fat until melted. Blend flour into fat; cook, stirring constantly, just until bubbly. Stir in 4 cups of the broth and mushrooms.

5. Cook, stirring constantly, until gravy thickens and bubbles 1 minute. Pour over the chicken. Serve over hot biscuits.

NOTE: Any leftover broth may be used for chicken soup for the next day.

KETTLE CHICKEN

A hearty meal-in-one that's great for cold winter nights.

Makes 8 servings.

2 broiler-fryers (about 2½ pounds each), cut up
2 tablespoons butter or margarine
2 tablespoons vegetable oil
4 cups water
1 medium-size onion, chopped (½ cup)
1 medium-size carrot, pared and sliced thin (½ cup)
1 stalk celery, chopped (½ cup)
2 teaspoons salt
1 teaspoon leaf basil, crumbled
6 peppercorns
4 whole cloves
1 bay leaf
6 tablespoons flour
1 package (10 ounces) frozen peas
Mashed potatoes

1. Brown chicken parts, part at a time, in butter or margarine and oil in a kettle or Dutch oven. Remove chicken pieces as they brown, then return all to kettle. Add water, onion, carrot, celery, salt, basil, peppercorns, cloves and bay leaf.
2. Heat to boiling; reduce heat; cover. Simmer 45 minutes, or until chicken is tender. Remove chicken and reserve.
3. Strain broth into a 4-cup measure; add water, if needed, to make 4 cups. Press vegetables through a sieve into broth.
4. Skim fat from broth, returning 6 tablespoons to kettle; stir in flour; heat, stirring constantly, just until bubbly. Stir in the 4 cups of broth; continue cooking and stirring until gravy thickens and bubbles 1 minute. Season to taste with salt and pepper, if needed. Add peas and chicken; reheat to boiling. Lower heat; simmer 10 minutes. Serve with mashed potatoes.

Pies

CRISSCROSS CHICKEN PIE

This would be grandmother's idea of a stick-to-the-ribs dinner.

Bake at 400° for 20 minutes, then at 350° for 25 minutes.
Makes 6 servings.

1 broiler-fryer (3 pounds), cut up
3 cups water
Handful of celery tops
2 teaspoons salt
6 peppercorns
Curry Cream Sauce
1 package (10 ounces) frozen peas, cooked
    and drained
1 pimiento, chopped
2 cups sifted flour
⅓ cup shortening
⅔ cup milk

1. Simmer chicken with water, celery tops, 1 teaspoon salt and peppercorns in kettle 1 hour, or until tender. Remove from broth and let cool until easy to handle.
2. Strain broth into a 4-cup measure; add water, if needed, to make 3 cups. Make Curry Cream Sauce.
3. Slip skin from chicken, then remove meat from bones. (It comes off easily while still warm.) Cut into bite-size pieces; toss with peas, pimiento and 2 cups of Curry Cream Sauce in medium-size bowl. Set aside for Step 5. (Save remaining sauce to reheat and serve over pie.)
4. Sift flour and 1 teaspoon salt into medium-size bowl; cut in shortening with pastry blender until mixture is crumbly; stir in milk with a fork just until dough holds together.
5. Turn out onto lightly floured pastry cloth or board; knead lightly 5 or 6 times. Roll out ⅔ of dough to a rectangle, 16x12; fit into a baking dish, 10x6x2. Spoon filling into shell.
6. Roll out remaining pastry to a rectangle about 14x7; cut into 9 long strips, each about ¾ inch wide, with knife or pastry wheel. Lay 5 strips lengthwise over filling. Halve remaining 4 strips; weave across long strips to make a crisscross top. Trim overhang to 1 inch; fold under; flute.
7. Bake in hot oven (400°) 20 minutes; reduce heat to moderate (350°). Bake 25 minutes longer, or until golden. Cut into 6 servings. Serve with remaining hot Curry Cream Sauce.

CURRY CREAM SAUCE: Melt 6 tablespoons (¾ stick) butter or margarine over low heat in medium-size saucepan. Stir in 6 tablespoons flour, 1 teaspoon salt, 1 teaspoon curry powder and ⅛ teaspoon pepper. Cook, stirring all the time, just until mixture bubbles. Stir in 3 cups chicken broth slowly; continue cooking and stirring until sauce thickens and boils 1 minute. Stir in 1 tall can evaporated milk. Makes about 4½ cups.

OLD-FASHIONED CHICKEN PIE

It's so good it's no wonder this dish has been around for ages.

Bake at 400° for 30 minutes.
Makes 8 servings.

2 broiler-fryers (about 2½ pounds each)
Water
2 teaspoons salt
¼ teaspoon pepper
2 cups sliced carrots
1 package (10 ounces) frozen peas
¼ cup (½ stick) butter or margarine
6 tablespoons flour
1½ cups biscuit mix
½ cup dairy sour cream
1 egg
2 teaspoons sesame seeds

1. Place chickens in a large heavy kettle or Dutch oven; add 2 cups water, salt, pepper and carrots. Heat to boiling; reduce heat; cover; simmer 45 minutes. Add peas; simmer 15 minutes longer, or until chicken is tender. Remove chicken to a bowl to cool.
2. Skim fat from chicken broth-vegetable mixture; reserve 2 tablespoons fat. Melt butter or margarine with reserved chicken fat in a medium-size saucepan; stir in flour; cook, stirring constantly, just until bubbly. Stir in chicken broth-vegetable mixture; continue cooking and stirring until gravy thickens and bubbles 1 minute.
3. When chickens are cool enough to handle, pull off skin and slip meat from bones; cut meat into bite-size pieces; stir into gravy; pour into an 8-cup baking dish, 8x8x2.

4. Combine biscuit mix and sour cream in a small bowl; stir to form a stiff dough; turn out onto a lightly floured board; knead a few times; roll out dough to ¼-inch thickness; trim to make an 8½-inch square; cut into 8 strips, each about one inch wide.

5. Using 4 of the strips, make a lattice design on top of the chicken mixture, spacing evenly and attaching ends firmly to edges of the dish. Place remaining strips, one at a time, on edges of dish, pinching dough to make a stand-up rim; flute rim. (Or, roll out dough to a 9-inch square and place over chicken mixture; turn edges under, flush with rim; flute to make a stand-up rim. Cut slits near center to let steam escape.)

6. Combine egg with 1 tablespoon water in a cup; mix with a fork until well blended; brush mixture over strips and rim; sprinkle with sesame seeds.

7. Bake in hot oven (400°) 30 minutes, or until chicken mixture is bubbly-hot, and crust is golden. Serve immediately.

DEEP-DISH CHICKEN PIE

Not for dieters but guaranteed to fill up a famished family.

Bake at 425° for 30 minutes.
Makes 6 servings.

6 medium-size potatoes, pared, quartered
6 medium-size carrots, scraped and quartered
1 small onion, chopped (¼ cup)
¼ cup chopped green pepper
2 tablespoons butter or margarine
1 can condensed cream of chicken soup
3 cups chunks of cooked chicken (boiled, roasted or broiled)
Biscuit Wedge Topping

1. Cook potatoes and carrots in boiling salted water in large saucepan 15 to 20 minutes, or until tender; drain, saving 1 cup of liquid for next step.

2. While vegetables cook, sauté onion and green pepper in butter or margarine until soft in saucepan; stir in chicken soup and 1 cup saved liquid.

3. Spoon vegetables and chicken into 8-cup casserole; pour sauce over.

4. Bake in hot oven (425°) 15 minutes while making Biscuit Wedge Topping; arrange biscuits on top of hot mixture; bake 15 minutes longer, or until biscuits are golden.

BISCUIT WEDGE TOPPING: Sift 1½ cups sifted flour, 2 teaspoons baking powder and ½ teaspoon salt into medium-size bowl; cut in ¼ cup (½ stick) butter or margarine; add ½ cup milk all at once; stir just until blended. Turn dough out onto lightly floured pastry cloth or board; knead lightly ½ minute; roll out to a 7-inch round; cut into 6 wedges; brush tops lightly with milk; sprinkle with ¼ teaspoon poppy seeds.

JUMBO CHICKEN POPOVER

This turns out to be an oversize puffy popover containing browned chicken parts.

Bake at 350° for 1 hour.
Makes 4 servings.

1 broiler-fryer (about 3 pounds)
4 tablespoons plus 1½ cups flour
2 teaspoons salt
1 teaspoon paprika
¼ teaspoon pepper
Fat for frying
1½ teaspoons baking powder
4 eggs
1½ cups milk
3 tablespoons melted butter or margarine
Cream Gravy

1. Cut chicken into 8 pieces—2 breasts, 2 wings, 2 thighs, 2 drumsticks. Cut away back and any small bones from breasts; simmer bones with neck and giblets in 1 cup water in small saucepan. Strain to make broth for Cream Gravy (for recipe, turn to chapter on GRAVIES).

2. Shake chicken pieces with 4 tablespoons flour, 1 teaspoon salt, paprika and pepper in paper bag to coat lightly.

3. Brown, a few at a time, in hot fat in heavy frying pan; drain on paper towel.

4. Sift 1½ cups flour, baking powder and 1 teaspoon salt into medium-size bowl.

5. Beat eggs slightly in second medium-size bowl; blend in milk and melted butter or margarine. Stir into dry ingredients; beat with rotary beater until smooth.

6. Pour batter into buttered shallow 8-cup baking dish; arrange chicken in batter.

7. Bake in moderate oven (350°) 1 hour, or until golden. (Keep oven door closed for full hour.) Serve with Cream Gravy.

They come from Europe, South America, Asia and Africa, yet they're completely at home here. They're chicken recipes that blend cooking secrets from many old worlds with ingredients found in your local supermarket. And while the names may sound foreign, the preparation is no more difficult than for other, more familiar American recipes. Some, in fact, have become as much a part of our cuisine as fried chicken and chicken pot-pie. So the next time you feel like getting away from it all, serve one of these dishes. They're your passport to international flavor–and there's no packing or unpacking involved.

Special Imports

TAGINE

In Morocco, ginger, paprika and olives are favorite seasoners for the ever-popular chicken.

Makes 6 servings.

 2 broiler-fryers (about 2 pounds each), cut up
4 tablespoons (½ stick) butter or margarine
4 medium-size onions, chopped (2 cups)
3 teaspoons salt
1½ teaspoons ground ginger
1 teaspoon paprika
¼ teaspoon pepper
Water
1 jar (7 ounces) stuffed green olives, drained
    and sliced
2 tablespoons flour
Bulgar
¼ cup chopped parsley
6 thin lemon wedges

1. Wash the chicken pieces; pat dry. Brown, a few pieces at a time, in butter or margarine in a heavy kettle or Dutch oven; remove all from kettle.
2. Stir onions into drippings in kettle; sauté until soft. Stir in salt, ginger, paprika, pepper and 1 cup water. Return chicken; cover.
3. Simmer, basting several times with liquid in kettle, 45 minutes, or until chicken is tender.
4. While chicken simmers, combine sliced olives with water to cover in a small saucepan; heat to boiling; drain. Keep hot for Step 7.
5. Remove chicken from the kettle; keep hot. Pour liquid into a 2-cup measure; let stand about 1 minute, or until fat rises to top, then skim off. Add water to liquid, if needed, to make 1½ cups; return to kettle; heat to boiling.
6. Blend flour and ¼ cup water until smooth in a cup; stir into boiling liquid. Cook, stirring constantly, until gravy thickens and boils 1 minute.
7. When ready to serve, combine olives with Bulgar; spoon onto a heated serving platter; arrange chicken on top; sprinkle with chopped parsley. Arrange lemon wedges, petal fashion, in center. Pass gravy separately.

BULGAR (Cracked Wheat)

Makes 6 servings.

3½ cups water
½ cup (1 stick) butter or margarine
3 teaspoons salt
1 package (1 pound) bulgar wheat
2 medium-size eggplants
1 large onion, chopped (1 cup)
¼ cup vegetable oil

1. Heat water with butter or margarine and 2 teaspoons of the salt to boiling in a large heavy saucepan; slowly stir in wheat. Cook, stirring several times, 5 minutes, or until liquid is almost absorbed; cover.
2. Continue cooking very slowly, stirring several times with a fork, 45 minutes, or until wheat is very light and fluffy.
3. While wheat cooks, slice eggplants 1 inch thick; pare and cut into 1-inch cubes.
4. In a large frying pan sauté onion in vegetable oil until soft; stir in eggplant and remaining 1 teaspoon salt; cover. Cook slowly, stirring often, 30 minutes.
5. Add cooked wheat; toss lightly with two forks to mix well and to fluff up the wheat.

GLAZED BUTTERFLY CHICKEN

Breasts, fragrant with a fruit-curry glaze.

Bake at 350° for 1½ hours.
Makes 8 servings.

Curry-Fruit Glaze (from page 108)
8 whole chicken breasts (12 ounces each)
6 tablespoons (¾ stick) butter or margarine
1 teaspoon ground ginger
½ cup flaked coconut

1. Make Curry-Fruit Glaze and set aside.
2. Cut away rib bones from chicken breasts, leaving the V-shape bone at neck.
3. Melt butter or margarine in a large shallow baking pan; stir in ginger. Roll chicken in mixture to coat well. then arrange, skin side up, in a single layer in pan. Tuck edges of each breast under to give a rounded shape. Spoon glaze over.
4. Bake, uncovered, in moderate oven (350°), basting often with glaze mixture in pan, 1 hour and 20 minutes, or until richly glazed.
5. Top with coconut; bake 10 minutes more.

CHICKEN PAPRIKA WITH PARSLEY DUMPLINGS

Sour cream gravy and dumplings make chicken extra special and extra hearty.

Makes 8 servings.

2 broiler-fryers (about 2½ pounds each), cut up
⅓ cup flour
2 teaspoons salt
¼ teaspoon pepper
2 tablespoons butter or margarine
1 tablespoon vegetable oil
1 large onion, chopped (1 cup)
2 envelopes instant chicken broth OR 2 teaspoons granulated chicken bouillon
1 tablespoon paprika
2 cups water
1 cup (8-ounce carton) dairy sour cream
¼ cup cream for whipping
Parsley Dumplings

1. Shake chicken in a mixture of flour, salt and pepper in a plastic bag to coat well. (Save any remaining seasoned flour mixture for gravy.)
2. Brown chicken, part at a time, in butter or margarine and vegetable oil in a kettle or Dutch oven; remove all from kettle. Pour off drippings, then measure 1 tablespoonful and return to kettle.
3. Stir in onion; sauté until soft. Stir in chicken broth or bouillon, paprika and water. Heat, scraping brown bits from bottom, to boiling; return chicken; cover. Simmer 30 minutes, or until chicken is tender. Remove from broth to a shallow pan; reheat broth to boiling.
4. Measure saved seasoned flour, adding more flour, if needed, to make 2 tablespoons. Blend with a small amount of water to a paste in a cup; stir into broth. Cook, stirring constantly, until gravy thickens and boils 1 minute.
5. Blend sour cream and cream in a small bowl; stir into kettle; return chicken. Reheat slowly to boiling while mixing Parsley Dumplings.
6. Drop dough in 8 mounds on top of chicken; cover tightly. Cook 20 minutes. (Do not lift lid of kettle while the dumplings cook.) Serve from kettle.

PARSLEY DUMPLINGS: Sift 1½ cups sifted regular flour, 2 teaspoons baking powder and ¾ teaspoon salt into a medium-size bowl; stir in 3 tablespoons chopped parsley. Combine ¾ cup milk and 2 tablespoons melted butter or margarine in a cup; stir into flour mixture just until moist. (Dough will be soft.)

CHICKEN PAPRIKASH

The esteemed concoction of paprika-flavored chicken in sour cream with noodles is one of Hungary's great contributions to the world of food.

Makes 8 servings.

2 broiler-fryers (about 3 pounds each)
1 large onion, chopped (1 cup)
2 tablespoons butter or margarine
2 tablespoons paprika
1 tablespoon flour
3 teaspoons salt
¼ teaspoon pepper
1 can (8 ounces) tomatoes
1 package (1 pound) noodles
1 cup (8-ounce carton) dairy sour cream
1 tablespoon chopped parsley

1. Cut the chickens into serving-size pieces.
2. Sauté onion in butter or margarine until soft in a large skillet with a cover. Stir in paprika and flour; cook, stirring constantly, 1 minute. Stir in salt, pepper and tomatoes (breaking with spoon).
3. Add chicken and giblets (except livers), turning to coat pieces well; cover. Simmer 30 minutes. Turn chicken pieces; add livers; simmer 15 minutes longer, or until chicken is tender.
4. Meanwhile, cook noodles, following label directions; drain; spoon onto hot serving platter. Remove chicken from skillet with a slotted spoon. Arrange on platter with noodles; keep warm.
5. Spoon sour cream into a medium-size bowl. Heat sauce in skillet to boiling; stir slowly into sour cream, blending well. Spoon over chicken. Garnish with chopped parsley.

POLYNESIAN HILO PLATTER

Many flavors join harmoniously in the stuffing and glaze of this exotic roast chicken.

Bake at 350° for 2 hours.
Makes 6 to 8 servings.

2 roasting chickens (about 4 pounds each)
4 cups Hilo Stuffing
3 tablespoons butter or margarine, melted
1½ cups Curry-Fruit Glaze

1. Rinse chickens inside and out with cold water; drain, then pat dry. Stuff neck and body cavities lightly with Hilo Stuffing. Smooth neck skin over stuffing and skewer to back; tie legs to tail with strings.
2. Place chickens on a rack in roasting pan; brush with melted butter or margarine.
3. Roast in moderate oven (350°) for 1 hour.
4. Spoon part of the Curry-Fruit Glaze over each chicken to make a thick coating. Continue roasting, basting 2 or 3 times with remaining glaze, 1 hour, or until drumsticks move easily and chickens are glazed.
5. Remove to a heated serving platter; cut away strings and remove skewers.

HILO STUFFING

Makes 4 cups, or enough to stuff two 4-pound chickens.

1 cup uncooked white rice
4 tablespoons (½ stick) butter or margarine
1 medium-size onion, chopped (½ cup)
2 envelopes instant chicken broth OR
　2 chicken bouillon cubes
2½ cups water
½ cup chopped macadamia nuts (from a
　6-ounce jar)
½ cup flaked coconut

1. In a large saucepan, sauté rice in butter or margarine, stirring often, just until it is golden.
2. Stir in onion, chicken broth or bouillon cubes and water; heat to boiling, crushing cubes, if using, with a spoon; cover. Simmer 20 minutes, or until rice is tender and liquid is absorbed.
3. Sprinkle with nuts and coconut; toss lightly to mix.

CURRY-FRUIT GLAZE

Makes 1½ cups, or enough to glaze two 4-pound chickens.

4 slices bacon, diced
1 medium-size onion, chopped (½ cup)
2 tablespoons flour
1 tablespoon sugar
2 teaspoons curry powder
½ teaspoon salt
1 tablespoon bottled steak sauce
1 cup water
2 tablespoons lemon juice
1 jar (4 ounces) baby-pack strained apples-
　and-apricots

1. Sauté bacon until almost crisp in a medium-size saucepan; remove and drain on paper toweling.
2. Stir onions into drippings in saucepan; sauté until just soft. Stir in flour, sugar, curry powder and salt; heat until bubbly.
3. Stir in remaining ingredients and bacon. Simmer, stirring several times, 15 minutes, or until thick.

CHICKEN CACCIATORE

Men especially like this zesty Italian dish. It's also a good choice for guests, because it waits well.

Makes 8 servings.

2 broiler-fryers (about 3 pounds each),
　quartered
¾ cup flour
3 teaspoons salt
¼ teaspoon pepper
6 tablespoons olive oil or salad oil
2 medium-size onions, chopped (1 cup)
1 clove garlic, minced
1 can (about 2 pounds) Italian tomatoes
1 tablespoon sugar
1 teaspoon basil
½ teaspoon thyme
2 medium-size green peppers, halved, seeded
　and sliced

1. Wash the chicken quarters; pat dry. Shake with flour, salt and pepper in a paper bag to coat well.
2. Brown pieces, a few at a time, in olive oil or salad oil in a large frying pan; remove all from pan.

3. Stir onion and garlic into drippings in pan and sauté until soft; stir in tomatoes, sugar, basil and thyme; heat to boiling.
4. Return chicken to pan; spoon some of the tomato sauce over; lay sliced green peppers on top; cover.
5. Simmer, basting several times with sauce in pan, 1½ hours, or until chicken is tender.

RISOTTO ALLA MILANESE

This is a continental specialty that can be ready for the table in less than 1 hour.

Makes 6 servings.

4 slices bacon, diced
1 pound chicken livers, halved
¼ cup all-purpose flour
1 teaspoon salt
¼ teaspoon pepper
1 large onion, chopped (1 cup)
1 cup uncooked regular rice
2 envelopes or teaspoons instant chicken broth
1 teaspoon leaf basil, crumbled
1 bay leaf
2½ cups water
Chopped parsley

1. Cook bacon until crisp in a large skillet. Remove bacon with a slotted spoon and reserve.
2. Shake chicken livers in a plastic bag with flour, salt and pepper.
3. Brown chicken livers in bacon drippings. Remove with slotted spoon and reserve.
4. Sauté onion in same skillet until soft. (If there is no fat remaining in the skillet, add 2 tablespoons vegetable oil.) Stir in rice, chicken broth, basil, bay leaf and water.
5. Heat to boiling. Lower heat; stir rice mixture well; cover.
6. Simmer 10 minutes. Spoon the browned chicken livers over rice. Return cover and simmer 20 minutes longer, or until liquid is absorbed and rice is tender; remove bay leaf. Sprinkle with reserved bacon and chopped parsley.

TWIN CHICKENS PARISIENNE

Stuffed with parsley, simmered in mushroom sauce, the birds are then bathed in gravy and presented on a bed of noodles.

Makes 6 to 8 servings.

2 whole broiler-fryers (about 3 pounds each)
1 teaspoon salt
½ teaspoon sugar
2 bunches parsley, washed and trimmed
2 tablespoons butter or margarine
1 can (3 or 4 ounces) whole mushrooms
¼ teaspoon pepper
2 tablespoons flour
¾ cup cream
Hot cooked noodles

1. Rinse chickens inside and out with cold water; drain, then pat dry. Sprinkle insides with ½ teaspoon of the salt and sugar; place parsley in body cavities, packing in lightly. Skewer neck skin to back; twist wing tips flat against skewered neck skin; tie the legs to tails with string.
2. Brown in butter or margarine in a heavy kettle or Dutch oven; turn breast side up.
3. Drain liquid from mushrooms into a 1-cup measure; add water to make ¾ cup; pour over chickens. Sprinkle with remaining ½ teaspoon salt and pepper; cover tightly. (Set mushrooms aside for Step 6.)
4. Simmer, basting several times with liquid in kettle, 1 hour and 15 minutes, or until tender. Remove from kettle and keep hot while making gravy.
5. Pour liquid from kettle into a 2-cup measure; let stand about a minute, or until fat rises to top, then skim off into a cup. Add water to liquid, if needed, to make 1 cup.
6. Measure 2 tablespoons of the fat and return to kettle; blend in flour; stir in the 1 cup liquid. Cook, stirring constantly, until gravy thickens and boils 1 minute. Stir in mushrooms and cream; heat slowly just to boiling. Darken with a few drops bottled gravy coloring, if you wish.
7. Spoon noodles into a heated large serving bowl. Take out skewers and cut string from chickens; arrange chickens on top of noodles; spoon gravy over all. Garnish with parsley, if you wish. Carve chickens into serving-size pieces.

MEXICALI CHICKEN

Chicken and peppers are steeped in a tangy tomato sauce—cook this in your gayest casserole.

Bake at 350° for 1½ hours.
Makes 8 servings.

2 broiler-fryers (about 3 pounds each), cut up
2 tablespoon butter or margarine
2 tablespoons olive oil or vegetable oil
1 large onion, chopped (1 cup)
1 large sweet green pepper, quartered, seeded
    and chopped
1 large sweet red pepper, quartered, seeded
    and chopped
3 teaspoons chili powder
¼ cup flour
1 can (about 2 pounds) Italian tomatoes
3 teaspoons salt
1 teaspoon sugar
¼ teaspoon pepper

1. Wash chicken pieces and dry. Brown, part at a time, in butter or margarine and olive oil or vegetable oil in a large frying pan; remove all from pan and set aside while making the sauce.
2. Stir onion and green and red peppers into drippings in pan; sauté until soft. Stir in chili powder; cook 1 minute longer.
3. Sprinkle flour over top, then blend in; stir in tomatoes, salt, sugar and pepper. Cook, stirring constantly, until sauce thickens and boils 1 minute.
4. Layer browned chicken, topping each with part of the sauce, into a 12-cup baking dish; cover.
5. Bake in moderate oven (350°) 1 hour; uncover. Bake 30 minutes longer, or until chicken is tender and sauce is thickened slightly. Garnish with rings of red and green pepper, if you wish.

ARROZ CON POLLO

Chicken with rice, Spanish style, includes tomatoes, onion, mushrooms, pimientos—and a nip of garlic.

Bake at 350° for 1 hour and 10 minutes.
Makes 4 servings.

1 broiler-fryer (about 3 pounds), cut up
¼ cup salad or olive oil
1 cup raw rice
1 large onion, chopped (1 cup)
2 cloves garlic, minced
1 strand saffron, crushed
2 cans (about 1 pound each) tomatoes
1 can (3 or 4 ounces) chopped mushrooms
1 can (about 4 ounces) pimientos, diced
2 tablespoons chopped parsley
1½ teaspoons salt
⅛ teaspoon pepper

1. Brown chicken on all sides in hot oil in large heavy frying pan; drain on absorbent paper; place in 3-quart baking dish; save for Step 4.
2. Sauté rice in same frying pan, stirring often, about 5 minutes, or until golden-brown; add onion and garlic; sauté over low heat 10 minutes, or just until tender.
3. Stir in saffron, tomatoes, mushrooms, diced pimientos, parsley, salt and pepper; heat to boiling, stirring often.
4. Pour hot tomato mixture over chicken in casserole; cover.
5. Bake in moderate oven (350°) 30 minutes; uncover; bake 40 minutes longer, or until chicken is tender and liquid is absorbed.

CHICKEN SAUTE NORMANDY STYLE

Chicken simmered in apple cider and served with a delicious cream and egg sauce.

Makes 6 servings.

2 broiler-fryers (about 1½ pounds each)
1 tablespoon vegetable oil
2 tablespoons butter or margarine
2 tablespoons applejack
1 medium-size onion, finely chopped (½ cup)
½ cup sliced celery
2 tablespoons chopped parsley
1 teaspoon salt
¾ teaspoon leaf thyme, crumbled
⅛ teaspoon pepper
1 cup apple cider
2 egg yolks
1 cup light cream

1. Cut chickens into serving-size pieces. Brown well in oil and butter or margarine in a large kettle; remove from heat.

2. Warm the applejack in a small saucepan until small bubbles appear around edge. (Do not boil.) Carefully ignite with a wooden match held at arm's length. Quickly pour over chicken, shaking gently until flames die. Remove chicken to a heated platter; keep warm.

3. Sauté onion and celery until soft in same kettle. Stir in parsley, salt, thyme, pepper and cider; heat to boiling. Return chicken pieces; reduce heat; cover. Simmer 45 minutes, or until chicken is tender; remove from heat. Remove chicken pieces from cooking liquid to a heated serving platter; keep hot.

4. Beat egg yolks slightly in a small bowl; blend in light cream. Gradually add cooking liquid, beating vigorously; pour back into saucepan. Cook, over medium heat, stirring constantly, 1 minute, or until sauce thickens slightly. Pour a little of the sauce over chicken pieces. Pass remaining sauce separately.

CHICKEN TEMPURA

This delicately cooked Japanese-style chicken has a golden-rich batter coating.

Makes 8 servings.

2 broiler-fryers (2 to 3 pounds each)
2 cups water
2 teaspoons salt
1 teaspoon poultry seasoning
¼ teaspoon pepper
2 eggs
½ cup milk
1 cup sifted flour
Fat for frying

1. Cut each chicken into 8 pieces (2 breasts, 2 wings, 2 thighs, 2 drumsticks); cook 15 minutes in 2 cups water seasoned with 1 teaspoon salt, poultry seasoning and pepper. (Save broth to simmer backs, necks and giblets to make soup for another meal.)

2. Drain chicken on paper towels; remove all skin and cut out any small rib bones; dry thoroughly.

3. Beat eggs slightly with milk in bowl; beat in flour and 1 teaspoon salt until smooth.

4. Melt enough fat (about 3 pounds) to make a 2-inch depth in large heavy saucepan; heat to 375°. or use an electric fryer, following manufacturer's directions.

5. Dip chicken, one piece at a time, into batter (tongs are a useful tool); let any excess batter drip back into bowl; fry 2 or 3 pieces at a time, turning once, about 4 minutes, or until golden; drain on paper towels; keep hot in warm oven while frying remaining chicken.

CHICKEN KIEV

These great Russian-style chicken breasts take fussing, so fix them ahead for a special dinner.

Makes 6 servings.

1½ sticks (6 ounces) butter or margarine
6 whole chicken breasts (about 12 ounces each)
4 tablespoons finely chopped parsley
½ teaspoon sugar
2 eggs
1 cup fine dry bread crumbs
1 teaspoon salt
⅛ teaspoon pepper
Shortening or salad oil for frying

1. Cut the butter or margarine into 12 even-length sticks; chill in freezer while fixing chicken, for butter should be very cold.

2. Pull skin from the chicken breasts; halve breasts and cut meat in one piece from bones. Place each half, boned side up, between waxed paper and pound very thin with a mallet or rolling pin to form a "cutlet." (Do not pound holes in meat.)

3. Place 1 piece very cold butter or margarine, 1 teaspoon parsley and a dash of the sugar on end of each cutlet; fold sides over to seal in butter, then roll up. Hold in place with wooden picks.

4. Beat eggs slightly in a pie plate; mix bread crumbs, salt and pepper in a second pie plate. Dip stuffed rolls in egg, then in crumb mixture to coat well. Chill at least an hour. (This much can be done ahead.)

5. When ready to fry, melt enough shortening or pour in enough salad oil to make a 2-inch depth in an electric deep-fat fryer or large saucepan; heat to 350°.

6. Fry rolls, 3 or 4 at a time and turning often, 7 minutes, or until tender and crisply golden. Lift out with a slotted spoon; drain well. Keep hot until all rolls are cooked.

CHINESE CHICKEN SALAD

Chinese fried noodles and soy dressing give the touch of authenticity to this Oriental-style salad.

Makes 6 servings.

1 whole broiler-fryer (about 3 pounds)
2 cups water
Handful of celery tops
1 teaspoon salt
6 peppercorns
1½ cups Soy Dressing
1 bunch fresh broccoli (about 2 pounds)
6 cups broken salad greens
1 cup chopped celery
2 green onions, sliced
5 large radishes, sliced
1 can (3 ounces) Chinese fried noodles
1 hard-cooked egg, shelled

1. Simmer chicken with water, celery tops, salt and peppercorns in kettle 1 hour, or until tender. Take chicken from broth and let drain in shallow pan just until cool enough to handle. (Strain broth and save for soup.)
2. Remove skin from chicken, then pull meat from frame in large pieces. (It comes off easily while still warm.) Cut into bite-size pieces; place in shallow pan; pour ¼ cup Soy Dressing over. Cover; chill at least an hour to blend flavors.
3. Trim and discard outer leaves from broccoli. Cut off ends to make about 4-inch-long stalks; split large ones lengthwise. Cook, covered, in about 1-inch depth boiling salted water in large frying pan 15 minutes, or until crisply tender; drain well.
4. Place in shallow pan; pour ½ cup Soy Dressing over. Cover; chill at least an hour.
5. When ready to serve, pile salad greens, celery, green onions and radishes, saving about 8 slices for Step 7, into large shallow salad bowl. Pour remaining ¾ cup Soy Dressing over; toss lightly to mix.
6. Arrange marinated broccoli with stems toward center in a ring on top; fill ring with marinated chicken. Spoon noodles around broccoli.
7. Press white of egg, then yolk through a sieve onto separate sheets of waxed paper. Spoon white on top of chicken; top with saved radish slices, overlapping slightly; garnish with sieved egg yolk.

SOY DRESSING: Combine ½ cup soy sauce, ½ cup salad oil or peanut oil and ½ cup wine vinegar or cider vinegar with 1 teaspoon salt and ½ teaspoon ground ginger in small jar with tight-fitting cover; shake to mix well. Makes 1½ cups.

CLASSIC CHICKEN ALMOND

An Oriental favorite of white meat, delicate vegetables and toasted nuts. You can start it the day before, finish it up quickly at suppertime.

Makes 6 servings.

3 whole chicken breasts (about 12 ounces each), halved
1 large onion, peeled and sliced
1½ teaspoons salt
⅛ teaspoon pepper
Water
2 tablespoons vegetable oil
1½ cups chopped celery
1 package (10 ounces) frozen peas
1 can (3 or 4 ounces) sliced mushrooms
2 tablespoons cornstarch
½ teaspoon ground ginger
2 tablespoons soy sauce
Toasted slivered almonds (from a 5-ounce can)

1. Combine chicken breasts, 2 slices of the onion, salt, pepper and 1 cup water in a large saucepan; cover. Simmer 20 minutes, or until chicken is tender.
2. Remove from broth and cool until easy to handle; strain broth into a small bowl. Pull skin from chicken and take meat from bones in one piece; chill, then cut into thin strips. Chill broth separately, then skim fat, if needed.
3. When ready to finish cooking, sauté remaining onion in vegetable oil in a large frying pan 2 to 3 minutes; push to side. Stir in celery and sauté 2 to 3 minutes; push to side. Place peas, mushrooms and liquid and chicken strips in separate piles in pan; pour in broth; cover. Steam 10 minutes, or until peas are crisply tender.
4. Lift vegetables from pan with a slotted spoon; place in a serving bowl; lift out chicken strips and arrange on top of the vegetables.

5. Blend cornstarch and ginger with soy sauce in a cup; stir in 2 tablespoons water until smooth. Stir into liquid in pan; cook, stirring constantly, until sauce thickens and boils 3 minutes.
6. Spoon over chicken and vegetables; sprinkle with almonds. Garnish with thin strips of pimiento and drained canned mushroom caps and celery slices threaded onto kebab sticks, and serve with hot cooked rice or noodles, if you wish.

MAKE-AHEAD NOTE: Chicken may be cooked as much as a day ahead and chilled in its broth to keep moist. Chop celery ahead too, and place in a transparent bag in the refrigerator until ready to cook.

MANDARIN SUPPER

Cubed chicken, Chinese-style fried rice and soy-seasoned broccoli make this meal-in-a-skillet.

Makes 6 servings.

2 chicken breasts (about 12 ounces each)
1 tablespoon packaged shrimp spice
1 tablespoon instant minced onion
1 teaspoon salt
2 cups water
1 cup uncooked rice
1 bunch fresh broccoli (about 1½ pounds)
2 large onions, chopped (2 cups)
6 tablespoons peanut oil or vegetable oil
4 tablespoons soy sauce
2 tablespoons wine vinegar or cider vinegar
¼ teaspoon ground ginger
¼ cup coarsely chopped salted peanuts

1. Combine chicken breasts, shrimp spice, instant onion, salt and water in a large saucepan; cover. Simmer 30 minutes, or until chicken is tender. Remove from broth and cool until easy to handle. Strain broth into a 4-cup measure; add water if needed to make 2¼ cups. Pull skin from chicken and take meat from bones; cut in cubes.
2. Combine the 2¼ cups chicken broth and rice in a medium-size saucepan. Cook 25 minutes, or until rice is tender and liquid is absorbed.
3. While rice cooks, trim broccoli; split any large stalks lengthwise, then cut into 2-inch lengths. Cook in boiling salted water in a saucepan 15 minutes; drain; keep warm.

4. Sauté chopped onions in 4 tablespoons of the peanut oil or vegetable oil until soft in a large frying pan; stir in cooked rice. Sauté, stirring constantly, 5 minutes; add chicken; toss lightly to mix. Arrange cooked broccoli around edge in pan.
5. Combine remaining 2 tablespoons peanut oil or vegetable oil, soy sauce, wine vinegar or cider vinegar and ginger in a cup; drizzle over broccoli. Sprinkle peanuts over rice. Serve warm right from the skillet it cooked in.

HONG KONG CHICKEN ALMOND

A simple version of the traditional Oriental dish.

Makes 4 servings.

2 whole chicken breasts (about 12 ounces each)
3 tablespoons salad oil
1 cup sliced celery
½ clove garlic, minced
2 envelopes instant chicken broth OR 2 chicken bouillon cubes
1½ cups water
1 tablespoon soy sauce
1 tablespoon chopped crystallized ginger
1 package (8 ounces) frozen Chinese pea pods
2 tablespoons cornstarch
¼ cup toasted slivered almonds (from a 5-ounce can)
3 cups hot cooked rice

1. Pull skin from chicken breasts; halve the breasts and cut meat in one piece from bones, then slice meat into long thin strips.
2. Heat salad oil in a large frying pan; add chicken and sauté, stirring constantly, 5 minutes. Stir in celery and garlic; sauté 3 minutes more, or until meat is almost tender.
3. Stir in chicken broth or bouillon cubes, water, soy sauce and ginger; heat to boiling, crushing cubes, if using, with a spoon; add pea pods; cover. Simmer 5 minutes.
4. Smooth cornstarch with a little water to a paste in a cup; stir into chicken mixture. Cook, stirring constantly, until mixture thickens and boils 3 minutes.
5. Spoon into a serving dish; sprinkle with almonds. Serve with rice.

Chicken is one of the most portable of foods. Hot or cold, it's the ideal choice for both indoor and outdoor eating. Previous chapters have offered chicken dishes that adapt well to being transported. The recipes in this chapter, however, are especially designed for carrying anywhere you choose.

We've divided the chapter into 3 sections that cover just about every outdoor occasion. The first, Patio Dinners, is a series of recipes you'll want to try on your barbecue or outdoor grill. (They can also be prepared indoors and then taken out.) This section is followed by Salads, and here there's no limit to the possibilities. Chicken salad is a welcome partner for bridge luncheons, warm summer night suppers or for winter dinners.

Last, but not least, Chicken Sandwiches.

Need we say more?

Indoor-Outdoor Chicken

Patio Dinners

CHICKEN ROMA

Boned breast meat is filled with salami stuffing and grilled ever so slowly.

Makes 6 servings.

6 chicken breasts, weighing about 12 ounces each
2 tablespoons finely chopped green onion
½ cup (1 stick) butter or margarine
1½ cups fresh bread crumbs
¼ pound soft salami, finely chopped

1. Bone chicken breasts, leaving skin in place. Place flat, skin side down, on a cutting board.
2. Sauté onion in 3 tablespoons of the butter or margarine until soft in a small frying pan; stir in crumbs and salami until moist.
3. Divide stuffing into 6 parts; spoon along hollows in chicken breasts. Fold edges of chicken over stuffing to cover completely; fasten with wooden picks.
4. Melt remaining butter or margarine in a small saucepan on grill; brush part over chicken. Place breasts on grill, buttered side down, about 6 inches above hot coals. Grill 20 minutes. Brush again with melted butter or margarine; turn. Grill 20 minutes longer, or until chicken is tender and golden. Place on a large serving platter; remove picks. Garnish with carrot curls and sprigs of chicory, if you wish.

NOTE: If traveling a distance to your eating spot, make stuffing and chill well, then stuff into chicken breasts and keep chilled until cooking time.

CHICKEN ON A SPIT

Currant jelly glazes this chicken as it twirls on the rotisserie.

Makes 4 to 6 servings.

2 cups ready-mix bread stuffing
½ cup (1 stick) butter or margarine, melted
⅔ cup water
1 roasting chicken (about 4 pounds)
½ cup currant jelly, melted

1. Prepare stuffing mix with ⅓ cup of the melted butter or margarine and water, following label directions on package.
2. Wash chicken, then dry. Stuff neck and body cavities lightly; skewer neck skin to body; secure body cavity closed and tie legs tightly to tail.
3. Place chicken on spit; brush with remaining butter or margarine. Set spit in position over hot coals; start spit turning.
4. Roast 1 hour; brush with melted jelly. Continue roasting, brushing often with more jelly, 15 minutes longer, or until chicken is tender and richly glazed.

GRILLED CHICKEN BREASTS SUPREME

This exotic chicken from the Far East is especially good with Tibetan rice and a tangy fruit sauce.

Makes 4 servings.

4 whole chicken breasts
½ cup flour
1 teaspoon salt
⅛ teaspoon pepper
⅛ teaspoon nutmeg
1 egg
1 tablespoon water
1 cup finely ground cashew nuts (½ pound)
4 green onions, chopped
2 tablespoons chopped parsley
4 tablespoons (½ stick) butter or margarine, melted
Tibetan Rice
3 cups Piquant Fruit Sauce

1. Wash and dry chicken; cut out any small rib bones and breastbones so breasts will lie flat, butterfly style. Shake in mixture of flour, salt, pepper and nutmeg in paper bag to coat well.
2. Beat egg with water in pie plate; place ground cashew nuts in second pie plate. Dip chicken in egg mixture, then in nuts.
3. Place each breast, skin side up, on a 12-inch square of heavy foil. Sprinkle with green onions and parsley; drizzle melted butter or margarine over.
4. Wrap foil around chicken and seal tightly with a drugstore fold; place on grill above hot coals. Grill, turning often, 1 hour, or until chicken is tender.

5. Split foil envelopes open; place each breast on a bed of Tibetan Rice; serve with Piquant Fruit Sauce.

TIBETAN RICE

Makes 4 servings.

¼ cup raw rice
2 tablespoons salad oil
½ teaspoon turmeric
½ teaspoon curry powder
½ teaspoon salt
¼ cup seedless raisins
Water
1 can condensed chicken broth
   OR 2 chicken bouillon cubes

1. Stir rice into salad oil in top of medium-size double boiler; heat over direct heat, stirring constantly, until rice is well coated with the oil.
2. Blend in turmeric, curry powder and salt; stir in raisins. Add enough water to the broth to make 1½ cups (or use bouillon cubes dissolved in 1½ cups boiling water); stir into rice mixture.
3. Cover; cook over simmering water 1 hour, or until rice is fluffed and tender and liquid is absorbed.

PIQUANT FRUIT SAUCE

Makes about 3 cups.

2 tablespoons brown sugar
1 teaspoon cornstarch
1 teaspoon salt
1 can (1 pound, 4 ounces) pineapple chunks
½ cup orange juice
1 tablespoon lemon juice
¼ cup water
1 can (about 11 ounces) mandarin orange sections, drained

1. Blend brown sugar, cornstarch and salt in medium-size saucepan; stir in pineapple and syrup, orange and lemon juices, and water.
2. Cook, stirring constantly, until sauce thickens slightly and boils 3 minutes. Stir in mandarin orange sections; heat just to boiling.

ROSEMARY CHICKEN

Serve this flavory chicken on the patio for a summer supper.

Bake at 400° for 1 hour.
Makes 4 servings.

2 broiler-fryers (2 pounds each), cut up
1 large onion, cut into thick slices
⅔ cup catsup
⅓ cup vinegar
4 tablespoons (½ stick) butter or margarine
1 clove garlic, minced
1 teaspoon rosemary, crushed
1 teaspoon salt
¼ teaspoon dry mustard

1. Place chicken, skin side down, in a single layer in a buttered shallow baking pan; top with onion slices.
2. Mix all remaining ingredients in a small saucepan; heat just to boiling; pour over chicken.
3. Bake in hot oven (400°) 30 minutes. Turn chicken, skin side up; baste with sauce in pan. Continue baking, basting once or twice, 30 minutes longer, or until tender and richly glazed.

SIMPLE SIMON

Chicken baked in a cheese-cracker coating—delicious hot or cold.

Bake at 375° for 1 hour.
Makes 6 servings.

1 package (about 6 ounces) cheese crackers, crushed fine
2 teaspoons seasoned salt
½ cup salad oil
2 broiler-fryers (about 3 pounds each), cut in serving-size pieces

1. Place cracker crumbs in a pie plate; stir in seasoned salt. Pour salad oil into a second pie plate.
2. Dip chicken pieces into salad oil, then into crushed crumbs to coat well. Place in a single layer in an ungreased large shallow pan.
3. Bake in moderate over (375°) 1 hour, or until tender and golden-brown. Serve warm or cold.

STUFFED WHIRLYBIRD

Rotisserie chicken with two stuffings.

Makes 4 servings.

1 roasting chicken (about 4 pounds)
Fruit Stuffing OR packaged Spanish Rice
   Stuffing
Butter or margarine (1 to 2 tablespoons)
Salt
Pepper
Ginger-Honey Glaze

1. Wash and dry chicken.
2. Stuff breast and body cavities with either Fruit Stuffing (recipe below) or Spanish Rice Stuffing (follow label directions).
3. Secure body and neck cavities tightly closed; tie legs and wings tightly to body. Rub bird with softened butter or margarine and sprinkle with salt and pepper.
4. Place on rotisserie spit and roast 1 hour, then begin basting with Ginger-Honey Glaze. Continue roasting, basting often, 30 to 45 minutes longer, or until chicken is richly browned and tender.

GINGER-HONEY GLAZE: Combine ½ cup soy sauce, 6 tablespoons honey and 2 teaspoons ground ginger in a small saucepan. Heat, stirring constantly, just to boiling. Makes enough for two roasting chickens.

FRUIT STUFFING

Makes 7 cups.

1 can (1 pound) sliced apples
Water
½ cup (1 stick) butter or margarine
1 package (2 cups) ready-mix bread stuffing
1 cup chopped peanuts
½ cup seedless raisins

1. Drain sliced apples; add water to apple liquid to make 1 cup; heat to boiling in large saucepan.
2. Stir in butter or margarine until melted; add ready-mix bread stuffing, sliced apples, peanuts and raisins, tossing lightly to mix.
3. Stuff chicken. Wrap any remaining stuffing in foil; cook on grill about 1 hour, while chicken roasts.

DUNKING CHICKEN

Fine finger food—crackly crisp outside, juicy inside—for picnic or patio meals.

Makes 6 servings.

2 broiler-fryers (about 2 pounds each), cut up
1 cup flour
2 teaspoons salt
½ teaspoon pepper
Bacon drippings
Orange Curry Dunk
Zippy Tomato Dunk

1. Wash and dry chicken pieces well. Shake in mixture of flour, salt and pepper in paper bag to coat well.
2. Heat bacon drippings in large frying pan or electric skillet. It'll take about 1 cup, for fat should be about ½ inch deep. (If you like, use part shortening.)
3. Place chicken in a single layer in hot fat; cover lightly. Cook over *low heat* 20 minutes, or until golden; turn; cover again and cook 20 minutes to brown other side. (If using an electric skillet, follow manufacturer's directions.) Remove browned chicken and set aside while cooking any remaining pieces, adding more drippings, if needed, to keep fat ½ inch deep.
4. Drain fat from frying pan, leaving just enough to keep chicken from sticking; return all chicken to pan. Cover; cook, turning once or twice, over very low heat 30 minutes longer, or until tender.
5. Serve hot or cold, with dunking sauces.

ORANGE CURRY DUNK

Makes 2 cups.

1 cup orange marmalade
⅓ cup vinegar
¼ cup granulated sugar
2 tablespoons brown sugar
1 tablespoon curry powder
1 tablespoon Worcestershire sauce
1 teaspoon salt
½ teaspoon ground ginger

Combine all ingredients in small saucepan; heat to boiling, then simmer, stirring constantly, until marmalade is melted and sauce is blended. Serve warm or cold.

ZIPPY TOMATO DUNK

Makes 1½ cups.

1 can (8 ounces) tomato sauce
½ cup finely chopped green pepper
½ cup finely chopped celery
2 tablespoons vinegar
2 tablespoons light molasses
1 tablespoon Worcestershire sauce
¼ teaspoon bottled red-pepper seasoning

Combine all ingredients in small saucepan; heat to boiling, then simmer, stirring constantly, 5 minutes, or until vegetables are softened and sauce is blended.

HERB SPITTED CHICKEN

Fresh herbs are a feature of this outdoor chicken.

Makes 4 servings.

3 tablespoons minced fresh rosemary
3 tablespoons minced fresh tarragon
OR 2 tablespoons leaf rosemary, crumbled
2 tablespoons leaf tarragon, crumbled
Dry white wine or chicken broth
½ cup (1 stick) butter or margarine
1 teaspoon salt
¼ teaspoon freshly ground pepper
1 roasting chicken (about 3½ to 4 pounds)

1. Combine fresh rosemary and tarragon in a small bowl. If you are using dried herbs, combine with ⅓ cup dry white wine or broth in a small bowl. Let stand 1 hour. Strain; reserve liquid. Add butter or margarine to the herbs; blend well.
2. Sprinkle the cavity of the chicken with part of the salt and pepper and put in about 1 tablespoon herb butter. Carefully loosen the skin over the breast with your fingers and press in about 1 to 2 tablespoons of the herb butter. Truss the bird, balance it on the spit and fasten it securely.
3. Melt the remaining herb butter and brush over bird. Sprinkle it with remaining salt and pepper. Combine the remaining herb butter with an equal quantity of wine or broth, or, if using dried herbs, with reserved wine or broth.
4. Roast the chicken for about 2½ hours, basting it frequently with the butter-wine mixture. Skim off the fat and pour a little juice over each piece of carved chicken.

BONANZA-BOBS

Thread the chunks on skewers with green pepper and onions and you're all set for the outdoor grill.

Makes 8 servings.

4 whole chicken breasts
4 green peppers, cut in pieces
2 cans (1 pound each) onions, well drained
2 teaspoons monosodium glutamate
2 teaspoons salt
½ cup butter or margarine, melted
1 tablespoon dried leaf tarragon
1 tablespoon lemon juice

1. Bone chicken breasts; remove skin. Cut each breast half into 6 to 8 chunks, about 1½ inches square.
2. Alternate chunks on 8 skewers with green pepper and onions. Sprinkle with monosodium glutamate and salt.
3. Combine melted butter, tarragon and lemon juice. Brush over kabobs; grill 3 inches from heat for 5 minutes. Turn and grill 5 minutes longer, brushing occasionally with butter mixture.

NAPOLI CHICKEN BROIL

Grilled chicken breasts brushed with a butter mixture—great indoors or out.

Makes 8 servings.

1 cup (2 sticks) butter or margarine
2 envelopes Italian-flavor salad dressing mix
¼ cup lime juice
8 chicken breasts, weighing about 12 ounces each

1. Melt butter or margarine in a small saucepan; stir in salad dressing mix and lime juice. Brush part over both sides of chicken.
2. Place the chicken, skin side down, on grill about 10 inches above hot coals. Grill, turning and brushing pieces often with more butter mixture, 40 minutes, or until tender and richly glazed.

NOTE TO INDOOR COOKS: Place chicken pieces, skin side up, on rack in broiler pan; brush with butter mixture. Broil, 4 to 6 inches from heat, brushing several times with butter mixture, 15 minutes; turn. Brush again; broil 15 minutes longer.

Salads

CLASSIC CHICKEN SALAD

Big, juicy chunks of chicken you can serve with either of two dressings.

Makes 8 servings.

2 broiler-fryers, whole or cut in serving-size
   pieces
3 cups water
1 onion, sliced
4 celery tops
2 bay leaves
2 teaspoons monosodium glutamate
2 teaspoons salt
2 cups sliced or chopped celery

1. Put chickens in a large kettle or Dutch oven. Add water and all ingredients except the chopped celery; heat to boiling; cover tightly. Reduce heat and simmer 1 hour, or until tender.
2. Remove from heat; strain broth. Refrigerate chicken and broth at once. When chicken is cool, remove meat from bones; cut meat into large chunks.
3. Mix cut-up chicken with chopped celery; add either Creamy Mayonnaise Dressing or Old-Fashioned Cooked Dressing; mix well. Serve on salad greens and garnish with tomato wedges, carrot curls, olives or radish roses, if you wish.

CREAMY MAYONNAISE DRESSING: Blend together ⅔ cup mayonnaise, ⅓ cup dairy sour cream, ½ teaspoon salt, ¼ teaspoon pepper and 1 teaspoon lemon juice. Makes 1 cup dressing.

OLD-FASHIONED COOKED DRESSING:
Mix together in top of double boiler 2 tablespoons flour, 1 teaspoon sugar, 1 teaspoon dry mustard, ½ teaspoon salt and ⅛ teaspoon pepper. Add 1 egg, 2 tablespoons butter or margarine, ¾ cup milk, 2 tablespoons vinegar and 1 tablespoon lemon juice; beat with rotary beater or wire whisk until well mixed. Cook, stirring constantly, over boiling water until slightly thickened, about 8 minutes. Refrigerate. Makes 1¼ cups dressing.

CHICKEN-CORN SALAD

Filling fare with all white meat chicken, hard-cooked eggs, corn nuggets and tender macaroni.

Makes 6 servings.

2 chicken breasts (about 12 ounces each)
2 cups water
1 slice onion
Few celery tops
1¼ teaspoons salt
3 tablespoons cider vinegar
2 teaspoons sugar
¼ teaspoon pepper
½ cup vegetable oil
1 package (8 ounces) small macaroni shells
1 can (12 or 16 ounces) whole-kernel corn,
   well drained
1 cup thinly sliced celery
1 large head Boston lettuce
3 hard-cooked eggs, shelled and coarsely
   chopped
¼ cup mayonnaise or salad dressing
3 tablespoons chopped parsley

1. Combine chicken breasts with water, onion, celery tops and ¼ teaspoon of the salt in a medium-size saucepan; cover. Simmer 30 minutes, or until chicken is tender. Remove from broth and cool until easy to handle. (Save broth to add to soup for another day.)
2. Pull skin from chicken and take meat from bones; cut meat into bite-size pieces.
3. Combine vinegar, sugar, remaining 1 teaspoon salt, pepper and vegetable oil in a jar with a tight fitting lid; shake well to mix. Drizzle 1 tablespoon over chicken; chill.
4. Cook macaroni in boiling salted water, following label directions; drain well. Combine with corn, celery and 1 tablespoon of the dressing in a large bowl; toss to mix well; chill. (Set remaining dressing aside for Step 7.)
5. When ready to serve, line 6 soup plates or shallow salad bowls with lettuce; shred remaining lettuce into pieces in centers. Spoon macaroni mixture on top.
6. Add chopped eggs to chicken mixture; toss lightly to mix; spoon over macaroni.
7. Beat remaining dressing into mayonnaise or salad dressing and parsley in a small bowl; pass separately.

CURRIED CHICKEN CORONET

A partylike rich chicken-salad mousse delicately spiced with curry.

Makes 8 servings.

2 whole chicken breasts (about 2 pounds)
2 cups water
1 medium-size onion, sliced
Handful of celery tops
1½ teaspoons salt
3 peppercorns
1 envelope unflavored gelatin
2 eggs, separated
½ cup chopped toasted almonds
1 teaspoon curry powder
¼ teaspoon pepper
1 cup mayonnaise
1 cup cream for whipping
1 can (about 13 ounces) frozen pineapple
    chunks, thawed and drained
½ cup flaked coconut

1. Combine the chicken breasts, water, onion, celery tops, 1 teaspoon salt and peppercorns in large saucepan; simmer, covered, 45 minutes, or until chicken is tender. Let stand until cool enough to handle, then skin chicken and take meat from bones. Dice chicken fine (you should have about 2 cups diced chicken).
2. Strain stock into a bowl; measure out 1 cupful; pour into a medium-size saucepan and cool. (Save any remaining stock for soup for another day.)
3. Soften gelatin in cooled stock in saucepan; heat, stirring constantly, until dissolved.
4. Beat egg yolks slightly in small bowl; slowly stir in dissolved gelatin. Return mixture to saucepan and cook, stirring constantly, 1 minute, or until slightly thickened; remove from heat.
5. Stir in diced chicken, almonds, curry powder, ½ teaspoon of salt and pepper, blending well. Chill 30 minutes, or until the mixture is syrupy-thick; blend in the mayonnaise.
6. Beat egg whites until stiff in large bowl; fold in chicken mixture until no streaks of white remain.
7. Beat cream until stiff in medium-size bowl; fold into chicken mixture.
8. Pour into a 6-cup ring mold; chill several hours, or until firm.

9. Unmold onto serving plate; fit a shallow bowl into center of mold; fill with pineapple chunks; sprinkle with coconut.

CHICKEN-APPLE SALAD

Mayonnaise and cream furnish the base for this Netherlands original.

Makes 4 servings.

1 broiler-fryer (about 3 pounds), cut up
2 cups water
1½ teaspoons salt
1 package (10 ounces) frozen broccoli spears
1 tablespoon bottled French dressing
2 medium-size apples
1 cup chopped celery
1 small onion, chopped fine (¼ cup)
½ cup mayonnaise or salad dressing
1 tablespoon lemon juice
Dash of pepper
½ cup cream for whipping
Iceberg lettuce
2 tomatoes, cut in wedges
2 hard-cooked eggs, shelled and sliced

1. Place chicken in a large frying pan; add water and 1 teaspoon of the salt. Heat to boiling; cover. Simmer 50 minutes, or until chicken is tender. Remove from broth; cool until easy to handle, then skin chicken and take meat from bones; cut into bite-size pieces. Place in a large bowl; chill.
2. Cook broccoli spears, following label directions; drain. Place in a pie plate; drizzle with French dressing; let stand a half hour to season and blend flavors.
3. Pare apples; quarter, core and dice. Add to chicken with celery and onion.
4. Blend mayonnaise or salad dressing with lemon juice, remaining ½ teaspoon salt and pepper in a small bowl. Beat cream until stiff in a second small bowl; fold into mayonnaise mixture; fold into the chicken mixture.
5. Line a large serving platter with lettuce. Spoon chicken mixture in a mound down center. Arrange broccoli spears on one side, tomato wedges on other side and egg slices at each end.

PYRAMID PLATTER

This main-course salad is a giant triple-decker built on chicken. To top it off, the work can all be done ahead of time.

Makes 4 servings.

3 chicken breasts (about 12 ounces each)
2 cups water
¼ cup chopped celery
1 small onion, chopped (¼ cup)
2 teaspoons salt
¼ teaspoon cayenne
1 pound sliced bacon
Romaine
4 large tomatoes, sliced thin
2 individual-portion wedges (about 1¼
    ounces each) Roquefort cheese, crumbled
2 small ripe avocados
Lime juice
½ cup refrigerated Thousand Island dressing
    (from an 8-ounce jar)
½ cup dairy sour cream (from an 8-ounce
    carton)
Paprika

1. Combine chicken breasts, water, celery, onion, salt and cayenne in a large frying pan; heat to boiling; cover. Simmer 30 minutes, or until chicken is tender. Remove from broth; cool. Chill about 45 minutes. Pull off skin and carefully remove meat from bones; cut meat into thin slices.
2. Sauté bacon until limp in a large frying pan. Pick up end of each bacon strip in tines of fork; wind around fork. Return bacon curls to frying pan to crisp and brown. Drain bacon on paper toweling.
3. Line a platter with part of the romaine leaves. Arrange layers of chicken slices in a neat circle over romaine; layer tomato slices in a smaller circle over chicken. Sprinkle cheese over tomatoes.
4. Halve and pit avocados; sprinkle with lime juice.
5. Mix Thousand Island dressing with sour cream in a small bowl; spoon into avocado halves; sprinkle with paprika. Place 2 avocado halves at each end of platter. Arrange 3 of the bacon curls on top of cheese and remainder at sides of pyramid.
6. To serve, place one filled avocado half on each serving plate and surround with portions of the pyramid layers; garnish with bacon curls.

CHICKEN VERONIQUE

Fresh green grapes and apricots, plus a tangy cucumber dressing, add style to a favorite.

Makes 6 servings.

4 chicken breasts (about 12 ounces each)
Few celery tops
2 teaspoons salt
6 peppercorns
1 bay leaf
1 envelope instant chicken broth
    OR 1 chicken bouillon cube
1 cup water
1 cup chopped celery
1 cup seedless green grapes, halved
2 cups Cucumber Dressing
Bibb lettuce
6 apricots, washed, halved and pitted

1. Combine the chicken breasts, celery tops, salt, peppercorns, bay leaf, instant chicken broth or bouillon cube and water in a large frying pan; heat to boiling; cover. Simmer 30 minutes, until meat is tender.
2. Cool in broth until easy to handle, then remove and pull off skin; take meat from bones; cube. Place in a large bowl. (Strain broth and chill for making soup another day.)
3. Add celery and grapes to chicken; drizzle with about half of the Cucumber Dressing; toss lightly to mix. Chill at least an hour to season.
4. When ready to serve, line a large bowl with lettuce; pile chicken mixture in center; frame with apricot halves. Serve with remaining dressing.

CUCUMBER DRESSING: Combine 6 tablespoons mayonnaise or salad dressing, 1½ teaspoons salt, 1 teaspoon chopped fresh dill, ¼ teaspoon pepper, 6 tablespoons lemon juice and 1 cup buttermilk in a small bowl; beat until well-blended. Stir in 1 small cucumber, pared, diced and drained well. Chill at least an hour to season. Makes about 2 cups.

PARISIAN CHICKEN BOWL

Halved chicken breasts are glazed, French style, and served cold with seasoned vegetables for this fancy bowl.

Makes 6 servings.

3 whole chicken breasts (12 ounces each)
1 small onion, sliced
1 teaspoon salt
⅛ teaspoon pepper
1 bay leaf
2 cups water
1 envelope unflavored gelatin
½ cup mayonnaise or salad dressing
6 pitted ripe olives
1 package (10 ounces) frozen Fordhook lima
   beans
½ cup bottled Italian salad dressing
4 cups broken mixed salad greens
3 medium-size tomatoes, peeled and sliced
3 hard-cooked eggs, shelled and quartered

1. Combine chicken breasts with onion, salt, pepper, bay leaf and water in a large saucepan; cover. Simmer 30 minutes, or just until tender.
2. Remove from broth, cool until easy to handle, then pull off skin. Remove meat from each half of breast in one piece; place in one layer in a shallow dish. Chill.
3. Strain broth into a 2-cup measure; chill just until fat rises to top, then skim.
4. Soften gelatin in 1 cup of the broth in a small saucepan. (Save any remaining to add to soup.) Heat gelatin mixture, stirring constantly, just until gelatin dissolves; pour into a small bowl. Blend in mayonnaise or salad dressing; chill, stirring several times, 20 minutes, or until as thick as unbeaten egg white.
5. Spoon part over chilled chicken breasts to make a thick layer, then repeat with remaining until chicken is evenly glazed. Cut each olive into 6 slivers, arrange, petal fashion, on top of each glazed chicken breast; chill until gelatin is firm.
6. Cook lima beans, following label directions; drain. Toss with ¼ cup of the Italian dressing in a small bowl; cover. (This much can be done early in the day, or even a day ahead.) If making ahead, store in the refrigerator until ready to use.
7. When ready to serve, place salad greens in a large shallow bowl; drizzle remaining ¼ cup Italian dressing over; toss lightly to mix. Top with tomato slices; mound lima beans in center, then arrange chicken breasts, spoke fashion, around beans; place quartered eggs around edge of bowl. Garnish with a cherry-tomato flower, if you wish. To make, cut a cherry tomato into eighths from tip almost to stem end; separate "petals" slightly; stuff with a ripe olive and top with a sprig of parsley.

CHICKEN SALAD DELUXE

Tender chicken is brightly flavored with a sour cream-mayonnaise combination.

Makes 4 servings.

1 broiler-fryer (about 3 pounds)
4 cups water
1 small onion, sliced
Few celery tops
¼ teaspoon salt
⅓ cup mayonnaise or salad dressing
⅓ cup dairy sour cream
1 tablespoon lemon juice
¼ teaspoon pepper
¾ cup chopped celery
1 medium-size onion, chopped (½ cup)
¼ cup chopped dill pickle
Lettuce
Paprika

1. Combine chicken with water, sliced onion, celery tops and salt in a kettle or Dutch oven. Heat to boiling; reduce heat; cover; simmer about 1 hour, or until chicken is tender. Remove from broth and cool until easy to handle. (Save broth to start a soup another day.)
2. Skin the chicken and take meat from bones. Cut meat into bite-size pieces; put in a medium-size bowl.
3. Blend mayonnaise or salad dressing, sour cream, lemon juice and pepper in a small bowl. Combine celery, onion and dill pickle with chicken; add the dressing; toss until evenly coated. Cover; chill at least an hour to season and blend flavors.
4. Line salad bowl with lettuce leaves. Spoon salad into bowl. Sprinkle with paprika.

WINTER CHICKEN SALAD

White meat, carrots and celery team up in a warm salad for cold weather.

Makes 6 servings.

3 chicken breasts (about 12 ounces each)
1 pound carrots, pared and sliced thin
2 cups sliced celery
1 small onion, chopped (¼ cup)
¼ cup water
1 envelope instant chicken broth
OR 1 chicken bouillon cube
2 teaspoons salt
½ cup mayonnaise or salad dressing
Potato chips

1. Pull skin from chicken breasts, then cut meat from bones; dice meat.
2. Combine with carrots, celery, onion, water, chicken broth or bouillon cube and salt in a large frying pan; heat to boiling; cover.
3. Simmer 30 minutes, or until chicken is tender. Drain off any broth and save to add to soup or stew. Fold mayonnaise or salad dressing into chicken mixture.
4. Spoon onto a large serving platter; frame with potato chips and garnish with parsley, if you wish.

AVOCADO CHICKEN SALAD

Chilled, seasoned chicken and delicate avocado: A combination everybody loves.

Makes 6 servings.

1 stewing chicken (about 4 pounds), cooked
4 tablespoons salad oil
2 tablespoons fresh lime juice
¼ teaspoon ground ginger
1 large head of iceberg lettuce, washed and dried
1 cup sliced celery
1 large ripe avocado

1. Cool chicken until easy to handle; remove skin and white and dark meat from frame in chunks as big as possible, then slice into thin bite-size pieces. (You should have about 4 cups.) Place in medium-size bowl. Save broth for making soup another day.
2. Combine salad oil, lime juice and ginger in a cup; sprinkle over chicken; toss to coat well; cover; chill.

3. At serving time, place a large lettuce leaf on each plate; shred remaining lettuce; toss with celery, and divide evenly onto lettuce leaves. Top with mounds of marinated chicken.
4. Peel avocado, remove seed and cut into thin lengthwise slices; arrange 3 on top of each mound of chicken to garnish.

BARBECUED CHICKEN SUPPER SALAD

You can use ready-cooked meat and salad from your supermarket for this hearty hot-weather meal.

Makes 4 servings.

2 containers (1 pound each) prepared macaroni salad
1 package (4 ounces) shredded Cheddar cheese
1 can (8 ounces) lima beans, drained
½ cup chopped celery
½ teaspoon fines herbes
1 small head chicory, washed, drained
2 medium-size tomatoes, cut in wedges
2 ready-to-eat barbecued chickens, weighing about 2 pounds each
Sweet mixed pickles
Stuffed green olives

1. Combine macaroni salad, cheese, lima beans, celery and herbes in a large bowl; toss lightly to mix well. Chill about an hour to season.
2. Just before serving, line a large platter with chicory leaves; break remaining into bite-size pieces in center; spoon macaroni salad on top. Tuck tomato wedges around salad.
3. Cut chickens in half with kitchen scissors; place, skin side up, around edge of platter.
4. Thread pickles and olives, alternately, onto wooden picks; stick, kebab style, into macaroni salad. Serve with rye bread-and-butter sandwiches, if you wish.

CHICKEN MOUSSE

This refreshing gelatin salad is packed with fruits and vegetables to compliment the chicken.

Makes 16 servings.

2 large chicken breasts (about 1 pound each)
2 cups water
1 small onion, peeled and sliced
Few celery tops
1 teaspoon salt
1 bay leaf
4 peppercorns
1 can (about 9 ounces) pineapple tidbits
2 envelopes unflavored gelatin
1 cup mayonnaise or salad dressing
1 tablespoon lemon juice
1 teaspoon prepared mustard
½ pound cooked ham
1 can (5 ounces) water chestnuts, drained

1. Combine chicken breasts, water, onion, celery tops, salt, bay leaf and peppercorns in a large saucepan; heat to boiling; cover. Simmer 30 minutes, or until chicken is tender.
2. While chicken cooks, drain syrup from pineapple into a 1-cup measure; add water, if needed, to make ½ cup. Stir in gelatin to soften. Set pineapple aside.
3. Remove chicken from broth; strain broth into a 4-cup measure; add water, if needed, to make 3 cups. Return to same saucepan; stir in softened gelatin.
4. Heat slowly, stirring constantly, until gelatin dissolves; remove from heat. Blend in mayonnaise or salad dressing, lemon juice and mustard.
5. Pour into a shallow pan. Freeze 20 minutes, or just until firm about 1 inch from edges but still soft in middle.
6. While gelatin mixture chills, pull skin from chicken and take meat from bones; dice meat. (There should be about 1½ cups.) Dice ham and water chestnuts; combine with diced chicken and pineapple in a medium-size bowl.
7. Spoon partly frozen gelatin mixture into a chilled large bowl; beat until thick and fluffy. Fold in chicken-ham mixture; spoon into an 8-cup ring mold. Chill several hours, or until firm.
8. When ready to serve, loosen salad around edge and center ring with a knife; dip mold *very quickly* in and out of hot water. Cover with a large serving plate; turn upside down; gently lift off mold. Fill center of ring with salad greens, if you wish.

SUMMER CHICKEN DIVAN

A winter casserole turns cool for summer salad days.

Makes 6 servings.

3 chicken breasts (about 12 ounces each)
1 small onion, peeled and sliced
1 teaspoon salt
Dash of pepper
Water
2 packages (10 ounces each) frozen asparagus spears
1 envelope Parmesan salad dressing mix
Vegetable oil
Cider vinegar
1 head Boston lettuce, separated into leaves
2 cans (3 or 4 ounces each) whole mushrooms, drained
½ cup mayonnaise or salad dressing
2 hard-cooked egg yolks

1. Combine chicken, onion, salt, pepper and 2 cups water in a large frying pan; cover. Simmer 30 minutes, or until chicken is tender. Remove from broth; cool until easy to handle, then pull off skin. Remove meat from each half of breast in one large piece; set aside. (Strain broth and chill for soup another day.)
2. While chicken cooks, cook asparagus, following label directions; drain; place in a shallow dish.
3. Prepare salad dressing mix with vegetable oil, vinegar and water, following label directions; drizzle ½ cup over asparagus; let stand 30 minutes to season.
4. Line a large shallow serving dish with lettuce; arrange asparagus spears over lettuce, then place chicken breasts, overlapping, in a row on top of asparagus. Pile mushrooms at each end.
5. Blend mayonnaise or salad dressing into remaining dressing in asparagus dish; drizzle over chicken. Press egg yolks through a sieve on top.

Sandwiches

STUFFED SALAD ROLLS

A tasty jumble of chopped chicken, cheese and celery, piled on frankfurter rolls.

Makes 4 servings, 2 rolls each.

2 cups chopped lettuce
1 cup diced cooked chicken
½ cup diced process American or
    Swiss cheese
½ cup chopped celery
½ cup mayonnaise
2 tablespoons pickle relish
¼ teaspoon curry powder
8 frankfurter rolls, split, toasted and buttered

1. Combine lettuce with chicken, cheese and celery in medium-size bowl.
2. Blend mayonnaise, pickle relish and curry powder in small bowl; stir into salad mixture to coat well; pile into prepared rolls.

CHICKEN CHEESE CLUBS

Chicken, bacon and Muenster—a flavory combo—spiked with tomatoes and cucumber.

Bake at 450° for 5 minutes.

Makes 4 sandwiches.

12 slices bacon (½ pound)
2 medium-size tomatoes, each cut in 4 slices
½ small cucumber, sliced
12 slices whole-wheat bread, toasted
    and buttered
¼ cup prepared sandwich spread
8 slices cooked chicken
4 slices Muenster cheese (from an 8-ounce
    package)
8 pitted ripe olives
8 small sweet pickles

1. Sauté bacon until crisp in a large frying pan; drain on paper toweling.
2. Place tomato and cucumber slices and bacon, dividing evenly, on 4 pieces of the toast; add another slice of the toast; spread with sandwich spread.
3. Top with chicken slices, then cheese and remaining toast, buttered side down. Place sandwiches on a cooky sheet.

4. Bake in a very hot oven (450°) 5 minutes, or until cheese melts slightly.
5. Press wooden picks into sandwiches to hold; cut each sandwich diagonally into quarters. Top picks with olives and pickles.

CHICKEN LIVER BOUNTIES

Here's a sandwich to please gourmets. Cook the livers gently, then combine with broiled tomatoes and crisp bacon.

Makes 6 sandwiches.

6 slices bacon
1 pound chicken livers
2 tablespoons flour
¼ teaspoon seasoned salt
1 can (3 or 4 ounces) chopped mushrooms
3 large tomatoes, each cut in 6 slices
3 large hamburger buns, split

1. Sauté bacon just until crisp in a large frying pan; drain on paper toweling, then crumble. Drain off all drippings, then measure 2 tablespoons and return to pan. (Set bacon aside for Step 5.)
2. Halve chicken livers; snip out any veiny parts or skin with scissors. Shake livers with flour and seasoned salt in a paper bag to coat.
3. Brown slowly in drippings in frying pan; stir in mushrooms and liquid. Heat, stirring constantly, to boiling; cover. Simmer 3 minutes, or just until livers lose their pink color.
4. While livers cook, place tomato slices and bun halves in a single layer on rack in broiler pan. Broil 3 to 4 minutes, or until tomatoes are heated through and buns are toasted.
5. Place 2 tomato slices on each bun half; spoon hot liver mixture over, dividing evenly. Top each with another tomato slice; sprinkle with crumbled bacon. Garnish with parsley, if you wish.

2. Cook slowly, stirring constantly, 5 minutes, or until thickened: Remove from heat; stir in butter or margarine until melted. This dressing will keep well in a tightly covered jar in the refrigerator.

CLUB NIGHT CASSEROLE

This agreeable casserole will please all comers. It's best started the day before.

Bake at 350° for 50 to 60 minutes.
Makes 8 to 12 servings.

1 stewing chicken (about 5 pounds), not cut up
3½ cups water
1 medium-size onion, sliced
1 carrot, scraped and halved
Handful of celery tops
2 teaspoons salt
1 bay leaf
6 cups cooked rice (1½ cups raw)
6 tablespoons chicken fat
6 tablespoons flour
1 cup light or table cream
2 cans (3 or 4 ounces each) sliced mushrooms
1 can (about 4 ounces) pimientos, diced
1 cup (about a 5-ounce can) toasted slivered almonds
1 cup buttered soft bread crumbs (2 slices)

1. Combine chicken, water, onion, carrot, celery tops, salt and bay leaf in large kettle; cover; simmer 1 to 1½ hours, or until tender.
2. Cool chicken in stock; remove, and skin. Take meat from bones; cut meat into bite-size pieces; place in medium-size bowl. Pour ½ cup stock over to keep chicken moist; cover and chill.
3. Strain remaining stock into a medium-size bowl; chill; skim off fat and save for Step 5. (This much can be done the day before.)
4. When ready to complete dish, heat 1 cup stock and pour over cooked rice in large bowl; let stand while making sauce.
5. Melt chicken fat from Step 3 in medium-size saucepan, adding butter or margarine, if needed, to make 6 tablespoons. Remove from heat; blend in flour; stir in 2 cups stock.

6. Cook over low heat, stirring constantly, until sauce thickens and boils 1 minute. Remove from heat; gradually stir in cream, mushrooms and their liquid, pimientos, almonds and chicken; season to taste with salt and pepper.
7. Make alternate layers of chicken and rice mixtures in buttered 12-cup casserole; sprinkle buttered bread crumbs around edge.
8. Bake in moderate oven (350°) 50 to 60 minutes, or until sauce bubbles around edges and crumbs are golden-brown.

JAMBALAYA

A kettle of contrasts from Creole country: Chicken, ham, vegetables, rice.

Makes 12 servings.

2 broiler-fryers (about 2 pounds each), cut up
3 cups diced cooked ham (1 pound)
4 tablespoons (½ stick) butter or margarine
2 cloves garlic, sliced
3 large onions, chopped (3 cups)
1 package (1 pound) frozen deveined shelled raw shrimps
3 cans (about 1 pound each) stewed tomatoes
2 teaspoons salt
¼ teaspoon liquid red-pepper seasoning
1 large bay leaf
3 cups thinly sliced celery
2 cups uncooked rice
¼ cup chopped parsley

1. Wash chicken pieces; pat dry.
2. Brown ham lightly in butter or margarine in a heavy roasting pan. Stir in garlic and onions; sauté 5 minutes, or until soft. Add chicken and shrimps.
3. Combine the tomatoes, salt, red-pepper seasoning and bay leaf in a large bowl; pour over ham and chicken.
4. Heat to boiling; cover. Simmer 30 minutes. Stir in celery and rice, making sure all rice is covered with liquid.
5. Simmer 30 minutes longer, or until chicken and rice are tender; remove bay leaf. Stir in parsley.

3. Drain syrup from pineapple into a cup. Add pineapple and grapes to chicken. Blend 2 tablespoons of the syrup with ½ cup mayonnaise or salad dressing and remaining ½ teaspoon salt in a small bowl; fold into chicken mixture. Chill.
4. Halve avocado; pit and peel. Mash in a small bowl; stir in crumbled bacon, ¼ cup of the remaining mayonnaise or salad dressing and red-pepper seasoning. (Fix avocado mixture no longer than an hour ahead so that it keeps its bright color.)
5. Cut each loaf of bread lengthwise into 3 even slices; spread with remaining ¼ cup mayonnaise or salad dressing.
6. Spread avocado mixture on bottom slices and chicken salad on middle slices; stack loaves back in shape; cover with top slices. Cut loaf crosswise into 8 thick double-decker sandwiches.

CHICKEN STROGANOFF ROUNDS

To round out a light supper menu, just add raw relishes and a simple dessert.

Makes 6 servings.

1 broiler-fryer (about 3 pounds), cut up
1 medium-size onion, chopped (½ cup)
½ cup chopped celery
2 tablespoons butter or margarine
1 package Stroganoff sauce mix
1 cup (8-ounce carton) dairy sour cream
6 split hamburger buns, toasted

1. Simmer chicken, covered, in 2 cups lightly salted boiling water in a large frying pan 40 minutes, or until tender. Remove chicken from bones; dice meat. Measure 1 cup of the broth and set aside.
2. Sauté onion and celery in butter or margarine until soft in same frying pan; stir in chicken.
3. Blend sauce mix with the 1 cup chicken broth in a small bowl; stir into chicken mixture. Heat to boiling; cover. Simmer 10 minutes.
4. Stir about 1 cup of the hot sauce mixture into sour cream in a small bowl; stir back into pan. Heat very slowly just until hot. Spoon over toasted buns to serve open-face style.

CHICKEN-CHEESE PUFF

A unique sandwich idea that's made with your own homemade puff.

Bake at 375° for 55 minutes.
Makes 4 servings.

1 cup milk
4 tablespoons (½ stick) butter or margarine
1 teaspoon onion salt
¼ teaspoon pepper
1 cup sifted regular flour
4 eggs
1 package (6 ounces) sliced Swiss cheese, diced
2 cups diced cooked chicken
1 cup finely chopped celery
½ cup mayonnaise or salad dressing
1 can (4½ ounces) deviled ham
2 tablespoons lemon juice

1. Heat milk, butter or margarine, ½ teaspoon of the onion salt, and pepper just to boiling in a medium-size saucepan. Add flour all at once; stir vigorously with a wooden spoon 2 minutes, or until batter forms a thick smooth ball that follows spoon around pan. Remove from heat.
2. Beat in eggs, 1 at a time, until batter is shiny-smooth.
3. Set aside ¼ cup of the diced cheese; stir remainder into mixture in saucepan. Drop batter by heaping tablespoonfuls onto a large cooky sheet to form a rectangle about 12x5. (Batter will spread during baking to make a long loaf.) Sprinkle with the ¼ cup cheese.
4. Bake in moderate oven (375°) 45 minutes, or until puffed and golden.
5. While puff bakes, combine chicken and celery in a large bowl. Blend mayonnaise or salad dressing, deviled ham, lemon juice and remaining ½ teaspoon onion salt in a small bowl; fold into chicken mixture.
6. Cut a thin slice from top of puff; scoop out any bits of soft dough from bottom with a teaspoon. Spoon chicken mixture into bottom; set top back in place.
7. Bake 10 minutes longer, or until filling heats through. Carefully slide onto a large serving platter; cut crosswise into 4 thick slices.

How many times have you told yourself there's no incentive to cook dinner when you're the only one who's home? You'll open a can of stew, toss a tv dinner in the oven or make a sandwich. These are easy solutions. But we offer better ones with the recipes in this chapter. They'll help make lonesome hours a little more pleasant without a great deal of work. And because they can be made ahead of time and kept waiting in the refrigerator or oven, they're also ideally suited for nights when your husband is going to be late for dinner or when you're out and he's home alone.

For a week when you'll be alone for several nights we offer recipes that make enough for 2 or 3 solo dishes. A bonus with these multiple-serving recipes: If a friend calls at the last minute, you can invite her over for dinner!

Dishes for One

SUPERMARKET CHICKEN SUPPER

A ready-barbecued chicken and prepared macaroni salad from the supermarket can make 2 dinners for a loner.

Makes 1 serving for 2 meals.

1 container (1 pound) prepared macaroni salad
½ package (4 ounces) shredded Cheddar cheese
½ small can (7 to 8 ounces) lima beans, drained
¼ cup chopped celery
¼ teaspoon fines herbes
½ small head chicory, washed, dried and separated into leaves
1 medium-size tomato, cut in wedges
1 ready-to-eat barbecued chicken (about 2 pounds)
Sweet mixed pickles
Stuffed green olives

1. Combine macaroni salad, cheese, lima beans, celery and herbes in a large bowl; toss lightly to mix well. Chill at least an hour to season.
2. Line a platter with chicory leaves; break remaining into bite-size pieces in center; spoon half the macaroni salad on top. Tuck tomato wedges around salad. Put rest of salad in a covered refrigerator container for next meal.
3. Cut chicken in half with kitchen scissors; place one half, skin side up, on platter beside salad. Wrap other half in transparent wrap and place in meat keeper compartment of refrigerator for tomorrow's meal.
4. Garnish with pickles and olives, and serve with rye bread-and-butter sandwiches, if you wish.

LONE RANGER CHICKEN

The sauce will help keep this chicken from drying out—either in the oven or the refrigerator—until it's needed for a single dinner.

Bake at 400° about 1 hour.
Makes 1 serving for 2 meals.

2 large chicken breasts OR 2 legs with thighs
Butter or margarine
Savory Sauce

1. Wash chicken pieces; pat dry; remove skin if you wish.
2. Arrange chicken pieces in a single layer in a well-buttered shallow baking pan.
3. Spoon Savory Sauce over so chicken pieces are well coated.
4. Bake, uncovered, in hot oven (400°) about 1 hour, or until chicken is tender.
5. Remove one breast or leg with half the sauce, and cool; then refrigerate in a covered jar for reheating tomorrow (or perhaps the next day, but better not keep it longer than that).
6. Leave other breast or leg tightly covered in the oven (with the heat off) to be eaten within an hour or two, or refrigerate in a small covered baking dish for reheating the same night.

SAVORY SAUCE

Makes 1½ cups.

1 can (8 ounces) tomato sauce
1 small onion, chopped
½ teaspoon garlic powder
2 tablespoons soy sauce
1 tablespoon sugar
½ teaspoon dry mustard
Dash cayenne pepper

Mix all ingredients in a medium-size bowl.

LONER'S SALAMI-CHICKEN DUO

These spicy drumsticks taste delicious hot or cold.

Makes 1 serving for 2 meals.

2 chicken drumsticks with thighs
1 slice (1 ounce) salami
2 tablespoons flour
½ teaspoon salt
¼ teaspoon paprika
¼ teaspoon leaf oregano, crumbled
Dash pepper
3 tablespoons vegetable oil

1. Cut through chicken legs at joints to separate drumsticks and thighs, then cut an opening along bone of each drumstick and in meaty part of each thigh with a sharp knife to make a pocket for stuffing.

2. Cut salami into 4 strips; stuff 1 strip into each piece of chicken.

3. Shake pieces, a few at a time, in mixture of flour, salt, paprika, oregano and pepper in a bag to coat evenly.

4. Cook pieces slowly in vegetable oil in a medium-size frying pan 20 minutes; turn; cover loosely. Cook 20 minutes longer, or until tender and crisply golden. Remove from pan and drain on paper towel. Wrap tightly in foil and place in oven or refrigerator to keep.

SINGLE SAM'S SALAD SANDWICH

Delicious chicken salad makes 2 summer suppers (or 1 for a hungry husband).

Makes 1 serving for 1 or 2 meals.

1 whole chicken breast (about 12 ounces),
    OR 1 can (5 or 6 ounces) boned chicken, diced
1 cup water
1 small onion, sliced
Handful of celery tops
½ plus ¼ teaspoon salt
Pepper
½ cup diced celery
¼ cup slivered almonds
4 tablespoons mayonnaise
1 tablespoon milk
⅛ teaspoon dry mustard
1 or 2 large Vienna rolls
Butter or margarine
Lettuce
Cherry tomatoes

1. If using chicken breast, place it in a medium-size saucepan with the water, onion, celery tops, ½ teaspoon salt and a dash of pepper. Simmer, covered, 20 to 30 minutes, or until chicken is tender. Let stand until cool enough to handle, then skin chicken and take meat from bones. Dice chicken (you should have about 1 cup).

2. Combine chicken, celery and almonds in medium-size bowl. Mix mayonnaise, milk, ¼ teaspoon salt, mustard and a dash of pepper; stir into chicken mixture, tossing lightly to mix. If making 2 portions, chill 1 portion on a plate until serving time; place remainder in a covered refrigerator container in coldest part of refrigerator for tomorrow's meal.

3. At mealtime, split Vienna roll and butter it. Line buttered roll with lettuce; fill with salad. Garnish with cherry tomatoes.

BOWLING-NIGHT SALAD

Stash these cooling little salads in the refrigerator for someone's dinner tonight—and tomorrow night.

Makes 3 individual molds.

1 broiler-fryer (about 2½ pounds), cut up
3 cups water
½ small onion, sliced
Few celery tops
1½ teaspoons salt
3 peppercorns
1 envelope unflavored gelatin
¼ cup apple juice
½ cup mayonnaise or salad dressing
¼ cup diced celery
2 tablespoons chopped toasted slivered almonds
2 tablespoons chopped stuffed green olives
Boston lettuce

1. Combine chicken, water, onion, celery tops, salt and peppercorns in a kettle; cover. Simmer 1 hour, or until chicken is very tender; remove from broth. Strain broth into a 2-cup measure.

2. Soften gelatin in apple juice in a medium-size saucepan; stir in 1½ cups of the broth. (Chill any remaining broth to add to soup for another meal.)

3. Heat gelatin mixture slowly, stirring constantly, until gelatin dissolves; remove from heat. Cool for Step 5.

4. Pull skin from chicken and take meat from bones; dice fine. (There should be about 2 cups.)

5. Blend mayonnaise or salad dressing into gelatin mixture in saucepan; pour into an ice-cube tray. Freeze 20 minutes, or until firm about 1 inch in from edges.

6. Spoon into a chilled large bowl; beat until fluffy thick. Fold in diced chicken, celery, almonds and olives. Spoon into 3 individual molds. Chill several hours or until firm.

7. Salad can be eaten from the mold, or unmolded onto a lettuce-lined plate and garnished with melon crescents.

No one likes to diet. But,
fortunately, today even
the most stringent diets are
more creative and palat-
able than ever before.
Take chicken. By itself it
offers the dieter real
flavor and high protein
in exchange for very few
calories and little fat.
And with thought and
planning, it becomes down-
right gourmet.
Because it's a short-
fibered, easily-digested
meat, chicken is also ideal
for anyone on a geriatric
or convalescent diet. The
low- or no-salt dieter can
enjoy chicken, too, because
it responds so well to all
other seasonings.
A 3-ounce portion of skinless, boneless broiled
chicken breast has only 115
calories; with skin, it has
only 185. Have a piece of
chicken. You'll enjoy your
diet as well as the results!

Chicken on a Diet

SKINNY-GIRL PAELLA

A low-calorie version of the favorite from sunny Valencia.

Bake at 350° for 1 hour.
Makes 6 servings.

1 broiler-fryer (about 2 pounds), cut in serving-size pieces
1 large onion, chopped (1 cup)
1 clove garlic, minced
1 cup uncooked rice
6 small slices salami (about 2 ounces), diced
2 teaspoons salt
1 teaspoon sugar
¼ teaspoon pepper
⅛ teaspoon crushed saffron
1 can (about 1 pound) tomatoes
1½ cups water
1 envelope instant chicken broth OR 1 chicken bouillon cube
1 pound fresh shrimps, shelled and deveined, OR 1 package (12 ounces) frozen deveined shelled raw shrimps
1 can (4 ounces) pimientos, drained and cut in large pieces

1. Pull skin from chicken pieces, if you wish. Place chicken, meaty side down, in a single layer on rack of broiler pan.
2. Broil, 4 inches from heat, 10 minutes; turn; broil 10 minutes longer, or until lightly browned; set aside for Step 4.
3. Pour drippings from broiler pan into a medium-size frying pan. Stir in onion and garlic; sauté until soft; spoon into a 12-cup baking dish with rice, salami, salt, sugar, pepper and saffron.
4. Combine tomatoes with water and instant chicken broth or bouillon cube in same frying pan; heat to boiling, crushing bouillon cube, if used, with a spoon. Stir into rice mixture with shrimps. Arrange chicken and pimientos on top; cover.
5. Bake in moderate oven (350°) 1 hour, or until liquid is absorbed and chicken is tender. Garnish with parsley and serve with chopped green onions to sprinkle on top, if you wish.

Dieter's portion: ½ breast, 5 shrimps, and 1 cup rice mixture—406 calories.

CHICKEN SALAD PLATE

Cottage cheese as you've never known it before.

Makes 6 servings.

2 pounds chicken breasts
2 cups water
1 slice of onion
Few celery tops
2 teaspoons salt
3 tablespoons vinegar
1 teaspoon paprika
¼ teaspoon seasoned pepper
¼ teaspoon garlic powder
¾ cup low-fat cottage cheese (from an 8-ounce carton)
3 tablespoons buttermilk
1 small onion, chopped (¼ cup)
1 cup pared and chopped cucumber
2 tablespoons chopped pimiento
1 head Boston lettuce, washed, dried and separated into leaves
18 radishes, trimmed
3 hard-cooked eggs, quartered

1. Combine chicken breasts with water, onion slice, celery tops and 1 teaspoon of the salt in a large saucepan; cover. Simmer 30 minutes, or just until tender.
2. Remove chicken from broth; cool until easy to handle but still warm, then pull off skin and take meat from bones; cut into cubes. Place in a medium-size bowl.
3. Combine vinegar, remaining 1 teaspoon salt, paprika, seasoned pepper and garlic powder in a small bowl. Add to chicken and toss lightly until well mixed. Chill in refrigerator at least 1 hour.
4. Combine cottage cheese, buttermilk and chopped onion in an electric-blender container; cover. Whirl until creamy-smooth. Spoon into a small bowl and refrigerate until serving time.
5. When ready to serve, combine chicken mixture with cucumber, pimiento and cottage cheese dressing. Toss lightly to mix.
6. Place lettuce leaves to form cups on 6 serving plates; place ⅔ cup of chicken salad in each lettuce cup. Arrange 3 radishes and 2 egg quarters attractively on each plate.

Dieter's Portion: The amount specified in Step 6—215 calories.

BONELESS CHICKEN CACCIATORE

Plump chunks of chicken and bright green strips of pepper in a spicy tomato sauce spiked with wine. How could this be diet fare?

Makes 6 servings.

2 broiler-fryers (about 1½ pounds each)
2 cups water
2 cans (8 ounces each) tomato sauce
1 tablespoon leaf oregano, crumbled
½ cup dry white wine
1 medium-size onion, chopped (½ cup)
1 large green pepper, halved, seeded and
  sliced
1 clove of garlic, minced
½ teaspoon salt
¼ teaspoon pepper

1. Simmer chicken in water in a large covered saucepan for 30 minutes. Remove. Cool until easy to handle. Pour stock into a 4-cup measure. Refrigerate. Remove meat from chicken. Discard skin and bones. Skim any fat from chicken stock.
2. Put chicken, 2 cups of the stock and remaining ingredients in a saucepan, cover. Simmer 20 minutes. Uncover. Allow to simmer, stirring occasionally, until sauce has thickened, about 10 minutes.

Dieter's Portion: 1/6 of the chicken—248 calories.

LOW-CALORIE CHICKEN ORIENTALE

A sweet-and-sour chicken dish that's off the "forbidden list," thanks to today's easy-to-use sugar substitutes.

Bake at 325° for 55 minutes.
Makes 6 servings.

2 broiler-fryers (1½ pounds each), cut up
1 can (1 pound) unsweetened pineapple
  chunks in pineapple juice
3 tablespoons wine vinegar
1 tablespoon soy sauce
½ teaspoon dry mustard
1 teaspoon salt
¼ teaspoon pepper
2 green peppers, seeded and cut in strips
1 tablespoon cornstarch
2 tablespoons water

1. Place chicken pieces skin side up in a shallow baking dish and surround with pineapple chunks.
2. Mix juice with vinegar, soy sauce, mustard, salt and pepper and pour over chicken. Bake, uncovered, in moderate oven (325°) for 40 minutes, basting occasionally. Add pepper strips.
3. Combine cornstarch and water in a cup. Stir into liquid in baking dish and bake an additional 15 minutes, or until bubbly.

Dieter's Portion: 1/6 of the chicken—248 calories.

CHICKEN-LIVER RAGOUT

Your diet seems like something in the past when you try this dish.

Makes 4 servings.

3 slices bacon, cut in 2-inch pieces
1 pound chicken livers, halved
2 medium-size onions, peeled and quartered
2 medium-size green peppers, quartered and
  seeded
1 tablespoon flour
½ teaspoon paprika
1 cup water
2 envelopes instant chicken broth
  OR 2 chicken-bouillon cubes
¼ teaspoon leaf thyme, crumbled
1 small bay leaf
2 cups hot cooked noodles

1. Sauté bacon until crisp in a medium-size frying pan; remove and drain on paper toweling. Pour off all drippings.
2. Sauté livers slowly in same pan 3 to 5 minutes, or just until they lose their pink color; remove and set aside for Step 4.
3. Stir onions and green peppers into frying pan. Sprinkle with flour and paprika, then stir in water, chicken broth, thyme and bay leaf; cover. Simmer 15 minutes, or until onions are tender; remove bay leaf.
4. Add chicken livers to sauce; heat 5 minutes, or until bubbly.
5. Spoon noodles onto serving plates; top with liver mixture; sprinkle with bacon.

Dieter's Portion: ¼ of the chicken liver-noodle combination—323 calories.

DIETER'S DELIGHT

A masterpiece, and fun to make: Chilled chicken breasts in a gelatin glaze decorated with vegetable flowers.

Makes 6 servings.

3 chicken breasts (about 12 ounces each), halved
2 envelopes instant chicken broth OR
    2 chicken bouillon cubes
1½ cups water
3 teaspoons leaf tarragon
1 tablespoon instant minced onion
Few sprigs of parsley
1 envelope unflavored gelatin
6 carrot slices
2 green onion tops, cut in strips
Fresh spinach leaves

1. Combine chicken breasts, instant broth or bouillon cubes, and water in a large saucepan. Tie tarragon, onion and parsley in a cheesecloth bag; add to saucepan; cover. Simmer 30 minutes, or until chicken is tender. Remove from broth and cool until easy to handle; pull off skin; chill. Chill broth until fat rises to top, then skim off.
2. Soften gelatin in ½ cup of the broth in a small saucepan; heat, stirring constantly, until gelatin dissolves; remove from heat. Stir in remaining broth.
3. Place chicken breasts in a single layer on a wire rack set in a shallow pan.
4. Measure ½ cup of the gelatin mixture; set cup in a small bowl of ice and water; chill just until as thick as unbeaten egg white. Brush over chicken breasts to coat. (Keep remaining gelatin at room temperature.)
5. Arrange a flower in gelatin on each chicken breast, using a carrot slice for blossom and a long strip of green onion top for stem and short pieces for leaves. Chill until firm.
6. Measure out another ½ cup of the gelatin mixture and chill until thickened; brush over decorations on chicken; chill until firm. Chill remaining gelatin mixture; brush over chicken a third time to make a thick coating, then chill several hours.
7. When ready to serve, arrange chicken on a spinach-lined large platter. Garnish with cherry tomatoes cut to form flowers.

Dieter's portion: One-half chicken breast— 196 calories.

WEIGHT-WORRIER'S FRICASSEE

A happy combination of rich-tasting gravy and sensible calorie count.

Makes 6 servings.

3 whole chicken breasts (about 12 ounces each), halved
1 small onion, chopped (¼ cup)
½ cup finely chopped celery
2 teaspoons salt
⅛ teaspoon pepper
1 cup water
2 tablespoons instant-type flour
½ cup skim milk

1. Simmer the chicken, covered, with onion, celery, salt, pepper and water in a medium-size frying pan 30 minutes, or until tender; remove to a heated serving platter.
2. Mix flour and skim milk in a cup; stir into hot broth in pan. Cook, stirring constantly, until gravy thickens and boils 1 minute. Serve in a separate bowl.

Dieter's portion: ½ chicken breast and ¼ cup gravy—200 calories.

POT AU FEU (Dinner in a Pot)

A low-calorie version of a French classic.

Makes 4 servings.

1 pound boneless round steak
3 cups water
1 can condensed beef broth
1 large onion, chopped (1 cup)
1 clove of garlic, minced
2 teaspoons salt
4 sprigs parsley
1 bay leaf
6 peppercorns
½ teaspoon leaf thyme
1 whole chicken breast, weighing about 12 ounces
4 large carrots (about ½ pound)
2 zucchini
3 cups celery sticks

1. Trim all fat from beef. Place steak in a heavy kettle or Dutch oven. Add water, beef broth, onion and garlic. Place parsley, bay leaf, peppercorns and thyme on a small piece of cheesecloth; bring up corners to enclose herbs; tie securely; add to kettle.

2. Heat to boiling; lower heat; cover. Simmer 1 hour. Add chicken breast; simmer 30 minutes, or until meats are tender. Remove meats; keep warm.

3. While meats cook, pare carrots and cut in sticks; trim zucchini, cut in sticks.

4. Reheat broth in kettle to boiling; add carrots; cover. Cook 15 minutes. Add zucchini and celery sticks; cook 15 minutes longer, or until tender. Remove.

5. Strain broth into a large bowl, pressing onion and garlic through sieve into liquid; let stand about a minute, or until fat rises to top, then skim off.

6. Carve meats; combine with broth and vegetables in a heated tureen.

Dieter's Portion: ¼ of recipe—380 calories.

STREAMLINED CHINESE CHICKEN

Meal-in-one teams white meat with pineapple and vegetables.

Makes 6 servings.

3 whole chicken breasts (about 2½ pounds)
3 tablespoons soy sauce
1 tablespoon salad oil or peanut oil
1 can (1 pint, 2 ounces) unsweetened pineapple juice
4 tablespoons cornstarch
1 can (8 ounces) diet-pack pineapple chunks
2 cans (3 or 4 ounces each) sliced mushrooms
½ teaspoon salt
1 package (10 ounces) frozen peas, thawed
6 cups shredded Chinese cabbage (about 1 head)
3 cups cooked hot rice

1. Remove skin and bones from chicken breasts; slice meat into long thin strips.

2. Place soy sauce in pie plate; dip chicken strips into sauce; brown quickly in salad oil or peanut oil in large frying pan.

3. Stir just enough unsweetened pineapple juice into cornstarch in cup to make a smooth paste; save for Step 5.

4. Stir remaining pineapple juice, and pineapple chunks and mushrooms with liquid into chicken in pan; heat to boiling.

5. Stir in cornstarch mixture and salt; cook, stirring constantly, until sauce boils 3 minutes. Cover; simmer 15 minutes.

6. Stir in peas; arrange cabbage on top. Cover; cook 8 minutes, or until peas and cabbage are tender. Serve over cooked hot rice.

Dieter's portion: 1 cup chicken mixture and ½ cup rice—398 calories.

SWEET-AND-SOUR CHICKEN

The Oriental way to diet . . . delicious.

Makes 4 servings.

2 whole chicken breasts (about 12 ounces each)
3 tablespoons teriyaki sauce or soy sauce
1 tablespoon vegetable oil
2 medium-size yellow squash, trimmed and sliced
1 package (9 ounces) frozen cut green beans, thawed
2 cups water
2 tablespoons lemon juice
1 can (8½ ounces) diet-pack pineapple tidbits
2 tablespoons cornstarch
1 can (6 ounces) water chestnuts, sliced
Granulated or liquid low-calorie sweetener

1. Pull skin from chicken breasts, cut meat from bones; cut into thin strips.

2. Marinate chicken with teriyaki sauce or soy sauce in a bowl for 15 minutes.

3. Heat oil in a large skillet; remove chicken from sauce; brown quickly in hot oil. Add yellow squash and green beans. Sauté, stirring gently, 3 minutes, or just until shiny-moist. Add remaining teriyaki sauce or soy sauce, water, lemon juice; cover; steam 5 minutes.

4. While vegetables steam, drain liquid from pineapple into small cup; stir in cornstarch to make a smooth paste.

5. Add pineapple tidbits and sliced water chestnuts to skillet; heat just to boiling. Stir in cornstarch mixture; cook, stirring constantly, until mixture thickens and bubbles 3 minutes. Stir in your favorite low-calorie sweetener, using the equivalent of 1 tablespoon sugar. Serve with Chinese noodles, if you wish (70 calories per ⅓ cup).

Dieter's Portion: ½ chicken breast and ¼ of all other ingredients—306 calories.

BARBECUE CHICKEN

Broiled chicken with a flavorful basting sauce.

Makes 4 servings.

1 broiler-fryer (2½ pounds), cut up
1 can (about 5 ounces) tomato juice (¾ cup)
1 small onion, grated (¼ cup)
2 tablespoons tarragon vinegar
1 tablespoon prepared mustard
1 tablespoon Worcestershire sauce
½ teaspoon salt
¼ teaspoon pepper
Granulated or liquid low-calorie sweetener

1. Preheat broiler.
2. Place chicken, skin side down, in a single layer on rack in broiler pan.
3. Combine tomato juice, onion, vinegar, mustard, Worcestershire sauce, salt, pepper and your favorite low-calorie sweetener, using the equivalent of 1 tablespoon sugar, in a small bowl. Brush some over chicken.
4. Place broiler pan about 8 inches from heat. Broil, basting often with sauce, 20 minutes; turn skin side up. Continue broiling, basting often with sauce, 20 minutes longer, or until chicken is richly browned and tender.
5. Serve with cooked rice, if you wish (92 calories per ½ cup serving).

Dieter's Portion: ¼ of chicken—259 calories.

CALICO CHICKEN FRICASSEE

Simmered chicken with a creamy gravy.

Makes 4 servings.

1 broiler-fryer (2 pounds), cut up
1 pound carrots, diagonally cut
   (about 2 cups)
1 large onion, chopped (1 cup)
1 cup thin-sliced celery
1 cup hot water
1 envelope instant chicken broth OR
   1 teaspoon granulated chicken bouillon
2 teaspoon salt
1 teaspoon leaf sage, crumbled
1 cup frozen peas (from plastic bag)
2 tablespoons flour
½ cup skim milk
2 tablespoons chopped parsley

1. Place chicken pieces skin side down in a large skillet over *very low* heat. (Do not add fat.) Cook until chicken is a rich brown on skin side, about 10 minutes; turn and brown on other side.
2. Add carrots, onion and celery to skillet; toss to coat with drippings from chicken. Cook and stir 10 minutes.
3. Add hot water, instant chicken broth, salt and sage; mix well; return chicken; cover; simmer 10 minutes; add peas, simmer another 10 minutes, or until chicken and vegetables are tender. Remove chicken; keep warm.
4. Mix flour and skim milk to a smooth paste in a small bowl; stir into vegetables; heat to bubbling, stirring constantly. Cook 1 minute, or until thickened and bubbly. Stir in parsley; spoon onto serving dish; top with chicken.

Dieter's Portion: ¼ of chicken—306 calories.

SLIM-JIM HAWAIIAN CHICKEN

Cooked to a turn in a zippy soy-and-onion sauce. No fat needed.

Bake at 350° for 1½ hours.
Makes 6 servings.

3 small broiler-fryers (about 1½ pounds
   each)
1 small onion, chopped (¼ cup)
¼ cup soy sauce
1½ cups water
6 slices diet-pack pineapple (from a
   1-pound, 4-ounce can)
2 tablespoons chopped parsley

1. Arrange split chickens, skin side down, in a large shallow baking pan. Mix onion, soy sauce and water in a small bowl; pour over chicken.
2. Bake in moderate oven (350°) 45 minutes; turn chicken; bake, basting several times with soy mixture in pan, 45 minutes longer, or until brown and tender.
3. Drain pineapple slices well on paper toweling; roll edge of each in chopped parsley. Serve with chicken.

Dieter's portion: 1 chicken half with 1 pineapple slice—287 calories.

DEVILED CHICKEN

Onion and mustard make this a tangy way to diet.

Makes 4 servings.

2 chicken breasts (about 14 ounces each), halved
½ teaspoon salt
¼ teaspoon paprika
1 medium-size onion, peeled and sliced
1 can (about 2 ounces) deviled ham
2 tablespoons dry white wine
½ teaspoon prepared mustard

1. Wash chicken; dry well. Place, skin side down, in a single layer in a large frying pan; sprinkle with salt and paprika. Place onion slices on top; cover tightly. (No need to add any water.)
2. Cook over low heat 30 minutes. Push onion to side of pan; turn chicken.
3. Blend deviled ham, wine and mustard in a cup; spoon over chicken; cover.
4. Cook 20 minutes longer, or until chicken is tender. Place on a heated serving platter; spoon onion and remaining liquid in pan over top.

Dieter's Portion: ½ chicken breast and ¼ of the sauce and onion—240 calories.

ORANGE CHICKEN

A taste of honey . . . and much more.

Bake at 375° for 50 minutes.
Makes 4 servings.

4 chicken legs with thighs (about 8 ounces each)
1 teaspoon salt
¼ teaspoon pepper
¼ cup orange juice
1 tablespoon honey
1 teaspoon Worcestershire sauce
¼ teaspoon dry mustard

1. Place chicken, skin side up, in a single layer in a shallow baking pan; sprinkle with salt and pepper.
2. Bake in moderate oven (375°) 30 minutes.
3. Blend orange juice, honey, Worcestershire sauce and mustard in a cup; brush part over chicken.

4. Continue baking, brushing again with remaining orange mixture, 20 minutes, or until chicken is tender and richly glazed.

Dieter's Portion: 1 chicken leg with thigh—216 calories.

OVEN-BAKED "SOUTHERN FRIED" CHICKEN

Crisp and crunchy-perfect chicken every time, thanks to an inexpensive easy-do "convenience mix" you make yourself and keep in the pantry to use as needed.

Makes 6 servings.

½ cup "Skinny Shake" (recipe follows)
2 broiler-fryers (about 2½ pounds each), cut up

1. Measure out ½ cup of "Skinny Shake" mix and put it in a heavy paper bag. Moisten the pieces of chicken with water and shake them up in the bag, a few pieces at a time.
2. Arrange chicken, skin side up, in a single layer on a non-stick baking pan and bake in a moderate oven (375°) about 45 minutes, adding absolutely no other fats or oils. Don't be alarmed if the chicken seems dry for the first 20 minutes; then the "Skinny Shake" starts to work, and at the end of the baking period, it will be crisp and perfect.

BASIC "SKINNY SHAKE" (recipe makes enough to coat about 20 cut-up chickens or about 30 servings of fish fillets): Empty one 16-ounce container (about 4 cupfuls, dry measure) of bread crumbs into a deep bowl and stir in ½ cupful of vegetable oil with a fork or pastry blender until evenly distributed. Add 1 tablespoon salt, 1 tablespoon paprika, 1 tablespoon celery salt and 1 teaspoon pepper. This is a good seasoning for chicken, fish or chops. Or season it to suit yourself: Onion or garlic powder, sesame or poppy seeds, dried herbs, lemon pepper . . . use your imagination!

Dieter's Portion: 1/6 of the chicken—244 calories.

COQ AU VIN (Chicken With Wine)

This is Family Circle's method of frying chicken without fat, and using the natural fat from the chicken (calories already counted) to sauté vegetables.

Bake at 350° for 30 minutes.
Makes 4 servings.

1 broiler-fryer (2½ pounds), cut up
1 large onion, chopped (1 cup)
1 clove of garlic, minced
1¾ cups water
½ cup dry red wine
1 teaspoon salt
1 teaspoon leaf tarragon, crumbled
1 bay leaf
½ pound small white onions, peeled
2 envelopes instant beef broth or 2 teaspoons
    granulated beef bouillon
1 pound fresh mushrooms
2 tablespoons flour

1. Place chicken pieces, skin side down, in a large skillet over *very low* heat. (Do not add fat.) Cook slowly until skin side is a rich brown, about 10 minutes; turn and brown other side.
2. Remove chicken from skillet with tongs and place in an 8-cup casserole. Remove 2 tablespoons of the chicken drippings from skillet.
3. Sauté chopped onion and garlic slowly, until soft, in remaining drippings in skillet; stir in 1 cup of the water, red wine, salt, tarragon and bay leaf. Heat to boiling. Pour over chicken in casserole; cover.
4. Bake in a moderate oven (350°) for 30 minutes, or until the chicken is tender.
5. While chicken bakes, return reserved chicken drippings to skillet; brown peeled onions slowly. Leave 6 of the mushrooms whole, for garnish; halve remainder; add all to skillet. Toss to coat with pan drippings.
6. Add instant beef broth and ½ cup boiling water to skillet; cover. Simmer 5 minutes. Remove mushrooms with a slotted spoon and reserve. Continue cooking onions, 15 minutes, or until tender and broth has evaporated, leaving a rich brown residue. (Watch carefully lest they scorch.)

7. Place cooked chicken, mushrooms and onions in a heated serving dish. Remove bay leaf. Pour liquid from casserole into skillet. Heat to boiling. Blend flour with ¼ cup cold water to make a smooth paste. Stir flour mixture into boiling liquid in skillet. Continue cooking and stirring until mixture thickens and bubbles 1 minute. Pour over chicken and vegetables. Garnish chicken with whole mushrooms and chopped parsley, if you wish.

Dieter's Portion: ¼ of broiler-fryer—339 calories.

SLICK CHICK

Each dieter rates a half golden-glazed chicken plus spicy apple stuffing in this too-good-to-be-true roast.

Roast at 375° for 1½ hours.
Makes 4 servings.

2 small whole broiler-fryers (about 1½
    pounds each)
1½ teaspoons salt
1 large onion, chopped (1 cup)
¼ cup water
¼ teaspoon ground coriander
¼ teaspoon curry powder
3 medium-size apples, pared, quartered,
    cored and chopped
Granulated or liquid no-calorie sweetener
1 teaspoon paprika
½ cup chicken broth

1. Rinse chickens inside and out with cold water; drain, then pat dry. Sprinkle insides with ½ teaspoon of the salt.
2. Simmer onion in water in a medium-size frying pan 5 minutes, or until soft; stir in coriander, curry powder, apples, another ½ teaspoon of the salt and your favorite no-calorie sweetener, using the equivalent of 1 teaspoon sugar.
3. Cook, stirring often, over medium heat 10 minutes, or until apples are slightly soft. Remove from heat.
4. Stuff neck and body cavities of chickens lightly with apple mixture. Smooth neck skin over stuffing and skewer to back; tie legs to tail with string. Place chickens, side by side, in a roasting pan.
5. Mix remaining ½ teaspoon salt and paprika in cup; sprinkle over chickens.

6. Roast in moderate oven (375°), basting several times with chicken broth, 1½ hours or until drumsticks move easily and meaty part of a thigh feels soft. (If you want to garnish chickens with onions, thread wedges of peeled onion onto dampened wooden picks and insert into chickens for last half hour of cooking time.)
7. Remove chickens to a heated serving platter; cut away strings and remove skewers. Garnish platter with parsley and a few thin apple slices, if you wish. Cut chickens in half, divide stuffing evenly.

Dieter's portion: ½ **chicken plus half of stuffing from 1 chicken—421 calories. (Crash dieters can omit the stuffing.)**

NO-FAT FRY WITH ONIONS

This magic chicken cooks golden brown with no fat, no turning.

Makes 4 servings.

1 broiler-fryer (about 2 pounds), cut in
    serving-size pieces
1 teaspoon salt
⅛ teaspoon pepper
2 large onions, sliced
½ cup water

1. Place chicken, skin side down, in a single layer in a large frying pan.
2. Sprinkle with salt and pepper; place onion slices on top; cover tightly. (No need to add any fat.)
3. Cook over low heat 30 minutes. Tilt lid slightly so liquid will evaporate; continue cooking 20 minutes longer, or until chicken is tender and golden.
4. Place chicken on a heated serving platter, pushing onions back into pan; stir in water, mixing with browned bits from bottom of pan; cook until liquid evaporates. Spoon over chicken.

Dieter's portion: ¼ **of the chicken and about** ¼ **cup onions—221 calories.**

PEACHY LOW-CALORIE CHICKEN

Chicken pieces baked with fruit and a seasoned glaze that add almost no calories.

Bake at 400° about 1 hour.
Makes 6 servings.

3 whole chicken breasts, split
3 chicken drumsticks
3 chicken thighs
1 can (about 1 pound) diet-pack cling
    peach halves
2 tablespoons lemon juice
1 teaspoon soy sauce

1. Arrange chicken pieces in a single layer in shallow baking dish, 12x8x2.
2. Drain peach syrup into a cup (save halves for Step 3). Add lemon juice and soy sauce to syrup; brush about half over chicken.
3. Bake in hot oven (400°), brushing every 15 minutes with remaining peach syrup mixture and pan juices, 1 hour, or until chicken is tender and richly browned. Place peach halves around chicken; brush with pan juices; bake 5 minutes longer to heat peaches.

Dieter's portion: ½ **chicken breast, 1 drumstick or thigh, and** ½ **peach—210 calories.**

CHICKEN TERIYAKI

An inexpensive calorie-counter's delight.

Makes 6 servings.

6 chicken breasts (about 6 ounces each), split
½ cup lemon juice
¼ cup water
3 tablespoons soy sauce
¼ teaspoon ground ginger
1 teaspoon garlic salt

1. Marinate chicken breasts in sauce made by combining all other ingredients. After several hours, remove chicken from marinade; reserve marinade.
2. Barbecue chicken about 30 minutes, or until tender, on the hibachi or under your broiler; baste frequently with marinade.

Dieter's Portion: 1 breast—159 calories.

In previous chapters we offer you recipes for some great chicken dishes. Some include recipes for special gravies, sauces and glazes. Others ask you to turn to this chapter for a particular recipe. However, don't be misled. The recipes here are not designed to complement only one chicken dish from another chapter. They're also meant to be used inventively anytime you bake or roast a chicken. As you'll see, they're easy to make... contrary to what many people think when it comes to gravies, sauces and glazes. The next time you're thinking chicken, take a look at the recipes in this chapter first. They may change your mind about serving that chicken plain.

Gravies, Sauces, Glazes

BROWN GRAVY

Makes 1 cup.

	Thick	Thin
Fat (from pan meat was cooked in)	2 tbls.	1 tbls.
Flour	2 tbls.	1 tbls.
Liquid from cooked meat plus water or stock, if needed	1 cup	1 cup
Salt and pepper	to taste	to taste

1. Pour all liquid from pan into measuring cup; skim off fat; return to pan measured amount of fat needed; save liquid.
2. Blend flour and fat in pan.
3. Place pan over low heat; stir, scraping bottom of pan to loosen meat pieces, until fat-flour mixture is richly browned.
4. Remove from heat; stir in liquid.
5. Cook over low heat, stirring constantly, until gravy thickens and boils 1 minute.
6. Season to taste; color with bottled gravy coloring, if you wish; strain.

CREAM GRAVY

Makes 2 cups.

Melt 2 tablespoons chicken fat, butter or margarine in small saucepan; remove from heat. Blend in 2 tablespoons flour; stir in 1 cup light cream and 1 cup chicken broth. Cook until gravy thickens and boils 1 minute.

MILK GRAVY

Makes 2 cups.

2 tablespoons butter or margarine
2 tablespoons flour
1 cup milk
1 teaspoon meat-extract paste dissolved in 1 cup hot water
Salt and pepper

1. Melt butter or margarine in small saucepan; remove from heat.
2. Blend in flour; stir in milk and meat-extract paste dissolved in hot water.
3. Cook, stirring constantly, until mixture thickens and boils 1 minute; season to taste.

PAN GRAVY

Makes 1¼ cups.

Blend 2 tablespoons drippings from chicken with 2 tablespoons flour, 1 tablespoon brown sugar, and ½ teaspoon salt; stir in 1¼ cups water. Cook until gravy boils 1 minute.

QUICK CREAM GRAVY

Makes about 1½ cups.

Blend ¼ cup evaporated milk into 1 can (10 ounces) chicken gravy in small saucepan. Heat slowly, until bubbly-hot and smooth.

CREAM GIBLET GRAVY

Makes about 2½ cups.

Chicken giblets, back and neck
1½ cups plus 2 tablespoons water
1 small onion, sliced
2 tablespoons flour
1 cup evaporated milk
Salt and pepper

1. Combine giblets (except liver), back, neck, 1½ cups water and onion in pan; cover.
2. Simmer 1 hour. Add liver last 20 minutes.
3. Remove giblets and chicken pieces (reserve broth); cool; dice; save for Step 5.
4. Strain broth, adding water if needed to make 1 cup. Remove broth to saucepan; stir in flour blended with 2 tablespoons water.
5. Cook over low heat, until gravy boils 1 minute; stir in milk and chopped giblets and chicken; season with salt and pepper.

BARBECUE SAUCE

Makes 2½ cups.

2 cans (8 ounces each) tomato sauce
1 medium-size onion, chopped (½ cup)
1 clove garlic, minced
¼ cup soy sauce
2 tablespoons sugar
1 teaspoon dry mustard
⅛ teaspoon cayenne pepper

Mix all ingredients in a medium-size bowl.

PLUM SAUCE

Makes about 1 cup.

1 cup plum jam
1 tablespoon cider vinegar
1 teaspoon grated onion
½ teaspoon ground allspice
¼ teaspoon ground ginger

Combine all ingredients in a saucepan; heat slowly, stirring constantly, to boiling. Cool.

HAWAIIAN BARBECUE SAUCE

Makes 1¾ cups.

1 cup pineapple juice
¼ cup soy sauce
¼ cup vinegar
¼ cup salad oil
½ teaspoon ground ginger
1 tablespoon sugar

1. Combine ingredients well.
2. Brush on broiler-fryer halves or quarters frequently until they are done.

MORNAY SAUCE

Makes about 1¼ cups.

2 tablespoons butter or margarine
2 tablespoons flour
½ teaspoon salt
⅛ teaspoon pepper
½ cup milk
½ cup chicken stock
¾ cup grated sharp Cheddar cheese
½ teaspoon prepared mustard
½ teaspoon Worcestershire sauce
1 tablespoon chopped parsley

1. Melt butter or margarine in small saucepan; remove from heat.
2. Blend in flour, salt and pepper; stir in milk and chicken stock.
3. Cook over low heat, stirring constantly, until sauce thickens and boils 1 minute.
4. Add cheese, mustard and Worcestershire sauce; continue cooking, stirring occasionally, until cheese melts; remove from heat.
5. Stir in parsley. Serve hot.

DARK CHERRY SAUCE

Makes about 2 cups.

1 can (1 pound) pitted dark sweet cherries
2 tablespoons cornstarch
1 tablespoon prepared mustard
1 tablespoon molasses
Few drops red-pepper seasoning
Dash of salt
3 tablespoons lemon juice

1. Drain syrup from cherries into a 2-cup measure; add water to make 1½ cups.
2. Blend a few tablespoons syrup into cornstarch until smooth in a small saucepan; stir in remaining syrup, mustard, molasses, red-pepper seasoning and salt. Cook over low heat, stirring constantly, until mixture thickens and boils 3 minutes.
3. Stir in cherries and lemon juice; heat slowly just until bubbly. Serve hot.

DOUBLE ORANGE GLAZE

Makes about ¾ cup.

Combine ½ cup thawed frozen concentrated orange juice (from a 6-ounce can), ¼ cup orange marmalade and 2 tablespoons bottled meat sauce in a small saucepan. Heat slowly, stirring constantly, until marmalade melts and mixture is blended; remove from heat.

GOLDEN PINEAPPLE GLAZE

Makes about ¾ cup.

Combine ¼ cup pineapple syrup, ¼ cup orange juice, 2 tablespoons bottled meat sauce, 1 tablespoon melted butter.

GINGER-HONEY GLAZE

Makes about ¾ cup.

Combine ½ cup soy sauce, 6 tablespoons honey and 2 teaspoons ground ginger in small saucepan. Heat, stirring constantly, just to boiling.

3

FISH FOR ECONOMY

All too often fish is considered a meat substitute rather than a permanent part of the weekly menu. This chapter is designed to change all that. First, we tackle the one area that makes many people shy away from this delectable food, the question of how to buy fish—how much, what kind and in what form. On the following pages you'll find numerous suggestions along these lines, plus a page of drawings that shows you the most common market forms of fish. Then it's on to the recipes and, since fish adapts so beautifully to all kinds of seasonings, the possibilities here are almost endless. As for cooking, here, too, fish is adaptable. It's great fried, broiled, baked, poached or steamed. What more could you ask when, on top of all these merits, fish is also a money-saver!

WHAT TO LOOK FOR WHEN YOU BUY FRESH FISH

Fresh fish, like many other foods, is less costly at certain times of the year—depending on the variety of fish you're buying and the area you live in. Ask at your local market which fish are in season now and which are the best buys.

• Fresh fish may be purchased whole, dressed, in steaks, fillets or chunks (see page 49). When you buy it either whole or dressed, look for the following characteristics: Firm flesh; fresh and mild odor; bright, clear, full eyes (not cloudy, pink or sunken); red gills, free of slime; shiny skin with the color unfaded.

• Fillets, steaks and chunks should have firm textured flesh and a fresh, mild odor.

FROZEN FISH

May be bought by the pound whole, dressed, in steaks, fillets, chunks, portions and sticks. Throughout the year you'll see numerous varieties available.

• Look for the following characteristics as a guide to buying frozen fish of good quality: The flesh should be solidly frozen when you buy it and should not be discolored or have any freezer burn. It should have little or no odor.

• Keep frozen (at 0°) until ready to use. Store in its original wrapper. Follow label directions for thawing and cooking.

CANNED FISH

Comes in a wide variety of styles and often offers an economical alternative to fresh or frozen fish. Tuna, salmon, mackerel and sardines are the most abundant kinds of canned fish. Look for the following, all of the same quality, but at varying prices:

• Tuna, Fancy or Solid: A good choice for recipes where appearance is important, such as cold platters, this type of tuna is also the most expensive of tuna packs. Each can contains 3 or 4 large pieces packed in oil or water.

• Chunk-Style Tuna, unlike fancy, is cut into convenient-size pieces. It is more moderately priced than fancy and is good for salads.

• Flaked or grated tuna, excellent for sandwiches or dishes where appearance doesn't matter, is usually lower in price than fancy or chunk-style and offers the same nutritional qualities.

• Salmon is available in the following grades, listed in descending order according to price—red or sockeye; chinook or king salmon; medium-red, coho or silver salmon; pink salmon; and chum or keta salmon. The higher priced varieties are deeper red in color and have a higher oil content.

• Mackerel and Maine sardines are available in 15-ounce cans and 3¾ or 4-ounce cans repectively. Both offer economy.

STORAGE

• Fresh fish will keep in the refrigerator (at 35° to 40°) for one to two days before cooking.

• Frozen raw fish can be kept in the freezer (at 0°) in its original wrapper, up to six months.

• Cooked fish products can be stored in the refrigerator for three to four days and in the freezer for about three months.

• Canned fish should be stored in a cool, dry place for no more than a year.

GOOD FISH BUYS

Consider the less expensive kinds of fish: Turbot, cod, red snapper, pollock, flounder and haddock—instead of trout, halibut and sole. Also, whiting and ocean perch offer good value.

• Buy frozen fish rather than fresh, unless you live in a fishing area where prices of fresh fish are extremely good. And if you're willing to fillet any fish, you'll save about 50 percent.

• Remember that all white meat fillets can be interchanged in recipes if breaded, rolled, stuffed or topped with sauce. So choose the least expensive for such recipes.

HOW MUCH TO BUY PER SERVING

As a general guide, keep these amounts in mind when purchasing fish:

Whole	3/4 to 1 pound
Dressed or Pan-Dressed	1/2 pound
Fillets or Steaks	1/3 pound
Sticks	1/4 pound
Portions	1/3 pound
Canned	1/6 pound

TUNA SHORTCAKE

2 tablespoons butter or margarine
½ cup chopped green pepper
1 can condensed cream of mushroom soup
½ cup dairy sour cream
2 cans (7 ounces each) tuna, drained and flaked
¼ cup chopped stuffed olives
¼ teaspoon leaf basil, crumbled
2 teaspoon instant minced onion
2 cups all-purpose buttermilk biscuit mix
4 slices process American cheese (from an 8-ounce package)

1. Melt butter or margarine in a medium-size saucepan; sauté green pepper until tender, about 5 minutes. Add soup, sour cream, tuna, olives and basil. Heat just until hot; do not allow to boil.
2. Add onion to biscuit mix, then prepare mix, following label directions for biscuits. Spoon evenly into a greased 8-inch cake pan.
3. Bake in hot oven (400°) 15 minutes, or until golden. Loosen around edge with knife; turn out onto serving dish; split in half. Place cheese slices on cut surface of bottom half; spoon half the tuna mixture over the cheese; put top half in place; spoon remaining mixture over. Serve hot. Makes 6 servings.

TUNA FLORENTINE

6 tablespoons (¾ stick) butter or margarine
1 medium-size onion, chopped (½ cup)
¼ cup flour
½ teaspoon salt
  Dash nutmeg
2 cups milk
1 package (6 ounces) process Gruyère cheese, shredded
2 cans (7 ounces each) tuna, drained and flaked
2 packages (10 ounces each) frozen chopped spinach, thawed and drained
½ cup fine dry bread crumbs
¼ cup grated Parmesan cheese

1. Melt butter or margarine in a medium-size saucepan; sauté onion just until soft; stir in flour, salt and nutmeg; cook, stirring constantly, just until bubbly. Stir in milk; continue cooking and stirring until sauce thickens and bubbles 1 minute; remove from heat. Stir in shredded cheese, just until melted; add tuna.
2. Place spinach in the bottom of a lightly greased 6-cup baking dish; spoon tuna-cheese mixture over the top; top with crumbs and Parmesan cheese.
3. Bake in moderate oven (350°) 25 minutes, or until golden. Makes 8 servings.

COD PROVENCALE

1 large onion, chopped (1 cup)
1 clove of garlic, minced
3 tablespoons olive oil or vegetable oil
2 large ripe tomatoes
1 teaspoon salt
1 teaspoons leaf thyme, crumbled
¼ teaspoon pepper
1 package (1 pound) frozen cod fillets (not thawed)
  Boiled potatoes
  Cucumber slices
  Chopped parsley

1. Sauté onion and garlic in olive oil or vegetable oil until soft in a large skillet with a cover.
2. Peel, core and chop tomatoes; stir into onion mixture and cook 2 minutes; add salt, thyme and pepper.
3. Place frozen fish block in the sauce in skillet, spooning part of the sauce over fish; cover skillet.
4. Simmer 20 minutes, or until fish flakes easily with a fork. Transfer fish with a wide spatula to a heated serving platter; spoon sauce over and around fish. Surround with boiled potatoes and cucumber slices; garnish with chopped parsley. Makes 4 servings.

SALMON FLORENTINE

1 package (about 10 ounces) spinach
1 can (1 pound) pink salmon
3 tablespoons butter or margarine
3 tablespoons flour
½ teaspoon salt
½ teaspoon dillweed
1½ cups milk
1 egg, beaten
2 tablespoons lemon juice

1. Trim stems and any coarse leaves from spinach. Wash leaves well; place in a large saucepan; cover. (There's no need to add any water.)
2. Cook 1 minute over low heat, or just until spinach wilts; drain well; chop.
3. Drain salmon; remove skin and bones; break into small pieces.
4. Melt butter or margarine in a small saucepan; stir in flour, salt and dillweed. Cook, stirring constantly, just until bubbly. Stir in milk; continue cooking and stirring until sauce thickens and bubbles 1 minute. Stir half of hot mixture into beaten egg in a small bowl; return to saucepan; cook, stirring constantly, 1 minute, or until sauce thickens again. Stir in lemon juice.
5. Fold 1 cup of the hot sauce into salmon. Line 4 scallop shells or 4 individual foil baking dishes with chopped spinach. Spoon salmon mixture onto center of spinach. Spoon remaining hot sauce over salmon.
6. Broil, about 4 inches from heat, 3 minutes, or until tops are light brown and bubbly. Garnish with a slice of lemon and a sprig of parsley, if you wish. Makes 4 servings.

TUNA-POTATO PIE

1 package piecrust mix
3 medium-size potatoes
2 large onions
1 can (about 7 ounces) tuna
6 tablespoons (¾ stick) butter or margarine
1½ teaspoons salt
¼ teaspoon pepper
3 tablespoons chopped parsley
Milk

1. Prepare piecrust mix, following label directions, or make pastry from your favorite two-crust recipe. Roll out half the pastry to a 12-inch round on a lightly floured pastry cloth or board; fit into a 9-inch pie plate; trim overhang to ½ inch.
2. Pare potatoes and cut into very thin slices; peel onions and cut into thin slices; drain and flake tuna.
3. Layer potatoes, onions and tuna in shell, dotting each layer with part of the butter or margarine and sprinkling with part of the salt, pepper and parsley.
4. Roll out remaining pastry to an 11-inch round; cut slits near center to let steam escape;

cover pie. Trim overhang to ½ inch; turn edges under, flush with rim; flute to make a stand-up edge. Brush pastry with milk. Sprinkle with sesame seeds, if you wish.
5. Bake in moderate oven (375°) 55 minutes, or until potatoes are tender and pastry is golden. Cool at least 10 minutes before serving. Makes 6 servings.

FISHERMAN'S STEW

1 can (1 pound) small white potatoes, drained and diced
1 cup thinly sliced celery
2 tablespoons butter or margarine
2 cans frozen condensed oyster stew, thawed
2 cans (about 7 ounces each) tuna, drained and flaked coarsely
1 can (about 1 pound) green peas
3 cups milk
2 tablespoons instant minced onion
1 teaspoon salt
Few drops red-pepper seasoning
2 tablespoons chopped parsley

1. Sauté potatoes and celery lightly in butter or margarine in a heavy kettle.
2. Stir in oyster stew, tuna, peas and liquid, milk, instant onion, salt and pepper seasoning.
3. Heat very slowly, stirring several times, just to boiling. Ladle into heated soup bowls; sprinkle with parsley. Makes 6 servings.

BAVARIAN SMELTS

2 pounds smelts, fresh or frozen (not the breaded kind)
1 bottle or can (12 ounces) beer
Fat for frying
1 cup flour
1 teaspoon salt
¼ teaspoon pepper
Lemon wedges

1. Split, clean and remove heads from fresh smelts, or thaw frozen smelts. Pour beer over smelts in a large bowl; cover with transparent wrap; chill at least 1 hour.
2. Melt enough shortening, or pour in enough oil, to make a 1-inch depth in a skillet; heat to 375° on deep-fat thermometer. (To page 125.)

Fresh and frozen fish are sold in a variety of forms or cuts. Following is a rundown on the best known market forms, with tips on what you (or your market) need to do before the fish are ready for cooking. Suggestions for methods of cooking are also included.

1. WHOLE, FRESH: Just as the fish comes from the water. Before cooking, have the fish scaled and remove entrails. Then use whole or cut into fillets, steaks or chunks and bake, poach, broil, fry or steam.

2. DRESSED OR PAN-DRESSED, FRESH OR FROZEN: The entrails, head, tail and fins are already removed and the fish is scaled. Normally the larger varieties of fish are called dressed; the smaller ones, pan-dressed. The pan-dressed fish are ready to cook; the dressed fish may be cooked as is or cut into smaller sizes—fillets, steaks or chunks. Bake, poach, broil, fry or steam.

3. FILLETS, FRESH OR FROZEN: Ready-to-cook, these are the sides of the fish, cut lengthwise away from the backbone. The fillets may or may not be skinless. Bake, poach, broil, fry or steam.

4. BUTTERFLY FILLETS, FRESH OR FROZEN: These are the two sides of the fish cut lengthwise away from the backbone and held together by the uncut flesh and skin of the belly. They are ready to cook (cook same as single fillets).

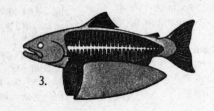

5. STEAKS, FRESH OR FROZEN: Meat cut from a large dressed fish in slices ⅝- to 1-inch thick. The only bone in this cut is a cross-section of the backbone. Steaks are ready to cook as purchased and may be baked, poached, broiled, fried or steamed.

6. FRIED FISH STICKS, FROZEN: Fish sticks are ready to heat-and-serve when you purchase them (either by deep frying or oven frying). They are cut from frozen fish blocks and then coated with a batter, breaded, partially cooked, packaged and frozen. In addition to fish sticks, you may also find that the frozen food section of your market carries fried fish portions and raw frozen fish portions which have been breaded. Both are also cut from frozen fish blocks and are ready to cook or heat-and-serve as directed on the package label.

3. Combine flour, salt and pepper in a pie plate. Remove smelts from beer with a slotted spoon; reserve beer. Roll smelts in seasoned flour; dip again in beer, then again in seasoned flour.

4. Fry smelts, turning once, 5 minutes, or until golden. Lift out with a slotted spoon; drain on paper toweling. Arrange on a heated serving platter or individual plates. Serve immediately with lemon wedges. Makes 6 servings.

ITALIAN FISH STEW

    ½ cup olive oil
    1 clove garlic, chopped
    1 tablespoon leaf basil, crumbled
    1 medium-size onion, chopped (½ cup)
    ½ teaspoon crushed red pepper
    ½ cup dry white wine
    1 can (2 pounds, 3 ounces) Italian tomatoes
    2 tablespoons tomato paste
    1 bottle (8 ounces) clam broth or juice
    2 teaspoons salt
    2 packages (1 pound each) frozen cod fillets, thawed
    1 package (1 pound) frozen haddock fillets, thawed
    1 pound fresh or frozen shrimp, shelled and deveined
    2 tablespoons tubettini or other small pasta
    2 tablespoons finely chopped parsley
    1 tablespoon grated lemon rind

1. Heat oil in a heavy kettle or Dutch oven; sauté garlic, basil, onion and crushed red pepper until onion is tender. Add wine; simmer about 5 minutes, or until liquid is somewhat reduced. Add tomatoes, tomato paste, clam broth and salt; simmer, uncovered, 20 to 30 minutes to thicken sauce.

2. Leave fish fillets in blocks; cut into large pieces. Add fish and shellfish to sauce. Cover; simmer 10 minutes, or until fish is just done (it will look opaque).

3. Remove fish to serving dish; keep warm. Add pasta to sauce. Cover; simmer 10 minutes longer, or until pasta is tender. Pour over fish in serving dish; garnish with chopped parsley and grated lemon rind. Stew may be ladled over slices of Italian bread rubbed with garlic for a heartier dish. Makes 8 servings.

PLANKED FLOUNDER FILLETS

    2 packages (1 pound each) frozen flounder fillets, thawed
    ¼ cup (½ stick) butter or margarine
    2 tablespoons lemon juice
    ½ teaspoon paprika
    Duchess Potatoes (recipe follows)
    1 package (10 ounces) frozen mixed vegetables, cooked, drained, and seasoned
    Buttery Cherry

    Watercress

1. Separate fish fillets carefully; arrange in a single layer on a cooky sheet.

2. Melt butter or margarine in a small saucepan; stir in lemon juice and paprika. Brush part of mixture on fish fillets.

3. Broil fillets about 4 inches from heat for about 5 minutes.

4. Transfer fillets from cooky sheet with wide spatula, layering in the center of a seasoned 15x10-inch plank (see note), or a flameproof platter.

5. Fill a pastry bag with Duchess Potatoes; pipe 6 nests of potatoes around the plank; border plank between nests with remaining potatoes. Brush remaining paprika-butter on fish.

6. Bake in hot oven (400°) 15 minutes, or until potatoes are tipped with golden-brown. At serving time, fill potato nests with seasoned mixed vegetables. Garnish plank with Buttery Cherry Tomatoes and watercress. Makes 6 servings.

NOTE: To season a new plank, rub it well with vegetable oil on top and sides; heat on rack in very slow oven (275°) 1 hour; cool; wipe off any excess oil.

DUCHESS POTATOES

    6 medium-size potatoes, pared
    ⅓ cup milk
    2 eggs
    2 tablespoons butter or margarine
    1 teaspoon salt

1. Cook potatoes in boiling salted water 15 minutes, or until tender in a large saucepan; drain. Return potatoes to pan and shake over low heat until dry and fluffy.

2. Mash potatoes; beat in milk, eggs, butter or

margarine and salt until fluffy-light. Cool. Makes 6 servings.

BUTTERY CHERRY TOMATOES—Remove stems from 1 cup cherry tomatoes. Melt 2 tablespoons butter or margarine in a small skillet. Saute tomatoes over low heat, stirring gently, just until skins burst. Sprinkle with 1 tablespoon chopped parsley. Add to plank containing Planked Flounder Fillets

GOLDEN STUFFED FLOUNDER FILLETS

2 pounds fresh or frozen flounder fillets (6 to 8 pieces)
½ cup (1 stick) butter or margarine
1 cup grated carrot
½ cup finely chopped celery
1 small onion, chopped (¼ cup)
¼ cup chopped parsley
2 cups soft bread crumbs
½ teaspoon salt
¼ teaspoon pepper
¼ teaspoon leaf thyme, crumbled
1 tablespoon butter or margarine
Sauce:
    Milk
2 tablespoons butter or margarine
2 tablespoons all-purpose flour
½ cup grated Swiss cheese
¼ teaspoon salt
⅛ teaspoon pepper

1. Thaw frozen fish fillets; pat dry.
2. Melt the ½ cup butter or margarine in a medium-size skillet. Saute carrot, celery, onion and parsley until tender. Toss with bread crumbs; season with ¼ teaspoon of the salt, ⅛ teaspoon of the pepper and thyme.
3. Sprinkle remaining ¼ teaspoon salt and ⅛ teaspoon pepper over fillets. Spoon stuffing evenly onto centers of fillets; fold over to enclose. Arrange in a buttered shallow 8-cup baking dish; dot with remaining tablespoon of butter or margarine. Cover baking dish tightly with a sheet of foil.
4. Bake in hot oven (400°) 12 minutes, or just until fish is opaque. Remove from oven and keep warm while preparing cheese sauce.
5. Make sauce: Drain liquid from fish into a 2-cup measure. Add milk to make 1¼ cups.
6. Melt butter or margarine in a saucepan; stir in flour. Cook, stirring constantly, until mixture is bubbly; add milk mixture. Cook over medium heat, stirring constantly, until sauce is thickened and bubbly. Add cheese, salt and pepper; stir until cheese is melted. Pour the cheese sauce over fillets in the baking dish.
7. Place dish under broiler 5 minutes, or until sauce is bubbly and lightly browned. Serve immediately, with a side portion of broccoli, if you wish. Makes 8 servings.

POACHED COD, PORTUGUESE STYLE

2 packages (1 pound each) frozen cod
½ cup dry white wine
½ cup water
3 lemon slices
1 teaspoon salt
    Dash pepper
1 tablespoon butter or margarine
3 tablespoons vegetable oil
1 clove garlic, crushed
1 large onion, sliced
2 small green peppers, halved, seeded and cut into strips
2 tomatoes, cut in wedges
½ cup pitted ripe olives
    Chopped parsley

1. Remove fish from freezer; cut each block of fish into 3 pieces with a serrated knife.
2. Combine fish, wine, water, lemon slices, salt and pepper in a large skillet; bring to boiling; lower heat. Simmer, covered, turning pieces once, 20 minutes, or until fish flakes easily when pierced with a fork. Remove fish to heated serving dish with a slotted spoon; keep warm while preparing sauce and vegetables. Remove and discard lemon slices.
3. Reduce cooking liquid by boiling rapidly, uncovered, 10 minutes, until it measures ½ cup. Add butter or margarine; swirl skillet until butter is melted and sauce is slightly thickened; pour over fish.
4. In second skillet, in hot oil, saute garlic and onion, stirring often, 5 minutes; add peppers, saute 10 minutes longer, or just until vegetables are tender. Stir in tomatoes and olives; heat 2 minutes. Arrange vegetables in serving dish with fish. Sprinkle with chopped parsley. Serve with crusty slices of French or Italian bread, if you wish. Makes 6 servings.

4

CASH IN ON CASSEROLES

The casserole is many things to many people. To some it's convenience. To the large family, it's the littlest leftover deliciously stretched into an entire meal. To others, it's a lifesaver when busy schedules force dinner into a holding pattern. And still others love casseroles because they hate pots. Added to these reasons for making casseroles, goes one other—the dollar. Nowhere else can so much economy be found under one lid— and it's economy of the best sort. The big, hearty servings beautifully disguise the fact that you're watching the budget. Our recipe for Meatless Moussaka is an example. This Greek classic, made with eggplant, tomatoes, cheese and tangy seasonings, will feed eight people for under $4. What's more, it's easy-to-make. Try the recipe for this casserole and all the others in this chapter. They're perfect answers to a worried budget.

Careful shopping does pay off. If you save only 5¢ on each meal, you'll save up to $50 by the end of the year. Casseroles offer an easy way to stretch these savings even further. Following are some tips to help you get started.

• Use instant nonfat dry milk whenever a casserole calls for a sauce or gravy with a milk base. It's much less expensive than whole milk, and you'll never know the difference!

• Use tag ends of bread for casserole toppings. Cut sliced bread into tiny cubes or pull apart into crumbs, toss with melted butter or margarine, grated cheese or mixed dry herbs. Then sprinkle on top of your casserole before baking. Another bread idea: Slice French bread very thin, butter slices and place, overlapping, around the rim of the casserole.

• Save bits of dry cereal in a jar, then crush or whirl in a blender for a ready-to-use casserole crumb topper.

• For a quick casserole that still watches the budget, try the following: Heat canned beans in a casserole then top with: crisp bacon or thin slices of ham or Canadian bacon; a sprinkle of grated Parmesan cheese or finely minced onion; paper-thin green-pepper rings; a drizzle of molasses sparked with mustard; heat-and-serve sausage links or thin pork chops.

• For a convenience-food casserole, try this: Start with precooked rice or macaroni, or curried, Spanish or Chinese fried-rice mix. Add one of the following—a can of drained flaked tuna, diced canned luncheon meat or cut-up leftover meat from a roast. Add canned tomato sauce and heat all together in the oven.

• Stir Worcestershire sauce to taste into canned chicken stew; heat to boiling; spoon into a baking dish. Top with a pastry crust flavored with a smidgen of sage. Bake in hot oven (400°) until golden.

• Prepare packaged Spanish-rice mix and place in a baking dish. Arrange canned Vienna sausages on top; sprinkle all generously with grated Cheddar cheese. Bake in hot oven (400°) 20 minutes, or until bubbly hot and cheese melts.

• Leftover meats and vegetables are naturals for casseroles, and they can cut costs dramatically over purchasing special ingredients.

• It's a good idea, therefore, to buy foods with leftovers in mind, to use for casseroles

• Use up leftover sauces and gravies in casseroles, combined with vegetables and meats.

SUBSTITUTIONS

When preparing casseroles from leftovers you may run across a necessary ingredient you don't have. The following chart is designed to help you make-do.

IF YOU DON'T HAVE:	SUBSTITUTE THE FOLLOWING:
1 whole egg	2 egg yolks or 2½ tablespoons sifted dry whole egg powder plus 2½ tablespoons lukewarm water
1 tablespoon flour (for thickening)	½ tablespoon cornstarch or 1 tablespoon granular tapioca or 2 teaspoons quick cooking tapioca or 2 tablespoons of granular cereal
1 cup sifted flour	1 cup unsifted minus 2 tablespoons
1 cup honey	1¼ cups sugar plus ¼ cup liquid*
1 cup corn syrup	1 cup sugar plus ¼ cup liquid*
1 cup milk	½ cup evaporated milk plus ½ cup water or approximately ¼ cup nonfat dry milk plus water to make 1 cup fluid milk or approximately ⅓ cup instant nonfat dry milk plus water to make 1 cup fluid milk
1 medium-size onion, chopped	1 tablespoon instant minced onion, rehydrated

*Use the same liquid called for in the recipe.

CHICKEN IN WALNUT SAUCE

    1 package (8 ounces) regular noodles
    2 broiler-fryers, weighing about 2 pounds each, cut in serving-size pieces
    2 teaspoons salt
    ½ teaspoon leaf rosemary, crumbled
    ¼ teaspoon pepper
    3 tablespoons butter or margarine
    1 medium-size onion, chopped (½ cup)
    4 tablespoons flour
    1¾ cups milk
    ¼ cup dry white wine
    1 can condensed cream of chicken soup
    1 can (4 ounces) walnuts, chopped
      Paprika

1. Cook noodles, following the label directions; drain well. Place in a refrigerator-to-oven baking dish, 13x9x2.
2. Season chicken with 1½ teaspoons of the salt, rosemary and pepper. Brown, part at a time, in butter or margarine in a large frying pan; place in a single layer over noodles.
3. Stir onion into drippings in pan; sauté until soft. Blend in flour; cook, stirring constantly, until bubbly. Stir in milk and wine; continue cooking and stirring until sauce thickens and boils 1 minute. Stir in soup, walnuts and remaining ½ teaspoon salt. Pour over mixture in baking dish. Sprinkle with paprika. Cover; chill.
4. About 1 hour and 15 minutes before serving time, place baking dish, covered, in moderate oven (350°).
5. Bake 1 hour and 15 minutes, or until bubbly and chicken is tender. Makes 8 servings.

CHOW MEIN CASSEROLE

    1 pound chicken breast fillets (boneless)
    2 tablespoons vegetable oil
    3 tablespoons soy sauce
    1 envelope or teaspoon instant chicken broth
    1 cup water
    1 divider pack (43 ounces) mushroom chow mein
    2 cups cooked rice
    1 can (3 ounces) chow mein noodles

1. Cut the chicken meat into strips ¼-inch wide.
2. Heat oil in a medium-size skillet 30 seconds. Add chicken. Stir-fry quickly until chicken turns white, about 5 minutes.
3. Stir in soy sauce, chicken broth, water and can of sauce from chow mein.
4. Drain and rinse can of vegetables; stir into chicken mixture; heat to bubbly-hot.
5. Layer half the cooked rice in buttered 8-cup casserole; add half the hot chicken mixture; repeat layering; sprinkle top with noodles.
6. Bake, uncovered, in hot oven (400°) for 15 minutes, or until bubbly-hot. Serve with additional soy sauce. Makes 4 servings.

BACON AND LIVER CASSEROLE

    6 slices bacon, chopped
    1 large onion, chopped (1 cup)
    ½ cup all-purpose flour
    1 teaspoon salt
      Dash of pepper
    2 pounds sliced beef liver
    2½ cups milk
    ½ cup packaged bread crumbs
    2 tablespoons margarine, melted

1. Combine bacon and onion in a large skillet. Cook until bacon is crisp and onion is tender. Remove with slotted spoon, reserving drippings in skillet.
2. Combine flour, salt and pepper; coat liver. Reserve remaining flour mixture.
3. Fry liver in reserved bacon drippings; cut into serving-size pieces. Place in 8-cup baking dish.
4. Blend reserved flour mixture with drippings in skillet; add milk. Cook over medium heat, stirring constantly, until the sauce thickens and bubbles.
5. Pour sauce over liver; sprinkle with bacon and onion mixture. Combine bread crumbs with margarine; sprinkle evenly over casserole.
6. Bake in moderate oven (350°) for 25 minutes, or until sauce is bubbly. Makes 8 servings.

TONGUE AND RICE CASSEROLE

    ¾ cup uncooked rice
    1 package (10 ounces) frozen peas, cooked and drained
    2 cups cubed, cooked, smoked tongue
    1 can condensed Cheddar cheese soup
    1 cup milk

¼ teaspoon salt
⅛ teaspoon pepper
½ cup packaged croutons

1. Cook rice, following label directions.
2. Combine rice, peas and tongue in a shallow 8-cup baking dish.
3. Blend cheese soup with milk in a medium-size bowl; add salt and pepper. Pour over rice mixture. Toss lightly to mix. Arrange croutons around edge of dish.
4. Bake in a moderate oven (375°) 30 minutes, or until sauce is bubbly and the top is lightly browned. Makes 6 servings.

FAST CHICKEN CREOLE

3 cups hot cooked rice
3 tablespoons butter or margarine
½ cup chopped green pepper
1 medium-size onion, chopped (½ cup)
½ cup thinly sliced celery
1 clove of garlic, mashed
1 can condensed chicken gumbo soup
1 can (1 pound) tomato wedges in tomato juice, drained
1 can (3 or 4 ounces) sliced mushrooms, drained
2 cans (5 ounces each) boned chicken, diced
¼ teaspoon leaf marjoram, crumbled
¼ teaspoon salt
1 package (4 ounces) shredded process American cheese

1. Place cooked rice in a lightly greased 8-cup baking dish.
2. Sauté green pepper, onion, celery and garlic in butter or margarine until tender in a large saucepan. Stir in remaining ingredients, except cheese. Pour mixture over rice, spreading evenly; sprinkle with cheese; cover.
3. Bake in moderate oven (350°) 30 minutes, or until bubbly-hot. Makes 4 servings.

SHEPHERDESS PIE

1 package (8 ounces) heat-and-serve sausage patties
2 tablespoons flour
2 cups water
1 envelope vegetable-beef soup mix

4 cups hot mashed potatoes
½ cup crumbled whole-wheat wafers

1. Cut each sausage patty into about 10 small pieces; brown, stirring frequently, in a medium-size skillet. Blend in flour; cook, stirring constantly, just until bubbly. Stir in water and soup mix; continue cooking and stirring until gravy thickens and boils 5 minutes.
2. Line bottom and sides of a buttered deep 6-cup baking dish with 3 cups of the mashed potatoes. Spoon in sausage and gravy; spoon remaining potatoes in mounds over top; sprinkle with crumbled wafers.
3. Bake in moderate oven (350°) 45 minutes, or until bubbly-hot. Sprinkle with finely chopped parsley, if you wish. Makes 4 servings.

ALSATIAN CASSEROLE OF PORK CHOPS, POTATOES AND ONIONS

6 slices bacon
4 loin pork chops, 1 inch thick
4 large boiling potatoes, pared and thinly sliced
2 medium-size onions, thinly sliced
1 teaspoon salt
¼ teaspoon pepper
1 teaspoon caraway seeds
¾ cup dry white wine
2 cloves garlic, lightly crushed
1 tablespoon chopped parsley

1. Fry 2 slices of the bacon in a large skillet until crisp; crumble and reserve. Trim fat from chops; brown chops in bacon drippings.
2. Arrange half the potatoes in a layer in a deep baking dish or Dutch oven, preferably earthenware or enameled cast iron. Top with half the onions; sprinkle with half the salt and pepper.
3. Place chops over onions, overlapping, to form a single layer. Add remaining potatoes and onions, salt and pepper.
4. Crush caraway seeds; add to baking dish with wine and garlic. Place remaining bacon over top. Cover with a double thickness of foil, then with lid.
5. Roast in slow oven (300°) 2½ hours, or until meat and potatoes are tender. Discard bacon; skim off fat, if necessary. Sprinkle with parsley and crumbled bacon. This is very good with mustard and beer. Makes 4 servings.

CALICO FRANKS

2 packages (8 ounces each) frozen mixed vegetables with onion sauce
1½ cups milk
1 pound frankfurters, sliced
1 cup soft bread crumbs (2 slices)
1 package (4 ounces) shredded Cheddar cheese

1. Combine frozen vegetables with milk in a large saucepan; heat, following label directions. Stir in frankfurters; spoon half into a 6-cup baking dish.
2. Mix bread crumbs and cheese in a small bowl; sprinkle half over layer in baking dish. Top with remaining vegetable mixture, then remaining crumb mixture.
3. Bake in moderate oven (375°) 30 minutes, or until casserole is bubbly in center and crumb topping is golden. Makes 4 servings.

TUNA PUFF

Instant mashed potatoes
Butter or margarine
Salt
Water
Milk
1 can (13 ounces) tuna, drained and flaked
4 eggs, beaten
⅓ cup grated Parmesan cheese
2 tablespoons fine dry bread crumbs
1 envelope white sauce mix
Water
1 tablespoon lemon juice
Dash seafood seasoning

1. Prepare 2 cups instant mashed potatoes with butter or margarine, salt, water and milk, following label directions.
2. Combine potatoes, tuna, eggs and cheese in a large bowl.
3. Butter a 4-cup baking dish, then sprinkle with crumbs. Fill with potato mixture.
4. Bake in moderate oven (350°) 1 hour, or until puffy and golden brown.
5. Prepare white sauce mix in a small bowl, following label directions. Add lemon juice and seafood seasoning, blending well. Serve separately to spoon over tuna puff. Makes 4 servings.

OLD WEST PORK CHOPS

6 pork chops, ¾ inch thick (about 1½ pounds)
3 tablespoons vegetable oil
1 large onion, cut into 6 slices
2 teaspoons chili powder
1 green pepper, chopped
1 cup uncooked regular rice
1 can (8 ounces) tomato sauce
1¼ cups water
2 teaspoons salt

1. Brown chops well on both sides in oil in a skillet; remove.
2. Brown onion slices on both sides in same pan; remove.
3. Stir in chili powder and cook 2 minutes; add green pepper, rice, tomato sauce, water and salt; heat to boiling.
4. Pour into a shallow 8-cup baking dish; arrange browned chops over rice and place an onion slice on each chop; cover dish.
5. Bake in moderate oven (375°) 1 hour, or until liquid is absorbed. Makes 6 servings.

CALIFORNIA TUNA BAKE

8 ounces rotini macaroni, cooked and drained
1 can (7 ounces) tuna, drained and flaked coarsely
1 package (10 ounces) frozen peas, cooked and drained
¼ cup sliced pimiento-stuffed olives
2 tablespoons minced onion
½ teaspoon salt
¼ teaspoon seasoned pepper
1 can condensed cream of mushroom soup
1 package (3 or 4 ounces) cream cheese, cubed

1. Combine macaroni, tuna, peas, olives and onion in a large bowl; toss lightly; sprinkle with salt and seasoned pepper; toss again. Stir in soup until evenly coated; fold in cream-cheese cubes. Spoon mixture into an 8-cup baking dish; cover.
2. Bake in moderate oven (350°) 30 minutes, or until bubbly-hot. Makes 4 servings.
NOTE—You may substitute elbow macaroni, small shells, or ditalini for the rotini, if you wish.

OLD ENGLISH CASSEROLE

8 ounces noodles, cooked and drained
1½ pounds ground beef
1 large-size onion, thinly sliced
1 tablespoon flour
½ teaspoon seasoned salt
¼ teaspoon lemon pepper
1 can (3 or 4 ounces) sliced mushrooms
1 can (1 pound) green beans, drained
1 can (15 ounces) tomato sauce special
1 cup grated Cheddar cheese

1. Place cooked noodles in a lightly greased 8-cup baking dish.
2. Brown beef in a large skillet; remove meat to a bowl; drain all but 1 tablespoon fat from skillet. Sauté onion in fat until tender in skillet; return beef.
3. Blend in flour, seasoned salt and lemon pepper. Stir in sliced mushrooms and liquid, green beans and tomato sauce. Spoon mixture over noodles, spreading evenly; sprinkle with cheese.
4. Bake in moderate oven (350°) 30 minutes, or until bubbly-hot. Makes 6 servings.

CHICKEN RISOTTO

2 tablespoons thinly sliced green onion
1 tablespoon butter or margarine
1 cup chopped celery
1¼ cups packaged precooked rice
1 can condensed cream of chicken soup
1½ cups milk
2 tablespoons soy sauce
1½ cups diced cooked chicken
1 can (3 or 4 ounces) chopped mushrooms, drained
1 can or jar (2 ounces) pimientos, drained and sliced
1 can (3 ounces) chow-mein noodles

1. Sauté onion in butter or margarine until soft in a large frying pan; stir in celery and rice; cook 1 minute longer.
2. Stir in soup, milk, soy sauce, chicken, mushrooms and pimientos; heat to boiling. Spoon into a 7-cup baking dish; cover.
3. Bake in moderate oven (375°) 20 minutes; uncover. Sprinkle noodles over top. Bake 10 minutes longer, or until noodles are hot. Makes 4 servings.

SHRIMPS WITH LEMON RICE

1½ cups uncooked regular rice
2 teaspoons ground turmeric
1 teaspoon mustard seeds
½ cup (1 stick) butter or margarine
½ pound fresh or frozen shrimps, shelled and deveined
2 packages (1 pound each) frozen cod or other white-fleshed fish fillets
1 can or jar (7 ounces) pimientos, drained and diced
1 teaspoon salt
1 cup dry white wine
3 tablespoons lemon juice

1. Cook rice, following label directions.
2. Heat turmeric and mustard seeds in butter or margarine in a large frying pan 2 to 3 minutes. Stir in shrimps; sauté 5 minutes; remove with a slotted spoon and place in a 12-cup refrigerator-to-oven baking dish.
3. Cut frozen fish into chunks; cook, turning once or twice, until fish flakes easily, about 10 minutes. Add to casserole.
4. Stir rice into drippings in pan; heat slowly, stirring constantly, until golden. Stir in pimientos and salt; spoon into baking dish.
5. Mix wine and lemon juice in a cup; stir into rice mixture. Cover; chill.
6. About 1 hour and 15 minutes before serving, place dish, covered, in moderate oven (350°).
7. Bake 1 hour and 15 minutes, or until hot. Makes 8 servings.

TUNA-CHEESE IMPERIAL

1 package (8 ounces) wide noodles
½ cup (1 stick) butter or margarine
5 tablespoons flour
1 teaspoon salt
¼ teaspoon pepper
2½ cups milk
1 package (8 ounces) cream cheese
1 can (about 7 ounces) tuna, drained
½ cup sliced pimiento-stuffed olives
2 tablespoons cut chives
1 package (6 ounces) sliced Muenster cheese
1½ cups bread crumbs (3 slices)

1. Cook noodles, following the label directions; drain and reserve.

2. Melt 5 tablespoons of the butter or margarine in a medium-size saucepan; stir in flour, salt and pepper; cook, stirring constantly, until bubbly. Stir in milk; continue cooking and stirring until sauce thickens and boils 1 minute. Slice cream cheese into sauce; stir until melted, then add tuna, olives and chives; remove from heat.

3. Pour about ¾ cup of the sauce into a greased 10-cup baking dish, then layer other ingredients on top this way: Half of the noodles, half of remaining sauce, 2 slices Muenster cheese, remaining noodles, half of remaining sauce, remaining Muenster cheese and remaining sauce.

4. Melt remaining 3 tablespoons butter or margarine in a small saucepan; add bread crumbs; toss lightly with a fork. Sprinkle over mixture in baking dish.

5. Bake in moderate oven (350°) 30 minutes, or until bubbly. Makes 6 servings.

MEATLESS MOUSSAKA

    2 large eggplants, sliced ½-inch thick but not
      peeled
    2 teaspoons salt
Tomato Sauce:
    3 medium-size onions, peeled and chopped
    1 clove garlic, peeled and crushed
    2 tablespoons olive or vegetable oil
    4 medium-size tomatoes, peeled, cored and
      coarsely chopped (reserve juice)
    ¼ teaspoon leaf rosemary, crumbled
    2 tablespoons minced fresh mint
      OR: 1 tablespoon mint flakes
    2 tablespoons minced parsley
    2 teaspoons sugar
    1 teaspoon salt
    ¼ teaspoon pepper
    1 can (8 ounces) tomato sauce
Cheese Filling:
    1 carton (1 pound) cream-style cottage cheese
    1 egg
    2 tablespoons grated Parmesan cheese
    ⅛ teaspoon leaf rosemary, crumbled
    ⅛ teaspoon mace
    ¼ teaspoon salt
    ⅛ teaspoon pepper
    4 tablespoons olive or vegetable oil
    ⅔ cup grated Parmesan cheese

1. Sprinkle both sides of each eggplant slice with salt; place between several thicknesses of

paper toweling; weight down; let stand 1 hour.

2. Meanwhile, make the Tomato Sauce: Stir-fry onions and garlic in oil in a large, heavy skillet over moderate heat about 8 minutes, until limp and golden. Add tomatoes, their juice and all remaining ingredients except tomato sauce and heat, uncovered, stirring occasionally, until tomatoes begin to release their juices. Cover; lower heat and simmer 1 hour, stirring occasionally; stir in tomato sauce and simmer, uncovered, 15 minutes longer.

3. Prepare Cheese Filling while Tomato Sauce simmers: Mix together all remaining ingredients except the 4 tablespoons oil and ⅔ cup Parmesan cheese; refrigerate until needed.

4. Brush both sides of each eggplant slice lightly with olive or vegetable oil, then broil quickly on each side to brown.

5. To assemble Moussaka, spoon half the Tomato Sauce over the bottom of a 13x9x2-inch baking pan; sprinkle generously with grated Parmesan, then arrange half the browned eggplant slices on top. Spread with cheese filling; sprinkle with Parmesan. Arrange remaining eggplant slices on top; sprinkle with Parmesan. Finally, cover with remaining Tomato Sauce and one last sprinkling of Parmesan.

NOTE: Dish can be prepared up to this point several hours ahead of time and refrigerated until about an hour before serving—in fact, it will be better if it is, because the flavors get together better.

6. Bake, uncovered, 45 to 50 minutes in moderate oven (375°), until bubbling and browned; remove from oven and let stand 15 minutes before cutting into squares. Makes 8 servings.

SWISS-TUNA SCALLOP

    2 cups coarsely crushed saltines
    1 can (1 pound) cream-style corn
    1 can (7 ounces) tuna, drained and flaked
    1 package (8 ounces) Swiss cheese, shredded
    ¼ cup diced pimiento
    1 cup milk
    2 tablespoons butter or margarine
    1 tablespoon minced onion

1. Combine saltines, corn, tuna, cheese and pimiento in a large bowl.

2. Combine milk, butter or margarine, and onion in a small saucepan; heat slowly until

butter melts. Pour over tuna mixture; toss lightly. Spoon into a greased 6-cup baking dish.
3. Bake in moderate oven (350°) 45 minutes, or until bubbly in center. Makes 4 servings.

CORNED BEEF AND POTATO CASSEROLE

1 can (12 ounces) corned beef
1 tablespoon prepared mustard
1 teaspoon caraway seeds, crushed slightly
1 teaspoon salt
⅛ teaspoon pepper
3 tablespoons butter or margarine
1 package (about 5 ounces) hash brown potatoes with onions
1¾ cups boiling water
2 medium-size tomatoes, sliced

1. Chop corned beef coarsely; place in a 6-cup casserole. Add mustard, caraway seeds, salt and pepper; toss to mix well. Dot top with butter or margarine.
2. Stir in potato and onion mix; pour water over; stir with a fork; cover.
3. Bake in moderate oven (375°) 20 minutes, stirring once after 10 minutes. Uncover; stir with a fork; place tomato slices, overlapping, in a ring around edge of casserole. Continue baking 10 minutes, or until potatoes are tender. Makes 4 servings.

HAM AND BROCCOLI ROYALE

1 cup uncooked regular rice
2 packages (10 ounces each) frozen broccoli spears
6 tablespoons (¾ stick) butter or margarine
2 cups fresh bread crumbs (4 slices)
2 large onions, chopped fine (2 cups)
3 tablespoons flour
1 teaspoon salt
¼ teaspoon pepper
3 cups milk
1½ pounds cooked ham, cubed (4 cups)
1 package (8 ounces) sliced process white American cheese

1. Cook rice, following label directions; spoon into a greased refrigerator-to-oven baking dish, 13x9x2.
2. Cook broccoli, following label directions;

drain well. Place in a single layer over the rice in baking dish.
3. Melt butter or margarine in a large frying pan; measure out 2 tablespoonfuls and sprinkle over bread crumbs in a small bowl; set aside.
4. Stir onions into remaining butter in frying pan; sauté until soft. Stir in flour, salt and pepper; cook, stirring constantly, until bubbly. Stir in milk; continue cooking and stirring until sauce thickens and boils 1 minute. Stir in ham; heat again just until bubbly; pour over layers in baking dish.
5. Place cheese slices over sauce; sprinkle buttered bread crumbs over all. Cover; chill.
6. About 45 minutes before serving time, uncover dish; place in moderate oven (350°).
7. Bake 45 minutes, or until bubbly and crumb topping is golden. Makes 8 servings.

TOMATO-CHEESE TART

½ package piecrust mix
1 cup shredded Cheddar cheese
2 packages (6 ounces each) process Gruyère cheese, shredded
3 ripe medium-size tomatoes
1 teaspoon salt
1 teaspoon leaf basil, crumbled
1 teaspoon leaf oregano, crumbled
⅛ teaspoon pepper
½ cup chopped green onions
2 tablespoons butter or margarine
2 tablespoons soft bread crumbs

1. Prepare piecrust mix, following label directions, adding ½ cup of the Cheddar cheese. Roll out to a 12-inch round on a lightly floured pastry board; fit into a 9-inch pie plate. Trim overhang to ½ inch; turn under; flute to make a stand-up edge. Prick well with fork.
2. Bake in hot oven (425°) 10 to 15 minutes, or until golden; cool.
3. Spoon remaining Cheddar cheese and Gruyère into piecrust. Slice tomatoes in half lengthwise and then into thin wedges. Arrange, slightly overlapping, in a circular pattern over the cheese. Sprinkle with salt, pepper, basil and oregano.
4. Sauté green onions in butter or margarine until tender in a small skillet. Spoon in the center of pie; sprinkle with bread crumbs.
5. Bake in moderate oven (325°) 20 minutes, or until tomatoes are tender. Makes 4 servings.

5

PASTA & RICE

They're great meat stretchers, but pasta and rice can also stand on their own. They combine well with so many flavors that an almost endless variety of dinners is possible when you use them. They look festive, too, whether the dish is a simple macaroni and cheese casserole or a more complicated dinner such as Homemade Tiny Ravioli which requires making your own pasta dough. But, like any art, this can be a satisfying experience, particularly if you enjoy puttering in the kitchen. Add a salad and bread and you've got a meal that will satisfy the heftiest appetite and the littlest budget. In addition to the recipes for pasta and rice, we've included some for bean dinners because they, too, offer a great deal for very little. All in all, there are three dozen recipes plus tips on buying, storing and saving even more money on these already economical foods.

CASSOULET

1 pound dried pea beans
6 cups water
1½ teaspoons salt
1 clove garlic, chopped
2 carrots, diced
4 medium-size onions, each studded with 1
    whole clove
1 sprig parsley
1 bay leaf
½ teaspoon leaf thyme, crumbled
3 slices salt pork
2 lamb shanks
1 cup sliced celery
1 can (8 ounces) tomato sauce
½ cup dry white wine
1 Polish ring sausage (Kielbasa)

1. Pick over and wash beans. Put beans and water in a heavy kettle. Bring to boiling; remove from heat. Let stand 1 hour.
2. Add salt, garlic, carrots, onions, parsley, bay leaf, thyme and salt pork to beans. Cover; bring to boiling. Lower heat; simmer 1 hour.
3. Add lamb shanks, celery, tomato sauce, wine and sausage. Simmer 1 hour and 30 minutes longer, or until meats are tender. Remove meat from lamb shanks; skin and slice sausage; remove bay leaf. Return meats to beans. Simmer, uncovered, to thicken, if necessary. Garnish with chopped parsley. Makes 8 servings.

CHICKEN-LIMA KETTLE MEAL

1 pound dried baby lima beans
6 cups water
1 chicken (2½ pounds), cut up
2 tablespoons vegetable oil
1 clove garlic, chopped
1 large onion, chopped (1 cup)
1 green pepper, seeded, coarsely chopped
1 cup coarsely chopped carrot
1 teaspoon paprika
2 teaspoons salt
¼ teaspoon pepper
1 bay leaf

1. Pick over and wash limas. Put limas and water in a heavy kettle. Bring to boiling; remove from heat. Let stand 1 hour.
2. Wash and dry chicken. Heat oil in a skillet;

add chicken pieces and brown well. Remove. Drain off all but 1 tablespoon of fat from skillet. Add garlic, onion, green pepper and carrot to same skillet; sauté until lightly browned. Add paprika; cook 2 minutes, stirring constantly.
3. Add browned chicken, sautéed vegetables, salt, pepper and bay leaf to limas. Cover; bring to boiling. Simmer 1 hour, or until chicken is tender. Makes 6 servings.

STUFFED SHELLS

32 large macaroni shells (from 1-pound
    package)
1 can or jar (about 1 pound) spaghetti sauce
1 small onion, grated (about 1 tablespoon)
1 tablespoon butter or margarine
2 cans (4½ ounces each) corned beef spread
3 hard-cooked eggs, peeled and sieved
1 egg, beaten
¼ cup chopped parsley

1. Cook shells, following label directions; drain.
2. Combine spaghetti sauce, grated onion and butter or margarine in a small sauce pan; heat just to boiling; remove from heat.
3. Combine corned beef spread, sieved eggs, beaten egg and parsley in a small bowl, stirring to blend. Fill shells using about 1 rounded teaspoonful mixture for each.
4. Pour about half the spaghetti-sauce mixture into a shallow 6-cup baking dish; arrange shells in a layer on sauce; top with remaining sauce.
5. Bake, uncovered, in hot oven (400°) for 30 minutes, or until bubbly-hot. Makes 4 servings.

WHITE CLAM SAUCE

1 medium-size onion, chopped (½ cup)
1 clove of garlic, minced
¼ cup olive oil or vegetable oil
2 cans (10½ ounces each) minced clams
½ cup chopped parsley

1. Sauté onion and garlic in oil until soft in a medium-size saucepan. Add clams with liquid and parsley; cook over low heat, just until hot.
2. For a special sauce, cool mixture slightly and place in electric-blender container; cover. Whirl 30 seconds. Reheat to serve. Serve over spaghetti, maruzzelle or fettuccine. Makes 3 cups.

MACARONI-CHEDDAR PUFF

1 cup uncooked elbow macaroni
6 tablespoons (¾ stick) butter or margarine
6 tablespoons flour
2 teaspoons dry mustard
1 teaspoon salt
1½ cups milk
1 tablespoon Worcestershire sauce
1½ cups grated Cheddar cheese (6 ounces)
6 eggs, separated

1. Cook macaroni, following label directions; drain; cool.
2. Melt butter or margarine in a medium-size saucepan; stir in flour, mustard and salt; cook, stirring constantly, until bubbly. Stir in milk and Worcestershire sauce; continue cooking and stirring until sauce thickens and boils 1 minute. Stir in cheese until melted; remove from heat. Let cool while beating eggs.
3. Beat egg whites just until they form soft peaks in a medium-size bowl.
4. Beat egg yolks until creamy-thick in a large bowl; beat in cheese sauce very slowly. Fold in egg whites until no streaks of white remain; fold in macaroni.
5. Spoon into a greased 8-cup soufflé dish or straight-side baking dish; gently cut a deep circle in mixture about 1 inch in from edge with a rubber spatula. (This gives the puff its high crown.)
6. Bake in slow oven (300°) 1 hour, or until puffy-firm and golden. Serve at once. Makes 6 servings.

VEAL AND SHELLS PLATTER

1 package (8 ounces) maruzzelle (small shells), or elbow macaroni
1 package (1 pound) frozen veal patties
4 tablespoons (½ stick) butter or margarine
¼ cup olive oil or vegetable oil
1 large onion, chopped (1 cup)
1 clove of garlic, minced
1 cup chopped parsley

1. Cook shells in a kettle, follow label directions; drain; return to kettle.
2. While shells cook, combine butter or margarine and oil in a large skillet and heat until foamy. Add onion and garlic; sauté until soft;

stir in parsley, cook 1 minute. Remove onion with slotted spoon; add to drained shells. Pour half the butter mixture over shells, tossing until evenly coated.
3. Cut veal patties in half. Brown, turning once, in oil remaining in skillet.
4. Pile shells into center of a heated platter and arrange veal around pasta. Drizzle drippings in skillet over veal. Serve with grated Parmesan cheese, if you wish. Makes 6 servings.

MADE-BY-YOU RAVIOLI

3 cups sifted all-purpose flour
2 teaspoons salt
3 eggs
2 tablespoons olive oil or vegetable oil
¼ cup water
  Ricotta Filling (recipe follows)
  Homemade Tomato Sauce
½ cup freshly grated Parmesan cheese

1. Sift flour and salt onto a large wooden board; make a well in center; add eggs, oil and water. Work liquids into flour with fingers to make a stiff dough. (Or make dough in a large bowl, but it's not as much fun.)
2. Knead dough on board (do not add additional flour) 10 minutes, or until dough is smooth and soft as perfectly kneaded bread dough.
3. Wrap dough in transparent wrap. Let stand 15 minutes. Cut into quarters; keep dough you are not working with wrapped, or it will dry out.
4. Roll out dough, one quarter at a time on the wooden board (do not use additional flour) to a rectangle, 12x4½. This takes a lot of pressure with rolling pin. Repeat with remaining quarters of dough.
5. Shape ravioli, following directions with Ravioli Form and fill with Ricotta Filling. Or: Place 12 teaspoonsful of filling, evenly spaced, on one rolled-out strip. Cover with a second rolled-out strip and cut between mounds of filling with a fluted pastry wheel. (Ravioli can be cooked at once or placed in a single layer on cooky sheets until ready to cook.)
6. Heat 6 quarts of water to boiling in a kettle; add 2 tablespoons salt and 1 tablespoon oil. Cook ravioli, 24 at a time, 10 minutes; remove with slotted spoon to heated serving dish; top with half the Homemade Tomato Sauce and grated Parmesan cheese. Repeat with remaining

ravioli, sauce and cheese. Makes about 48 ravioli or enough for 6 to 8 servings.

RICOTTA FILLING

1 cup ricotta cheese
OR: 1 container (8 ounces) cream-style cottage cheese
½ cup freshly grated Parmesan cheese
1 egg, beaten
2 tablespoons chopped parsley

Combine cheeses in a small bowl; stir in egg and parsley, blending well. Chill until ready to fill ravioli. Makes enough to fill 48 ravioli.

SHELL AND CHEESE PUFF

1 package (8 ounces) maruzzelle (small shells) or elbow macaroni
6 tablespoons (¾ stick) butter or margarine
¼ cup flour
1½ teaspoons salt
1½ teaspoons dry mustard
½ teaspoon paprika
2 cups milk
½ pound Cheddar cheese, shredded (2 cups)
6 eggs, separated
Sesame seeds

1. Cook shells in a kettle, following label directions; drain; return to kettle.
2. While shells cook, melt butter or margarine in a medium-size saucepan. Blend in flour, salt, mustard and paprika; cook, stirring constantly, just until bubbly. Stir in milk; continue cooking and stirring until sauce thickens and bubbles 1 minute. Stir in cheese until melted. Remove from heat; cool.
3. Beat egg whites just until they double in volume and form soft peaks in a large bowl.
4. Beat egg yolks until creamy-thick in a second large bowl; gradually add cooled sauce, stirring until well-blended. Stir in cooked, drained shells. Lightly stir in about 1 cup of the beaten egg whites; gently fold in remainder until no streaks of white remain.
5. Pour into an ungreased 8-cup soufflé or straight-side baking dish; gently cut a deep circle in mixture about an inch in from edge with spatula. (This gives the puff its tiered top.)

Sprinkle the puff mixture with sesame seeds.
6. Bake in moderate oven (350°) 1 hour, or until puffy-firm and golden. Makes 8 servings.

BEANS WITH PASTA

1 pound dried kidney beans
6 cups water
2 smoked ham hocks (about 1½ pounds)
1 medium-size onion, chopped (½ cup)
4 carrots, chopped
1 teaspoon salt
¼ teaspoon pepper
3 tablespoons tomato paste
2 cups uncooked macaroni shells
½ cup chopped parsley

1. Pick over and wash beans. Put beans and water in a heavy kettle. Bring to boiling; remove from heat. Let stand 1 hour.
2. Add ham hocks, onion, carrots, salt and pepper to beans. Cover; bring to boiling. Lower heat; simmer 2 hours, or until beans are tender. Add more hot water, if necessary, to prevent mixture from becoming too thick and sticking. Add tomato paste; simmer 10 minutes longer.
3. Cook pasta, following label directions; drain well. Remove meat from ham hocks; return to beans. Add pasta; mix lightly. Sprinkle with parsley. Makes 6 servings.

ITALIAN BEAN BAKE

1 package (1 pound) dried red kidney beans
6 cups water
1 large onion, chopped (1 cup)
1 pound ground beef
1 can (1 pound) tomatoes
2 teaspoons salt
1 teaspoon leaf marjoram, crumbled

1. Pick over beans and rinse. Place in a large saucepan and add water. Heat to boiling; boil 2 minutes; remove from heat and cover. Allow to stand 1 hour.
2. Add chopped onion to saucepan. Heat to boiling; reduce heat and simmer 1 hour.
3. While beans cook, brown ground beef in a large skillet; break into small pieces. Stir in tomatoes, salt and marjoram; simmer 5 minutes.
4. Drain beans, reserving liquid. Combine beans

and ground-beef mixture in a 10-cup casserole. Stir in 1 cup of reserved bean liquid. Cover.

5. Bake in slow oven (325°) 2½ hours; remove cover. Bake 30 minutes longer, or until beans are tender. (Should beans begin to get dry during baking, add some of the reserved bean liquid, just enough to moisten the surface.) Makes 8 servings.

BOSTON BAKED BEANS

1 package (1 pound) dried pea beans
6 cups water
1 large onion, chopped (1 cup)
½ cup firmly packed dark brown sugar
½ cup molasses
2 tablespoons prepared mustard
1 teaspoon salt
½ pound lean salt pork, thinly sliced

1. Pick over beans and rinse. Place in a large saucepan and add water. Heat to boiling; boil 2 minutes; remove saucepan from heat and cover. Allow to stand 1 hour.
2. Add chopped onion to saucepan. Heat to boiling; reduce heat and simmer 1½ hours, or until skins of beans burst when you blow on several in a spoon.
3. Stir brown sugar, molasses, mustard and salt into saucepan until well-blended. Layer beans and sliced salt pork into a 10-cup bean pot or casserole. Cover.
4. Bake in slow oven (325°) 3½ hours; remove cover. Bake 30 minutes longer, or until beans are a dark brown. (Should beans begin to get dry during baking, add hot water, just enough to moisten the surface.) Makes 8 servings.

SKILLET BEEF SCRAMBLE

1 cup elbow macaroni
1 large onion, chopped (1 cup)
1 tablespoon vegetable oil
1 pound ground chuck
1 can (19 ounces) chunky vegetable soup
1 tablespoon chopped parsley
1 teaspoon seasoned salt
¼ teaspoon pepper

1. Cook macaroni in boiling salted water, following label directions; drain; reserve.
2. Sauté onion in vegetable oil until soft in a

large skillet; crumble ground chuck into skillet; continue cooking until pink is gone from meat.
3. Stir in vegetable soup, parsley, salt, pepper and macaroni. Heat til bubbly. Makes 4 servings.

FRENCH LIMA BEAN CASSEROLE

1 package (1 pound) dried lima beans
4 cups water
1 pound cubed lamb shoulder
3 tablespoons vegetable oil
1 large onion, chopped (1 cup)
2 medium-size carrots, pared and chopped
2 envelopes instant chicken broth
2 teaspoons salt
1 teaspoon leaf rosemary, crumbled
¼ teaspoon pepper

1. Pick over beans and rinse. Place in a large saucepan and add water. Heat to boiling; boil 2 minutes; remove from heat and cover saucepan. Allow to stand 1 hour.
2. Brown lamb in oil in a large skillet; remove. Sauté onion and carrot until soft in same skillet.
3. Drain beans and measure liquid. Add enough water to make 3 cups. Stir bean liquid into skillet with instant chicken broth, salt, rosemary and pepper. Heat to boiling.
4. Layer beans and browned lamb in a 12-cup casserole. Pour liquid over casserole. Cover.
5. Bake in moderate oven (350°) 2 hours; remove cover. Bake 30 minutes longer, or until beans are tender and soft. Makes 8 servings.

HOMEMADE TOMATO SAUCE

1 large onion, chopped (1 cup)
1 clove of garlic, minced
¼ cup olive oil or vegetable oil
1 can (2 pounds, 3 ounces) Italian tomatoes
1 can (6 ounces) tomato paste
2 teaspoons leaf basil, crumbled
1 teaspoon salt
Dash of sugar
1 cup water

1. Sauté onion and garlic in oil until soft in a large saucepan; stir in tomatoes, tomato paste, basil, salt, sugar and water.
2. Heat to bubbling; reduce heat; simmer, uncovered, stirring frequently, 45 minutes, or until sauce has thickened. Makes about 5 cups.

HOW MUCH SHOULD YOU BUY?

The chart below shows how much the most popular kinds of macaroni, rice and beans will make when cooked.

Variety	Uncooked	Cooked
Macaroni (unbroken)	8 ounces	4 cups
Spaghetti (unbroken)	8 ounces	4 cups
Elbow Macaroni	2 cups	4 cups
Rotelle (spirals)	4 cups	4 cups
Farfalle (butterflies)	5 cups	4 cups
Shells (small)	2 cups	4 cups
Noodles (wide and regular)	6 cups	3 ½ cups
Noodles (fine)	5 cups	5 ½ cups
Regular white rice	1 cup	3 cups
Parboiled rice	1 cup	3 to 4 cups
Brown rice	1 cup	3 to 4 cups
Pre-cooked rice	1 cup	2 to 3 cups
Wild rice	1 cup	4 cups
Dried beans	1 cup	2 to 3 cups

STORAGE TIPS

• Unopened, macaroni should stay fresh for months when stored in a dry, cool cupboard. Once it's opened, however, it is best to keep it in a covered container. Follow the same advice when storing uncooked rice and beans.
• When refrigerating cooked rice, cover the rice so the grains will not dry out.
• Rice has excellent freezing qualities. It can be frozen plain or with any combination of foods suitable for freezing. It will keep frozen for 6 to 8 months.
• For each cup of cooked rice which has been refrigerated, add two tablespoons liquid. Simmer 4 to 5 minutes in a covered saucepan. For frozen rice, thaw and use same method.

MONEY-SAVING TIPS

• Buy rice in packages from a one-cup measure to a two- to five-pound box or bag. And remember, the larger the box, the lower the cost.
• Toss cooked rice or pasta with diced vegetables, meat and salad dressing for a supper salad.
• Add rice or pasta to your favorite soup for

extra heartiness or to make it go just a bit further.
• Combine rice, pasta or beans with cut-up meat or chicken from yesterday's roast, or with eggs, cheese or canned fish for a casserole to pull you through a before-payday squeeze.
• Mix varieties—white with brown rice or brown with wild rice, for a new flavor twist as well as for smart "stretching."

KNOW YOUR BEANS

Learn to know and use different kinds of beans for some great money-stretching meals. The commonest kinds are:
Great Northern—Large, white and oval-shape. They cook to jumbo size and are perfect for soup, baked beans, a casserole with meat, salads.
Limas—Color is gray-white to light green, with small ones called baby limas. Serve as a vegetable or combine with meat in a casserole.
Navy or pea beans—Small to medium and white. Popular for old-fashioned baked beans.
Marrow beans—Plump and white and shaped like a large peanut. Use in soups or casseroles.
Pinto beans—Light tan, mottled with pink or brown. Perfect in all bean dishes.
Yelloweye peas or beans—Small and white with a large yellow-brown spot. Preferred for baking.
Lentils—A relative of the bean family with a distinctive flat round dot shape colored yellow to dark brown. Make them into soup.
Split peas—Either green or yellow. And as their name implies, they come split. Use for soup.
Garbanzos—Medium-size, round, wrinkled and a rich cream color. Excellent in soup and in Spanish, Mexican and Italian recipes.
Idaho reds and kidney beans—Most popular for making chili. Idaho reds are sometimes called red Mexican or chili beans, and are dark red, medium-size and shaped like a kidney bean. Their big brother—the familiar kidney bean—varies in color from light to dark red. Use them, too, for casseroles, salads or a vegetable.
Blackeye peas or beans—Small and grayish white with a tiny black circle "eye." A favorite Southern vegetable.
Black beans—Small and really jet black. Also called purple hull beans. Use in Spanish recipes or as a meat substitute.
Cranberry beans—Red brown, plump and oval-shape with dark brown spots and stripes. Known also as October or Roman beans. Use in chili.

HOMEMADE RAVIOLI DOUGH

4 cups sifted all-purpose flour
¾ teaspoon salt
2 eggs, slightly beaten
2 tablespoons vegetable shortening
   Boiling water

1. Sift flour and salt into a large bowl; make a well in center and add eggs and shortening. Measure boiling water into a 1-cup measure.
2. Mix water gradually into flour to make a stiff dough. (It will take between ¾ cup and a scant 1 cup of water, depending on the moisture content of the flour and the size of the eggs.)
3. Turn dough out onto a lightly floured pastry board and knead 5 minutes, or until dough is very smooth and shiny. Cover dough with mixing bowl and allow to rest at least 10 minutes before rolling out. Makes 2 pounds of dough.

HOMEMADE TINY RAVIOLI

   Homemade Ravioli Dough (recipe above)
1 cup ricotta cheese OR: 1 cup dry cottage cheese
1 package (8 ounces) mozzarella cheese, shredded
½ cup grated Parmesan cheese
2 eggs, beaten
½ teaspoon salt
   Dash of freshly ground pepper
½ recipe Homemade Sauce (recipe follows)
   Grated Parmesan cheese

1. Prepare Homemade Ravioli Dough and allow to rest.
2. Combine ricotta or cottage cheese, shredded mozzarella cheese, grated Parmesan cheese, salt and pepper in medium-size bowl.
3. Divide dough in half; roll out each half to a 22x16-inch rectangle on lightly floured board.
4. Cut dough in half, crosswise; place ¼ teaspoon of filling at 1-inch intervals on half the dough. Lift up second half and place over filling. Cut ravioli with 1-inch round cutter (such as the center of a doughnut cutter). Save dough trims.
5. Repeat with second part of dough and then with all trims to make about 100 tiny ravioli. Place ravioli on a clean towel until ready to boil.
6. Heat a large kettle of salted water to boiling, adding about one quarter of the ravioli at a time; cook 7 minutes, or until ravioli float to the top. Remove from water with slotted spoon and serve with Homemade Sauce and grated Parmesan cheese. Makes 8 servings.

NOTE: Uncooked ravioli may be frozen in single layers on jelly-roll pans and frozen about 12 hours. The frozen ravioli may then be tumbled into plastic bags and returned to freezer. To cook: Follow same cooking directions as for fresh ravioli, but increase time 10 minutes.

HOMEMADE SAUCE

1 tablespoon vegetable oil
1 tablespoon olive oil
1 tablespoon butter or margarine
1 tablespoon lard
2 pounds boneless chuck or round, cut into ½-inch cubes
½ pound sweet Italian sausages, sliced
2 large carrots, finely chopped
1 small onion, chopped (¼ cup)
2 cloves garlic, crushed
2 cans (2 pounds, 3 ounces each) Italian tomatoes with tomato paste and basil leaf
3 teaspoons salt
1 teaspoon leaf oregano, crumbled
¼ teaspoon freshly ground pepper
2 tablespoons chopped parsley

1. Heat olive and vegetable oils, butter or margarine and lard in a large kettle. Brown round and sausage a few pieces at a time in kettle; remove as pieces brown with a spoon; reserve.
2. Sauté carrot, onion and garlic in same kettle until very soft; stir in tomatoes, salt, oregano and pepper; return meat to kettle.
3. Heat sauce slowly to boiling; lower heat; cover kettle. Simmer slowly 2 hours, or until meat is tender and sauce is thickened. Add parsley. Taste; add additional seasoning, if you wish. Makes 8 cups.

NOTE: Meatballs may be substituted for the beef and sausage.

PASTA WITH PINE NUTS AND RAISINS

1 can (1 pound) Italian tomatoes
¼ cup olive or vegetable oil
¾ cup raisins
¾ cup pine nuts

½ teaspoon salt
¼ teaspoon freshly ground pepper
1 package (1 pound) fusilli (spiral spaghetti)
  OR: 1 package (1 pound) thin spaghetti
¼ cup (½ stick) butter or margarine
1 cup grated Parmesan cheese

1. Heat tomatoes and oil in a small saucepan for 10 minutes, breaking up the tomatoes with the back of a spoon. Add raisins, pine nuts, salt and pepper. Simmer while cooking pasta.
2. Cook fusilli or spaghetti, following label directions; drain well. Return to kettle and toss with butter or margarine until evenly coated. Add tomato mixture and Parmesan cheese and toss until evenly coated.
3. Turn onto heated serving platter and serve with additional Parmesan cheese, if you wish. Makes 6 servings.

MARIA'S SPINACH ROLLS

Homemade Ravioli Dough (page 75)
3 packages (10 ounces each) frozen chopped spinach
1 container (15 ounces) ricotta cheese
  OR: 1 container (16 ounces) dry cottage cheese
1½ cups grated Parmesan cheese
¼ cup (½ stick) butter or margarine, melted
¾ teaspoon salt
¼ teaspoon freshly grated pepper
Few gratings whole nutmeg
Homemade Sauce, about 4 cups (page 75)
Grated Parmesan cheese

1. Prepare Homemade Ravioli Dough and allow to rest.
2. Cook frozen spinach, following label directions; drain very well in a strainer; combine with ricotta or cottage cheese, Parmesan cheese, melted butter or margarine, salt, pepper and nutmeg in a medium-size bowl.
3. Divide dough in thirds; roll out each third to a 22x10-inch rectangle on a lightly floured pastry board.
4. Spread one-third spinach mixture over dough; starting at a short end, begin to roll up dough, jelly-roll fashion; place seam-side down in the center of a triple-thick piece of cheesecloth; wrap cheesecloth around pasta roll to cover completely and tie ends with kitchen cord. Re-

peat with dough and filling to make 3 rolls.
5. Heat a large kettle of salted water to boiling; add one roll at a time and boil 20 minutes, or until roll floats to the top of the boiling water; remove with slotted spoon; repeat with other 2 rolls. Cool rolls on wooden board until cool enough to handle. (This much can be done the day ahead.)
6. Remove cheesecloth and cut each roll into 30 thin slices; overlap slices in a 12-cup baking dish; spoon 4 cups of Homemade Sauce over and sprinkle with grated Parmesan cheese; cover dish lightly with aluminum foil.
7. Bake in moderate oven (350°) 35 minutes, or until bubbly-hot. Makes 8 servings.

PASTA WITH CREAM AND SAFFRON

½ recipe for Homemade Ravioli Dough

  OR: 1 package (1 pound) fettuccine noodles
1 cup heavy cream
¼ teaspoon saffron threads, crumbled
2 egg yolks
2 thin slices cooked ham cut in julienne strips
  (1 cup)
¼ cup (½ stick) butter or margarine
Salt and pepper to taste

1. Prepare Homemade Ravioli Dough. Roll out to a 22x16-inch rectangle on lightly floured pastry board. Cut dough in half, crosswise; fold each half of dough into quarters, lengthwise; slice dough into ¼-inch-wide strips. Unwind strips and allow to dry on clean towels for 1 hour.
2. Heat 6 quarts of salted water to boiling in a large kettle.
3. While water comes to the boil: Heat cream slowly in a medium-size saucepan; remove from heat. Measure 3 tablespoons of the cream into a cup; add saffron and stir to blend well; beat egg yolks into saffron mixture; then beat this mixture into cream in saucepan; heat slowly, stirring constantly, just until mixture begins to thicken; add ham and allow to heat, but do not allow sauce to boil.
4. Cook noodles in boiling water 5 minutes; drain well. Return noodles to kettle; add butter or margarine and toss to coat evenly. Fold in sauce until well-blended. Turn onto heated serving platter. Makes 6 servings.

PASTA WITH POTATO

1 box (16 ounces) maccaroncelli or elbow
    macaroni
1 package (12 ounces) frozen French fried
    potatoes
    Vegetable oil
2 tablespoons butter or margarine
1 cup shredded mozzarella cheese (4 ounces)
½ cup grated Parmesan cheese
1 teaspoon salt
    Chopped parsley

1. Cook and drain noodles, following label directions.
2. While noodles are cooking, prepare potatoes, following label directions for frying in oil; drain on paper toweling.
3. Place noodles on a heated serving platter; add butter or margarine, mozzarella cheese, ¼ cup Parmesan cheese and salt; toss until noodles are coated with butter or margarine and cheeses are melted.
4. Spoon potatoes on top of noodles; sprinkle with remaining ¼ cup of Parmesan cheese and parsley. Makes 8 servings.

PASTA WITH BROCCOLI

1 bunch fresh broccoli (about 2 pounds)
    OR: 1 package (10 ounces) frozen broccoli
    spears
2 tablespoons olive or vegetable oil
2 large garlic cloves, halved
1 pepperoni sausage (about 8 ounces), diced
    (about 1½ cups)
1 package (1 pound) bow-tie noodles
¼ cup (½ stick) butter or margarine
1 cup grated Parmesan cheese

1. Trim fresh broccoli, removing leaves and cutting a thin slice from the bottom of each stem. Cut broccoli stems into julienne pieces, leaving the flowerettes whole. Wash broccoli flowerettes and stems.
2. Cook fresh broccoli stems in lightly salted boiling water in a large skillet 5 minutes; add flowerettes and cook 5 minutes longer, or until broccoli is crisply tender; drain well. Or: Cook frozen broccoli, following label directions; drain.
3. Heat oil in same skillet with garlic pieces for 5 minutes, but do not allow the garlic to brown.

(This is what gives garlic a bitter taste.) Remove garlic pieces with a slotted spoon; add diced pepperoni and cook about 5 minutes. Add broccoli and brown lightly.
4. Cook pasta, following label directions; drain and return to kettle. Add butter or margarine and toss to coat evenly. Add Parmesan cheese and toss well; then add broccoli-pepperoni mixture and toss them all gently to distribute evenly in pasta.
5. Turn out onto heated serving platter and serve with additional Parmesan cheese, if you wish. Makes 8 servings.

FETTUCINI ALFREDO

3 cups sifted all-purpose flour
2 teaspoons salt
3 eggs
3 tablespoons olive oil or vegetable oil
¼ cup cold water
    Cornstarch
½ cup (1 stick) butter or margarine, cut in
    small pieces
2 cups freshly grated Parmesan cheese
    Freshly ground black pepper

1. Sift flour and salt into a large bowl; make a well in center; add eggs, oil and water. Work liquids into flour with fingers to make a stiff dough.
2. Turn dough out onto a large pastry board. (Do not add additional flour.) Knead 10 minutes, or until dough is as smooth and soft as perfectly kneaded bread dough. Wrap dough in plastic wrap and allow to rest at room temperature 1 hour.
3. Sprinkle pastry board with cornstarch. Roll out dough, a quarter at a time, to a rectangle so thin you can read the cover of Family Circle through the dough.
4. Fold dough into quarters lengthwise. Slice dough across into ¼-inch—wide strips. Unwind strips and allow to dry on clean towels for 1 hour. Repeat with remaining quarters of dough.
5. Heat 6 quarts of water to boiling in a large kettle; add 2 tablespoons salt and 1 tablespoon oil. Cook fettucini 5 minutes, or until they are cooked to the tenderness you like. Drain well and turn out onto a heated serving platter.
6. Add pieces of butter or margarine and toss

with fork and spoon until butter melts. Add Parmesan cheese and continue to toss until fettucini are coated and glistening. For that final touch, grind black pepper over the top. Makes 4 servings.

SPAGHETTI PANCAKE

1 package (8 ounces) fusilli or thin spaghetti
4 eggs
1 tablespoon instant minced onion
1 teaspoon salt
1 teaspoon leaf oregano, crumbled
¼ teaspoon pepper
4 tablespoons (½ stick) butter or margarine
¼ cup grated Parmesan cheese

1. Cook fusilli in a kettle, following label directions; drain; return to kettle; cool slightly.
2. Beat eggs in a medium-size bowl; blend in instant onion, salt, oregano and pepper. Toss with cooled fusilli.
3. Heat butter or margarine in a large skillet. Add fusilli mixture; sprinkle with grated cheese. Cook over low heat about 5 minutes, or until underside is firm and golden.
4. Invert "pancake" onto a cooky sheet; then slide back into skillet; cook 5 minutes longer. Cut into 6 wedges in skillet. Serve with sweet Italian sausages and sautéed red and green peppers, if you wish. Makes 6 servings.

ZITI CASSEROLE

1 pound ziti
1 container (1 pound) ricotta cheese
¼ pound mozzarella cheese, diced
½ cup grated Parmesan cheese
1 egg
¾ teaspoon salt
¼ teaspoon pepper
6 cups Homemade Meat Sauce (recipe follows)

1. Cook ziti, following label directions.
2. While noodles are cooking, make filling: Combine ricotta, mozzarella, Parmesan, egg, salt and pepper in a large bowl.
3. Layers ziti, filling and meat sauce in a 13x9x2-inch baking dish, starting and ending with sauce.
4. Bake in moderate oven (350°) 40 minutes, or until bubbly-hot. Makes 8 servings.

HOMEMADE MEAT SAUCE

1 large onion, chopped (1 cup)
2 cloves garlic, minced
¼ cup vegetable oil
1 pound ground beef
2 Italian sausages, chopped
2 cans (2 pounds, 3 ounces each) Italian tomatoes
2 cans (6 ounces each) tomato paste
2 tablespoons sugar
1 tablespoon leaf oregano, crumbled
1 tablespoon leaf basil, crumbled
1 tablespoon salt
½ teaspoon pepper
¼ cup grated Parmesan cheese

1. Sauté onion and garlic in oil until soft in a large skillet; brown beef and sausage. Pour off all but 2 tablespoons fat in skillet.
2. Stir in tomatoes, tomato paste, sugar, oregano, basil, salt and pepper. Simmer, uncovered, stirring frequently, 45 minutes, or until sauce thickens. Stir in Parmesan cheese; cool.
3. Freeze in plastic containers in measured recipe portions. Makes 12 cups.

TORTELLINI

1 recipe Fettucini Alfredo
1 package (10 ounces) frozen chopped spinach, thawed
1 carton (1 pound) ricotta cheese OR: Cream-style cottage cheese
1 teaspoon salt
¼ teaspoon grated nutmeg
1 pound ground beef
2 cans (15 ounces each) special tomato sauce
½ cup dry red wine

1. Roll out Fettucini Alfredo dough, one-quarter at a time, on a pastry board lightly sprinkled with cornstarch, until thin enough to read the cover of Family Circle through the dough.
2. Cut out dough with a 3-inch round cutter. (You will get about 96 rounds.)
3. Press all water out of spinach and drain on paper toweling. Combine spinach, ricotta or cottage cheese, salt and nutmeg in a small bowl. Place ½ teaspoon on each round; fold in half and press edges tightly together to seal and twist into a crescent shape. Continue until all

rounds are filled. (You will have extra filling.)

4. Cook pasta, 24 at a time, in a large kettle of boiling water, to which 2 tablespoons salt and 1 tablespoon vegetable oil have been added, 10 minutes, or just until tender; drain.

5. Press ground beef into a large patty in a large skillet. Brown on one side for 5 minutes; turn and brown 5 minutes on second side. Drain off excess fat and chop into tiny pieces. Stir in tomato sauce and wine. Simmer 10 minutes.

6. Layer pasta, remaining filling and tomato mixture in a 13x9x2-inch baking dish.

7. Bake in moderate oven (350°) 30 minutes, or until casserole is bubbly-hot. Makes 8 servings.

HURRY-UP RICE SKILLET SUPPER

  1 package (about 10 ounces) frozen mixed vegetables
  2 tablespoons instant minced onion
  2 cups water
  ¼ teaspoon salt
  1 can condensed cream of celery soup
  1⅓ cups packaged precooked rice
  1 can (about 7 ounces) tuna, drained
  2 tablespoons dried parsley flakes
  ½ teaspoon leaf marjoram, crumbled
  1 teaspoon lemon juice

1. Cook frozen mixed vegetables with onion, water and salt in a large skillet 5 minutes.

2. Stir in soup until well-blended. Add rice, tuna, parsley and marjoram. Mix to blend; heat slowly to boiling, stirring constantly.

3. Cover skillet; lower heat. Simmer 5 minutes, or until rice is tender and mixture is creamy. Sprinkle with lemon juice. Makes 4 servings.

CHEDDAR CHEESE SAUCE

  4 tablespoons (½ stick) butter or margarine
  ¼ cup flour
  ¼ teaspoon salt
  Dash of pepper
  2½ cups milk
  1 teaspoon Worcestershire sauce
  ½ pound Cheddar cheese, shredded (2 cups)

Melt butter or margarine in a medium-size saucepan. Blend in flour, salt and pepper; cook, stirring constantly, just until bubbly. Stir in milk;

continue cooking and stirring until sauce thickens and bubbles 1 minute. Stir in cheese and Worcestershire sauce until cheese is melted. Serve with Manicotti Alla Veneziana
Makes about 2½ cups.

ZUCCHINI-TOMATO SAUCE

  1 large onion, chopped (1 cup)
  1 clove of garlic, minced
  1 pound zucchini, trimmed and chopped
  ¼ cup olive oil or vegetable oil
  2 large ripe tomatoes, peeled and chopped
  2 teaspoons leaf basil, crumbled
  1½ teaspoons salt
  ¼ teaspoon pepper
  Dash of sugar

1. Sauté onion, garlic and zucchini in oil until soft in a medium-size saucepan; stir in tomatoes, basil, salt, pepper and sugar.

2. Heat to bubbling; simmer 30 minutes, or until sauce thickens slightly. Serve over fettuccelle or spaghetti. Makes 3 cups.

RIGATI-EGGPLANT BAKE

  1 large eggplant, weighing about 2 pounds
  ½ cup olive oil or vegetable oil
  1 package (1 pound) rigati, or ziti, or elbow macaroni
  1 large onion, chopped (1 cup)
  1 jar (24 ounces) marinara sauce
  1 container (1 pound) cream-style cottage cheese
  ½ cup chopped parsley
  1 teaspoon Italian seasoning
  1 package (6 ounces) sliced provolone cheese

1. Trim ends from eggplant; cut into ½-inch slices; pare. Sauté slices, a few at a time, in part of the oil, until soft in a large skillet; drain on paper toweling.

2. Cook rigati in a kettle, following label directions; drain; return to kettle.

3. Sauté onion until soft in same skillet; stir in marinara sauce and simmer until piping-hot. Pour sauce over rigati in kettle and blend well.

4. Combine cottage cheese, parsley and Italian seasoning in a small bowl.

5. Place half the rigati mixture in a shallow 12-cup baking dish. Add half the eggplant, over-

lapping slices if necessary. Add cheese mixture, spreading evenly. Add remaining rigati mixture and top with remaining eggplant.

6. Bake in moderate oven (350°) 20 minutes. Cut provolone cheese into strips and arrange over eggplant.

7. Bake 10 minutes longer, or until cheese melts and the rigati mixture is bubbly-hot. Serve right from baking dish. Makes 8 servings.

GENOESE NOODLES

1 package (1 pound) noodles
½ cup (1 stick) butter or margarine, melted
2 cups parsley leaves, pressed down
1 tablespoon leaf basil
1½ teaspoons salt
¼ teaspoon pepper
1 clove garlic
2 tablespoons pine nuts (pignoli)
½ cup olive or vegetable oil
½ cup grated Parmesan cheese

1. Cook and drain noodles, following label directions; place on a heated platter.

2. While noodles cook, combine butter or margarine, parsley, basil, salt, pepper, garlic, nuts, oil and cheese in container of electric blender to make sauce. Whirl at high speed until smooth.

3. Pour sauce over noodles; toss lightly. Serve immediately. Makes 8 servings.

SPAGHETTI CARBONARA

1 pound spaghetti
½ pound sliced bacon, diced
1 large green pepper, halved, seeded and diced
3 eggs
½ teaspoon leaf marjoram, crumbled
½ teaspoon salt
Dash of pepper
4 tablespoons (½ stick) butter or margarine
1 cup grated Romano cheese

1. Cook spaghetti in boiling salted water; following label directions; drain and place on heated serving platter.

2. While pasta cooks, fry bacon until crisp in a skillet. Remove with a slotted spoon to paper

toweling. Drain off all but 2 tablespoons bacon fat from skillet. Saute green pepper in skillet until soft.

3. Beat eggs in a small bowl. Stir in marjoram, salt and pepper.

4. Toss butter or margarine with hot spaghetti until melted. Add seasoned eggs and toss until completely blended. Add bacon, green pepper and grated cheese. Toss once more and serve at once. Makes 6 servings.

MANICOTTI ALLA VENEZIANA

1 package (8 ounces) manicotti noodles
1 pound meat-loaf mixture
1 large onion, chopped (1 cup)
1 clove of garlic, minced
1 cup fresh bread crumbs (2 slices)
1 egg, beaten
½ cup chopped parsley
1 teaspoon leaf basil, crumbled
1 teaspoon salt
Dash of pepper
Cheddar Cheese Sauce (recipe on page 79)

1. Cook manicotti noodles, a few at a time, following label directions; lift out carefully with a slotted spoon; place in a large bowl of cold water until ready to use.

2. Shape meat-loaf mixture into a large patty in a large skillet; brown 5 minutes on each side, then break up into small pieces; remove with a slotted spoon to a medium-size bowl.

3. Saute onion and garlic until soft in drippings in skillet. Add to cooked meat with bread crumbs, egg, parsley, basil, salt and pepper, mixing until well-blended.

4. Lift manicotti noodles from water, one at a time; drain well. Fill each with part of the meat mixture, using a long-handled spoon.

5. Pour half the hot Cheddar Cheese Sauce into the bottom of a shallow 12-cup flameproof dish. Place filled manicotti over cheese sauce. Top with remaining sauce.

6. Broil, 4 inches from heat, 5 minutes, or until golden and bubbly. Makes 6 to 8 servings.

NOTE: Manicotti Alla Veneziana can be made early in the day and refrigerated. About 45 minutes before serving time, warm in moderate oven (350°) 30 minutes, then place under broiler until golden and bubbly.

6

CHEESE & EGG DISHES

Cheese and eggs offer big protein for little money. What's more, each can be used in an almost unlimited number of ways for either breakfast, lunch or dinner. Eggs, for instance, are one of the few foods that, without adding any other ingredient, can be made into a nutritional main course. And they can be cooked almost anyway you like—fried, baked, poached, soft-boiled or scrambled. Add leftovers and you've got the makings for a satisfying omelet. Add cheese and you've got a combination that's unbeatable in soufflés, casseroles, blintzes, etc. If you've been limiting eggs to breakfast and cheese to lunchtime sandwiches, take a look at the following nine pages. They include delightful dinner recipes and sage advice on getting the most for your money, plus tips on storing and cooking these around-the-clock foods.

MONEY-SAVING EGG TIPS

• What determines the price of eggs? Weight, among other things. For example: One dozen eggs in a carton marked EXTRA-LARGE must weigh, according to government standards, 27 ounces; those marked LARGE, 24 ounces; MEDIUM, 21 ounces; and SMALL, 18 ounces. Weight is not listed on the carton, but the size is, and that's your guarantee.

• How to figure cost per serving: Divide 12 into the cost per dozen. For example, if a dozen eggs cost 90¢, each egg actually cost 7.5¢. Therefore, an average 2-egg serving will cost you only 15¢. Nutritionists say that in buying a dozen large eggs at 90¢, the shopper is paying 60¢ a pound for high quality protein; eggs are a bargain.

• Egg Grades: Most supermarkets carry both AA and Grade A eggs and sometimes Grade B. All have the same nutritive value. The difference is in the appearance. The Grade B egg usually has a thinner white and a flatter yolk. Regardless of the size of the egg, AA and A grades are perfect for poaching, frying and cooking in the shell and, of course, are the highest priced. Grade B—at a lower price—is a smart buy for scrambling, making omelets or for use in any recipe where perfect appearance doesn't matter.

• When checking the prices of eggs of the same grade, but different size, keep this formula in mind: If the difference in the price per dozen between medium and large eggs of the same grade is 7¢ or more, the medium size is the better buy per pound. If the difference is 6¢ or less, the larger size egg is the better buy.

• Brown-shell eggs versus white-shell eggs. Both have the same nutritional quality and, depending on size, should be priced comparably. The color is determined by the breed of hen. Brown-shell eggs are preferred in some parts of our country; white shells, in other regions. Smart shoppers buy either or both.

• Do not wash eggs until you're ready to use them, otherwise you remove the shell film that helps keep them fresh. Store them in the refrigerator, as soon as you come home from the supermarket. The tote-home carton is fine for storage and provides a light covering. If you change the eggs to a special compartment in your refrigerator, place them large end up.

• If an egg is ruined because of improper cooking, it's money thrown away. Whatever your favorite way of cooking eggs, use low heat.

• Eggs tend to be most plentiful, and thus lower in price, during the winter. So, wintertime is often a time to think of main dishes from eggs.

• Save egg whites. Keep them chilled in a covered jar in the refrigerator. They will keep from 7 to 10 days. Beat whites with sugar until stiff, and use as a garnish for puddings.

• Save egg yolks. Place them in a covered jar with just enough water to cover; chill. Plan to use them within 2 to 3 days. Or poach the yolks right away, then rice them and use for garnishing salads. You can also hard-cook the yolks and store in a covered container for 4 to 5 days. Hard-cooked, they're perfect, mixed with mayonnaise, as a sandwich filling.

• The 2-egg omelet is one of the easiest, thriftiest ways to use any leftover meats, cheeses and vegetables.

MONEY-SAVING CHEESE TIPS

• To find the relative cost of various cheeses, compare the price of equal weights of cheese. As a general rule, you'll find aged or sharp natural cheeses usually cost more than mild ones; imported cheeses frequently cost more than domestic ones; and pre-packaged, sliced, cubed or grated cheeses may cost more than wedges or sticks. Also, large packages are usually your thriftiest buy.

• Save small or end pieces of cheese for garnishes. If the pieces become hard and dry, grate them and refrigerate in a covered container.

• If mold appears on natural cheeses, scrape it off. It's harmless and does not affect the taste of the cheese.

• Try cottage cheese and chives as a change from sour cream as a topping for baked potatoes. It's less expensive and has fewer calories.

• Cheese (except cottage, cream and Neufchâtel cheeses) tastes best when served at room temperature. Remove from refrigerator about 30 to 60 minutes before serving. However, cut off only what you plan to use; wrap and return the remainder to the refrigerator. Warm air only dries out cheese.

• Remember two points when cooking with cheese: Use low heat and avoid overcooking. Otherwise cheese will become stringy or tough —and could be the ruination of an otherwise good dinner. This is true whether the cheese is baked, broiled or cooked on top of the range.

THIRTY-MINUTE PIZZA

Vegetable oil
4 packages (8 ounces each) refrigerated crescent dinner rolls
1 can (15 ounces) spaghetti sauce
1 can (about 3 or 4 ounces) sliced mushrooms,
drained
½ cup sliced pitted ripe olives
1 teaspoon leaf oregano, crumbled
1 package (8 ounces) mozzarella cheese,
shredded
2 packages (8 ounces each) brown 'n' serve
sausages

1. Lightly oil two 14-inch round pizza pans.
Open crescent rolls following label directions.
Unroll and separate dough triangles. Fit triangles from 2 packages into each pizza pan.
2. Spread half of spaghetti sauce on each pizza.
Divide mushrooms and olives evenly over sauce;
sprinkle with oregano. Sprinkle cheese over both
pizzas.
3. Slice sausages diagonally; arrange in a pattern
on the cheese.
4. Bake in a hot oven (400°) 20 minutes, or until
crusts are golden brown. Garnish with a sprig
of fresh basil or parsley, if you wish. Makes two
14-inch pies.
TO REHEAT FROZEN PIZZA: Bake at 400° for 30
minutes, or until filling is bubbly.

SOUFFLÉED BROCCOLI ROULADE

4 tablespoons (½ stick) butter or margarine
½ cup flour
½ teaspoon salt
2 cups milk
4 eggs, separated
2 packages frozen broccoli
¾ cup shredded Swiss cheese
Swiss Cheese Sauce (recipe follows)

1. Grease a 15x10x1-inch jelly-roll pan; line with
wax paper; grease paper; dust with flour.
2. Melt butter or margarine in a medium-size
saucepan. Off heat, blend in flour and salt; stir
in milk. Cook, stirring constantly, until mixture
is very thick.
3. Beat egg whites until they form soft peaks in
a medium-size bowl. Beat egg yolks slightly in a
large bowl. Slowly beat hot mixture into egg
yolks, until blended. Fold beaten egg whites into
egg yolks until no streaks of yellow remain.
Spread evenly in pan.
4. Bake in moderate oven (325°) 45 minutes, or
until golden and top springs back when touched.
5. While omelet roll bakes, cook broccoli, following label directions; drain; cut into 1-inch
pieces. Reserve ½ cup for garnish.
6. Make Swiss Cheese Sauce.
7. Remove omelet roll from pan this way:
Loosen around edges with spatula; cover with
wax paper or foil. Place a large cooky sheet or
tray on top, then quickly turn upside down. Lift
pan; peel paper.
8. Arrange broccoli in a single layer on top of
roll; sprinkle with cheese and drizzle ½ cup hot
cheese sauce over. Starting at a 10-inch end,
roll up omelet, jelly-roll fashion, lifting wax
paper or foil as you roll to steady and guide it.
9. Lift roll onto a heated large serving platter
with two wide spatulas. Drizzle about ½ cup
more sauce over roll and garnish with broccoli.
10. Cut roll into thick slices. Pass remaining
sauce to spoon over. Makes 6 servings.

SWISS CHEESE SAUCE

⅓ cup butter or margarine
⅓ cup flour
½ teaspoon salt
⅛ teaspoon pepper
2 cups milk
¾ cup shredded Swiss cheese

1. Melt butter or margarine over low heat in a
medium-size saucepan. Stir in flour, salt and
pepper; cook, stirring constantly, just until mixture bubbles.
2. Stir in milk; continue cooking and stirring
until sauce thickens and bubbles 1 minute; stir
in cheese until melted. Keep warm. Makes 2½
cups, or enough for 6 servings of Souffléed
Broccoli Roulade.

ITALIAN FRITTATA

½ cup chopped green pepper
1 medium-size onion, chopped (½ cup)
4 tablespoons (½ stick) butter or margarine
1 large tomato, peeled and chopped
1 teaspoon salt
¼ teaspoon leaf oregano, crumbled
8 eggs
⅛ teaspoon pepper
2 ounces (2 slices) Provolone cheese (from a 6-ounce package), shredded

1. Sauté green pepper and onion in 2 tablespoons of the butter or margarine until soft, about 5 minutes, in a small skillet. Add tomato, ½ teaspoon of the salt and oregano. Cook slowly, 10 minutes, stirring occasionally, until all liquid is absorbed; reserve.
2. Beat eggs slightly in a medium-size bowl with remaining ½ teaspoon salt and pepper.
3. Heat a 10-inch skillet for 5 seconds. With a fork, swirl the remaining 2 tablespoons butter or margarine over bottom and sides of pan.
4. Pour in egg mixture. Cook, stirring with flat of fork and shaking pan back and forth until omelet is firm on bottom and almost set on top. Spread tomato mixture evenly over top. Sprinkle with cheese; cover skillet for about 2 minutes, or until cheese starts to melt. Cut in wedges to serve. Makes 4 servings.

CALICO CHEESE CASSEROLE

1 package (8 ounces) spaghetti
1 package (10 ounces) frozen mixed vegetables
6 tablespoons (¾ stick) butter or margarine
1½ cups soft white bread crumbs (3 slices)
4 tablespoons flour
1 teaspoon salt
3 cups milk
1 tablespoon prepared mustard
3 cups shredded sharp Cheddar cheese (¾ pound)
4 hard-cooked eggs, shelled and sliced

1. Break spaghetti into 3-inch pieces. Cook spaghetti and frozen mixed vegetables in separate saucepans, following label directions for each; drain well and return to saucepan spaghetti was cooked in.
2. Melt butter or margarine in a medium-size saucepan; measure 2 tablespoons into a small bowl and toss with bread crumbs.
3. Stir flour and salt into remaining butter in saucepan; cook, stirring constantly, until mixture bubbles; stir in milk and mustard. Continue cooking and stirring until mixture thickens and bubbles 1 minute. Stir in 2 cups of the cheese until melted.
4. Pour sauce over spaghetti in saucepan and stir until well blended. Spoon half the spaghetti mixture into an 8-cup shallow baking dish; top with egg slices; add remaining spaghetti. Sprinkle remaining 1 cup cheese over top of casserole and top with buttered bread crumbs.
5. Bake in moderate oven (350°) 30 minutes, or until casserole bubbles and crumbs are golden. Makes 6 servings.

BAKED SPINACH AND EGGS AU GRATIN

2 cups bread cubes (6 slices)
½ cup (1 stick) butter or margarine
2 packages (10 ounces each) frozen chopped spinach
1 medium-size onion, chopped (½ cup)
1 cup cubed Muenster cheese
2 teaspoons salt
⅛ teaspoon pepper
⅛ teaspoon ground nutmeg
¼ cup flour
1 cup milk
⅓ cup grated Parmesan cheese
8 eggs

1. Sauté bread cubes in 2 tablespoons of the butter or margarine in medium-size skillet until golden; place in the bottom of a lightly greased 6-cup baking dish. Sauté onion until tender in same skillet in 2 more tablespoons butter or margarine; reserve.
2. Cook spinach, following label directions, in medium-size saucepan; drain very well. Return to saucepan; add onion, Muenster cheese, salt, pepper and nutmeg. Spoon over bread cubes in baking dish.
3. Melt remaining butter or margarine in a small saucepan; stir in flour; cook, stirring constantly, just until mixture bubbles. Stir in milk slowly; continue cooking and stirring until sauce thickens and bubbles 1 minute. Remove from heat.
4. Stir in Parmesan cheese. Let mixture cool.

5. Separate 4 of the eggs. Beat egg whites in a medium-size bowl just until they begin to form soft peaks.

6. Beat egg yolks in a large bowl until thick and fluffy; beat in cooled white sauce mixture, a small amount at a time. Carefully fold in egg whites until no streaks of white remain.

7. Make 4 indentations with a spoon in the spinach mixture, 1 inch from edge of dish. Carefully break remaining eggs, one in each indentation. Spoon soufflé mixture completely over the top, right to the edge.

8. Bake in moderate oven (325°) 45 minutes, or until puffy-firm and golden. Serve at once. Makes 4 servings.

CHEESE BLINTZES

Batter:
  5 eggs
  2 cups sifted all-purpose flour
2½ cups milk
  ⅓ cup vegetable oil
Cheese Filling:
  1 container (2 pounds) cream-style cottage cheese
  2 eggs
  ⅓ cup sugar
1½ teaspoons vanilla
  ⅓ cup butter or margarine
Topping:
  1 can (1 pound, 5 ounces) cherry pie filling
  2 cups (1-pint carton) dairy sour cream

1. To make Batter: Beat eggs just until blended in a large bowl; sift flour over the eggs and beat in just until smooth; stir in milk and oil. Cover; chill for at least 45 minutes. While batter chills, prepare filling.

2. To make Cheese Filling: Combine cottage cheese, eggs, sugar and vanilla in large bowl. Beat at high speed with electric beater 3 minutes, or until smooth.

3. Heat a heavy 8-inch skillet slowly; test temperature by sprinkling on a few drops of water. When drops bounce about, temperature is right. Grease skillet lightly with part of the butter.

4. Measure batter, a scant ¼ cup at a time, into skillet, tilting it to cover the bottom completely.

5. Cook blintz 1 to 2 minutes, or until top is set and underside is golden; remove to a plate. Repeat with remaining batter to make 24 blintzes.

Sandwich each blintz with a piece of foil or wax paper to keep separated.

6. Place 3 tablespoons of the cheese filling down the center of the golden side of each blintz. Overlap two opposite sides over filling, then fold up ends toward middle on seam side.

7. Melt remaining butter or margarine in a large skillet. Brown blintzes, seam side down, turning to brown on other side. Keep warm until all blintzes have been browned. Serve blintzes warm, topped with cherry pie filling and a dollop of sour cream. Makes 12 servings.

TRIPLE CHEESE SOUFFLÉ

1½ cups shredded cheese (6 ounces)
  6 tablespoons (¾ stick) butter or margarine
  ⅓ cup flour
  1 teaspoon salt
  1 teaspoon onion powder
1½ cups milk
  Few drops hot red-pepper seasoning
  3 eggs, separated

1. Prepare an ungreased 6-cup soufflé or straight-side baking dish this way: Fold a piece of foil, 28 inches long, in half lengthwise; wrap around dish to make a 3-inch stand-up collar; hold in place with string and a paper clip.

2. Use any combination of cheese you have in your refrigerator, to make the 1½ cups. (We used Cheddar, Muenster and Parmesan.)

3. Melt butter or margarine in a medium-size saucepan; stir in flour, salt and onion powder; cook, stirring constantly, until mixture bubbles 1 minute; stir in milk and red-pepper seasoning; continue cooking and stirring until mixture thickens and bubbles 1 minute; stir in grated cheeses until melted; let cool while beating eggs.

4. Beat egg whites till they form soft peaks in a large bowl.

5. Beat egg yolks well in small bowl; beat in cooled cheese sauce very slowly until well blended. Fold this mixture into beaten egg whites until no streaks of white or yellow remain. Pour into prepared dish; make a deep circle in center with knife so soufflé will puff up high.

6. Bake in a slow oven (325°) for 1 hour, 15 minutes, or until puffy-firm and golden. Serve at once. Makes 6 servings.

CHEESE AND EGGPLANT CASSEROLE

1 large eggplant (about 1½ pounds)
3 tablespoons olive or vegetable oil
1 large onion, chopped (1 cup)
1½ cups soft white bread crumbs (3 slices)
1 teaspoon salt
1 teaspoon leaf oregano, crumbled
¼ teaspoon pepper
1 container (1 pound) cottage cheese
2 eggs
¼ cup chopped parsley
½ teaspoon salt
2 medium-size tomatoes, sliced
1 package (8 ounces) mozzarella cheese, sliced

1. Slice, pare and dice eggplant. Sauté in oil until soft; push to one side; sauté onion until soft; stir in bread crumbs, the 1 teaspoon salt, oregano and pepper; remove from heat.
2. Combine cottage cheese, eggs, parsley and the ½ teaspoon salt in a medium-size bowl.
3. Spoon half the eggplant mixture into an 8x8x2-inch baking dish; spread cottage cheese mixture over; top with remaining eggplant. Overlap slices of tomato over eggplant and top with slices of mozzarella cheese.
4. Bake in moderate oven (350°) 45 minutes; remove from oven and allow to set for 10 minutes before serving. Makes 6 servings.

PUFFY OMELET WITH CHEESE SAUCE

4 tablespoons (½ stick) butter or margarine
2 tablespoons flour
¾ teaspoon salt
1 cup milk
4 wedges process Gruyère cheese (from a 6-ounce package), shredded
4 eggs, separated
2 tablespoons water
Dash of pepper
1 tablespoon chopped green chili (from a 4-ounce can)

1. Make cheese sauce: Melt 2 tablespoons of the butter or margarine in a small saucepan; add flour and ½ teaspoon of the salt. Cook over low heat, stirring constantly, just until bubbly. Remove from heat; stir in milk slowly. Cook, stirring constantly, until sauce thickens and bubbles 1 minute. Remove from heat; stir in cheese little by little until melted and smooth. Cover; keep warm while preparing remaining ingredients.
2. Beat egg whites until stiff in a large bowl.
3. Beat egg yolks with remaining ¼ teaspoon salt and pepper until thick and lemon-colored in a small bowl; beat in water. Fold into egg-white mixture until no streaks of yellow remain.
4. Heat a 9-inch skillet or omelet pan with an ovenproof handle, 5 seconds over medium heat. With a fork, swirl remaining 2 tablespoons butter or margarine over bottom and sides.
5. Pour in egg mixture. Cook over low heat 5 minutes, or until mixture is set on the bottom and is golden-brown.
6. Bake in moderate oven (350°) 10 minutes, or until puffy and lightly golden on the top.
7. Loosen omelet around edge with a knife; lift onto heated large serving plate. Cut a gash with a knife down center of omelet; sprinkle green chili over one half. Spoon about ¾ cup of the cheese sauce over omelet; fold over with spatula. Spoon remaining sauce over the top. Serve at once. Makes 2 servings.

TWO-CHEESE GNOCCHI

5 cups water
1 teaspoon salt
1 cup enriched farina
2 eggs, beaten
1 cup shredded Swiss cheese
¼ teaspoon pepper
¼ cup (½ stick) butter or margarine
1 cup grated Parmesan cheese

1. Heat water with salt to boiling in a large saucepan; sprinkle in farina and stir until well blended; lower heat and simmer 15 minutes.
2. Remove saucepan from heat and beat in eggs, Swiss cheese and pepper. Return saucepan to heat and cook, stirring constantly, until mixture thickens, about 3 minutes.
3. Pour mixture into a buttered 15x9x1-inch baking pan; chill 30 minutes, or until set.
4. Cut mixture into 1½-inch diamonds and arrange, overlapping, in an 8-cup baking dish.
5. Melt butter or margarine in a small saucepan; drizzle over; sprinkle cheese on top.
6. Bake in hot oven (400°) 30 minutes, or until tips of gnocchi are golden. Makes 4 servings.

7

COMPANY MEALS

Right from the beginning with our cover photograph of Hearty Cassoulet, we knew you'd have company on your mind. After all, a food budget that only allows for the same number of people night after night, just isn't realistic. We've designed this chapter with reality in mind, and the recipes are geared to those times when you have at least eight people to feed—eight people you want to entertain well, but economically. Of course, if you're only planning a dinner for four or six, almost any recipe in this book will work. Or, you can prepare these larger dinners and know you'll have plenty for second helpings or for leftovers to stash in the freezer for that time when unexpected guests arrive. Try our recipes. They'll help put economy on the company menu—and the only thing your guests will know is that you're a marvelous cook.

HEARTY CASSOULET

- **1 package (1 pound) dried white Great Northern beans**
- **8 cups water**
- **2 large onions, peeled**
- **6 whole cloves**
- **2 stalks celery, with tops**
- **3 sprigs parsley**
- **2 bay leaves**
  Salt
- **½ pound salt pork, cut in ½-inch cubes**
- **1 pound lean breast of lamb, cut in 1½-inch pieces**
- **1 carrot, sliced**
- **2 cloves garlic, crushed**
- **1 can (6 ounces) tomato paste**
- **2 cups water**
- **2 envelopes or teaspoons instant chicken broth**
- **1 teaspoon leaf thyme**
- **4 pork chops (about 1¼ pounds)**
- **½ pound pork sausage, shaped into 8 small patties**

1. Place beans in a kettle; add 8 cups water; heat to boiling; cover. Cook 2 minutes; remove from heat; let stand 1 hour. Stud one of the onions with cloves, add to beans along with tops from celery, the parsley and bay leaves tied together with string; stir in 1 teaspoon salt; bring to boiling. Reduce heat and simmer, covered, 1 to 1½ hours, or until beans are tender. Drain, reserving liquid. Remove and discard parsley bundle.
2. Meanwhile, sauté salt pork until crisp in Dutch oven; remove and set aside. Pour off drippings; return 2 tablespoons to pan.
3. Brown lamb in hot drippings; remove and set aside. Slice remaining onion and celery stalks; add to drippings along with carrot and garlic; saute until golden, about 8 minutes. Return lamb and pork to Dutch oven. Stir in tomato paste, 2 cups water, instant chicken broth, thyme and 1 teaspoon salt; bring to boiling. Simmer, covered, 1 hour.
4. Add the beans and ½ cup of bean liquid to lamb mixture; adjust seasonings if needed. Turn into a 3-quart casserole.
5. Brown pork chops on both sides in a large skillet; add to bean mixture. Brown pork sausage patties in same skillet; set aside.
6. Bake in moderate oven (350°) 30 minutes.

Carefully stir beans, adding more bean liquid if too dry. Arrange sausage patties on top. Bake 30 minutes longer. Makes 8 servings.

CURRIED LAMB WITH GOLDEN PILAF

- **4 pounds lamb combination (neck and shoulder meat for stewing)**
- **2 cups water**
- **2 tablespoons vegetable oil**
- **3 cups cooking apples, pared, quartered, cored and chopped**
- **1 cup chopped celery**
- **5 teaspoons curry powder**
- **2 teaspoons salt**
  Golden Pilaf (recipe follows)

1. Cut meat from bones of lamb combination; cut meat into 1-inch pieces.
2. Place bones and water in a medium-size saucepan. Heat to boiling; reduce heat; cover. Simmer 30 minutes. Strain broth into a 2-cup measure (you should have 1½ cups); reserve.
3. Brown lamb pieces slowly, part at a time, in oil in a large skillet with a cover; remove meat with a slotted spoon and reserve.
4. Stir apple and celery into drippings in skillet; saute until soft; blend in curry powder and cook 1 minute. Stir in reserved lamb broth and salt. Heat to boiling; reduce heat; cover. Simmer 10 minutes. Mash this mixture with the back of a wooden spoon to make a smoother sauce.
5. Return reserved meat to skillet; cover; simmer 1 hour, or until meat is tender. Serve with Golden Pilaf. Makes 8 servings.

GOLDEN PILAF

- **2 cups uncooked regular rice**
- **¼ cup vegetable oil**
- **1 large onion, chopped (1 cup)**
- **2 envelopes instant chicken broth or 2 teaspoons granulated chicken bouillon**
- **2 teaspoons salt**
- **5 cups hot water**
- **½ cup golden raisins**

1. Sauté rice, stirring often, in oil until golden-brown in a large skillet; remove with spoon.

2. Sauté onion until soft in oil remaining in same pan; return rice to skillet with onion, chicken broth, salt, hot water and raisins.

3. Heat to boiling; reduce heat to low; cover. Simmer 35 minutes, or until liquid is absorbed and rice is tender. Makes 8 servings.

SPINACH LASAGNA

1 pound ground beef
½ pound sweet Italian sausages
2 large onions, chopped (2 cups)
1 clove of garlic, minced
1 can (2 pounds, 3 ounces) Italian tomatoes with tomato paste
3 teaspoons salt
2 teaspoons Italian herbs, crumbled
¼ teaspoon pepper
1 package (1 pound) lasagna noodles
2 eggs
2 packages (10 ounces each) frozen chopped spinach, thawed and drained well
1 carton (1 pound) cottage cheese
1 cup grated Parmesan cheese
2 packages (6 ounces each) sliced mozzarella cheese

1. Brown ground beef and Italian sausages in a large kettle; remove with a slotted spoon; reserve. Pour off all but 3 tablespoons of the fat. Saute onion and garlic until soft in fat in kettle. Return browned meat to kettle with Italian tomatoes, 2 teaspoons of the salt, Italian herbs and pepper. Simmer over low heat, stirring several times, 30 minutes.

2. While sauce simmers: Cook lasagna noodles, following label directions; drain and place in a bowl of cold water to keep separated.

3. Beat eggs in a large bowl; add drained spinach, cottage cheese and remaining 1 teaspoon of the salt.

4. When ready to assemble: Drain noodles on paper toweling; arrange 3 strips on the bottom of each of two 13x9x2-inch baking dishes. Spoon part of the cheese-spinach mixture over noodles; add part of meat sauce; sprinkle with grated Parmesan cheese. Continue layering until all ingredients have been used. Top each dish with slices of mozzarella cheese.

5. Bake in moderate oven (350°) 30 minutes, or until bubbly-hot. Garnish with sprigs of parsley, if you wish. Makes 12 servings.

NOTE: These dishes can be made early in the day. Assemble lasagna and keep in the refrigerator until 1 hour before party time. Place in cold oven and turn heat to 350°. Bake 1 hour, or until bubbly-hot.

ALGERIAN COUSCOUS

2 large onions, chopped (2 cups)
2 tablespoons olive oil
1 broiler-fryer (about 2½ pounds), cut up
1 pound lean lamb, cut into 1½-inch cubes
3 cups water
4 carrots, pared and cut into 1-inch pieces
3 teaspoons salt
¼ teaspoon pepper
¼ teaspoon ground ginger
1 three-inch piece stick cinnamon
1 teaspoon salt (for couscous)
1 cup water (for couscous)
1 package (1 pound, 1¾ ounces) couscous* (2¾ cups)
4 small zucchini, washed and cut into ½-inch slices
2 fresh tomatoes, chopped
1 can (1 pound, 4 ounces) chick peas, drained
1 cup seedless raisins
6 tablespoons (¾ stick) butter or margarine, melted

1. Sauté onions until golden in oil in a large skillet, about 5 minutes. Transfer to a stock pot or similar deep narrow kettle. Brown chicken and lamb in same skillet; transfer to stock pot as it browns.

2. Add water to skillet; bring to boiling, scraping off brown bits. Pour over meat. Stir in carrots, salt, pepper, ginger and cinnamon. Bring to boiling.

3. For couscous, dissolve salt in 1 cup water; sprinkle about ½ cup over couscous in a large bowl to moisten; place in a large, fine-mesh sieve. Hang sieve on edge of stock pot over stew, making sure the sieve does not touch stew. Cover tightly with foil to keep steam in. Simmer 40 minutes.

4. Remove sieve; stir zucchini, tomatoes, chick peas and raisins into stew. Sprinkle remaining salted water over couscous; mix or stir with a fork. Set sieve over stew again to steam. Simmer 30 minutes longer, or until meats and vegetables are tender. Thicken stew with a little flour mixed

with water, if you wish. Turn couscous into a large bowl; drizzle melted butter or margarine over; toss to mix.

5. To serve, spoon stew into center of a deep platter. Arrange the steamed buttered couscous around edge. Makes 8 servings.

*You may substitute brown or white rice or kasha and cook, following label directions.

GREEK LAMB STEW, AVGOLEMONO
(Lamb and Artichoke Stew)

- 3 pounds lean lamb, cut into 1½-inch cubes
- 2 tablespoons olive or vegetable oil
- 1 large onion, sliced
- ½ cup dry white wine
- 2 cups water
- 2 teaspoons salt
- ⅛ teaspoon pepper
- 1 bay leaf
- 1 tablespoon chopped fresh dill
  OR: 1 teaspoon dried dill weed
- 2 packages (9 ounces each) frozen artichoke hearts
- 2 tablespoons flour
- ¼ cup dry white wine
- 3 eggs
- ¼ cup fresh lemon juice

1. Brown lamb, part at a time (removing pieces to a bowl as they brown), in oil in heavy kettle or Dutch oven. Add onion; sauté until golden, about 5 minutes. Return meat to kettle. Add ½ cup wine; lower heat; cover. Simmer about 15 minutes.

2. Stir in water, salt, pepper and bay leaf. Simmer, covered, over low heat, 1 hour and 15 minutes, or until meat is tender.

3. Add dill and artichokes. Cook 10 minutes longer, or until artichokes are tender.

4. Remove bay leaf. Then remove meat and artichokes from cooking liquid with slotted spoon; arrange in a shallow serving casserole. Cover and keep hot while making sauce. Measure cooking liquid, there should be about 3 cups; add wine or water, if needed. Bring to boiling.

5. Blend flour and ¼ cup wine in a small cup; stir into boiling liquid. Cook and stir until sauce thickens and bubbles 1 minute.

6. Beat eggs with rotary beater or electric hand mixer until light and fluffy; beat in lemon juice. Gradually beat boiling sauce into egg mixture.

Return to saucepan; heat, stirring constantly, over low heat, 1 minute. (Sauce should not boil.)

7. To serve, pour sauce over meat and artichokes in casserole. Garnish casserole with lemon slices and sprigs of fresh dill, if you wish.

Makes 8 servings.

TWIN-MEAT RAGOUT

- 3 pounds lean boneless lamb shoulder, cut in 1-inch cubes
- 3 pounds veal shoulder, cut into cubes, about 1 inch each
- 2 large onions, peeled and sliced thin
- 1 large head iceberg lettuce, shredded
- 3 teaspoons salt
- ¼ teaspoon pepper
- 1½ teaspoons leaf rosemary, crumbled
- 5 envelopes instant chicken broth or 5 teaspoons granulated chicken bouillon
  Water
- 16 medium-size potatoes, pared
- 1 bag (2 pounds) frozen peas
- 4 medium-size yellow squashes, sliced
- 2 cups (1 pint) cherry tomatoes
- 1 tablespoon butter or margarine
- ¼ cup cornstarch

1. Combine lamb and veal with onions, lettuce, salt, pepper and rosemary in a large roasting pan. Sprinkle chicken broth or bouillon over top; pour 6 cups water into pan. Heat to boiling; cover. Simmer 1 hour. Place potatoes on top; simmer 1 hour longer, or until meats and potatoes are tender.

2. About 15 minutes before meats are cooked, cook peas and squashes in boiling salted water in separate medium-size saucepans just until crisply tender; drain.

3. Sauté tomatoes in butter or margarine in a medium-size frying pan, shaking pan often, 3 minutes, or just until hot.

4. Smooth cornstarch and about ½ cup water to a paste in a cup; stir into stew mixture. Cook, stirring constantly, until mixture thickens and boils 3 minutes.

5. Spoon stew mixture into two heated large serving dishes; spoon squash slices, then peas, in rings on top of each. Pile tomatoes in center. Garnish each tomato with a sprig of fresh rosemary, if you wish. Makes 16 servings.

GLAZED PORK SHOULDER

1 cook-before-eating smoked pork picnic
  shoulder (about 5 pounds)
  Water
1 tablespoon mixed pickling spices
1 cup firmly packed brown sugar
1 cup apple juice
¼ teaspoon ground cloves
½ cup chopped parsley

1. Place picnic shoulder in a kettle; add cold water to cover; add pickling spices.
2. Heat slowly to boiling; reduce heat; cover. Simmer 2½ hours, or until meat is tender when pierced with a two-tined fork. Remove from heat; allow meat to cool in liquid at least 30 minutes.
3. Place picnic shoulder in a shallow roasting pan. Cut skin from top of meat; score fat.
4. To make Parsley Sauce: Combine brown sugar, apple juice and cloves in a small saucepan. Heat to boiling; reduce heat; simmer 5 minutes. Remove sauce from heat; stir in chopped parsley. Brush part of sauce over meat.
5. Roast in moderate oven (375°), basting several times with part of sauce, 30 minutes, or until well-glazed.
6. Pass remaining Parsley Sauce separately. Serve with baked sweet potatoes and spiced pear halves, if you wish. Makes 12 servings.

BAKED OXTAIL RAGOUT

4 pounds oxtails
½ cup flour
1 teaspoon salt
1 teaspoon leaf savory, crumbled
¼ teaspoon pepper
¼ cup vegetable oil
1 large onion, chopped (1 cup)
1 can (12 ounces) carrot juice
1½ cups water
½ cup dry red wine
1 bay leaf

1. Cut oxtails into uniform length pieces.
2. Shake pieces in a mixture of flour, salt, savory and pepper in a plastic bag to coat well; reserve remaining seasoned flour for use in Step 4 (you should have about 2 tablespoons).
3. Brown pieces slowly, part at a time, in oil in a large skillet; remove pieces with a slotted spoon to an 8-cup baking dish.
4. Stir onion into drippings in skillet; sauté until soft. Stir in reserved seasoned flour; cook, stirring, just until bubbly. Stir in carrot juice, water and wine; continue cooking and stirring, until gravy thickens and bubbles 1 minute. Pour over meat in baking dish; add bay leaf; cover.
5. Bake in moderate oven (375°) 2 hours, or until meat separates easily from bones.
6. Ladle ragout into soap plates; serve with French bread, if you wish. Makes 8 servings.

TEXAS CHILI BEEF STEW

4 pounds beef short ribs
1 large onion, chopped (1 cup)
1 green pepper, halved, seeded and diced
2 cloves garlic, chopped
2 tablespoons chili powder
1 can (1 pound) tomatoes
1 can (4 ounces) green chilies, drained and
  chopped
1 envelope or teaspoon instant beef broth
1 cup boiling water
1 teaspoon salt
2 tablespoons flour
¼ cup water
2 cans (1 pound each) kidney beans, drained
1 can (1 pound) whole kernel corn, drained

1. Heat heavy kettle or Dutch oven; rub fat edges of short ribs over bottom until about 2 tablespoons of fat melt. Brown short ribs well on all sides; remove. Drain off fat.
2. Sauté onion, green pepper and garlic in same pan. Stir in chili powder; cook, stirring constantly, about 2 minutes. Add tomatoes and green chilies. Dissolve instant beef broth in boiling water; stir into tomato mixture. Return ribs to pan. Bring to boiling; lower heat; cover. Simmer 2 hours, or until meat is very tender and falls away from the bones.
3. Remove meat to serving bowl; keep warm. Carefully remove bones and skim fat from sauce in pan. Blend flour and water in a cup; mix well. Stir into sauce. Cook, stirring constantly, until sauce bubbles and thickens. Add kidney beans and corn; heat about 5 minutes. Spoon over meat in serving bowl. Makes 8 servings.

8

SOUPS 'N' STEWS

Slow-simmered soups and stews are two great ways to expand your menu and still trim the food budget. They're not difficult to prepare either, as the recipes in this chapter prove. Here you'll find ideas for one-pot seafood, meat, poultry and vegetable combinations, some made from scratch, others made with convenience-oriented foods that are perfect for busy nights. The Basic Beef Broth and Basic Chicken Broth recipes also offer you make-ahead flexibility. Then, as dinnertime rolls around, add leftover meats and vegetables or use the broths as the basis for a delicious onion soup, a chicken and vegetable stew or a stick-to-the-ribs beef and vegetable soup. The cost? Some of these specials can be made for less than 25¢ a serving. Others, though a bit more expensive, still provide your money's worth in flavor, nutrition and number of servings.

ONION SOUP

4 large onions, sliced (1½ pounds)
4 tablespoons (½ stick) butter or margarine
6 cups Basic Beef Broth (see below)
2 teaspoons salt
¼ teaspoon pepper
6 slices French bread, toasted
½ cup grated Parmesan cheese
¼ cup Gruyere or Swiss cheese

1. Saute onion in butter or margarine in Dutch oven 15 minutes, or until lightly browned. Stir in Beef Broth, salt and pepper. Bring to boiling; reduce heat; cover; simmer 30 minutes.
2. Ladle soup into 6 ovenproof soup bowls or 12-ounce custard cups, or an 8-cup casserole. Lay bread slices on top, sprinkle with cheeses.
3. Heat in very hot oven (425°) 10 minutes, then place under preheated broiler and broil until top is bubbly and lightly browned. Makes 6 servings.

BASIC BEEF BROTH

2½ pounds brisket, boneless chuck, or bottom round, in one piece
2 pounds shin of beef with bones
2 three-inch marrow bones
1 veal knuckle (about 1 pound)
Water
8 teaspoons salt
2 carrots, pared
2 medium-size yellow onions, peeled
2 stalks celery with leaves
1 turnip, pared and quartered
1 leek, washed well
3 large sprigs of parsley
12 peppercorns
3 whole cloves
1 bay leaf

1. Place beef, shin of beef, marrow bones and veal knuckle in a large kettle; add water to cover, about 4 quarts. Heat to boiling; skim off foam that appears on top. Add salt, carrots, onions, celery, turnip and leek; tie parsley, peppercorns, cloves and bay leaf in a small cheesecloth bag; add to kettle. Push under the liquid and add more water if needed.
2. Heat to boiling; cover; reduce heat; simmer very slowly 3½ to 4 hours, or until meat is tender. Remove meat and vegetables from broth.
3. Strain broth through cheesecloth into a large bowl. (There should be about 14 cups.) Use this broth in making Onion Soup (see left) or in any of our recipes calling for beef broth.
4. When meat is cool enough to handle, remove and dicard bones. Trim large piece of meat and save for another meal, if you wish. Cut trimmings and shin beef into bite-size pieces; serve as is, or use as the basic stock in Old-Fashioned Beef and Vegetable Soup (see page 99). To store in refrigerator up to 3 to 4 days, keep in covered container. To freeze, pack in small portions, 1 or 2 cups, in plastic bags or freezer containers, to use as needed.
5. To store in refrigerator, up to 4 days, leave fat layer on surface of broth until ready to use, then lift off and discard before heating. To freeze: Transfer broth to freezer containers, allowing space on top for expansion; freeze until ready to use (3 to 4 months maximum.) Makes 14 cups.

BASIC CHICKEN BROTH

2 broiler-fryers, 3 to 3½ pounds each
Chicken giblets
2 medium carrots, pared
1 large parsnip, pared
1 large onion, chopped (1 cup)
2 stalks celery
2 celery tops
3 sprigs parsley
1 leek, washed well
Water
2 tablespoons salt
12 peppercorns

1. Combine chicken, chicken giblets, carrots, parsnip, onion and celery in a large kettle; tie celery tops, parsley and leek together with a string; add to kettle. Add enough cold water to cover chicken and vegetables, about 12 cups.
2. Heat slowly to boiling; skim; add salt and peppercorns; reduce heat. Simmer very slowly 1 to 1½ hours, or until meat falls off the bones. Remove meat and vegetables from broth, discard the bundle of greens.
3. Strain broth through cheesecloth into a large bowl. (There should be about 12 cups.) Use this broth in the recipe for Mulligatawny Soup.
4. When cool enough to handle, remove and

discard skin and bones from chicken; cut meat into bite-size pieces; use as called for in following recipes, or use in salads, casseroles, etc. To store in refrigerator, up to 3 to 4 days, keep in covered container. To freeze, pack in small portions, 1 or 2 cups, in plastic bags or freezer containers, to use as needed.

5. To store in refrigerator, up to 4 days, leave fat layer on surface of broth until ready to use, then lift fat off and discard, or use in other cooking. To freeze, transfer broth to freezer containers, allowing space on top for expansion. Freeze until ready to use (3 to 4 months maximum). Makes 12 cups or enough for 2 soups, and even extra meat for a salad or casserole, if you wish.

MULLIGATAWNY SOUP

    3 medium carrots, pared and sliced
    2 stalks of celery, sliced
    6 cups Basic Chicken Broth
    3 cups cooked diced chicken (from Basic Chicken Broth)
    1 large onion, chopped (1 cup)
    4 tablespoons (½ stick) butter or margarine
    1 apple, pared, quartered, cored and chopped
    5 teaspoons curry powder
    1 teaspoon salt
    ¼ cup flour
    1 tablespoon lemon juice
    2 cups hot cooked rice
    ¼ cup chopped parsley
    6 lemon slices (optional)

1. Cook carrots and celery in 1 cup broth in a medium-size saucepan 20 minutes, or until tender. Add chicken; heat just until hot; cover; keep warm.
2. Saute onion until soft in butter or margarine in Dutch oven; stir in apple, curry powder and salt; saute 5 minutes longer, or until apple is soft; add flour. Gradually stir in remaining chicken broth; heat to boiling, stirring constantly; reduce heat; cover; simmer 15 minutes.
3. Add vegetables and chicken with the broth they were cooked in; bring just to boiling. Stir in lemon juice.
4. Ladle into soup plates or bowls; pass hot cooked rice and chopped parsley and lemon slices, if you wish, for each to add his own. Good with French bread. Makes 6 servings.

OLD-FASHIONED BEEF AND VEGETABLE SOUP

    1½ quarts Basic Beef Broth (see page 98)
      2 potatoes, peeled and diced (2 cups)
      2 carrots, pared and sliced
      1 cup sliced celery
      2 small onions, peeled and quartered
      1 can (1 pound) whole tomatoes
      2 teaspoons salt
      ⅛ teaspoon pepper
      ½ head green cabbage, shredded (2 cups)
      1 cup frozen corn (from a plastic bag)
      3 cups diced boiled beef (from Basic Beef Broth)
      1 tablespoon chopped parsley

1. Heat Beef Broth to boiling in a large saucepan or kettle; add potatoes, carrots, celery, onions, tomatoes, salt and pepper; heat to boiling again; lower heat; cover; simmer for 20 minutes.
2. Stir in cabbage, corn and meat; simmer 10 minutes longer or just until all vegetables are crisply tender. Sprinkle with parsley.
3. Ladle into soup bowls. Makes 8 servings.

BLACK BEAN SOUP

    4 cups dried black turtle beans (from two 1-pound bags)
    3½ quarts water
      ½ pound pepperoni, cut into ½-inch pieces
      3 large onions, sliced (3 cups)
      1 boneless smoked pork butt (about 2 pounds)
      2 cups dry red wine
      3 oranges, peeled and sectioned
      2 teaspoons salt
      ¼ cup chopped parsley

1. Combine beans with water in a large kettle; heat to boiling and boil 2 minutes; cover. Remove from heat; let stand 1 hour.
2. Heat beans to boiling again; add pepperoni and onions; reduce heat; cover. Simmer 2 hours, stirring occasionally, or until beans are tender. Add pork and wine. Simmer 1¼ hours longer, or until meat is cooked through.
3. Remove meat and keep warm. With a slotted spoon, remove pieces of sausage and about 3 cups of whole beans. Puree remaining beans in soup in a blender or press them through sieve.

Return beans to kettle along with sausage and the whole beans.

4. Add sections from 2 of the oranges and salt. Taste; add additional salt, if you wish. Bring to boiling; ladle into soup bowls. Garnish each serving with a section of reserved orange; sprinkle with parsley.

5. Slice pork butt thin and pass it around to eat, on a separate plate, with mustard and bread. Makes 12 servings.

NOTE: This dish can easily be made ahead of time because it freezes well. (Freeze soup and meats separately, sealing both in refrigerator-freezer containers.)

CIOPPINO

- 1 large onion, chopped (1 cup)
- 1 medium-size green pepper, halved, seeded and chopped
- ½ cup sliced celery
- 1 carrot, pared and shredded
- 3 cloves of garlic, minced
- 3 tablespoons olive oil
- 2 cans (1 pound each) tomatoes
- 1 can (8 ounces) tomato sauce
- 1 teaspoon leaf basil, crumbled
- 1 bay leaf
- 1 teaspoon salt
- ¼ teaspoon pepper
- 1 pound frozen halibut or turbot
- 1 dozen mussels in shell, if available
  OR: 1 can (10 ounces) clams in shell
- 1½ cups dry white wine
- 1 package (8 ounces) frozen, shelled, deveined shrimp
- ½ pound fresh or frozen scallops
- 2 tablespoons minced parsley

1. Sauté onion, green pepper, celery, carrot and garlic in olive oil until soft in a kettle or Dutch oven.

2. Stir in tomatoes, tomato sauce, basil, bay leaf, salt and pepper; heat to boiling; lower heat; cover; simmer 2 hours. Discard bay leaf.

3. While sauce simmers, remove the skin from the halibut or turbot; cut into serving-size pieces. Using a stiff brush, thoroughly scrub the mussels, cutting off their "beards," under running water to remove any residue of mud and sand. Reserve for use in Step 5.

4. Stir wine into sauce in kettle. Add the fish, shrimp and scallops. Simmer, covered, 10 minutes longer.

5. Place mussels or clams in a layer on top of fish in kettle; cover; steam 5 to 10 minutes, or until the shells are fully opened and fish flakes easily. (Discard any unopened mussels.)

6. Ladle into soup plates or bowls. Sprinkle with parsley. Serve with sourdough bread, or crusty French or Italian bread. Makes 8 servings.

NOTE: If fresh clams are available and reasonably priced, use 1 dozen in place of the canned clams. Be sure to rinse them well before adding to soup, and discard any that do not open once they have been cooked.

BOOTHBAY CHOWDER

- 3 slices bacon, chopped
- 1 large onion, chopped (1 cup)
- 4 medium-size potatoes, pared and diced (3 cups)
- 3 cups water
- 1 teaspoon salt
- ¼ teaspoon pepper
- 2 cans (10½ ounces each) minced clams
- 1 bottle (8 ounces) clam juice
- 1 envelope instant nonfat dry milk (for 1 quart)
- 3 tablespoons flour
- 2 tablespoons minced parsley

1. Cook bacon until crisp in a large heavy saucepan or Dutch oven. Remove bacon with slotted spoon; drain on paper toweling; reserve. Add onion to bacon drippings in saucepan; sauté until soft.

2. Add potatoes, 2 cups of the water, salt and pepper; cover. Simmer, 15 minutes, or until potatoes are tender. Remove from heat.

3. Drain liquid from clams into a 4-cup measure; reserve clams. Add bottled clam juice and remaining cup of water.

4. Combine dry milk with flour in a small bowl; stir briskly into clam liquids in cup. Add to potato mixture in saucepan. Cook, stirring constantly, over medium heat, until chowder thickens and bubbles 1 minute.

5. Add clams; heat just until piping-hot. Ladle into soup bowls. Sprinkle with parsley and reserved bacon. Serve with pilot crackers, if you wish. Makes 6 to 8 servings.

HUNGARIAN PORK GOULASH

2 pounds pork, cut in 1-inch cubes
2 tablespoons butter or margarine
1 large onion, chopped (1 cup)
1 tablespoon paprika
1 can condensed chicken broth
1 cup water
1 teaspoon caraway seeds
2 teaspoons salt
   Dash of pepper
1 can (1 pound, 11 ounces) sauerkraut
2 tablespoons flour
¼ cup water
1 cup dairy sour cream
   Chopped parsley

1. Brown pork, part at a time (removing pieces to a bowl as they brown), in butter or margarine in a heavy kettle or Dutch oven. Sauté onion until golden, about 5 minutes, in same pan, adding more butter or margarine, if needed. Stir in paprika; cook 1 minute longer. Return meat.
2. Stir in chicken broth, 1 cup water, caraway seeds, salt and pepper. Heat to boiling; lower heat; cover. Simmer 1 hour and 15 minutes.
3. Drain and rinse sauerkraut; stir into stew. Simmer 30 minutes longer, or until tender.
4. Blend flour and ½ cup water in a small cup; stir into simmering stew. Cook and stir until gravy thickens and boils.
5. Lower heat; stir in sour cream, a tablespoon at a time, to prevent curdling. Heat just until heated through. Do not boil. Sprinkle with parsley. Makes 6 servings.

PETITE MARMITE

   Turkey carcass with meat
   Giblets (from freezer)

1 pound beef, brisket or flanken
8 cups cold water
1 large onion, studded with 2 cloves
1 small parsnip, pared and quartered
4 carrots
1 stalk celery with leaves, chopped
4 sprigs parsley
1 large leek (white part only)
2 stalks celery
1 white turnip
2 teaspoons salt

¼ teaspoon freshly ground pepper
2 cups Sauce

1. Cut any large pieces of meat still on turkey and reserve; remove all skin from carcass and break into as small pieces as possible.
2. Place turkey carcass in deep kettle; add frozen giblets, beef and water.
3. Heat to boiling; lower heat; simmer, skimming foam from surface, until liquid is clear. Add onion, quartered parsnip and 1 of the carrots, chopped celery with leaves, and parsley.
4. Simmer 1½ hours, or until beef is tender; remove kettle from heat and allow to stand until beef is cool enough to handle.
5. Cut beef into tiny cubes; cut off all remaining turkey from carcass; dice giblets. Strain soup into a large bowl; allow to cool until all fat has floated to the top; skim off all fat. Rinse kettle and return liquid to kettle with cut-up meats.
6. Slice leek; cut remaining 3 carrots and 2 stalks celery into julienne strips and dice turnip; add to kettle with salt, pepper and sauce from Braised Turkey Persillade.
7. Heat soup to boiling; lower heat; cook 1 hour, or until vegetables are very tender. Taste; add additional salt and pepper, if you wish. Ladle into heated soup bowls. Makes 8 servings.

GREEK LAMB STEW

2½ pounds lamb shoulder, cubed
¼ cup vegetable oil
3 medium-size onions, chopped (1½ cups)
1 clove garlic, minced
1 can (1 pound, 12 ounces) tomatoes
1 can (8 ounces) tomato sauce
1 cup water
2 teaspoons salt
½ teaspoon ground marjoram
¼ teaspoon ground pepper
1 small eggplant, peeled and cubed
1 large green pepper, seeded and cubed
3 cups uncooked elbow macaroni (from a 1-pound package)

1. Brown meat lightly in oil in a Dutch oven. Remove cubes; add garlic and onions; sauté 5 minutes, or until soft.
2. Add lamb cubes, tomatoes, tomato sauce,

water, salt, marjoram and pepper; bring to boiling; lower heat and simmer, covered, 1 hour. Add eggplant, green pepper and macaroni; cook 30 minutes longer, or until meat and macaroni are tender. Makes 8 servings.

JAMBALAYA

    2 broiler-fryers, about 2 pounds each, cut up
    1 cup diced cooked ham
    4 tablespoons (½ stick) butter or margarine
    2 cloves garlic, minced
    2 large onions, chopped (2 cups)
    2 cans (1 pound each) stewed tomatoes
    2 teaspoons salt
    ½ teaspoon chili powder
    1 cup uncooked rice
    2 cups sliced celery

1. Brown chicken pieces lightly in butter or margarine in Dutch oven. Remove chicken pieces; brown ham lightly. Add garlic and onions; saute 5 minutes, or until soft. Return chicken.
2. Add stewed tomatoes, salt and chili powder to chicken mixture; bring to boiling; lower heat; simmer, covered, 30 minutes. Add rice and celery; cook 30 minutes longer, or until chicken and rice are tender. Makes 8 servings.

UKRAINIAN KETTLE

    1 bottom round beef roast (about 4 pounds)
    2 tablespoons vegetable oil
    1 large onion, diced (1 cup)
    2 teaspoons seasoned salt
    1 teaspoon seasoned pepper
    1 can condensed beef broth
    2 small yellow turnips (about 2½ pounds)
    1 cup sliced celery

1. Brown meat on all sides in oil in a kettle or Dutch oven. Add onion, seasoned salt and pepper, and beef broth. Heat to boiling; reduce heat; cover. Simmer 2 hours.
2. Pare turnips; cut into 1-inch cubes. Add with celery to meat, turning to coat with liquid in kettle. Cover; simmer 1 hour longer, or until meat and vegetables are tender.
3. Place pot roast on a carving board; cut into thick slices; arrange on a platter. Remove vegetables from kettle with a slotted spoon and arrange around meat. Spoon cooking liquid over all. Or, use cooking liquid to prepare a gravy (recipe follows). Makes 8 servings.
GRAVY: Pour cooking liquid into a 2-cup measure; add water, if needed, to make 2 cups; return to kettle and bring to boiling. Blend ¼ cup flour with ¼ cup water in a jar with a tight-fitting lid; shake to mix well; stir into boiling liquid. Cook, stirring constantly, until gravy thickens and bubbles 1 minute. Pour a little gravy over the meat and serve the remainder separately.

COPENHAGEN OXTAIL SOUP

    3 pounds oxtails, cut up
    3 teaspoons salt
    ⅛ teaspoon pepper
    1 large onion, chopped (1 cup)
    2 carrots, pared and sliced (1 cup)
    1 parsnip, pared and sliced (¾ cup)
    1 turnip, pared and sliced (1 cup)
    2 tablespoons brandy
    6 cups water
    ½ teaspoon leaf savory, crumbled
    1 bay leaf
      Eggs Mimosa (recipe follows)
      Chopped parsley

1. Spread oxtails in a single layer in shallow roasting pan. Season with salt and pepper. Roast in very hot oven (450°) 45 minutes, or until browned. Drain off fat, reserving 2 tablespoons.
2. Sauté onion, carrots, parsnip and turnip in reserved fat in kettle or Dutch oven, 10 minutes, or until soft. Add browned oxtails. Drizzle brandy over, ignite carefully with a lighted match. Add water to roasting pan in which oxtails were browned. Heat, stirring constantly, to dissolve browned bits; pour over oxtails and vegetables in Dutch oven; add savory and bay leaf. Bring to boiling; reduce heat; cover; simmer slowly 2 hours, or until meat separates easily from bones.
3. Ladle into soup bowls; place a half egg in each, sprinkle with parsley. Serve with crusty French bread. Makes 6 servings.
EGGS MIMOSA—Cut 3 hard-cooked eggs in half lengthwise. Carefully remove yolks, keeping whites whole. Press yolks through a sieve, spoon back into whites.

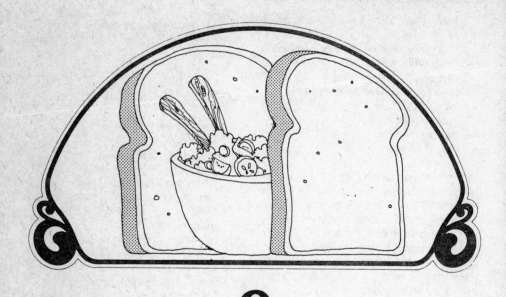

9
DINNER
SALADS & SANDWICHES

Serve lunch for dinner! Classically enjoyed as lunchtime fare or as an accompaniment to dinner, salads and sandwiches can be your dinner when a few extra touches are added. Our recipe for Salad Niçoise is a case in point. Starting with the basic greens and dressing, we added meat and cheese and turned this salad into a beautiful meal-in-one . . . for under 60¢ a serving. Then there's Bavarian Baked Potato Salad, a hot version of potato salad that includes frankfurters and cheese, and offers an even bigger budget break. The recipe makes enough for six people, at under 40¢ a serving. For sandwich-style dinners we offer Steak Medallions, Hot Tuna Heroes, Grilled Cheese for a Crowd, and many more. You'll find they're all geared to budget-watching but none scrimp on nutrition or inspiration. So have some lunch for dinner tonight!

• Don't wash away savings. For longer-lasting, fresher-tasting salad greens, don't wash them until you're ready to use them. Tomatoes and cucumbers get moldy and rot. Lettuce turns rusty and gets limp. Take only as much lettuce as you're going to need for your salad. Then wash and dry it, so dressings will cling to the leaves.

• For a change of pace in salads, along with a vitamin A boost, use escarole, chicory and spinach instead of iceberg lettuce. As another lettuce-and-tomatoes alternative, consider making your own coleslaw. Cabbage is reasonably priced and goes a long way. Use half for coleslaw, half for cooked cabbage and several outer leaves for rolled cabbage dinner.

• For further salad variety, look for the less familiar regional or seasonal greens. A few examples are: Prize head lettuce with red-edged leaves; lamb's lettuce; fennel, or finochio, with its distinctive anise flavor; the tender young dandelion, mustard and beet greens, plus Swiss chard. You can cook these greens, of course, but don't miss out on the unusual flavor touches that just a few, chopped up, will add to a salad.

• Save on salad dressings by making your own.

• Save on mayonnaise and salad dressing by buying the quart size. It's thriftier than two pints, even for the small family. Buy when your favorite brand is on sale—you may save as much as 10 to 20¢ a quart.

• Pick out fairly firm, medium-size heads of lettuce, for larger ones may be overgrown and tend to be slightly bitter. If you spot a reddish discoloration at stem end, don't be concerned, for this is nature's way of sealing the cut that was made when the head was picked.

• As a general rule, you can count on about 4 servings from a medium-size head of iceberg lettuce, or 1 pound of loose greens, or a 1½-pound head of cabbage.

• For cost-cutting on sandwiches, try baking your own breads, slicing cheeses yourself and buying luncheon meats unsliced.

FRUITS & VEGETABLES: GENERAL BUYING TIPS

• Be alert to price changes in fresh fruits and vegetables. A rule of thumb: Buy seasonal fresh foods when they're most plentiful in your area; the prices will normally be lower then. Also, buy only what you'll use in a short time (with the exceptions of onions and potatoes which will keep). In general, September is the peak of the harvest for many fruits and vegetables that are locally grown. At other times, frozen and canned fruits and vegetables may be your best buys.

• Prices of canned and frozen fruits and vegetables are influenced by seasonal changes just the way fresh fruits and vegetables are. Normally, there will be a substantial—perhaps even dramatic—drop in prices about the time a new crop is packed. During these weeks, which usually occur in late spring or summer, you might see six cans of vegetables on sale for $1.

• If you have any yard space to spare for growing vegetables, you'll be way ahead on savings when winter comes.

• Canned mushrooms cost *more* than fresh ones. Many people think the reverse is true, but the canned variety—even the pieces and stems—are 50 percent more expensive. If you like to cook with mushrooms, buy them fresh in large quantities when on sale, and freeze them.

• Fruits and vegetables that are reduced for quick sale rate consideration if you are buying them for immediate use. Also, don't hesitate to buy fruits that freeze well. Even near-overripe bananas can be frozen. The skin will blacken but the inside will still be fine for use in cakes, breads, etc. Or, you can remove the peel before freezing, blend the fruit with other ingredients and then freeze it.

• When oranges are in season, the cost is usually very reasonable, but it still pays to compare the price of the loose ones to the packaged fruit. (Generally the packaged fruit is less expensive.)

• When buying loose-packed frozen vegetables, it pays to look for the larger sizes. Those packed in clear plastic bags are especially good buys. For one thing, you can see exactly what you're buying. You also have the advantage of using whatever you need at any given time and placing the remainder back in the freezer. Savings of up to 40 percent are often possible.

• The difference between grades of canned fruits and vegetables is not a difference in quality, but of appearance. You do not need to buy fancy grades for stews, soups, pies, etc. Lower grades are just as nutritious, the flavor is often just as good and the price is usually lower. What is different may be the color (as in tomatoes or peas), size and uniformity of pieces (as in peach slices) or tenderness.

SALAD NICOISE

- 5 medium-size potatoes, cooked, drained and cooled
- ½ pound fresh green beans, cooked, drained and cooled
- ⅔ cup vegetable oil
- ⅓ cup wine vinegar
- 2 cloves garlic, crushed
- 1 tablespoon prepared mustard
- 1 tablespoon chopped parsley
- ½ teaspoon instant minced onion
- 1 teaspoon salt
- ¼ teaspoon ground pepper
- 2 large tomatoes, cut into slices
- 1 red onion, cubed
- 1 small green pepper, seeded and cubed
- 6 ripe olives, halved
- 3 hard-cooked eggs, shelled and sliced
- 1 can (2 ounces) anchovy fillets, drained
- 2 medium-size heads of romaine
- 1 can (14 ounces) tuna fish, drained

1. Peel potatoes and cut into thick slices. Place in a shallow dish. Place beans in a second shallow dish.
2. Combine oil, vinegar, garlic, mustard, parsley, onion, salt and pepper in a jar with a tight-fitting lid; shake well to mix. Drizzle ½ cup over potatoes and 2 tablespoonfuls over beans; let each stand at least 30 minutes to season.
3. Layer vegetables, eggs, anchovies and romaine in a large salad bowl. Break tuna into chunks; arrange on top. Pour rest of dressing over; toss lightly in order to blend flavors. Makes 6 servings.

CHICKEN SALAD

- 1 broiler-fryer, weighing about 3 pounds
- 2 cups water
- 1 teaspoon seasoned salt
- ¼ teaspoon seasoned pepper
- 1 large onion, chopped (1 cup)
  Few sprigs of parsley
- 1 can (4 ounces) pimiento, drained and chopped
- 1 small clove of garlic, finely chopped
- ¼ cup vegetable oil
- ¼ cup catsup
- 2 tablespoons vinegar
- 1 tablespoon prepared mustard

- ½ teaspoon salt
- ½ teaspoon leaf rosemary, crumbled
- 1 cup uncooked regular rice
- 1 package (10 ounces) frozen peas, cooked
  Romaine leaves, broken

1. Place chicken in a large kettle or Dutch oven with water to cover, seasoned salt and pepper, ½ cup of the chopped onion and parsley; bring to boiling; reduce heat; cover. Simmer 45 minutes, or until chicken is tender; remove chicken from kettle; cool; strain broth; reserve.
2. Remove meat from bones; cut into bite-size pieces. Place chicken in a large bowl with remaining ½ cup onion, pimiento and garlic.
3. Stir oil, catsup, vinegar, mustard, salt and rosemary in a small bowl until well blended; pour over chicken; toss and cover. Then let stand at room temperature to season, while cooking the rice.
4. Cook rice following label directions, using reserved chicken broth for part of the liquid. Cool.
5. Add cooked peas and rice to chicken; toss lightly. Serve on washed romaine leaves. Makes 6 servings.

STEAK MEDALLIONS

- 3 medium-size onions, peeled and sliced thin
- 2 medium-size green peppers, seeded and sliced into thin rings
- 4 tablespoons (½ stick) butter or margarine
- 4 cube steaks or individual boneless steaks, cut about ¼ inch thick
- 4 hero rolls
- 2 medium-size tomatoes, each cut in 8 slices
- ½ teaspoon seasoned salt
- ½ teaspoon seasoned pepper

1. Sauté onions and green peppers in 2 tablespoons of the butter or margarine until soft in a large frying pan; remove with a slotted spoon and keep warm.
2. Sauté steaks in same frying pan 2 minutes on each side, or until done as you like beef.
3. Split rolls almost through; open out flat. Spread with remaining 2 tablespoons butter or margarine; place on serving plates.
4. Place tomato slices and steaks on rolls; sprinkle with salt and pepper. Spoon onion mixture over steaks. Serve hot with corn chips and a cola beverage, if you wish. Makes 4 servings.

MACARONI AND HAM SALAD

  2 cups uncooked elbow macaroni
  2 cups cooked diced ham (½ pound)
  ½ cup chopped green pepper
  1 small onion, chopped (¼ cup)
  ¾ cup mayonnaise or salad dressing
  ½ teaspoon salt
  ⅛ teaspoon pepper
  1 pint cherry tomatoes, halved

1. Cook macaroni, following label directions; drain well. Cool.
2. Combine macaroni, ham, green pepper and onion in large bowl. Add mayonnaise, salt and pepper; toss to mix. Chill well.
3. Just before serving, halve 1 cup cherry tomatoes; add to salad; toss lightly to mix. Garnish with remaining tomatoes. Makes 8 servings.

SALMON MOUSSE

  2 envelopes unflavored gelatin
  2 cups water
  ¼ cup lemon juice
  1 envelope or teaspoon instant vegetable broth
  1 can (1 pound) salmon
  ¾ cup finely chopped celery
  ½ cup finely chopped seeded red pepper
  2 tablespoons chopped parsley
  2 tablespoons grated onion
  ½ teaspoon salt
  ¾ cup mayonnaise or salad dressing

1. Soften gelatin in 1 cup water in a medium-size saucepan. Heat, stirring constantly, until gelatin dissolves; remove from heat; cool; stir in 2 tablespoons lemon juice. Measure out ¾ cup of mixture and reserve.
2. Stir remaining 1 cup of water and instant vegetable broth into remaining mixture in saucepan. Heat, stirring constantly, just until hot.
3. Drain salmon and flake, removing bones and skin. Combine in medium-size bowl with celery, red pepper, parsley, grated onion, salt and mayonnaise or salad dressing. Stir in the ¾ cup gelatin mixture from Step 1. Reserve while preparing mold.
4. Pour half the remaining gelatin mixture into bottom of a 6-cup fish-shape mold; place in a large pan of ice and water; let stand, turning

mold often from side to side, to form a thin coat of gelatin on bottom and sides of mold.
5. Spoon salmon mixture over gelatin-coated mold, spreading to cover mold completely.
6. Chill in refrigerator 4 hours, or until firm.
7. When ready to serve, run a sharp-tip thin-blade knife around top of salad; dip mold very quickly in and out of hot water. Cover with a chilled serving plate; turn upside down; shake gently; lift off mold. Garnish with cucumber slices and red pepper slices, and serve with mayonnaise or salad dressing, if you wish. Makes 6 servings.

CHEF'S SALAD

  1 chicken breast, weighing about 12 ounces
  2 cups water
    Few celery tops
  1 small onion, halved
  1½ teaspoons salt
  ¾ cup chili sauce
  ½ cup mayonnaise or salad dressing
  1 teaspoon instant minced onion
  ½ teaspoon sugar
  6 cups broken mixed salad greens
  1 package (3½ ounces) sliced tongue, rolled in cone shapes
  1 package (8 ounces) sliced cooked ham, cut in thin strips
  1 package (8 ounces) sliced process Swiss cheese, cut in thin strips
  1 large tomato, cut into wedges
  1 small cucumber, pared and thinly sliced
  1 hard-cooked egg, sieved

1. Combine chicken breast, water, celery, onion and 1 teaspoon of the salt in a medium-size saucepan; heat to boiling; cover. Simmer 30 minutes, or until chicken is tender. Remove from broth; cool. Chill about 45 minutes. Skin and bone, then cut chicken in cubes.
2. Blend chili sauce, mayonnaise or salad dressing, instant minced onion, sugar and remaining ½ teapsoon salt in a small bowl. Chill dressing 30 minutes.
3. Place greens in a large salad bowl. Arrange tongue, ham, chicken, Swiss cheese, tomatoes and cucumber slices in sections on top. Sprinkle with sieved egg.
4. Just before serving, spoon on dressing; toss to mix. Makes 6 servings.

HOT TUNA HEROES

2 cans (about 7 ounces each) tuna fish
1 cup chopped celery
1 pound fresh peas, shelled (1 cup)
4 slices process Swiss cheese, cubed
¼ cup chopped parsley
¾ cup mayonnaise or salad dressing
6 hero rolls
4 tablespoons (½ stick) butter or margarine, melted

1. Drain tuna; separate into small-size chunks. Place in a medium-size bowl.
2. Add celery, peas, cheese and parsley; fold in mayonnaise or salad dressing.
3. Cut a slice from top of each roll; hollow out inside, leaving a ½-inch-thick shell. Brush insides of shells with melted butter or margarine; fill with tuna fish mixture. Wrap each separately in foil.
4. Bake in hot oven (400°) 15 minutes, or just until filling is hot. Thread a lemon wedge and 2 ripe olives onto a wooden pick to serve with each sandwich, if you wish. Serve hot. Makes 6 servings.

CHICKEN SALAD DELUXE

1 broiler-fryer (about 3 pounds)
4 cups water
1 small onion, sliced
  Few celery tops
¼ teaspoon salt
⅓ cup mayonnaise or salad dressing
⅓ cup dairy sour cream
1 tablespoon lemon juice
¼ teaspoon pepper
¾ cup chopped celery
1 medium-size onion, chopped (½ cup)
¼ cup chopped dill pickle
  Lettuce
  Paprika

1. Combine chicken with water, sliced onion, celery tops and salt in a kettle or Dutch oven. Heat to boiling; reduce heat; cover; simmer about 1 hour, or until chicken is tender. Remove from broth and cool until easy to handle. (Save broth to start a soup another day.)
2. Skin the chicken and take meat from bones.

Cut meat into bite-size pieces; place in a bowl.
3. Blend mayonnaise or salad dressing, sour cream, lemon juice and pepper in a small bowl. Combine celery, onion and dill pickle with chicken; add the dressing; toss until evenly coated. Cover; chill at least an hour to season and blend flavors.
4. Line salad bowl with lettuce leaves. Spoon salad into bowl. Sprinkle with paprika. Makes 4 servings.

BAVARIAN BAKED POTATO SALAD

5 medium-size potatoes (about 2 pounds)
1 pound frankfurters, cut into 1-inch pieces
2 tablespoons vegetable oil
1 medium-size onion, chopped (½ cup)
2 tablespoons flour
3 tablespoons brown sugar
1 teaspoon salt
1 teaspoon dry mustard
⅛ teaspoon pepper
1 cup water
⅓ cup vinegar
1 cup thinly sliced celery
½ cup chopped green pepper
¼ cup chopped pimiento
1 package (8 ounces) process sliced American cheese

1. Cook potatoes in boiling salted water in a large saucepan 30 minutes, or until tender; drain. Cool until easy to handle, then peel and dice. Place in a medium-size bowl.
2. Brown frankfurters in oil in a medium-size skillet; remove with a slotted spoon to the bowl with potatoes.
3. Saute onion in same skillet until soft. Combine flour, sugar, salt, mustard and pepper; stir into drippings; cook, stirring constantly, until bubbly. Stir in water and vinegar; continue cooking and stirring until dressing thickens and bubbles 1 minute.
4. Add celery, green pepper and pimiento; cook 1 minute longer. Pour over potatoes and frankfurters. Spoon one half of the potato mixture into an 8-cup baking dish; layer with 4 slices of cheese; spoon remaining potato mixture into dish. Top with remaining cheese slices cut into triangles.
5. Bake in moderate oven (350°) 15 minutes, or until cheese is melted. Makes 6 servings.

TIJUANA TOASTIES

6 flat corn-meal cakes (6 to a package)
1 pound ground beef
1 small onion, chopped (¼ cup)
2 tablespoons butter or margarine
2 teaspoons chili powder
1 teaspoon salt
2 cans (1 pound each) barbecue beans
1 cup shredded iceberg lettuce
1 package (4 ounces) shredded
   Cheddar cheese

1. Split corn-meal cakes with a sharp knife; place, cut sides up, on a cooky sheet.
2. Shape ground beef into a patty in a large frying pan. Cook 5 minutes on each side, then break up into small chunks; push to one side. Add onion and butter or margarine to pan; sauté 3 minutes, or until onion is soft. Stir in chili powder and salt; cook 1 minute. Stir in beans; heat slowly to boiling.
3. Heat corn cakes in broiler 2 to 3 minutes, or just until toasted; place 2 pieces on each of 6 serving plates. Spoon beef mixture on top. Sprinkle lettuce over half and grated cheese over remainder. Serve hot with corn chips, if you wish. Makes 6 servings.

HEIDELBERGS

1 can (1 pound, 11 ounces) sauerkraut
1 tart apple, halved, cored and diced
3 tablespoons sugar
1 package (¾ pound) smoked sausage links
1 tablespoon butter or margarine
½ cup mayonnaise or salad dressing
½ cup chili sauce
1 teaspoon instant minced onion
½ cup grated Cheddar cheese
8 large slices caraway rye bread

1. Drain liquid from sauerkraut. Combine sauerkraut with apple and sugar in a medium-size saucepan; heat to boiling; cover. Simmer 15 minutes to blend flavors; drain.
2. Split sausages lengthwise; sauté in butter or margarine until lightly browned in a medium-size frying pan.
3. Blend mayonnaise or salad dressing with chili sauce, onion and cheese in a small bowl.
4. Place 2 slices of bread on each of 4 serving plates; spread each with part of the mayonnaise mixture. Layer sauerkraut, remaining mayonnaise mixture and sausages on top. Garnish each with a sprig of parsley and serve with sour pickles, if you wish. Makes 4 servings.

GRILLED CHEESE FOR A CROWD

½ cup mayonnaise or salad dressing
¼ cup finely chopped dill pickle
24 slices white bread
3 packages (8 ounces each) sliced provolone cheese
½ cup (1 stick) butter or margarine, melted

1. Mix mayonnaise or salad dressing and pickle in a small bowl; spread 1 rounded teaspoonful on each slice of bread.
2. Place cheese on half the bread slices, cutting cheese to fit; top with remaining bread, spread side down. Brush sandwiches lightly on both sides with melted butter or margarine; place on cooky sheets.
3. Bake in extremely hot oven (500°) 5 minutes, or until golden and cheese is melted. (No need to turn.) Cut each sandwich in half diagonally; serve immediately on a large serving platter. Makes 12 servings.

RHINELAND POTATO SALAD

4 large potatoes
1 pound frankfurters
3 tablespoons vegetable oil
1 large onion, chopped (1 cup)
1 large green pepper, halved, seeded and chopped
1 large red pepper, halved, seeded and chopped
2 teaspoons salt
¼ teaspoon ground pepper
⅓ cup vinegar

1. Peel potatoes; cut into thin slices. Cook in boiling salted water 15 minutes, or just until tender; drain well.
2. Cut frankfurters into thin slices. Brown in oil in a large skillet; push to one side; add onion; sauté until soft. Add chopped peppers, salt, ground pepper and vinegar; cook, stirring constantly, for about 2 minutes.

3. Add drained potatoes to skillet; toss gently to mix. Spoon into serving bowl and serve warm. Makes 4 servings.

SPAGHETTI PORKERS

- 1 package (8 ounces) heat-and-serve sausages, cut in 1-inch pieces
- 2 cans (15 ounces each) spaghetti in tomato sauce
- ¾ teaspoon Italian seasoning
- 4 hero rolls, split and buttered
- 1 green pepper, seeded and cut in thin rings

1. Brown sausages in a medium-size frying pan; stir in spaghetti and Italian seasoning. Heat slowly, stirring once or twice, until bubbly.
2. Put rolls together with spaghetti filling, dividing evenly; top with green-pepper rings. Offer Parmesan cheese to sprinkle over filling, if you wish. Serve hot. Makes 4 servings.

GERMAN POTATO AND EGG SALAD

- 5 medium-size potatoes (about 2 pounds)
- 8 hard-cooked eggs, shelled and coarsely chopped
- 4 ounces Swiss cheese, cubed (1 cup)
- 1 cup cubed ham (or any leftover cold cut you wish)
- 2 tablespoons vegetable oil
- 1 medium-size onion, chopped (½ cup)
- 2 tablespoons flour
- 1 tablespoon sugar
- ¾ teaspoon salt
- 1 teaspoon dry mustard
- 1⅓ cups water
- ⅓ cup vinegar
- ½ cup chopped green pepper
- ¼ cup chopped pimiento

1. Cook potatoes in boiling salted water in a large saucepan 30 minutes, or until tender; drain. Cool until easy to handle, then peel and dice. Place in a 10-cup baking dish; add hard-cooked eggs and Swiss cheese.
2. Brown ham or other leftover meat in oil in a medium-size skillet; remove with a slotted spoon; reserve for Step 4.
3. Sauté onion in same skillet until soft. Combine flour, sugar, salt and dry mustard; stir into

drippings. Cook, stirring constantly, until bubbly. Stir in water and vinegar; continue cooking and stirring until dressing thickens and bubbles 1 minute.
4. Add green pepper and pimiento; cook 1 minute longer. Pour over potato and egg mixture; toss lightly until combined; sprinkle with the reserved ham.
5. Serve warm or bake in moderate oven (325°) 10 minutes, or until mixture is piping-hot. Serve from the baking dish or spoon onto individual plates in the kitchen. Makes 8 servings.

PÂTÉ SUPPER SANDWICHES

- ½ pound sliced bacon
- 1 pound chicken livers
- 2 tablespoons chopped onion
- 1 can (3 or 4 ounces) sliced mushrooms
- 1¼ teaspoons salt
- 2 teaspoons Worcestershire sauce
- 4 tablespoons (½ stick) butter or margarine
- 3 medium-size tomatoes, sliced thin
- 2 teaspoons sugar
- ¼ teaspoon pepper
- ¼ cup chopped parsley
- 12 large slices rye bread

1. Sauté bacon until crisp in a medium-size frying pan; remove and drain on paper toweling; keep warm. Pour all drippings from pan, then measure 2 tablespoonfuls and return to pan.
2. Stir chicken livers and onion into pan. Cook slowly, stirring constantly, 5 minutes, or until browned; stir in mushrooms and liquid, ¼ teaspoon of the salt, and Worcestershire sauce. Cook, stirring several times, 5 minutes, or until liquid evaporates. Mash mixture well with a fork.
3. While livers cook, melt butter or margarine in a jelly-roll pan; place tomatoes in a single layer in pan; sprinkle with sugar, remaining 1 teaspoon salt and pepper.
4. Heat in moderate oven (350°) 5 minutes, or just until hot; sprinkle with parsley.
5. Place each of 6 slices of bread on a serving plate; top with tomatoes, then drizzle buttery drippings from pan over tomatoes. Spread liver mixture over tomatoes, dividing evenly. Top with bacon and remaining bread slices. Cut each sandwich in half; serve hot with potato chips and dill pickles, if you wish. Makes 6 servings.

TUNA MOLD

1 package (10 ounces) frozen peas
1 can (7 ounces) solid-pack tuna
1 small onion, finely chopped (¼ cup)
¼ cup diced pimiento
1 envelope unflavored gelatin
¼ cup cold water
2 tablespoons sugar
½ teaspoon salt
⅛ teaspoon pepper
½ cup boiling water
¼ cup lemon juice
½ cup mayonnaise or salad dressing

1. Cook peas and drain. Drain and flake tuna. Combine peas, tuna, onion and pimiento; toss.
2. Soften gelatin in cold water. Add sugar, salt, pepper and boiling water; stir until gelatin is dissolved. Add lemon juice and mayonnaise or salad dressing; stir until smooth. Chill until syrupy.
3. Spoon tuna mixture into a 4-cup mold. Carefully pour gelatin mixture into mold. Insert a small spatula at intervals through the mixture to allow gelatin to reach the bottom of the mold.
4. Refrigerate until firm, about 3 hours. Unmold as in Salmon Mousse   Garnish with salad greens, if you wish. Makes 4 servings.

CHICKEN SALAD WITH CAPERS

2 chicken breasts (about 12 ounces each), cooked
½ cup chopped celery
2 tablespoons finely chopped onion
⅓ cup mayonnaise or salad dressing
1 tablespoon lemon juice
2 tablespoons drained capers
½ teaspoon salt
⅛ teaspoon pepper

1. Remove skin and bones from chicken breasts; cut meat into generous pieces (there should be about 3 cups).
2. Combine chicken, celery and onion in a medium-size bowl. Blend mayonnaise or salad dressing with lemon juice; add to chicken mixture with capers, salt and pepper. Toss well to coat. Chill well. Makes 4 servings.

HAM-AND-CHEESE WAFFLES

3 tablespoons prepared mustard
3 tablespoons mayonnaise or salad dressing
12 slices white sandwich bread
6 slices process American cheese (from an 8-ounce package)
6 slices spiced ham (from an 8-ounce package)
6 tablespoons (¾ stick) butter or margarine

1. Blend mustard and mayonnaise or salad dressing in a cup; spread over bread.
2. Cover each of 6 slices with cheese, then spiced ham; top with remaining bread. Spread outsides of sandwiches with butter or margarine.
3. Bake in preheated waffle iron 4 to 5 minutes, or until golden and cheese melts. Cut in half diagonally; place 3 halves on each serving plate. Serve hot with deviled eggs, bean salad and milk, if you wish. Makes 4 servings.

HAM, CHICKEN AND CHEESE LOAF

2 envelopes unflavored gelatin
½ cup cold water
½ teaspoon salt
⅛ teaspoon pepper
1 teaspoon grated onion
1 tablespoon lemon juice
1 cup boiling water
½ cup mayonnaise or salad dressing
1 cup dairy sour cream
1½ ounces Roquefort cheese, crumbled (½ cup)
2 cups diced cooked ham
2 cups diced cooked chicken
1 cup finely chopped celery

1. Soften gelatin in cold water. Add salt, pepper, onion, lemon juice and boiling water; stir until gelatin is dissolved. Add mayonnaise or salad dressing, sour cream and cheese; stir until smooth. Chill over ice and water, stirring constantly, until as thick as unbeaten egg white.
2. Fold in ham, chicken and celery. Turn into a 9x5x3-inch loaf pan.
3. Refrigerate until firm, about 3 hours. Unmold as in Salmon Mousse   Garnish with salad greens and radish roses, if you wish. Makes 8 to 10 servings.

10
MAKE LEFTOVERS COUNT

Everyone has leftovers. But not everyone knows what to do with them. As a result, they often end up in the garbage—and you end up spending more than you need to every week of the year. This chapter is devoted to showing you what to do with some of the most common types of leftover meats. We've also included several recipes that start with a roast and follow-up with a recipe for an equally delicious second meal. In other sections of the book, such as in the soup and casserole chapters, you'll find additional ideas for using leftovers effectively. All are geared to not only helping you get more for your money, but to making leftovers taste and look just as good as when you served the same foods the first time around.

BOEUF A LA MODE EN GELEE

3 medium carrots, pared and cut in ½-inch slices
1 pint Brussels sprouts, washed and trimmed
2 cans condensed beef broth
1⅓ cups water
2 envelopes unflavored gelatin
3 tablespoons Madeira or dry sherry
6 drops liquid red-pepper seasoning
1 pound cooked roast beef or steak, sliced thin
Watercress
Horseradish Dressing (recipe follows)

1. Cook carrots and Brussels sprouts separately in boiling salted water, 15 minutes or until tender. Drain; chill.
2. Combine beef broth and water in medium-size bowl. Soften gelatin in 1 cup of broth, about 5 minutes, in a small saucepan. Heat, stirring constantly, until gelatin dissolves; stir into remaining broth in bowl. Add Madeira and red-pepper seasoning. Cut Brussels sprouts in half lengthwise.
3. Pour ¾ cup of the gelatin mixture into an 11x7x1½-inch pan or an 8-cup shallow mold; place in a larger pan of ice and water until gelatin is sticky-firm. Arrange part of the Brussels sprouts and carrots in decorative pattern along sides of pan. Make 12 rolls or bundles of meat slices; place 6 down center of pan, spacing evenly; spoon several tablespoons of remaining gelatin mixture over vegetables and meat. Arrange some of remaining Brussels sprouts against sides of pan. Add enough gelatin mixture to almost cover meat. Chill until sticky-firm.
4. Arrange remaining meat and vegetables on top of first layer in pan; set pan on shelf in refrigerator; carefully spoon remaining gelatin over to cover meat and vegetables completely. Chill until firm, several hours or overnight.
5. Just before serving, loosen gelatin around edges with a knife; dip pan quickly in and out of hot water; wipe off water. Cover pan with serving plate; turn upside down; shake gently; lift off mold. Border with watercress, if you wish. Serve with Horseradish Dressing. Makes 6 servings.

HORSERADISH DRESSING—Combine ¾ cup mayonnaise or salad dressing; 1 hard-cooked egg, sieved; 1 tablespoon tarragon vinegar; and 1 teaspoon prepared horseradish in a small bowl; stir to blend well. Cover; refrigerate to blend flavors. Makes 1 cup.

CORNISH BEEF HASH AND EGG PIE

3 medium-size onions, chopped (1½ cups)
2 tablespoons butter or margarine
2½ cups chopped cooked corned beef (¾ pound)
3 cups chopped boiled potatoes
1 teaspoon Worcestershire sauce
½ teaspoon salt
¼ teaspoon pepper
1 package piecrust mix
¼ cup milk
6 eggs

1. Sauté onion in butter or margarine until soft in medium-size skillet, about 5 minutes.
2. Combine corned beef, potatoes, onions, Worcestershire sauce, salt and pepper in a large bowl; toss to mix well with a fork.
3. Prepare piecrust mix, following label directions or make pastry from your favorite two-crust recipe. Roll out ½ of pastry to a 12-inch round on a lightly floured board; fit into a 9-inch, deep pie plate. Trim any crust overhang to ½ inch.
4. Spoon hash mixture into prepared pastry shell, mounding center higher than sides. Scoop a hollow about 1½ inches wide, 1 inch in from edge all around. Drizzle milk over hash. Break eggs into hollow, spacing evenly.
5. Roll out remaining pastry to an 11-inch round; cut several slits near center to let steam escape; cover pie. Trim overhang to ½ inch; turn edge under, flush with rim; flute edge. Roll out trimmings to make fancy cutouts for top, if you wish. Brush top and cutouts with milk.
6. Bake in very hot oven (450°) for 10 minutes, reduce heat to 400° and bake 15 minutes longer, or until pastry is golden. Cut into wedges and serve hot. Makes 6 servings.

HAM AND LIMA CASSEROLE

2 tablespoons butter or margarine
1 small onion, chopped (¼ cup)
1 can (1 pound) tomatoes
½ teaspoon salt

⅛ teaspoon pepper
2 package (10 ounces each) frozen baby lima
  beans, cooked and drained
2 cups cubed, cooked ham
1 tablespoon butter or margarine, melted
¼ cup packaged bread crumbs

1. Melt the 2 tablespoons butter or margarine in large skillet; sauté onion until tender. Stir in tomatoes, salt and pepper.
2. Arrange limas and ham in layers in a shallow 8-cup baking dish. Pour tomato mixture over limas and ham. Combine the 1 tablespoon melted butter and bread crumbs in a small bowl; sprinkle over top of casserole.
3. Bake in a moderate oven (375°) 30 minutes, or until sauce is bubbly. Makes 6 servings.

SWEET AND PUNGENT PORK

3½ cups cooked pork (1¼ pounds), cut into
  ¾-inch cubes
1 tablespoon soy sauce
1 egg, slightly beaten
  Oil for frying
½ cup cornstarch (for coating)
Sauce:
1 large onion, chopped (1 cup)
1 large green pepper, halved, seeded and cut
  into strips
3 carrots, pared and sliced very thin,
  (about 1 cup)
1 tablespoon vegetable oil
1 tablespoon cornstarch
1 cup water
5 tablespoons vinegar
¼ cup firmly packed light brown sugar
1 envelope or teaspoon instant chicken broth
1 can (about 13 ounces) pineapple tidbits

1. Combine pork with soy sauce in a medium-size bowl; toss to mix with fork; cover. Let stand at room temperature 30 minutes. Add egg, toss to coat meat well with egg.
2. Pour enough vegetable oil to make 1-inch depth in a medium-size skillet or saucepan; heat to 375° on deep-fat thermometer.
3. Place ½ cup cornstarch in a plastic bag; add pork cubes and shake bag until meat is well coated with cornstarch.
4. Sauté pork, about a third at a time, in the hot oil 3 minutes, or until golden brown and

coating is crisp. Lift out with a slotted spoon; drain on paper toweling. Keep warm.
5. Sauté onion, green pepper and carrots in oil in large skillet 2 to 3 minutes, or until vegetables are crisply tender.
6. Mix 1 tablespoon cornstarch with 2 table-spoons water in cup. Add remaining water, vinegar, sugar and chicken broth to skillet; bring to boiling; cover; reduce heat; simmer 5 minutes. Stir in pineapple and cornstarch mixture; bring to boiling, stirring constantly; cover; cook just until thickened, about 1 minute.
7. Just before serving, combine the sweet-and-pungent sauce with pork. Then serve with hot cooked rice and additional soy sauce, if you desire. Makes 6 servings.

HAM AND POTATOES AU GRATIN

2 tablespoons butter or margarine
1 small onion, chopped (¼ cup)
2 tablespoons flour
1¾ cups milk
½ teaspoon salt
⅛ teaspoon pepper
1½ pounds potatoes, pared and diced,
  (about 3 cups)
4 wedges Gruyère cheese (from a 6-ounce
  package), shredded
6 slices cooked ham (about ¼-inch thick)

1. Melt butter in saucepan; sauté onion until tender. Stir in flour; cook until bubbly. Add milk. Cook over medium heat, stirring constantly, until sauce thickens. Add salt and pepper.
2. Layer diced potatoes and cheese in a buttered, deep, 6-cup baking dish. Pour over sauce; mix lightly. Cover.
3. Bake in a moderate oven (350°) 1 hour, or until potatoes are tender. Uncover; top with ham slices; cover. Bake 15 minutes longer. Makes 6 servings.

ADRIATIC LAMB PIE

2 hot Italian sausages (6 ounces)
3 small yellow onions, peeled and quartered
1 small green pepper, halved, seeded and
  diced (½ cup)
2½ cups cooked cubed lamb

2 tablespoons vegetable oil
1 small eggplant, pared and cubed (3 cups)
3 tablespoons flour
1 can (1 pound) tomatoes
2 cups water
1 envelope or teaspoon instant beef broth
1 teaspoon salt
½ teaspoon leaf basil, crumbled
½ teaspoon leaf rosemary, crumbled
2 zucchini, washed, trimmed and sliced
1 package (8 ounces) refrigerated buttermilk biscuits

1. Slice sausages into 1-inch pieces; brown in large skillet. Add onions and pepper, sauté until soft in drippings from sausage. Remove sausage and vegetables with slotted spoon to a 12-cup baking dish.
2. Brown lamb in same skillet. Remove to baking dish. Add oil and eggplant to skillet; sauté 5 minutes; sprinkle with flour. Stir in tomatoes, water, beef broth, salt, basil and rosemary. Bring to boiling, stirring constantly. Boil 1 minute. Pour over meat in baking dish; add zucchini. Mix well.
3. Roll buttermilk biscuits on a lightly floured pastry board into pencil-thin strips. Arrange on top of stew in a lattice pattern.
4. Bake in moderate oven (375°) 40 minutes, or until pastry is golden brown and pie is bubbly-hot. Makes 6 servings.

DEVILED BEEF SLICES

8 slices cooked beef (¼-inch thick)
2 tablespoons prepared mustard
1 egg
½ teaspoon salt
Few drops red-pepper seasoning
2 tablespoons water
1 cup seasoned fine dry bread crumbs
4 tablespoons vegetable oil

1. Spread beef slices with the prepared mustard.
2. Beat egg in a pie plate. Stir in salt, red-pepper seasoning and water. Sprinkle bread crumbs on wax paper.
3. Dip beef slices first into seasoned egg and then into bread crumbs.
4. Heat oil in a large skillet. Brown beef slices on one side; turn and brown on second side. Serve on a heated platter. Makes 4 servings.

SAVORY STUFFED CABBAGE

1 pound cooked lamb, ground
2 cups cooked rice
1 egg
1 clove garlic, crushed
1 teaspoon salt
¼ teaspoon leaf thyme, crumbled
¼ teaspoon leaf rosemary, crumbled
⅛ teaspoon pepper
1 can (15 ounces) special tomato sauce
1 head of cabbage (about 3½ pounds)
2 tablespoons butter or margarine
1 large onion, chopped (1 cup)
2 teaspoons sugar
½ teaspoon salt
½ cup water

1. Combine lamb, rice, egg, garlic, salt, thyme, rosemary, pepper and ⅔ cup of the tomato sauce in large bowl; mix well with fork.
2. Trim outside leaves from cabbage. Cut a small slice about 3 inches in diameter from top end; set aside. With a sharp-tip knife and hands, hollow out cabbage leaving a shell about ½ inch thick. (Chop cut-out pieces coarsely and cook separately to serve along with stuffed cabbage or save to cook as a vegetable for another day.)
3. Spoon lamb mixture into shell, pressing it down firmly, fit top back into place; tie with a string.
4. Saute onion in hot butter or margarine in medium-size frying pan until soft, about 5 minutes; add remaining tomato sauce, sugar, salt and water. Bring to boiling, stirring constantly. Remove from heat.
5. Place cabbage, core end down, in a deep flameproof casserole or Dutch oven; pour sauce over; cover. (If cabbage is too high, use an inverted bowl or foil to cover.)
6. Bake in moderate oven (350°), basting 2 or 3 times with sauce, for 1 hour and 30 minutes.
7. Place stuffed cabbage on a heated serving platter; remove string. Spoon some of sauce over cabbage; pass remaining sauce in a separate bowl. Cut cabbage into wedges for serving. Garnish with parsley, if you wish.
SERVING IDEA—Save several of the pretty large outer cabbage leaves. Blanch them in boiling salted water, just before cabbage is served, then wrap leaves around cabbage before serving. Makes 6 servings.

BONED ROAST CAPON

½ pound cooked ham
3 tablespoons dry sherry
1 tablespoon finely chopped shallots or green onion
1 capon, turkey or chicken (about 6 pounds)
2 cups water
   Giblets
½ teaspoon salt
1 pound ground veal
3 eggs
9 tablespoons milk
¼ cup coarsely chopped pistachio nuts
3 tablespoons chopped parsley
1 teaspoon salt
¼ teaspoon pepper
¼ teaspoon leaf thyme, crumbled
   Dash of ground allspice
   Olive Gravy (recipe follows)

1. Cut ham into ½-inch-thick strips; place in a small bowl with sherry and shallots to marinate for about 1 hour.
2. Place capon, breast side down, on cutting board. With a sharp, thin-bladed knife, cut alongside backbone through skin and flesh to the bone. Then, following rib cage with the tip of the knife, cut meat from back and breast bones on both sides, leaving wings and thigh and leg bones intact. Lift out rib cage.
3. Break the rib bones into smaller pieces; place in roasting pan. Roast in hot oven (450°) 20 minutes, or until richly browned. Drain off fat; place bones in a large saucepan with water, neck, gizzard and heart and the ½ teaspoon salt. Cover; simmer about 1 hour. Remove and discard bones; chop gizzard and heart; reserve broth.
4. Combine ⅓ of ground veal, liver from capon, 1 egg and 3 tablespoons of the milk in container of electric blender. Whirl at high speed, just until smooth; turn out into a large bowl. Repeat twice with remaining veal, egg and milk. Stir nuts, parsley, remaining salt, pepper, thyme and allspice into meat mixture.
5. Spread capon, skin side down, on cutting board. Using a darning needle and cotton string, make a few stitches, starting at leg end, to sew skin back together for about 2 inches. Sprinkle with 1 tablespoon of the sherry marinade from Step 1. Arrange a few strips of ham on the capon; spread ⅓ of veal mixture down the center;

arrange ⅓ of remaining ham on top; repeat twice.
6. Continue sewing together until filling is completely enclosed, bringing neck skin down the back to reshape capon as close to original as possible. Tie with string in several places; tie legs together. Place, breast side up, in a small roasting pan; fold a piece of foil and place loosely, as a tent, over bird.
7. Insert meat thermometer into center of filling. Roast in moderate oven (350°), basting often with pan drippings, 2 hours and 25 minutes, or until meat thermometer registers 160°. After about 1½ hours, remove foil to let bird brown nicely. Transfer to a heated platter and keep warm while making gravy. Makes 6 servings plus leftovers.
OLIVE GRAVY—Add reserved broth to roasting pan; bring to boiling over medium heat, scraping off browned bits; strain into a 2-cup measure. Measure 3 tablespoons fat into a small saucepan. Discard rest of fat. Stir 3 tablespoons flour into fat in saucepan; stir over medium heat until flour turns light brown. Blend in drippings (about 1½ cups) and 2 tablespoons Madeira. Cook, stirring constantly, until mixture thickens and bubbles, 3 minutes. Parboil 1 cup stuffed green olives in water to cover for 5 minutes; drain. Add to gravy, along with reserved chopped gizzard and heart. Makes about 2 cups.
Leftover Specialty: Souffleed Chicken Supreme (recipe follows).

SOUFFLEED CHICKEN SUPREME

1 can condensed cream of shrimp soup
1 cup milk
2 cups cut-up cooked chicken (see Boned Roast Capon)
3 tablespoons butter or margarine
¼ cup flour
¾ cup milk
4 eggs, separated
1 teaspoon salt
   Few drops red-pepper seasoning
¼ teaspoon cream of tartar

1. Blend soup with 1 cup milk. Combine with chicken in 8-cup shallow baking dish.
2. Melt butter or margarine in small saucepan. Blend in flour; cook, stirring constantly, until bubbly. Stir in ¾ cup milk; continue cooking

and stirring until mixture thickens and bubbles 1 minute; cool.

3. Beat yolks with salt and pepper seasoning in a large bowl. Beat in hot mixture.

4. Beat whites with cream of tartar just until stiff peaks form. Fold whites, ½ at a time, into yolk mixture just until well combined. Spoon soufflé mixture over chicken in baking dish.

5. Bake in moderate oven (375°) 40 minutes, or until puffed and browned. Makes 6 servings.

ROAST LAMB, MIDDLE-EASTERN STYLE

    1 five-pound leg of lamb
    1 bunch green onions
    1 large lemon
    1 small bunch fresh mint
  1½ teaspoons salt
    ¼ teaspoon freshly ground pepper
    3 cups boiling water
    4 tablespoons flour

1. Trim all but a thin layer of fat from lamb. Place lamb, trimmed side up, on rack in shallow roasting pan.

2. Chop onions, whole lemon and mint leaves until very fine; blend with 1 teaspoon of the salt and pepper.

3. Press all but ¼ cup of mixture onto surface of lamb. Place roasting pan on rack in oven; pour 3 cups boiling water into pan.

4. Roast in hot oven (425°) 15 minutes; reduce heat to slow (325°) and roast 1 hour and 45 minutes, basting several times with water in pan, for rare lamb. Roast 30 minutes longer for medium lamb. Remove roast from pan to heated serving platter and sprinkle with reserved green onion mixture. Keep in warm place while making gravy.

5. Strain liquid in roasting pan into 4-cup measure; allow to stand 5 minutes; skim off all fat. Return liquid to roasting pan; heat to boiling. Combine flour with ½ cup cold water to make a smooth paste; stir into bubbling liquid. Cook, stirring constantly, until mixture thickens and bubbles 3 minutes. Season with remaining ½ teaspoon salt and serve in heated gravy boat.

6. Garnish platter with lemon wedges and green onions, if you wish. Makes 6 servings plus leftovers.

Leftover Specialty: Moussaka a La Turque (recipe is in the next column; it serves 6).

MOUSSAKA A LA TURQUE

    2 large eggplant (about 1¼ pounds each)
    2 large onions, chopped (2 cups)
    1 clove garlic, minced
    4 tablespoons olive or vegetable oil
    ½ pound fresh mushrooms, chopped
    2 cups cooked lamb (see Roast Lamb,
         Middle-Eastern Style)
    3 teaspoons salt
    ¼ teaspoon pepper
    1 teaspoon leaf oregano, crumbled
    3 eggs
    2 cups soft white bread crumbs (4 slices)

1. Halve eggplant lengthwise; place, cut side down, in a 15x10x1-inch baking pan. Place baking pan on rack in oven; pour boiling water in pan to a depth of one-half inch.

2. Bake in moderate oven (375°) 30 minutes, or until eggplant is soft when pressed with fingertip. Remove eggplant from baking pan; drain on paper toweling.

3. Scoop out inside of eggplant, being careful not to break the skin. (A grapefruit knife does this very easily.) Chop eggplant into small pieces.

4. Sauté onion and garlic in oil until soft in a large skillet; add mushrooms; sauté 3 minutes. Add eggplant and sauté until liquid in pan has evaporated. (Both the mushrooms and eggplant give off liquid when cooked.) Stir in lamb, salt, pepper and oregano; cook 3 minutes; remove from heat.

5. Beat eggs in a large bowl; stir in bread crumbs, then eggplant mixture, until well-blended.

6. Line an 8-cup charlotte mold or straight-sided mold or bowl with eggplant shells, skin side out; spoon eggplant mixture into shells; fold shells over mixture. Cover mold with a double thickness of foil.

7. Place mold on a rack or trivet in a kettle or steamer; pour in boiling water to half the depth of the mold.

8. Bake in moderate oven (375°) 1 hour and 30 minutes; remove mold from water and remove foil cover; allow to stand on wire rack 10 minutes.

9. Unmold onto heated serving platter; remove any excess moisture from platter. Garnish with chopped parsley and a tomato rose, if you wish. Serve immediately. Makes 6 servings.

POTTED PORK ROAST

1 seven-pound loin of pork
3 cups dry red wine
1 large onion, chopped (1 cup)
6 whole cloves
6 whole allspice
1 three-inch piece stick cinnamon
½ cup light corn syrup
4 tablespoons flour
½ teaspoon salt
Duchess Potatoes (recipe follows)
Buttered carrots
Buttered zucchini

1. Trim excess fat from pork; place in a glass or plastic container (not aluminum) large enough to hold roast.
2. Heat 1 cup of the wine, onion, cloves, allspice and cinnamon to boiling in a small saucepan. Lower heat; simmer 5 minutes. Combine with remaining wine; pour over pork.
3. Cover container. Refrigerate pork overnight, turning several times in the marinade.
4. Place pork on rack in a shallow roasting pan; score remaining fat in a diamond pattern. Pour marinade over pork.
5. Roast in slow oven (325°), basting often with marinade, 3 hours and 20 minutes, or until a meat thermometer inserted into meat registers almost 170°.
6. Brush roast with corn syrup; roast 10 minutes longer, or until roast is glazed and meat thermometer reads 170°. Place roast on heated platter and keep warm while making sauce.
7. Strain liquid from roasting pan into a 4-cup measure; allow to stand 5 minutes; skim off all fat. Return liquid to pan and heat to bubbling. Combine flour with 1 cup cold water to make a smooth mixture; pour into bubbling liquid in roasting pan.
8. Cook, stirring constantly, until mixture bubbles 3 minutes. Taste; season with salt, if necessary. Pour into heated gravy boat.
9. Serve roast with Duchess Potatoes, buttered carrots and buttered zucchini. Garnish with orange slices and watercress, if you wish. Makes 6 servings plus leftovers.
DUCHESS POTATOES—Pare 2 pounds potatoes; cut into small pieces. Cook in boiling, salted water until tender, about 20 minutes. Mash potatoes; beat in 3 tablespoons butter or margarine, ½ teaspoon salt and 2 beaten eggs. Press out

through pastry bag into 6 mounds on buttered cooky sheet. Bake in hot oven (425°) for 15 minutes, or until lightly golden. Makes 6 servings. Leftover Specialty: Oriental Pork Platter (recipe follows).

ORIENTAL PORK PLATTER

12 thin slices cooked pork (see Potted Pork Roast)
½ cup dry sherry
¼ cup soy sauce
3 tablespoons peanut or vegetable oil
2 medium-size onions, sliced
2 medium-size green peppers, halved, seeded and cut into cubes
2 yellow squash, sliced
½ pound fresh mushrooms, sliced
OR: 1 can (6 ounces) sliced mushrooms
1½ cups water
1 envelope or teaspoon instant chicken broth
2 teaspoons salt
1 can (8 ounces) water chestnuts, drained and sliced
1 can (4 ounces) pimiento, drained, chopped
2 tablespoons cornstarch
¼ cup cold water
Hot cooked rice

1. Place pork slices in a shallow pan; combine sherry and soy sauce and pour over meat. Allow to marinate 30 minutes.
2. Heat oil in a large skillet; brown pork quickly in oil; remove from skillet and keep warm.
3. Sauté onion in same skillet just until soft; add green pepper and yellow squash; sauté 2 minutes; add mushrooms and sauté 2 minutes. Add marinade from pork, 1½ cups water, chicken broth and salt.
4. Heat to boiling; cover skillet; lower heat; simmer 5 minutes, or just until vegetables are crisply tender. Add the water chestnuts and the pimiento.
5. Combine cornstarch and cold water to make a smooth paste. Stir into bubbling liquid in skillet. Cook, stirring constantly, 1 minute. Return pork slices; heat 1 minute, or just until thoroughly hot.
6. Line a heated serving platter with hot cooked rice and spoon vegetable mixture over, reserving some of the sauce; arrange pork slices over vegetables; spoon sauce over. Makes 4 servings.

11

GREAT DESSERTS

There's good reason why cake is one of the very first things any cook learns to create. What could be more popular, easier to make and, at the same time, endless in its flavor possibilities? Made from scratch or from a mix, it takes well to frosting or to a simple sprinkling of sugar on top. It offers a sweet ending to a meal or a not-too-sweet taste treat in mid-afternoon. Consider all these things and you'll realize that one chapter of recipes is just not enough to do justice to this favorite.

Cake Making Tips

KINDS OF PANS

Cake pans are made in standard sizes, and most are marked by size on the bottom. You may substitute one size for the other in most cakes (see chart below). However, the baking time may vary slightly. The most popular cake pans used are those shown here.

Round—8 and 9 inch
Square—8 and 9 inch
Bundt tube pan—9 inch
Angel cake tube pan—9 and 10 inch
Oblong—13x9x2 inch
Loaf—9x5x3 inch

To be sure your cake pans are the diameter and depth called for in a recipe, measure them with a ruler.

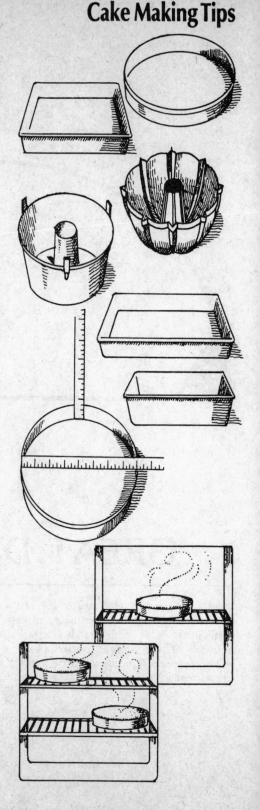

ALTERNATE PAN CHART

If Your Recipe Calls For:	You May Use:
Three 8x1$\frac{1}{2}$-inch round pans	Two 9x9x2-inch square pans
Two 9x1$\frac{1}{2}$-inch round pans	Two 8x8x2-inch square pans OR: One 13x9x2-inch oblong pan
One 9x5x3-inch loaf pan	One 9x9x2-inch square pan

PREPARING PANS

Use a generous coating of vegetable shortening (unless otherwise specified) and a light dusting of flour for an even, golden crust. For foam cakes, pans are never greased, since the airy cake batter needs to cling to the sides of the pan as it expands.

WHERE TO PUT PANS IN OVEN

When baking one layer or an oblong, place in center of rack.

When baking two layers, use two racks in center third of oven, layers in opposite corners.

When baking three or four layers, use two racks in center third of oven. Stagger pans in opposite corners of both racks so they do not block heat circulation in oven.

For a tube cake, lower rack to bottom third of oven. Place pan in center.

FROSTING THE CAKE

An easy way to frost a cake is to put the cake plate on something you can turn. Place cake plate on a large bowl or sugar canister, then turn as you frost. Of course, if you have a lazy Susan, that is even better. Now ready to frost.

1. First, brush off all the loose crumbs.
2. For layer cakes, frost cakes with flat (bottom) sides together. Cake will be even and steady.
3. Frost entire outside of assembled cake with a very thin layer of frosting and let it set about 20 minutes. The thin coating holds crumbs in place and keeps them from mixing with the final frosting.
4. Frost sides of cake first, then frost top, swirling frosting for that grand finale.

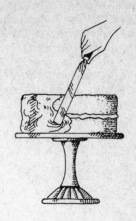

Cake Making Tips That Save You Time

When making a Mocha Log, work quickly in rolling up the warm cake, lifting towel from the back to make the cake roll and keep it from cracking. Once it's started, you'll be surprised how easily the cake just turns over and over—almost by itself. Wrap the towel tightly around the cake and let it stand to cool completely.

To split an angel or chiffon cake into even layers, measure first, then mark your cutting lines with wooden picks. For cutting, use a serrated long-blade knife with a sawing motion.

Have trouble with layers scooting apart after they're filled? Just anchor them in place with long thin metal skewers, and when top of cake is finished, take them out and smooth frosting.

Meringue rosettes are easy-to-make with a teaspoon if you don't have a pastry bag. Spoon up a bit of meringue, then drop into place, swirling upward to a peak.

If a layer humps a bit in the center, shave off flat with a sharp knife. Brush any loose crumbs from edge with a pastry brush so they won't muss frosting; or, trim a thin slice from edges.

Cakes Are Easy To Decorate

Crisscross Pattern: Draw parallel lines in frosting, about 1 inch apart, using a knife or spatula. Turn cake and draw lines at right angles to first series.

Shadow Design: Drip melted chocolate (prepared as for feather design) from a teaspoon around edge of frosted cake; let chocolate run down sides.

Make a Feather Top: Frost cake and drizzle melted chocolate (melt 2 squares with ½ teaspoon shortening) across frosting, in lines about 1 inch apart. Draw edge of spatula across lines.

Spoon Trick: Push the tip of a teaspoon lightly into soft frosting, as shown in drawing. Withdraw spoon quickly to keep lines sharp; repeat, keeping spoon marks in straight line.

Plaid Design: Use a table fork to make a plaid effect on frosting. Pull fork toward you in parallel lines, equally spaced. Turn cake and make lines at right angles to these.

FOAM CAKES

COFFEE CHIFFON CAKE

Bake at 325° for 1 hour and 10 minutes.
Makes one 10-inch tube cake.

- 2⅓ cups sifted cake flour
- 1⅓ cups sugar
- 3 teaspoons baking powder
- ½ teaspoon salt
- ½ cup vegetable oil
- 5 egg yolks
- ¾ cup cold water
- 1 tablespoon instant coffee powder
- 1 cup (7 to 8) egg whites
- ½ teaspoon cream of tartar
  Mocha Glaze (recipe follows)

1. Sift flour, 1 cup of the sugar, baking powder and salt into a medium-size bowl. Make a well and add in order: Oil, egg yolks, water and coffee; beat with a spoon until smooth.
2. Beat egg whites and cream of tartar in large bowl with electric mixer until foamy-white and double in volume. Beat in remaining ⅓ cup sugar, 1 tablespoon at a time, until meringue stands in firm peaks.
3. Gradually pour egg yolk mixture over beaten whites, gently folding in until no streaks of white remain. Spoon into ungreased 10-inch tube pan.
4. Bake in slow oven (325°) 1 hour and 10 minutes, or until top springs back when lightly pressed with fingertip.
5. Invert pan, placing tube over a quart-size soft-drink bottle; let cake cool completely. When cool, loosen cake around outside edge and tube and down sides with a spatula. Cover pan with serving plate; turn upside down; shake gently; lift off pan. Drizzle Mocha Glaze over top of cake, letting it run down the side.

MOCHA GLAZE

Makes enough for top of one 10-inch tube cake.

- 2 tablespoons butter or margarine
- 2 squares (1 ounce each) unsweetened chocolate
- 1 teaspoon instant coffee powder
- ⅛ teaspoon ground cinnamon
- 1 cup sifted 10X (confectioners') sugar
- 2 tablespoons hot water

1. Melt butter with chocolate in a small heavy saucepan over very low heat; stir until blended.
2. Remove mixture from heat; stir in coffee and the cinnamon.
3. Add sugar alternately with hot water, beating until smooth.

OLD-FASHIONED SPONGE CAKE

Bake at 325° for 1 hour.
Makes one 9-inch tube cake.

- 1 cup sifted cake flour
- 1 teaspoon baking powder
- ½ teaspoon salt
- 6 eggs, separated
- 1 cup sugar
- 1 teaspoon grated orange rind

1. Sift flour, baking powder and salt onto wax paper; reserve.
2. Beat egg whites in large bowl with electric mixer at high speed until foamy-white and double in volume. Beat in ½ cup of the sugar, 1 tablespoon at a time, until meringue stands in soft peaks.
3. Beat egg yolks in small bowl at high speed until thick and lemon-color. Beat in remaining ½ cup of the sugar, 1 tablespoon at a time, until mixture is very thick and fluffy. Beat in orange rind.
4. Fold flour mixture, ⅓ at a time, into egg yolk mixture with a wire whip or rubber scraper until completely blended.
5. Fold flour-egg-yolk mixture into meringue until no streaks of white or yellow remain. Pour into an ungreased 9-inch tube pan.
6. Bake in slow oven (325°) 1 hour, or until top springs back when lightly pressed with your fingertip.
7. Invert pan, placing tube over a quart-size soft-drink bottle; let cake cool completely. Loosen cake around the edge and the tube and down the sides with a spatula.
8. Cover pan with a serving plate; shake gently; turn upside down; lift off pan. Sift 10X sugar over top, if you wish; slice and serve the sponge cake with sweetened fresh fruit.

PETALED DAFFODIL CAKE

Bake at 325° for 1 hour.
Makes 1 ten-inch round cake.

10 eggs
1 teaspoon cream of tartar
½ teaspoon salt
1⅓ cups granulated sugar
1 teaspoon vanilla
1 cup sifted cake flour
½ teaspoon grated lemon rind
1 cup heavy cream
¼ cup 10X (confectioners') sugar
Yellow food coloring

1. Separate eggs, placing whites in a large bowl, and 4 of the yolks in a medium-size bowl. (Chill remaining 6 yolks in a covered jar to add to scrambled eggs.)
2. Add cream of tartar and salt to egg whites; beat with electric mixer until foamy-white and double in volume. Beat in granulated sugar, 1 tablespoon at a time, beating all the time until sugar dissolves and meringue forms soft peaks; beat in vanilla.
3. Sift flour, ¼ at a time, over top and gently fold in.
4. Add lemon rind to the 4 yolks in bowl; beat until thick. Spoon half of the white batter on top and fold in until no streaks of white remain.
5. Spoon batters by tablespoonfuls, alternating colors, into a 10-inch angel-cake pan. (Do not stir batters in pan.)
6. Bake in slow oven (325°) 1 hour, or until golden and top springs back when lightly pressed with fingertip.
7. Hang cake in pan upside down over a soda-pop bottle; cool completely. Loosen cake around edge and tube with a knife; invert onto a large serving plate.
8. Combine cream with 10X sugar and a few drops food coloring in a medium-size bowl; beat until stiff.
9. Spread part over side and top of cake to make a thin smooth layer. Next, take up spoonfuls of frosting on the back of a teaspoon and press onto cake in rows to make petal shapes. Start at the bottom of cake and make one row all the way around, then continue on up to edge. Finish top the same way, working from outside edge toward center. Chill cake until serving time. Cut in wedges to serve.

CHOCOLATE-CHERRY ROLL

Bake at 400° for 10 minutes.
Makes 8 servings.

4 eggs
1 teaspoon vanilla
¾ cup sugar
½ cup sifted cake flour
⅓ cup unsweetened cocoa powder
1 teaspoon baking powder
½ teaspoon salt
1 quart cherry ice cream
Chocolate Whipped Cream (recipe follows)

1. Butter a 15x10x1-inch baking pan; line with wax paper; butter paper.
2. Beat eggs with vanilla until fluffy-thick and lemon colored in large bowl with electric mixer at high speed. Gradually beat in sugar until mixture is very thick.
3. Sift flour, cocoa powder, baking powder and salt over bowl. Fold in until well-blended. Spread the mixed batter evenly in prepared baking pan.
4. Bake in hot oven (400°) 10 minutes, or until top springs back when lightly touched with fingertip.
5. Loosen cake around edges of pan with a sharp knife. Invert pan onto a clean towel lightly dusted with 10X (confectioners') sugar; peel off wax paper. Cut off edges of cake if they are too crisp to roll.
6. Starting at one end, roll up cake, jelly-roll fashion; wrap in towel. Cool cake completely on a wire rack.
7. Soften ice cream slightly. Unroll cooled cake carefully; spread evenly with softened ice cream; reroll. Place on a cooky sheet. Freeze at least 1 hour.
8. Frost roll with Chocolate Whipped Cream. Freeze until serving time. Cut into 8 thick slices.

CHOCOLATE WHIPPED CREAM

1 cup heavy cream
3 tablespoons instant cocoa mix (with sugar)

Beat cream and cocoa in a small bowl until stiff. Spread on filled Chocolate-Cherry Roll at once. Freeze until ready to serve at dessert time.

MADE FROM MIXES

ORANGE WALNUT CAKE

Bake at 350° for 50 minutes.
Makes 1 eight-inch round cake.

*1 package yellow cake mix
 2 teaspoons grated orange rind
 ½ cup orange juice
 ¾ cup water
 ½ cup finely chopped walnuts
   Orange Glaze (recipe follows)

1. Grease an 8-inch springform pan; flour lightly, tapping out any excess.
2. Combine cake mix, *2 eggs, orange rind and juice, and water in a large bowl; beat, following label directions; stir in walnuts. Pour into prepared pan.
3. Bake in moderate oven (350°) 50 minutes, or until top springs back when lightly pressed with fingertip. Cool in pan on a wire rack 10 minutes. Loosen cake around edge with a knife; release spring and carefully lift off side of pan. Place cake on a wire rack; cool completely. Remove cake from base; place on a serving plate.
4. Make Orange Glaze. Spoon over top of cake, letting mixture drizzle down side. Sprinkle thin strips of orange rind over top.

ORANGE GLAZE: Blend 1 cup sifted 10X (confectioners' powdered) sugar and 1 tablespoon orange juice until smooth in a small bowl; stir in 1 tablespoon more orange juice, part at a time, until glaze is thin enough to pour.

MOCHA TUNNEL CAKE

Makes 8 servings.

1 package white angel-cake mix
  Water
1 pint chocolate ice cream
2 pints coffee ice cream
  Toasted slivered almonds

1. Prepare angel-cake mix with water, bake in a 10-inch angel-cake pan, cool, and remove from pan, following label directions on the mix.

2. Hollow out cake this way: Cut a deep circle around top of cake about ¾ inch in from edge, then cut a second circle about ¾ inch from center hole. Cut ring into large sections and lift out, loosening at bottom with a fork. Place shell on a cooky sheet.
3. Spoon chocolate ice cream, a little at a time, into hollow in cake; cut small slices from ring and fit over ice cream to make a smooth top. (Wrap remaining pieces of cake and set aside for nibbles.) Place cake in freezer while preparing "frosting."
4. Beat coffee ice cream in a large bowl just until soft enough to spread; frost cake all over; sprinkle with almonds. (Work quickly so ice cream doesn't melt.)
5. Freeze at least four hours, or overnight. When ready to serve, place on a serving plate; cut into wedges.

ALMOND FRUIT BASKET

Bake at 350° for 45 minutes.
Makes 1 ten-inch round cake.

1 package angel-cake mix
  Water
1 can (about 14 ounces) frozen pineapple, thawed and drained
1 package (about 12 ounces) frozen peaches, thawed and drained
2 tablespoons rum or brandy
⅔ cup apricot preserves
¾ cup sliced almonds, toasted
4 bananas

1. Prepare cake mix with water, following label directions; pour batter into a 10-inch angel-cake pan.
2. Bake in moderate oven (350°) 45 minutes, or until a long wooden skewer inserted near center comes out clean.
3. Hang cake in pan upside down over a soda-pop bottle; cool completely. Loosen the cake around edge and tube with a knife; invert onto a large serving plate.
4. Combine pineapple, peaches and rum or brandy in a medium-size bowl; toss lightly. Chill at least an hour to blend flavors.
5. Starting ½ inch in from outer edge of cake, cut a coneshape piece from center, using a sharp knife and a sawing motion; lift out and wrap the piece to serve for another dessert.

6. Heat preserves just until bubbly in a small saucepan; press through a sieve into a small bowl. Brush over outside of cake to glaze evenly; press almonds into glaze.

7. Just before serving, peel bananas and slice; add to chilled fruits; spoon into hollow in cake. Garnish with maraschino cherries, if you wish. Cut cake in wedges, serving some of the fruit with each piece.

ORANGE SUNBURST

Makes 1 ten-inch round cake.

1 package orange chiffon-cake mix
 Eggs
 Water
½ cup sugar
¼ cup light rum
¾ cup orange marmalade
 Fluffy Orange Frosting (recipe follows)
½ cup chopped pistachio nuts
2 seedless oranges, pared, sectioned and drained

1. Prepare cake mix with eggs and water, bake in a 10-inch angel-cake pan, cool and remove from pan, following label directions. Split cake horizontally; lift off top layer; turn cut edge up.
2. Combine sugar and ½ cup water in a small saucepan. Heat, stirring constantly, to boiling, then simmer 2 minutes; cool slightly; stir in rum. Spoon over cake layers.
3. Spread ½ cup of the orange marmalade over bottom layer; place on a serving plate. Top with remaining layer, cut side down.
4. Prepare Fluffy Orange Frosting; spread over side and top, making deep swirls with spatula.
5. Heat remaining ¼ cup orange marmalade until melted in a small saucepan; place pistachio nuts on wax paper. Dip one end of each orange section into marmalade, then into pistachio nuts. Arrange on top of cake. Cut in wedges.

FLUFFY ORANGE FROSTING: In the top of a large double boiler, combine 2 unbeaten egg whites, 1¼ cups sugar, 1 tablespoon light corn syrup and ¼ cup thawed frozen concentrate for orange juice; place top over simmering water. Cook, beating constantly with an electric beater at high speed, 10 minutes, or until frosting stands in firm peaks; remove from heat.

TOASTED ALMOND BUTTER TORTE

Bake at 350° for 35 minutes.
Makes 1 nine-inch cake.

1 package yellow cake mix
 Eggs
 Water
1 package (6 ounces) sliced almonds
1 package creamy fudge frosting mix
½ cup (1 stick) butter or margarine
1 tablespoon instant coffee
1 package creamy vanilla frosting mix
1½ cups sifted 10X (confectioners') sugar

1. Prepare cake mix with eggs and water; bake in two 9x1½-inch layer cake pans. Cool, and remove from pans, following label directions.
2. While cake bakes, spread almonds in a shallow pan; heat in same oven 12 minutes, or until lightly toasted; set aside.
3. Prepare fudge frosting mix with ¼ cup of the butter or margarine and warm water, following label directions.
4. Dissolve instant coffee in ¼ cup warm water in a medium-size bowl; add vanilla frosting mix and remaining ¼ cup butter or margarine; prepare, following label directions; stir in 10X sugar until smooth. Put cake layers together with coffee frosting. Place on a serving plate. Spread chocolate frosting on side and top of cake; sprinkle all over with reserved toasted almonds. Slice and serve.

CHIFFON CAKE TOWER

Makes 8 to 10 servings.

1 eight- or nine-inch packaged chiffon cake
1 can (5 ounces) vanilla pudding
1 jar (10 ounces) cherry preserves
1 package vanilla glaze mix

1. Split cake into 4 layers. Place first layer on serving plate; spread with ⅓ of pudding, then spread about 4 tablespoons of preserves over pudding. Top with next layer. Repeat with remaining pudding, preserves and cake, ending with cake.
2. Prepare glaze, following label directions. Spread on top of cake, letting it drizzle down the side of cake. Garnish top with preserves, if you wish; refrigerate until ready to serve.

FRUITCAKES

PLANTATION FRUITCAKE

Bake at 300° for 2 hours.
Makes 1 nine-inch tube cake.

- **2 cups seedless raisins**
- **1 can (1 pound) cling peaches, drained and chopped**
- **1 cup vegetable shortening**
- **1 cup firmly packed brown sugar**
- **½ cup cream sherry or orange juice**
- **1 jar (1 pound) mixed candied fruits**
- **2 cups chopped walnuts**
- **4 eggs, beaten**
- **2½ cups sifted all-purpose flour**
- **1 teaspoon baking powder**
- **1½ teaspoons salt**
- **1 teaspoon ground cinnamon**
- **½ teaspoon ground cloves**
- **¼ cup light corn syrup**

1. Butter a 9-inch bundt pan. Dust with flour; tap out excess.
2. Combine raisins, peaches, shortening, brown sugar and sherry or orange juice in a medium-size saucepan; heat just to boiling. Remove from heat; cool.
3. Add candied fruit and nuts to cooked mixture; stir in beaten eggs.
4. Sift flour, baking powder, salt, cinnamon and cloves onto wax paper; stir into fruit mixture. Spoon into prepared pan.
5. Bake in slow oven (300°) 2 hours, or until center springs back when pressed with fingertip. Cool in pan on wire rack 15 minutes; turn out of pan; cool completely. Heat corn syrup just until bubbly in a small saucepan. Brush syrup over cake.

EASY NOËL FRUITCAKE

Bake at 350° for 1 hour.
Makes 1 medium-size tube cake or 1 loaf cake.

- **1 package (17 ounces) apricot nut bread mix**
- **1 jar (1 pound) mixed candied friuts**
- **1 cup chopped pecans**
- **½ cup seedless raisins**
- **½ cup whole blanched almonds (optional)**
- **¼ cup light corn syrup**

1. Butter a 6-cup fancy tube pan or a 9x5x3-inch loaf pan; line bottom with wax paper; butter paper. (If tube pan is not flat on bottom, butter very well; dust with flour; tap out excess.)
2. Prepare the mix, following label directions, adding fruit, pecans and raisins with dry mix. Turn into pan. Arrange almonds on batter.
3. Bake in moderate oven (350°) 1 hour, or until top springs back when lightly pressed.
4. Cool in pan on wire rack 10 minutes. Turn out of pan; remove wax paper, cool completely.
5. Heat corn syrup just until bubbly in small pan; brush over cake. Decorate with candied cherries, if you wish.

DUBLIN HOLLY CAKE

Bake at 325° for 1 hour, 30 minutes.
Makes 1 ten-inch tube cake.

- **1 jar (1 pound) candied mixed fruits**
- **1 package (11 ounces) currants**
- **1½ cups chopped walnuts**
- **2 tablespoons grated orange rind**
- **4 cups sifted all-purpose flour**
- **2 teaspoons apple-pie spice**
- **1 teaspoon baking soda**
- **1 teaspoon salt**
- **1 cup (2 sticks) butter or margarine**
- **1½ cups firmly packed brown sugar**
- **3 eggs**
- **1 cup stout or dark ale**

1. Butter a 10-inch tube pan; dust with flour; tap out excess.
2. Combine candied fruits, currants, chopped walnuts and orange rind in a very large bowl.
3. Sift flour, apple-pie spice, baking soda and salt onto wax paper. Sprinkle ¼ cup of mixture over fruits and nuts and toss to coat.
4. Beat butter or margarine, brown sugar, eggs in large bowl with electric mixer at high speed, 3 minutes, until fluffy.
5. Stir in remaining flour mixture alternately with stout or ale, beating after each addition.
6. Pour batter over prepared fruit and nuts and fold just until well-blended. Spoon into pan.
7. Bake in slow oven (325°) 1 hour and 30 minutes, or until center springs back when lightly pressed with fingertip. Cool in pan on wire rack for 15 minutes; loosen around edge and tube with a knife; turn out onto wire rack; cool.

CHOCOLATE CURLS

Makes enough curls to decorate a 9-inch cake.

Melt 7 squares semisweet chocolate in a small bowl over hot water, stirring often. Turn out onto cold cooky sheet. Spread out to a 6x4-inch rectangle. Refrigerate just until set. Pull a long metal spatula across chocolate, letting the soft chocolate curl up in front of the spatula. Place curls on wax paper. It takes a little practice, so count on a few to be less than perfect; put these on the cake first. Save prettiest curls for the top.

GOLDEN FRUITCAKE

Bake at 325° for 1 hour and 40 minutes.
Makes 1 ten-inch cake.

- 2 packages (1 pound, 1 ounce each) poundcake mix
- 4 eggs
  Milk or water
- 1 jar (8 ounces) candied red cherries, chopped
- 1 cup whole blanched almonds, chopped
- ½ cup golden raisins, chopped
- ¼ cup cognac
- 1 can (3½ ounces) flaked coconut
- 2 tablespoons grated orange rind
- 1 tablespoon grated lemon rind
  Orange Frosting (recipe follows)

1. Butter a 10-inch angel-cake pan; flour lightly, tapping out any excess.
2. Prepare both packages of poundcake mix with eggs and milk or water, following label directions.
3. Combine cherries, almonds and raisins in a medium-size bowl; stir in cognac. Fold into batter with coconut and orange and lemon rinds. Spoon into prepared pan.
4. Bake in slow oven (325°) 1 hour and 40 minutes, or until top springs back when lightly pressed with fingertip. Cool 10 minutes in pan on a wire rack. Loosen cake around edge and tube with a knife; turn onto rack; turn right side up; cool completely.
5. Make Orange Frosting; spread over top of cake, letting mixture run down side. Decorate with candied cherries, angelica and almonds.

ORANGE FROSTING: Combine 1½ cups sifted 10X (confectioners') sugar, 1 tablespoon cognac and 1 tablespoon orange juice in a small bowl; beat until smooth. Spread over top and side of Golden Fruitcake.

DIAMOND HEAD FRUITCAKE

Bake at 275° for 2 hours.
Makes 2 medium-size fruitcakes.

- 3 jars (4 ounces each) candied pineapple, chopped
- 3 jars (4 ounces each) candied orange peel, chopped
- 1 can (4 ounces) flaked coconut
- 1½ cups golden raisins
- 1 cup chopped pecans or macadamia nuts
- 2½ cups sifted cake flour
- 1 teaspoon baking powder
- ½ teaspoon salt
- ½ cup (1 stick) butter or margarine
- 1 cup sugar
- 4 eggs
- ½ cup pineapple juice
- ¼ cup light corn syrup
  Red and green candied cherries
  Pecan halves

1. Butter two 8½x4½x2½-inch loaf pans; dust lightly with flour; tap out any excess.
2. Combine fruits and nuts in a large bowl.
3. Sift flour, baking powder and salt onto wax paper. Sprinkle ¼ cup of mixture over fruits and nuts; toss to coat.
4. Beat butter or margarine, sugar and eggs in large bowl with electric mixer at high speed for 3 minutes, until fluffy.
5. Stir in remaining flour mixture alternately with pineapple juice, beating after each addition, until the batter is quite smooth.
6. Pour batter over prepared fruits and nuts and fold just until well-blended. Spoon batter into prepared pans.
7. Bake in very slow oven (275°) for 2 hours, or until centers spring back when lightly pressed with fingertip.
8. Cool cakes in pans on wire rack for 15 minutes; loosen around edges with a knife; turn out onto wire racks; cool completely.
9. To decorate: Heat corn syrup in small saucepan just until bubbly; brush over cakes. Garnish with halved candied cherries and pecan halves.

TORTES AND SPECIALS

MOCHA CHESTNUT TORTE

Bake at 325° for 30 minutes.
Makes 12 servings.

 4 eggs, separated
 1 cup sugar
 ¼ cup cold brewed coffee
 ½ teaspoon vanilla
 1 cup sifted cake flour
 1½ teaspoons baking powder
 ¼ teaspoon salt
 1 package (6 ounces) semisweet chocolate
   pieces
 1 can (1 pound) chestnuts
 2 egg yolks
 2 tablespoons hot brewed coffee
 ½ teaspoon vanilla
 ½ cup (1 stick) butter or margarine
 3 cups heavy cream
 ½ cup sifted 10X (confectioners') sugar
 ½ cup unsweetened cocoa powder
   Chocolate Leaves (recipe follows)
   Chestnut Filling (recipe follows)
   Maraschino cherries

1. Butter bottoms only of 2 nine-inch round layer-cake pans. Line with wax paper; butter paper.
2. Beat egg whites in large bowl of electric mixer until foamy-white. Add ½ cup of the sugar gradually, beating all the time until meringue stands in stiff peaks.
3. Beat egg yolks in small bowl with electric mixer until thick and lemon color; gradually beat in remaining ½ cup sugar until mixture is very thick and light. Stir in cold coffee. Fold yolk mixture gently into meringue until no streaks of white remain.
4. Put flour, baking powder and salt into sifter; sift over egg mixture, a small amount at a time. Fold in gently. Pour into prepared pans.
5. Bake in slow oven (325°) 30 minutes, or until tops spring back when lightly pressed with fingertip.
6. Invert cake pans with their edges resting on the bottom of custard cups (to keep sponge layers high and light); cool. Remove from pans; peel paper. Split each layer into 2 thin layers.
7. Make Chocolate Leaves: Melt semisweet

chocolate in top of a double boiler over simmering water. Spread ½ the chocolate in a thin even layer on foil on a cooky sheet; chill. Cut out leaf shapes for decorating. Reserve remaining chocolate for Chestnut Filling.
8. Make Chestnut Filling: Drain chestnuts, reserving liquid. Reserve 8 whole chestnuts for decoration. Place 2 egg yolks, 3 tablespoons liquid from chestnuts, remaining chestnuts, coffee, remaining melted chocolate and vanilla in container of an electric blender. Whirl until smooth, scraping sides of container once or twice. Blend in small pieces of butter or margarine until smooth. Chill until spreadable.
9. Put cake layers together with Chestnut Filling. Combine 2 cups of the cream, cocoa and ½ cup 10X sugar in a medium-size bowl; beat until stiff. Spread on top and side of cake.
10. Beat remaining 1 cup cream with remaining 1 tablespoon 10X sugar in a small bowl until stiff. Fill a pastry bag fitted with a notched tube; decorate cake as you wish. Garnish with reserved chestnuts, chocolate leaves and maraschino cherries. Refrigerate until serving time. Sift 10X sugar over top, if you wish.

ZUGER KIRSCHTORTE

Makes 12 servings.

The Sponge Cake:
 4 whole eggs
 2 egg yolks
 ¾ cup granulated sugar
 ½ cup sifted all-purpose flour
 6 tablespoons sifted cornstarch
 5 tablespoons butter or margarine, melted
   and cooled to lukewarm

1. Preheat oven to 350 degrees. Butter a 9-inch cake pan and dust lightly with flour. The cake pan must have at least a 2-inch rim. If it does not, tie on a collar of waxed paper or aluminum foil, buttered or use a 9-inch springform pan.
2. In a large bowl, combine the eggs, egg yolks and sugar and beat at high speed until thick and light yellow. The mixture will triple in volume.
3. Sift together the flour and cornstarch and with a spatula fold into the egg mixture. Add the melted and cooled butter or margarine and mix only until it is completely absorbed.
4. Pour the batter into the cake pan and bake

350° for 25 to 30 minutes, or until golden brown on top and springy to the touch. Cool the cake in the pan for 5 to 10 minutes and unmold onto a sugared square of wax paper.

The Almond Meringue:

½ cup egg whites (4 egg whites)
1 cup granulated sugar
⅓ cup blanched almonds, ground
½ tablespoon flour

5. Reduce oven to 275°. Beat whites with ⅓ cup of sugar until they form soft peaks. Gradually add another ⅓ cup sugar until it is absorbed and the egg whites form stiff peaks.
6. Mix together ⅓ cup sugar, ground almonds and flour, and fold into the beaten egg white mixture until thoroughly blended.
7. Using waxed freezer wrap (or baking paper), cut off two square pieces and with a pencil, trace an 8-inch circle on each square. Dust lightly with flour and place each square on a baking sheet. Using a pastry bag with a small tube, cover the circles with meringue. Start with a small dot in the center and continue circling until the drawn circle is completely covered (like a coiled rope). Or use a spatula and spread the meringue ½ inch thick.
8. Bake (275°) for about 30 minutes, or until a light gold color and crisp. Turn off the oven and let the meringues cool in the oven.

Kirsch Syrup:

¼ cup sugar
½ cup water
2 tablespoons kirsch

9. Bring the sugar and water to a boil and then let cool. Add kirsch.

Additional Ingredients:

Basic Butter Cream (recipe follows) flavored with 1 tablespoon kirsch
½ cup blanched, sliced toasted almonds (for decoration)

10. To assemble cake, cut off a paper-thin layer of the brown crust from the top and bottom of the sponge cake. (This permits the syrup to soak into the sponge cake easily.) Brush top,

bottom and side of the cake with the kirsch syrup.
11. Cover one meringue with ¼ inch of butter cream. Place the kirsch-soaked sponge cake on top of the meringue. Spread the top of the sponge cake with about another ¼ inch of butter cream. Place the second meringue on top of the butter cream. Spread the rest of the butter cream all around the sides of the cake. Holding the bottom of the cake in one hand, press the toasted almonds around the side of the cake. Lightly sift confectioners' sugar on top of the cake, if you wish.

Basic Butter Cream:

Yield: 2 cups
1 cup granulated sugar
¾ cup water
4 egg yolks
1 cup sifted 10X (confectioners') sugar
½ pound unsalted butter

In a saucepan, bring the granulated sugar and water to a boil and cook until it reaches 234 degrees on a candy thermometer, or a medium soft-ball stage.

Place egg yolks in a large bowl and stir in confectioners' sugar. Add the hot, boiled sugar mixture in a thin stream and beat at medium speed, until cooled.

In another bowl, whip the butter until creamy, then beat into the egg yolk mixture until well blended and light. (Keep cool, but do not refrigerate until on cake.)

NOTE: There are cakes and there is Zuger Kirschtorte. Whether you're on a diet or not, I doubt if you will be able to resist the flavor of this cake, which is not overly sweet, and a perfect climax to a festive dinner. This is a traditional torte or cake of Switzerland.

The Sponge Cake will absorb a quantity of the Kirsch syrup and not become soggy, just more delicious. This sponge cake may be used for many types of tortes, for birthday cakes or for any festive cake.

The Basic Butter Cream is versatile. You can flavor it with chocolate, mocha or nut. It is the perfect frosting for cakes and petits fours. Just follow the recipe, step by step and be sure that the egg yolk-sugar syrup mixture has cooled completely before you beat in the butter.

OATMEAL CRUNCHES

Bake at 375° for 12 minutes.
Makes about 4 dozen.

1½ cups sifted all-purpose flour
½ teaspoon baking soda
½ teaspoon salt
   Dash of mace
 1 cup shortening
1¼ cups firmly packed brown sugar
 1 egg
¼ cup milk
1¾ cups quick-cooking rolled oats
 1 cup chopped walnuts
 1 cup raisins

1. Measure flour, soda, salt and mace into a sifter.
2. Cream shortening with brown sugar until fluffy in a large bowl; beat in egg and milk. Sift in flour mixture, blending well to make a thick batter; fold in oats, walnuts and raisins.
3. Drop by teaspoonfuls, 3 inches apart, on greased cooky sheets.
4. Bake in moderate oven (375°) 12 minutes, or until lightly golden. Remove from cooky sheets; cool completely on wire racks.

CHINESE ALMOND COOKIES

Bake at 350° for 15 minutes.
Makes 3½ dozen cookies.

 1 cup vegetable shortening
 1 cup sugar
 2 eggs
 1 tablespoon water
 3 teaspoons almond extract
 3 cups sifted all-purpose flour
1½ teaspoons baking soda
¼ teaspoon salt
 1 package (6 ounces) whole blanched
   almonds

1. Beat shortening and sugar until light and fluffy in a large bowl with electric mixer.
2. Beat eggs in a small bowl with a fork until thoroughly blended; remove 2 tablespoons egg into a cup; add 1 tablespoon water; set aside.
3. Add beaten eggs and almond extract to shortening-sugar mixture, blending thoroughly.
4. Sift flour, baking soda and salt onto wax paper. Beat into the shortening-sugar mixture.
5. Shape into 1½-inch balls using 1 level measuring tablespoon of cooky dough. Place 2 inches apart on lightly greased cooky sheets.
6. Flatten cooky with fingertips into a 2-inch round. Place 1 blanched almond into the center of each cooky. Brush top of each cooky with reserved egg and water.
7. Bake in moderate oven (350°) 15 minutes, or until firm. Remove to wire racks to cool.

PEPPERMINT PINWHEELS

Bake at 350° for 10 minutes.
Makes 5 dozen cookies.

 2 cups sifted all-purpose flour
½ teaspoon baking powder
½ teaspoon salt
¾ cup (1½ sticks) butter or margarine
¾ cup sugar
 1 egg yolk
 1 teaspoon vanilla
½ teaspoon mint extract
   Few drops red food coloring

1. Sift flour, baking powder and salt onto wax paper.
2. Beat butter or margarine with sugar until fluffy light in a large bowl; beat in egg yolk and vanilla.
3. Stir in flour mixture, a third at a time, blending well after each addition, to make a soft dough.
4. Divide dough in half, and to half add the peppermint extract and enough red food coloring to tint the dough a deep pink.
5. Roll out each color dough to a 16x10-inch rectangle, between sheets of wax paper. Remove top sheet of wax paper from pink dough; place dough top side down on top of plain dough; peel off paper.
6. Roll up dough tightly, jelly-roll fashion. Wrap in wax paper or foil; chill several hours until very firm. (Or you may freeze dough and take out of freezer one half hour before baking.)
7. When ready to bake, unwrap dough and cut into ¼-inch thick slices with a sharp knife; place on ungreased cooky sheets.
8. Bake in moderate oven (350°) 10 minutes, or until cookies are firm, but not browned. Remove from cooky sheets to wire racks; cool.

DATE CHEWS

Bake at 350° for 25 minutes.
Makes about 6 dozen cookies.

- ¾ cup sifted all-purpose flour
- ½ teaspoon baking powder
- ¼ teaspoon salt
- 3 eggs
- 1 cup sugar (for dough)
- 2 tablespoons orange juice
- 1 package (8 ounces) pitted dates, chopped
- 1 cup chopped pecans
- ¼ cup chopped candied orange peel
  Sugar (for coating)

1. Sift flour, baking powder and salt onto wax paper.
2. Beat eggs until foamy-light in a large bowl; slowly beat in the 1 cup sugar; continue beating until mixture is fluffy-thick. Stir in orange juice.
3. Fold in flour mixture, dates, pecans and orange peel. Spread evenly in a 13x9x2-inch buttered baking pan.
4. Bake in moderate oven (350°) 25 minutes, or until golden and top springs back when lightly pressed with fingertip. Cool in pan on a wire rack 15 minutes.
5. Cut lengthwise into 9 strips and crosswise into 8 to make 72 pieces, about 1x1½. Roll each in sugar in a pie plate to coat generously.

OUR BEST-EVER BROWNIES

Bake at 350° for 30 minutes.
Makes 16 brownies.

- 2 squares unsweetened chocolate
- ½ cup (1 stick) butter or margarine
- 2 eggs
- 1 cup sugar
- 1 teaspoon vanilla
- ½ cup sifted all-purpose flour
- ⅛ teaspoon salt
- ¾ cup chopped walnuts
- 1 package (6 ounces) semisweet chocolate pieces
- ½ cup dairy sour cream

1. Melt chocolate and butter or margarine in a small saucepan over low heat; cool.
2. Beat eggs in small bowl with electric mixer

until fluffy. Gradually beat in sugar until mixture is fluffy-thick. Stir in chocolate mixture and vanilla.
3. Fold in flour and salt until well-blended; stir in walnuts. Spread evenly in 8x8x2-inch buttered baking pan.
4. Bake in moderate oven (350°) 30 minutes, or until shiny and firm on top. Cool completely in pan on a wire rack.
5. Melt chocolate pieces in top of a double boiler over hot water. Stir until smooth. Remove from heat; stir in sour cream until well-blended. Spread frosting on cooled brownies. Cut into 2-inch squares.

BROWN-EDGE LEMON WAFERS

Bake at 375° for about 10 minutes.
Makes about 5 dozen 3-inch cookies.

- ¼ cup sugar
- 3 teaspoons grated lemon rind
- 2 cups sifted all-purpose flour
- 2 teaspoons baking powder
- ½ teaspoon salt
- ½ cup shortening
- 1 cup sugar
- 1 egg
- ½ teaspoon vanilla
- ½ cup water
- ¼ cup lemon juice

1. Blend sugar and 1 teaspoon of the lemon rind in cup; reserve.
2. Measure flour, baking powder and salt into sifter.
3. Cream shortening in medium-size bowl until soft; gradually add sugar (for dough), creaming well after each addition.
4. Blend in egg, remaining lemon rind and vanilla; beat until mixture is light and fluffy.
5. Sift and add dry ingredients alternately with water and lemon juice, blending until smooth after each addition. Dough will be very soft.
6. Drop dough by teaspoonfuls onto buttered cooky sheets, keeping mounds about 2 inches apart. Sprinkle lightly with lemon-sugar mixture.
7. Bake in moderate oven (375°) about 10 minutes, or until edges of cookies are light brown.
8. Remove from cooky sheets; cool on wire racks. Store in tightly covered container.

GINGERBREAD COOKIES

Bake at 350° for 8 minutes.
Makes 6 dozen cookies.

5½ cups sifted all-purpose flour
 1 teaspoon baking soda
 1 teaspoon salt
 2 teaspoons ground cinnamon
 1 teaspoon ground ginger
 1 teaspoon ground cloves
 ½ teaspoon ground nutmeg
 1 cup vegetable shortening
 1 cup sugar
 1 cup molasses
 1 egg
 1 teaspoon vanilla
   Royal Frosting (recipe follows)

1. Sift flour, baking soda, salt and spices onto wax paper.
2. Beat vegetable shortening with sugar until fluffy-light in a large bowl; beat in molasses, egg and vanilla.
3. Stir in flour mixture, a third at a time, blending well after each addition, to make a soft dough. Wrap dough in foil and chill 4 hours, or overnight.
4. Roll out dough, one quarter at a time, to a ⅛-inch thickness on a lightly floured pastry board. Cut with 3-inch cooky cutters.
5. Place, approximately 1 inch apart, on ungreased cooky sheets.
6. Bake in moderate oven (350°) 8 minutes, or until cookies are firm but not too dark. Remove to wire racks with spatula; cool. Decorate with Royal Frosting and allow frosting to harden before storing.

ROYAL FROSTING

Makes about 1½ cups.

 2 egg whites
 1 teaspoon lemon juice
3½ cups sifted 10X (confectioners') sugar

Beat egg whites and lemon juice until foamy in a medium-size bowl. Slowly beat in sugar, until frosting stands in firm peaks and is stiff enough to hold a sharp line when cut through with a knife. Keep frosting covered with a damp paper towel to keep from drying before using.

FLORENTINES

Bake at 325° for 12 minutes.
Makes 2 dozen.

 ⅓ cup butter or margarine
 ⅓ cup honey
 ¼ cup sugar
 2 tablespoons milk
 ⅔ cup sifted all-purpose flour
 1 cup (8 ounces) mixed candied fruits
 1 can (3½ ounces) sliced almonds
 3 squares semisweet chocolate
 1 tablespoon butter or margarine

1. Melt ⅓ cup butter or margarine in pan; remove from heat; stir in honey, sugar, milk.
2. Add flour, candied fruits and almonds; stir until well-blended.
3. Return saucepan to very low heat. Cook, stirring constantly, until mixture begins to thicken (about 2 minutes). Remove from heat.
4. Drop mixture by teaspoonfuls, 2 inches apart, onto well-greased cooky sheets.
5. Bake in slow oven (325°) 12 minutes, or until golden-brown around edges. Cool slightly on cooky sheets, then remove and cool completely.
6. Melt chocolate squares and 1 tablespoon butter or margarine in a metal cup over simmering water. Spread the bottom of half the cookies with chocolate and top each with a second cooky. Allow to become firm before storing.

MELT-AWAYS

Bake at 325° for 20 minutes.
Makes about 4 dozen balls.

 ½ cup butter or margarine
 3 tablespoons 10X (confectioners') sugar
 1 cup sifted all-purpose flour
 1 cup finely chopped walnuts

1. Cream butter or margarine with sugar in medium-size bowl; gradually add flour, mixing in thoroughly; stir in nuts; chill.
2. Form teaspoonfuls of dough into marble-size balls by rolling lightly between palms of hands; place on ungreased cooky sheets.
3. Bake in moderate oven (325°) 20 minutes, or until pale golden.
4. Remove from cooky sheet; while still hot, roll in additional confectioners' sugar; cool.

LEMON-DATE DIAMONDS

Bake at 325° for 35 minutes.
Makes 3 dozen cookies.

1 ¼ cups sifted all-purpose flour
1 ½ teaspoons baking powder
 ½ teaspoon salt
 ½ teaspoon pumpkin-pie spice
 2 eggs
 1 cup granulated sugar
 2 tablespoons vegetable oil
 1 package (8 ounces) pitted dates, chopped
 ½ cup chopped pecans
 1 cup 10X (confectioners') sugar
 1 tablespoon milk
 1 tablespoon lemon juice

1. Measure flour, baking powder, salt and pumpkin-pie spice into a sifter.
2. Beat eggs and granulated sugar just until blended in a large bowl; stir in vegetable oil, dates and pecans. Sift flour mixture over top, then blend in. Spread in a 13x9x2-inch buttered baking pan.
3. Bake in slow oven (325°) 35 minutes, or until golden and a wooden pick inserted in center comes out clean. Cool in pan on a wire rack.
4. Beat 10X sugar with milk and lemon juice until smooth in a small bowl; spread over cookies. Let stand until frosting is firm.
5. Cut into diamond shapes or bars.

ALMOND MACAROONS

Bake at 325° for 20 minutes.
Makes about 3 dozen cookies.

 1 can (8 ounces) almond paste
 2 egg whites
   Dash of salt
 1 teaspoon vanilla
 1 cup sifted 10X (confectioners') sugar
   Granulated sugar
   Sliced almonds
   Red candied cherries, quartered

1. Butter a large cooky sheet; dust with flour; tap off any excess.
2. Break up almond paste with fingers into large bowl.
3. Add egg whites, salt and vanilla. Beat with electric mixer at low speed until mixture is smooth and the ingredients are well-blended.
4. Add confectioners' sugar slowly, continuing to beat at low speed, until a soft dough forms.
5. Fit a pastry bag with a round tip. Fill bag with dough.
6. Pipe dough out in small rounds, or drop by teaspoonfuls on prepared cooky sheet. (Macaroons will spread very little when they bake.)
7. For a crackly top: Dip fingertip into water; pat over tops; sprinkle with granulated sugar. Decorate tops with almonds and cherries.
8. Bake in slow oven (325°) for 20 minutes, or until golden-brown.
9. Remove to wire racks with a spatula; cool.

WALNUT SUGARPLUMS

Makes about 2 dozen 2-ounce cakes.

 1 package (8 ounces) pitted dates
 1 cup seeded muscat raisins
 1 jar (4 ounces) chopped candied pineapple
 1 jar (4 ounces) chopped candied citron
 ½ cup (1 stick) butter or margarine
 1 cup 10X (confectioners') sugar
 2 tablespoons light corn syrup
 1 tablespoon lemon juice
 ¼ cup finely chopped candied or crystallized ginger
 2 packages (5 ounces each) shortbread cookies, crushed (about 3 cups)
 2 teaspoons ground cinnamon
 1 cup chopped walnuts
   Walnut halves

1. Chop dates and raisins; dice pineapple and citron.
2. Cream butter or margarine with 10X sugar until fluffy-light in a large bowl; beat in corn syrup and lemon juice. Stir in dates and raisins, then pineapple, citron and ginger.
3. Mix crushed cookies, cinnamon and chopped walnuts in a medium-size bowl; sprinkle over fruit mixture; stir in until completely blended. (Mixture will be stiff.)
4. Pack into tiny souffle or nut cups (1½-ounce size). Garnish each with a walnut half. Set cups in a large shallow pan or on a tray for easy handling; cover tightly with waxed paper or transparent wrap. Chill until firm. Keep refrigerated until ready to serve or give.

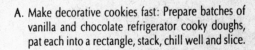

A.

A. Make decorative cookies fast: Prepare batches of vanilla and chocolate refrigerator cooky doughs, pat each into a rectangle, stack, chill well and slice.

B. Juice cans make good molds for refrigerator cookies. Pack dough in the can and chill. At baking time, remove the bottom of the can. (Use a can opener that cuts a smooth edge.) Press against bottom to push out dough—just enough to make one $1/8$- to $1/4$-inch thick cooky. Cut with a sharp knife and place dough on an ungreased cooky sheet. Repeat procedure until all dough is used.

B.

C. Ball cookies will be even in size if you pat the dough into a long roll first, then divide it: First in half, then quarters, then eighths and sixteenths, depending on what size cooky you want.

D. With only one batch of dough, you can make a whole plateful of different-looking treats. Here's how: After shaping the dough, leave some plain, press others, crisscross fashion with a fork. Make a hollow in some with your thumb or the handle of a wooden spoon to fill with jam after baking, or top with a big walnut half.

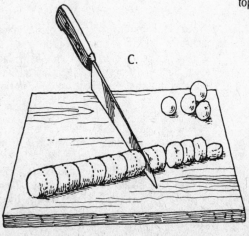

C.

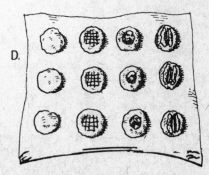

D.

195

PINE NUT MACAROONS

Bake at 375° for 10 minutes.
Makes about 2½ dozen cookies.

- **1 cup blanched almonds**
- **1 cup sugar**
- **2 egg whites**
- **½ teaspoon almond extract**
- **1 jar (8 ounces) pine nuts (pignoli)**

1. Dry blanched almonds thoroughly by placing them in a warm oven (350°) for 5 to 10 minutes. Grind as fine as possible, until powdery, while still warm.
2. Combine ground almonds and sugar in a medium-size bowl; add unbeaten egg whites and almond extract; beat thoroughly.
3. Drop by teaspoonfuls onto generously buttered and floured cooky sheets, leaving 1 inch between cookies. Smooth into rounds. Top each cooky with approximately ½ teaspoon pine nuts, pressing nuts into cooky. Let stand 3 hours.
4. Bake in moderate oven (375°) for 10 minutes. Remove cookies from oven; let stand on cooky sheets for 5 minutes; carefully remove with wide spatula (if cookies stiffen, put back into oven for a few seconds to soften). Store in airtight container when thoroughly cooled.

SPRINGERLE

Bake at 300° for 15 minutes.
Makes about 6 dozen small square cookies or about 3 dozen larger rectangles.

- **Anise seeds**
- **4 eggs**
- **2 cups sugar**
- **4 cups sifted all-purpose flour**
- **1 teaspoon baking soda**
- **2 teaspoons anise extract**

1. Butter cooky sheets; sprinkle with anise seeds.
2. Beat eggs with sugar until fluffy-light and thick in a large bowl. (Beating will take 5 minutes with an electric mixer. This step is important so your cookies will have a frosty top layer.) Stir in flour, a third at a time, soda and anise extract, blending well to form a stiff dough.
3. Roll out, about a third at a time, ½-inch thick,

on a lightly floured pastry cloth or board with a plain rolling pin.
4. Flour springerle rolling pin or individual molds. Roll pin slowly only once over dough; pressing down firmly enough to make clear designs. Dough will now be about ¼-inch thick. If using individual molds, press firmly into dough; carefully lift off mold.
5. Cut along lines to separate designs. Cut around borders of individual designs. Lift each cooky carefully; moisten bottom with a drop of water. Place 1 inch apart on prepared cooky sheets. Brush excess flour from tops.
6. Let cookies stand, uncovered, overnight.
7. Bake in slow oven (300°) 15 minutes, or until firm and dry. (Cookies should not brown.) Remove to wire racks; cool. Store in a tightly covered container about a week to mellow.

CRISP MOLASSES COOKIES

Bake at 350° for 8 minutes.
Makes 8 dozen cookies.

- **3¾ cups sifted all-purpose flour**
- **1 teaspoon baking soda**
- **½ teaspoon salt**
- **2 tablespoons cocoa**
- **2 teaspoons ground ginger**
- **1 tablespoon ground cinnamon**
- **2 teaspoons ground cloves**
- **1 cup (2 sticks) butter or margarine, softened**
- **1 cup sugar**
- **1 egg**
- **½ cup molasses**
- **Royal Frosting**

1. Sift flour, baking soda, salt, cocoa, ginger, cinnamon and cloves onto wax paper.
2. Beat butter or margarine until fluffy; add sugar gradually, beating well after each addition. Add egg and molasses; beat well. Stir in flour mixture; blend well. Wrap in plastic wrap or foil; refrigerate several hours, or overnight.
3. Roll out small portions of dough on a floured pastry board; cut into plain or fancy shapes with cooky cutters; brush excess flour off dough. Place on lightly buttered cooky sheets.
4. Bake in moderate oven (350°) for 8 minutes, or until edges are browned. Let cookies cool a few minutes on cooky sheets. Remove to wire racks with spatula; cool.

196

SUGAR COOKIES

Bake at 375° for 10 minutes.
Makes 4½ dozen cookies.

1 cup (2 sticks) butter or margarine, softened
1 cup sugar
2 eggs, room temperature
2½ teaspoons vanilla
3½ cups sifted all-purpose flour
2¼ teaspoons baking powder
¼ teaspoon salt

1. Beat butter or margarine and sugar in a large bowl at high speed on electric mixer. Add eggs and vanilla; beat until light and fluffy.
2. Sift flour, baking powder and salt onto wax paper. Stir into butter-sugar mixture.
3. Shape dough into 1-inch balls (1 level table-spoon). Place on lightly buttered cooky sheets.
4. Butter bottom of glass or jar, dip in the 3 tablespoons sugar. Flatten each cooky to ¼ inch thickness with bottom of glass.
5. Bake in moderate oven (375°) 10 minutes, or until edges are lightly browned. Cool.

LEBKUCHEN

Bake at 350° for 10 minutes.
Makes about 5 dozen cookies.

¾ cup honey
¾ cup firmly packed dark brown sugar
1 egg
2 teaspoons grated lemon rind
3 tablespoons lemon juice
3½ cups sifted all-purpose flour
1 teaspoon salt
1 teaspoon ground cinnamon
1 teaspoon ground nutmeg
½ teaspoon ground allspice
½ teaspoon ground ginger
¼ teaspoon ground cloves
½ teaspoon baking soda
1 cup (8 ounces) citron, finely chopped
1 cup chopped unblanched almonds
  Sugar Glaze (recipe follows)

1. Heat honey to boiling in a small saucepan; pour into a large bowl. Cool about 30 minutes.
2. Stir brown sugar, egg, lemon rind and lemon juice into cooled honey; blend well.
3. Sift flour, salt, cinnamon, nutmeg, allspice,

ginger, cloves and baking soda onto wax paper. Stir into honey mixture a third at a time. Add citron and almonds. Dough will be stiff but sticky. Wrap in foil or transparent wrap; refrigerate several hours, or until firm.
4. Roll out dough, ⅛ at a time, on a lightly floured pastry board, to a 6x5-inch rectangle. Cut into 8 rectangles, 2½x1½ inches. Place 1 inch apart on greased cooky sheets.
5. Bake in moderate oven (350°) 10 minutes, or until firm. Remove to wire racks.
6. While cookies are hot, brush with hot Sugar Glaze. When cookies are cool, decorate with almond halves, candied cherry halves and pieces of citron, if you wish. Use confectioners' sugar and water mixed to a smooth paste as "glue." Store cookies in wax-paper-separated layers in a covered container for 2 weeks to mellow.

SUGAR GLAZE: Combine ¾ cup granulated sugar and ⅓ cup water in a saucepan. Bring to boiling; lower heat; simmer 3 minutes. Remove from heat; stir in ¼ cup 10X (confectioners') sugar. Makes about ¾ cup.

CHOCOLATE CHIP COOKIES

Bake at 375° for 10 minutes.
Makes 4½ dozen cookies.

¾ cup (1½ sticks) butter or margarine
½ cup sugar
½ cup firmly packed brown sugar
1 egg
1 teaspoon vanilla
2 cups sifted all-purpose flour
½ teaspoon baking soda
¼ teaspoon salt
1 package (6 ounces) semisweet chocolate pieces
½ cup coarsely chopped walnuts

1. Beat butter or margarine, sugars, egg and vanilla in a large bowl with an electric mixer until light and fluffy.
2. Sift flour, baking soda and salt onto wax paper. Beat into butter-sugar mixture. Stir in chocolate pieces and walnuts.
3. Drop by teaspoonfuls onto buttered cooky sheets. Bake in moderate oven (375°) 10 minutes, or until cookies are lightly browned. Remove with spatula to wire racks to cool.

CHOCOLATE BLANC-MANGE

Makes 6 servings.

1 cup sugar
⅓ cup cornstarch
¼ teaspoon salt
3 squares unsweetened chocolate, cut up
3 cups milk
1½ teaspoons vanilla

1. Combine sugar, cornstarch, salt and chocolate in medium-size pan; gradually stir in milk.
2. Cook over medium heat, stirring constantly, until chocolate melts and mixture comes to boiling and is thickened. Boil 1 minute. Remove from heat; stir in vanilla. Pour into a 3-cup mold. Cover with plastic wrap; refrigerate until cold, about 3 hours.
3. When ready to serve, run a knife around top; dip mold very quickly in and out of hot water. Cover with serving plate; turn upside down; shake gently; lift off mold. Garnish with whipped cream and maraschino cherries, if desired.

STEAMED DATE-WALNUT PUDDING

Steam for 2 hours and 30 minutes.
Makes 8 servings.

1½ cups sifted all-purpose flour
1 teaspoon baking powder
¾ teaspoon baking soda
½ teaspoon salt
¼ teaspoon ground cinnamon
⅛ teaspoon mace
1 egg
½ cup sugar
3 tablespoons butter or margarine
1 cup orange juice
¼ cup orange marmalade
1 tablespoon grated lemon rind
1 teaspoon vanilla
1 cup chopped walnuts
1 cup chopped dates
½ cup candied cherries, chopped
Hard-Sauce Pinwheels (recipe follows)

1. Butter a 6-cup pudding mold or heat-proof bowl; sprinkle with sugar.
2. Sift flour, baking powder, baking soda, salt, cinnamon and mace on wax paper.
3. Beat egg in a large bowl; beat in sugar, butter

or margarine, orange juice, marmalade, lemon rind and vanilla.
4. Combine walnuts, dates and cherries with flour mixture; stir into egg mixture. Turn into prepared mold or bowl; cover with lid of mold or with foil, or a double thickness of wax paper and fasten with string to hold tightly.
5. Place on rack in a large kettle (or, make a doughnut shape of crumpled foil to fit bottom of kettle to serve as a rack); pour in boiling water to half-way point on mold. Cover kettle. Keep water gently boiling; add more boiling water, if necessary. Steam 2½ hours.
6. Cool pudding 10 minutes on wire rack; turn out onto serving plate. Serve warm with Hard-Sauce Pinwheels.
7. To reheat: Place pudding on sheet of heavy foil; bring foil up and gather at top, folding securely, to make pouch. Place pudding on rack in same kettle it was cooked in. Pour 2 inches of boiling water into kettle; cover; simmer for 30 minutes, or until heated through.

HARD-SAUCE PINWHEELS

Makes 8 servings.

½ cup (1 stick) butter or margarine, softened
2 cups sifted 10X (confectioners') sugar
2 tablespoons brandy
Red food coloring

1. Beat butter or margarine until fluffy in small bowl of electric mixer. Gradually beat in confectioners' sugar and brandy.
2. Divide mixture in half; tint 1 portion deep pink (the color will deepen somewhat as mixture stands).
3. Turn both tinted and plain portions onto separate sheets of wax paper; spread into rectangles. Cover with second sheets of wax paper; refrigerate. Carefully roll both portions of hard sauce between wax paper sheets to equal size rectangles, about ⅜-inch thick; refrigerate the rectangles again.
4. Remove top wax paper sheets; invert pink portion on plain portion. Remove wax paper. Carefully roll up from long side with help of bottom sheet of wax paper; wrap tightly in fresh wax paper sheet (roll, rather than try to lift finished roll, onto the fresh sheet). Refrigerate several hours, or overnight. Cut into slices and arrange around the Date-Walnut Pudding.

Gelatin Mold Tricks You Should Know

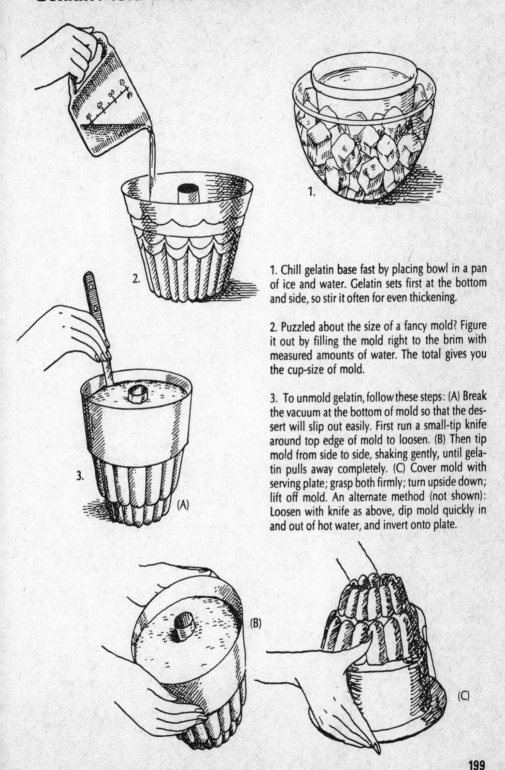

1. Chill gelatin base fast by placing bowl in a pan of ice and water. Gelatin sets first at the bottom and side, so stir it often for even thickening.

2. Puzzled about the size of a fancy mold? Figure it out by filling the mold right to the brim with measured amounts of water. The total gives you the cup-size of mold.

3. To unmold gelatin, follow these steps: (A) Break the vacuum at the bottom of mold so that the dessert will slip out easily. First run a small-tip knife around top edge of mold to loosen. (B) Then tip mold from side to side, shaking gently, until gelatin pulls away completely. (C) Cover mold with serving plate; grasp both firmly; turn upside down; lift off mold. An alternate method (not shown): Loosen with knife as above, dip mold quickly in and out of hot water, and invert onto plate.

HOLIDAY PLUM PUDDING

Steam for 5 hours and 30 minutes.
Makes 12 to 16 servings.

 1 package (8 ounces) pitted dates
 1 package (8 ounces) dried figs
 1 package (8 ounces) dried apricots
 ½ pound walnuts
 1 package (15 ounces) raisins
 1 jar (4 ounces) chopped candied citron
 1 cup sifted all-purpose flour
 3 teaspoons pumpkin-pie spice
 1 teaspoon salt
 4 eggs
 1 cup firmly-packed light brown sugar
 ½ pound ground suet
2½ cups soft white bread crumbs (5 slices)
 ½ cup brandy
 ½ cup corn syrup
 Eggnog Sauce (recipe follows)

1. Butter a 10-cup mold; dust evenly with granulated sugar, tapping out any excess.
2. Chop dates, figs, apricots and walnuts into small pieces. Combine with raisins and candied citron in a very large bowl.
3. Sift flour, pumpkin-pie spice and salt onto wax paper.
4. Beat eggs and brown sugar in large bowl of electric mixer at high speed, 3 minutes, until fluffy; lower speed and mix in ground suet, bread crumbs, brandy and corn syrup. Stir in flour mixture until well blended.
5. Pour egg mixture over fruits and nuts and stir until well blended. Spoon into prepared mold. Cover with lid of mold or with foil, or a double thickness of wax paper and fasten with string to hold tightly.
6. Place mold on a rack or trivet in a kettle or steamer (or, make a doughnut shape of crumpled foil to fill bottom of kettle to serve as a rack); pour in boiling water to half the depth of pudding mold; cover tightly.
7. Steam 5½ hours, or until pudding is firm and a long skewer inserted in center comes out clean. (Keep water boiling gently during entire cooking time, adding more boiling water, if needed.)
8. Cool pudding in mold 30 minutes. Loosen around edge with a knife; invert onto wire rack. Serve with Eggnog Sauce.
9. To reheat: Follow directions for Steamed Date-Walnut Pudding

EGGNOG SAUCE

Makes about 2 cups.

 2 egg yolks
 ½ cup sugar
 1 tablespoon flour
 Dash of salt
 2 tablespoons heavy cream
 ¼ cup (½ stick) butter or margarine, softened
 2 tablespoons brandy
 ½ cup heavy cream

1. Beat egg yolks and sugar until thick and lemon-colored in top of double boiler; stir in flour, salt and the 2 tablespoons cream.
2. Cook over simmering water, adding butter or margarine, 1 tablespoon at a time, stirring constantly, 10 minutes, or until butter melts and sauce thickens. Remove from heat; add brandy; cover; chill.
3. To serve: Beat remaining cream until stiff in a small bowl; fold into chilled egg mixture. Serve sauce with Holiday Plum Pudding.

YANKEE FRUIT COBBLER

Bake at 400° for 50 minutes.
Makes 8 servings.

 6 medium-size apples
1½ cups sugar
 ⅓ cup flour
 ½ teaspoon ground nutmeg
 2 cups cranberry-juice cocktail
 2 cups biscuit mix
 ⅔ cup milk
 1 teaspoon grated lemon rind

1. Pare apples, quarter, core and slice into a shallow 8-cup baking dish. Combine 1¼ cups of the sugar, flour and nutmeg in a small bowl; stir in cranberry juice until smooth. Pour over apples; cover.
2. Bake in hot oven (400°) 30 minutes, or until apples are tender.
3. Combine biscuit mix, 2 tablespoons of the remaining sugar, and milk in a medium-size bowl; stir just until evenly moist. Drop by tablespoonfuls in 8 mounds over hot apples. Mix remaining 2 tablespoons sugar and lemon rind in a cup; sprinkle over biscuits.
4. Bake 20 minutes longer, or until biscuits are golden. Serve the cobbler while still warm.

CREME BRULEE

Bake at 300° for 1 hour and 15 minutes.
Makes 4 servings.

2 cups light cream·or table cream
¼ cup granulated sugar
¼ teaspoon salt
2 eggs
1½ teaspoons vanilla
2 tablespoons brown sugar

1. Heat cream to scalding in top of a double boiler over simmering water; stir in granulated sugar and salt; remove from heat.
2. Beat eggs slightly in a medium-size bowl; slowly stir in scalded cream mixture and vanilla. Strain into a broilerproof shallow 3-cup baking dish.
3. Set dish in a large pan; place on oven shelf; pour boiling water into pan to within 1 inch of top of dish.
4. Bake in slow oven (300°) 1 hour and 15 minutes, or until center is almost set but still soft. (Do not overbake; custard will set as it cools.) Remove from water; cool; chill.
5. Just before serving, press brown sugar through a sieve on top of chilled custard. Place dish in a pan of ice. Broil 3 to 4 minutes, or until sugar starts to melt and bubble up. Spoon into dessert dishes.

ORANGE UPSIDE-DOWN PUDDING

Bake at 325° for 30 minutes.
Makes 6 servings.

2 eggs, separated
½ cup sugar
4 tablespoons (½ stick) butter or margarine
¼ cup thawed undiluted frozen orange juice concentrate
½ teaspoon vanilla
2 tablespoons flour
¼ teaspoon salt
1 cup milk

1. Beat egg whites until foamy-white and double in volume in a small bowl; beat in 2 tablespoons of the sugar, 1 tablespoon at a time, until meringue stands in firm peaks.
2. Cream butter or margarine with remaining sugar until fluffy in a medium-size bowl; beat

in egg yolks, thawed orange juice and vanilla.
3. Stir in flour and salt, then slowly stir in milk. Gently stir in meringue until fluffy-smooth; spoon into 6 buttered 6-ounce custard cups.
4. Set cups in a large shallow pan; place on oven shelf; pour boiling water into pan to depth of an inch.
5. Bake in slow oven (325°) 30 minutes, or until tops spring back when lightly pressed with fingertip. Remove cups from pan of water; cool.
6. To unmold, loosen puddings around edge with a knife; invert into serving dishes. Serve warm or cold.

CUSTARD CROWN

Bake at 325° for 2 hours.
Makes 8 servings.

¼ cup golden raisins
1 jar (4 ounces) chopped candied pineapple
¼ cup apricot preserves
2 packages (3 ounces each) ladyfingers
6 eggs
½ cup sugar (for custard)
2½ cups milk
¼ cup Cointreau
1 cup heavy cream
2 tablespoons sugar (for cream)
1 teaspoon vanilla

1. Place raisins in a small saucepan; cover with water. Heat to boiling; remove from heat. Let stand 5 minutes; drain.
2. Chop raisins with pineapple and preserves until almost smooth and pastelike.
3. Butter a straight-side 6-cup mold; line bottom with waxed paper. Separate ladyfingers; lay enough in mold to cover bottom; spread with 3 tablespoons of the fruit mixture. (A spoon makes the job go fast.) Stand more ladyfingers, touching each other, around side of mold to line completely.
4. Beat eggs slightly in a medium-size bowl; stir in the ½ cup sugar, milk and Cointreau.
5. Ladle 1 cup of the custard mixture into mold. Top with another layer of ladyfingers, spread with 3 tablespoons fruit mixture, and pour in ½ cup custard mixture. Continue layering with remaining ladyfingers and fruit and custard mixtures until all are used.
6. Cover mold with foil, transparent wrap or double-thick waxed paper; tie with string.

7. Set mold in a large pan; place on oven shelf; pour boiling water into pan to within 1 inch of top of mold.
8. Bake in slow oven (325°) 2 hours, or until firm on top.
9. Cool on wire rack 1 hour, then chill at least 4 hours, or even overnight.
10. To unmold, loosen dessert around edge with a small knife; invert onto a serving plate; lift off mold.
11. Beat cream with the 2 tablespoons sugar and vanilla until stiff in a medium-size bowl. Fit a fancy tip onto a pastry bag; spoon whipped cream into bag. Press out in ribbons around side of mold and in circles of rosettes on top, building up to a peak.
12. Garnish mold with a tiny wedge of green candied pineapple, if you wish.

MOCHA UPSIDE-DOWN PUDDING

Bake at 350° for 35 minutes.
Makes 6 to 8 servings.

    4 tablespoons (½ stick) butter or margarine
    1 cup sifted all-purpose flour
    ¾ cup sugar
    3 tablespoons instant coffee
1½ teaspoons baking powder
    Dash of salt
    1 egg
    ½ cup milk
    ½ cup instant cocoa mix
1¼ cups boiling water

1. Melt butter or margarine in a small saucepan; cool.
2. Mix flour, ½ cup of the sugar, instant coffee, baking powder and salt in a large bowl.
3. Beat egg slightly in a small bowl; stir in milk and cooled butter or margarine; blend into flour mixture until smooth. Pour into a buttered 6-cup baking dish.
4. Combine cocoa mix and remaining ¼ cup sugar in a small bowl; sprinkle over batter; pour boiling water slowly over top.
5. Bake in moderate oven (350°) 35 minutes, or until center springs back when lightly pressed with fingertip. Cool 15 minutes; spoon into serving dishes, topping each with some of the sauce. Serve the pudding while still warm with cream or vanilla ice cream, if you wish.

RAISIN-BREAD PUDDING

Bake at 350° for 45 minutes.
Makes 4 servings.

    2 cups milk, scalded
    2 tablespoons butter or margarine
    ¼ cup sugar
    2 eggs
    2 teaspoons vanilla
    6 slices raisin bread, cubed

1. Combine milk, butter or margarine, and sugar in a small bowl.
2. Beat eggs slightly in a medium-size bowl; slowly stir in milk mixture and vanilla. Pour over bread in a buttered 4-cup baking dish. Let stand 15 minutes.
3. Set baking dish in a shallow pan; place on oven shelf; pour boiling water into pan to a depth of 1 inch.
4. Bake in moderate oven (350°) 45 minutes, or until puffy-firm. Serve warm with cream.

SPICED BREAD PUDDING

Bake at 350° for 45 minutes.
Makes 6 servings.

    3 cups milk, scalded
    3 tablespoons butter or margarine
    3 cups fresh white-bread crumbs
    ⅓ cup presweetened wheat germ
    ½ teaspoon ground cinnamon
    ¼ teaspoon ground nutmeg
    ¼ teaspoon salt
    3 eggs
    ⅓ cup firmly packed light brown sugar
    1 teaspoon vanilla

1. Combine milk and butter or margarine in a large bowl. Stir in crumbs, wheat germ, spices and salt; let stand 5 minutes; beat til smooth.
2. Beat eggs slightly in a large bowl; stir in brown sugar, vanilla and bread mixture. Let stand 15 minutes. Spoon into 6 six-ounce buttered baking dishes.
3. Set baking dishes in a shallow pan; place on oven shelf; pour boiling water into pan to a depth of 1 inch.
4. Bake in moderate oven (350°) 45 minutes, or until set. Serve warm with whipped cream sprinkled with some presweetened wheat germ.

ZABAGLIONE

Makes about 3 cups.

⅔ cup dry white wine
⅓ cup sugar
4 egg yolks

1. Pour wine over sugar in a large metal bowl set over a saucepan of simmering water. Bottom should not touch the water. (Or use a metal double boiler with a wide top.) Add egg yolks.
2. Cook over simmering water, beating constantly with an electric beater at low speed, 5 minutes, or just until mixture mounds slightly; remove bowl from pan of water at once.
3. Continue beating at low speed 5 minutes longer, or until mixture is almost cold. Serve in stemmed glasses, or cover and chill to serve over fruit. Chill no longer than 3 hours so sauce holds its airy-lightness.

HOLIDAY STEAMED FIG PUDDING

Makes 8 servings.

1 package (8 ounces) dried figs
½ cup (1 stick) butter or margarine
¾ cup sugar
3 eggs
½ cup cream sherry
¼ cup molasses
1 teaspoon ground cinnamon
½ teaspoon salt
4 slices slightly dried bread, crumbled
1 cup chopped pecans
Foamy Sauce (recipe follows)

1. Rinse figs; drain. Place in a small saucepan and cover with water. Heat to boiling; reduce heat and simmer 35 minutes. Remove from liquid and cool until easy to handle; chop into tiny pieces.
2. Beat butter or margarine, sugar and eggs together in a large bowl of mixer, at high speed for 3 minutes, until light and fluffy.
3. Stir in sherry, molasses, cinnamon and salt (mixture will look curdled). Add bread crumbs, figs and pecans; stir until well-blended.
4. Grease a 4-cup mold; sprinkle with sugar. Spoon mixture into mold. Cover the top of mold with a double thickness of foil; tie foil around mold with a string to seal tightly.

5. Place mold on a rack or trivet (or make a "ring" of crumpled foil) in a kettle or steamer; pour in boiling water to half the depth of pudding mold; cover kettle tightly.
6. Steam 3 hours, or until a long thin metal skewer inserted near center comes out clean. (Keep water boiling gently during entire cooking time, adding more boiling water, if needed.)
7. Cool mold 5 minutes; loosen pudding around edge with a knife; unmold onto serving plate; cool slightly. Spoon Foamy Sauce over and serve.
NOTE: Pudding can be made ahead of time and stored, when cool, wrapped in foil. To reheat pudding, keep wrapped in foil; place on cooky sheet; heat in moderate oven (350°) for 20 minutes.

FOAMY SAUCE

Makes about 3 cups.

1 egg
⅓ cup butter or margarine, melted
1½ cups 10X (confectioners') sugar
1 teaspoon vanilla
1 teaspoon rum extract
1 cup heavy cream

1. Beat egg until thick in a medium-size bowl; gradually beat in melted butter or margarine until well-blended. Stir in 10X sugar with vanilla and rum extract until smooth.
2. Beat cream until stiff in a second bowl. Fold cream into sugar mixture. Chill until serving time. Spoon some sauce over pudding and pass the remaining sauce in a bowl.

PEACH IMPERATRICE

Makes 6 servings.

1 cup cooked regular rice
1½ cups milk
1 can (1 pound, 13 ounces) sliced cling peaches, drained
½ cup sugar
1 envelope unflavored gelatin
3 egg yolks
1 cup heavy cream

1. Combine rice and 1 cup of the milk in a small saucepan. Heat slowly, stirring constantly,

until all milk is absorbed; spoon into a bowl.
2. Set aside 8 to 10 peach slices; mash remainder in a small bowl.
3. Mix sugar and gelatin in a medium-size saucepan; beat in egg yolks, peach puree and remaining ½ cup milk. Heat slowly, stirring constantly, to boiling; fold into rice mixture. Chill, stirring often, until completely cold.
4. Beat cream until stiff in a medium-size bowl. Fold into chilled peach mixture; spoon into a 6-cup mold. Chill several hours, or until firm.
5. Unmold onto a serving plate. Garnish with additional whipped cream and saved peaches.

QUEEN OF PUDDINGS

Bake at 350° for 1 hour.
Makes 6 servings.

4 eggs
¾ cup sugar
Dash of salt
¼ teaspoon ground cinnamon
2 teaspoons vanilla
1 tablespoon butter or margarine, melted
4 cups milk
4 cups cubed white bread (10 slices)
1 cup apricot preserves
½ cup strawberry preserves

1. Separate 2 eggs; reserve egg whites. Combine egg yolks, remaining 2 eggs, ½ cup of sugar, salt, cinnamon, vanilla and butter or margarine in a large bowl; stir in milk. Place bread cubes in a lightly buttered 8-cup baking dish; pour egg mixture over the bread cubes and let stand for 15 minutes.
2. Set dish in a baking pan; place on oven rack; pour boiling water into pan to depth of one inch.
3. Bake in moderate oven (350°) 50 minutes, or until knife inserted ½ inch from edge of pudding comes out clean. (Center will be almost set, but still soft. Do not overbake, for custard will set as it cools.)
4. Beat egg whites until foamy-white and double in volume in a small bowl; beat in remaining ¼ cup sugar, 1 tablespoon at a time, until meringue stands in firm peaks.
5. Spoon ½ cup apricot preserves over hot pudding. Using a pastry bag with a large notched tip, press meringue into puffs on top of pud-

ding, as close together as possible, so no pudding shows. (This will keep the pudding from overcooking.) Place in same pan of hot water.
6. Bake in moderate oven (350°) for 10 minutes, or just until peaks turn golden; cool completely, at least 2 hours.
7. Just before serving: Melt remaining apricot and strawberry preserves in separate saucepans over low heat. Strain separately through a sieve; cool slightly. Carefully drizzle apricot preserves and strawberry preserves over meringue.

WINE JELLY WITH FRUITS

Makes 8 servings.

3 cups water
1 three-inch piece of stick cinnamon
3 whole allspice
1 package (6 ounces) lemon-flavored gelatin
1 cup dry white wine
1 can (about 11 ounces) mandarin-orange segments, drained
1 can (1 pound) purple plums, drained and pitted
1 can (1 pound) apricot halves, drained
Maraschino cherries
Mint leaves

1. Heat water with cinnamon stick and allspice to boiling in a small saucepan; remove spices.
2. Dissolve gelatin in boiling water in a bowl; stir in wine; keep at room temperature.
3. Place an 8-cup mold in a pan of ice and water; pour 1 cup of gelatin mixture into mold and chill until as thick as unbeaten egg white. Arrange mandarin-orange segments in a pattern in gelatin; chill until sticky-firm.
4. Pour 1½ more cups of the room-temperature gelatin into mold and chill until as thick as unbeaten egg white. Arrange purple plums in a pattern in gelatin; chill until sticky-firm.
5. Pour remaining room-temperature gelatin into mold and chill until as thick as unbeaten egg white. Fill the centers of apricot halves with maraschino cherries and arrange in a pattern in gelatin. Chill in refrigerator at least 4 hours.
6. To unmold: Loosen jelly around edges with a knife; dip mold very quickly in and out of a pan of hot water. Wipe water off mold; shake gently to loosen. Cover with plate; turn upside down; lift off mold. Garnish with mint.

CARAMEL CUPS

Bake at 325° for 50 minutes.
Makes 6 servings.

1 cup sugar
6 tablespoons water
2½ cups milk
6 eggs
2 egg yolks
¼ teaspoon salt

1. Combine ½ cup of the sugar and 4 table-spoons of the water in a small heavy saucepan. Heat slowly to boiling, then cook, without stir-ring, just until mixture turns golden. (Watch carefully, for it will caramelize quickly.) Very slowly stir in remaining 2 tablespoons water.
2. Pour about 1 tablespoonful of the hot cara-mel mixture into each of 6 six-ounce custard cups. Tip and turn cups quickly to coat bottom and sides thinly. Let stand while preparing the custard.
3. Heat milk very slowly to scalding in a medi-um-size saucepan.
4. Beat whole eggs and egg yolks slightly in a large bowl; stir in remaining ½ cup sugar and salt; slowly stir in scalded milk. Strain into a 4-cup measure; pour into caramel-coated cups.
5. Set cups in a large pan; place on oven shelf; pour boiling water into pan to within 1 inch of top of cups.
6. Bake in slow oven (325°) 50 minutes, or until center is almost set but still soft. (Do not over-bake; custard will set as it cools.) Remove cups from water; cool. Chill at least 4 hours.
7. To unmold, loosen custards around edges with a small knife; invert onto dessert plates. (Shake cups, if needed, to loosen custards at bottom.) Garnish each with fresh or thawed frozen peach slices, if you wish.

FLOATING ISLAND

Bake at 275° for 25 minutes.
Makes 6 servings.

3 eggs
Dash of salt
6 tablespoons sugar (for meringue)
2 cups milk
¼ cup sugar (for custard)
1 teaspoon vanilla

1. Butter a 6-cup ovenproof mixing bowl or deep baking dish; sprinkle with sugar, then tap out any excess.
2. Separate eggs, placing whites and yolks in separate medium-size bowls.
3. Beat egg whites with salt until foamy-white and double in volume. Sprinkle in the 6 table-spoons sugar, 1 tablespoon at a time, beating all the time until sugar completely dissolves and meringue stands in firm peaks. Spoon the me-ringue into prepared bowl, smoothing carefully against the side.
4. Set bowl in a baking pan; place on oven shelf; pour boiling water into pan to depth of about an inch.
5. Bake in very slow oven (275°) 25 minutes, or until firm and golden. Remove at once from water; cool; chill.
6. While meringue bakes, scald milk slowly in the top of a double boiler over direct heat. Beat egg yolks with the ¼ cup sugar until light and fluffy; very slowly stir in scalded milk; pour back into top of double boiler.
7. Cook, stirring constantly, over simmering water 10 minutes, or until custard thickens slightly and coats spoon; remove from heat. Stir in vanilla; cool; chill.
8. When ready to serve, place several spoonfuls of the custard into a shallow dish. Invert me-ringue into dish, then pour remaining custard around meringue. Garnish with small spoonfuls of your favorite jelly, if you wish. For serving, spoon meringue into dessert dishes, then spoon custard over top.

KITCHEN TIP: HOW TO SEPARATE EGGS

1. To separate an egg, first get out two small bowls. Then, holding the egg in one hand, tap it sharply in the middle with a knife or on the edge of one of the bowls.
2. Hold the egg over one bowl; pull the shell apart and tilt the shell so that the yolk remains in half of shell.
3. Pour yolk back and forth from one half of the shell to the other until all white runs into one bowl. Drop the yolk into the second bowl.
4. To separate more than one egg for a recipe, use two fresh bowls for each egg, following the same 1-2-3 method.

CHERRY CHEESE PIE

Bake at 350° for 10 minutes.
Makes 1 nine-inch pie.

- 1 package (about 7 ounces) vanilla wafers, crushed
- ½ cup (1 stick) butter or margarine, melted
- 1 package (8 ounces) cream cheese, softened
- 1 can (14 or 15 ounces) sweetened condensed milk
- ⅓ cup lemon juice
- 1 teaspoon vanilla
- 1 can (1 pound, 5 ounces) cherry pie filling
- ½ teaspoon almond extract
- 1 cup heavy cream

1. Blend vanilla-wafer crumbs with melted butter or margarine in a medium-size bowl. Press over bottom and side of a 9-inch pie plate.
2. Bake in moderate oven (350°) 10 minutes, or until set. Cool completely on a wire rack.
3. Beat cream cheese until smooth in a large bowl; slowly beat in condensed milk, then lemon juice and vanilla. Spread evenly in shell.
4. Blend cherry pie filling and almond extract in a medium-size bowl; spoon over cheese filling. Chill at least 3 hours.
5. Just before serving, beat cream until stiff in a medium-size bowl; spoon in a ring around edge on pie.

MACADAMIA NUT PIE

Bake at 325° for 1 hour and 10 minutes.
Makes 1 nine-inch pie.

- ½ package piecrust mix
- 4 eggs
- ⅔ cup sugar
- ¾ cup light corn syrup
- ¼ cup honey
- 3 tablespoons butter or margarine, melted and cooled
- ½ teaspoon vanilla
- 1¼ cups chopped macadamia nuts

1. Prepare piecrust mix, following label directions, or make pastry from your favorite single-crust recipe. Roll out to a 12-inch round on a lightly floured pastry cloth or board; fit into a 9-inch pie plate. Trim overhang to ½ inch; turn under, flush with rim; flute for a stand-up edge.

2. Combine eggs, sugar, corn syrup, honey, butter or margarine and vanilla in large bowl of electric mixer; beat about 5 minutes at medium speed, or until light and frothy. Stir in nuts.
3. Pour nut mixture into prepared pastry shell.
4. Bake in slow oven (325°) 1 hour and 10 minutes, or until crust is golden and filling is set at edges but still slightly soft in center. (Do not overbake.) Cool completely on a wire rack. Garnish with whipped cream and additional chopped macadamia nuts, if you wish.

CRANBERRY-PEACH PIE

Bake at 400° for 45 minutes.
Makes 1 nine-inch pie.

- ¾ cup sugar
- 2 tablespoons flour
- 1 teaspoon grated lemon rind
- ¼ teaspoon ground cinnamon
- 2 cans (about 1 pound each) sliced cling peaches, drained
- 2 cups fresh cranberries, washed and stemmed
- 1 package piecrust mix
- 1 egg, well beaten
- ½ cup 10X (confectioners') sugar
- 2 teaspoons water

1. Mix sugar, flour, lemon rind and cinnamon in a medium-size bowl; add peaches and cranberries. Toss lightly to coat fruit.
2. Prepare piecrust mix, following label directions, or make pastry from your favorite double-crust recipe. Roll out half to a 12-inch round on a lightly floured pastry cloth or board; fit into a 9-inch pie plate; trim overhang to ½ inch. Spoon cranberry-peach mixture into prepared pastry shell.
3. Roll out remaining pastry to an 11-inch round; cut a fancy design or several slits near center to let steam escape; cover pie. Trim overhang to ½ inch; turn edges under, flush with rim; flute to make a stand-up edge.
4. Mix egg with 1 tablespoon water in a bowl; brush over pastry for a rich glaze when baked.
5. Bake in hot oven (400°) 45 minutes, or until top is golden-brown and juices bubble up. Cool on a wire rack.
6. While pie is still warm, mix 10X sugar with water until smooth in bowl. Drizzle over pie.

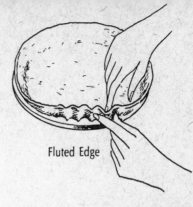

Fluted Edge

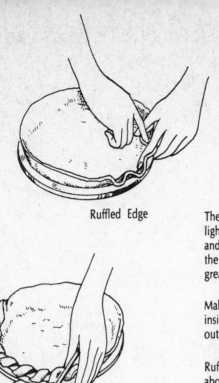

Ruffled Edge

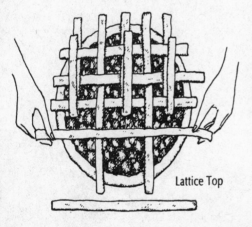

Rope Edge

The real beauty of any pie lies in its tasty filling and light, flaky crust. But appearance is important, too, and here we show you numerous ways to heighten the eye appeal of your favorite pies—without a great deal of effort.

Make a Fluted Edge: Press right forefinger along inside of rim between thumb and forefinger on outside. Repeat about every inch.

Ruffled Edge: Place left thumb and forefinger about 1/2 inch apart on the inside of rim, and with right forefinger on the outside, pull pastry in.

Rope Edge: Twisting slightly, press a slim pencil (or wooden skewer) diagonally into pastry all around edge to make even, widely spaced ridges.

For a Lattice Top to Use on Cherry Pie: Cut pastry strips from leftover piecrust dough. Lay half the strips evenly across top of filled pie. Handle carefully to avoid stretching or tearing dough. Then weave the first cross strip, over and under, through center. Each time you add another strip, fold back every other right-angle strip.

Lattice Top

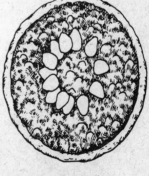

Cream Cheese Petals

Decorative Piecrusts and Trims

One-Crust Pie Edging

Cream Cheese Petals: Beat a bit of sugar and spice into cream cheese; measure level teaspoonfuls and push off spoon with your thumb. Place the petals, rounded sides up, in a double ring on top of a fruit-filled tart.

Cheese Curls: Shave thin strips from a small block of process Cheddar, using a vegetable parer or knife. Roll the strips around your finger; slide off gently and chill. Pile onto an apple pie.

Braided Edge: Cut thin pastry strips from leftover piecrust dough. Braid three, piecing enough together to go around pie plate. Brush pastry rim with water; press braid on top.

Double Scallop

Double Scallop: Press the tip of a teaspoon into pastry rim in two even rows, one close to edge of pie plate, the other a little further in.

Braided Edge

For a Fancy One-Crust Pie Edging: Fit the bottom crust into pie plate, leaving an overhang of 1½ inches. With scissors to speed up the job, snip even saw-tooth cuts all around and fold edge over filling toward center.

Cheese Curls

LEMON MERINGUE PIE

Bake the shell in a 450° oven for 8 to 10 minutes. Bake the meringue puffs at 425° for 3 to 5 minutes.
Makes 1 eight-inch pie.

½ **package piecrust mix**
1⅓ **cups sugar (for filling)**
⅓ **cup cornstarch**
¼ **teaspoon salt**
1¾ **cups water**
4 **eggs, separated**
2 **tablespoons butter or margarine**
1 **tablespoon grated lemon rind**
½ **cup lemon juice (about 4 lemons)**
¼ **teaspoon cream of tartar**
½ **cup sugar (for meringue)**

1. Prepare piecrust mix, following label directions, or make pastry from your favorite single-crust recipe. Roll out to a 10-inch round on a lightly floured pastry board; fit into an 8-inch pie plate. Trim overhang to ½ inch; turn under, flush with rim. Flute edge or scallop the edge with an inverted teaspoon, pressing down hard for each cut to form design.
2. Bake in hot oven (450°) 8 to 10 minutes, or until golden brown; cool.
3. Combine 1⅓ cups sugar, cornstarch and salt in a medium-size pan; gradually stir in water.
4. Cook over medium heat, stirring constantly, until mixture comes to boiling and is thickened. Boil 1 minute. Remove from heat.
5. Beat egg yolks slightly in a small bowl; slowly blend in about ½ cup of the hot cornstarch mixture; slowly stir back into remaining mixture in saucepan. Cook, stirring constantly, over low heat 2 minutes; remove from heat. (Do not overcook.) Stir in butter or margarine, lemon rind and lemon juice; pour into cooled pastry shell. Cover with plastic wrap; refrigerate until cold, about 3 hours.
6. Beat egg whites with cream of tartar until foamy-white and double in volume in a medium-size bowl; sprinkle in remaining ½ cup sugar, 1 tablespoon at a time, beating all the time until sugar dissolves completely and meringue stands in firm peaks.
7. Using a pastry bag with a large notched tip, press meringue into 10 to 12 large puffs on a greased and lightly floured cooky sheet. If you do not have a pastry bag, you can spoon the meringue into puffs on a floured cooky sheet.
8. Bake in hot oven (425°) 3 to 5 minutes, or just until peaks turn golden. Cool on cooky sheet. When the puffs are cool, carefully place on the cold pie with a small spatula. Garnish with lemon slices, if you wish.

BLACK BOTTOM PIE

Bake shell at 400° for 15 minutes.
Makes 1 nine-inch pie.

½ **package piecrust mix**
2 **tablespoons cornstarch**
1¼ **cups sugar**
3 **cups milk**
6 **egg yolks, well beaten**
1½ **teaspoons vanilla**
2 **squares unsweetened chocolate, melted**
1 **envelope unflavored gelatin**
¼ **cup cold water**
3 **tablespoons rum**
4 **egg whites**

1. Prepare piecrust mix, following label directions, or make pastry from your favorite single-crust recipe. Roll out to a 12-inch round on a lightly floured pastry board; fit into a 9-inch pie plate. Trim overhang to ½ inch; turn under, flush with rim; flute to make a stand-up edge. Prick shell well with a fork.
2. Bake in hot oven (400°) 15 minutes, or until pastry is golden. Cool completely in pie plate on a wire rack.
3. Combine cornstarch and ¾ cup of the sugar in a medium-size saucepan: stir in milk slowly. Cook over low heat, stirring constantly until thickened. Blend a small amount of the hot mixture into beaten egg yolks; add to hot mixture in saucepan. Cook 2 minutes longer, stirring constantly, until custard coats spoon. Remove from heat; stir in vanilla.
4. Measure out 2 cups of the custard into a medium-size bowl; stir in chocolate; cool. Pour into baked pastry shell. Chill.
5. Soften gelatin in water in a custard cup; add to remaining hot custard; stir until dissolved. Stir in rum. Place bowl in a larger bowl partly filled with ice and water to speed setting. Chill, stirring often, until slightly thickened.
6. Beat egg whites until foamy-white and double in volume in a medium-size bowl; beat in

remaining ½ cup sugar, 1 tablespoon at a time, until meringue stands in firm peaks.

7. Fold meringue into chilled gelatin mixture; chill again just until mixture mounds. Spoon over chocolate layer.

8. Chill several hours, preferably overnight, until firm. Garnish with whipped cream and chocolate sprinkles, if you wish.

PINWHEEL PUMPKIN PIE

Bake at 425° for 15 minutes, then at 350° for 35 minutes.
Makes 1 nine-inch pie.

- ½ package piecrust mix
- 2 eggs
- 1 can (1 pound) pumpkin
- ½ cup granulated sugar
- ½ cup firmly packed brown sugar
- 1 teaspoon ground cinnamon
- ¼ teaspoon ground cloves
- ¼ teaspoon ground nutmeg
- 1 teaspoon salt
- 1 tall can evaporated milk
- 1 can (1 pound, 13 ounces) sliced cling peaches
- 1 jar (12 ounces) peach preserves

1. Prepare piecrust mix, following label directions, or make pastry from your favorite single-crust recipe. Roll out to a 12-inch round on a lightly floured pastry board; fit into a 9-inch pie plate. Trim overhang to ½ inch; turn under, flush with rim; flute to make a stand-up edge.

2. Beat eggs slightly in a large bowl; stir in pumpkin, granulated and brown sugars, cinnamon, cloves, nutmeg, salt and evaporated milk. Pour into prepared pastry shell.

3. Bake in hot oven (425°) 15 minutes. Lower oven temperature to moderate (350°); continue baking 35 minutes, or until custard is almost set but still soft in center. (Do not overbake; custard will set as it cools.) Cool pie completely on a wire rack.

4. Drain syrup from peach slices; pat fruit dry with paper toweling.

5. Heat preserves until hot in a small saucepan; press through a sieve into a small bowl. Holding each peach slice on a fork, dip into preserves, then arrange in a ring around edge on pie. Chill the pie well until serving time.

PARISIENNE FRUIT TART

Bake at 400° for 20 minutes.
Makes 8 servings.

- 1 package (10 ounces) frozen patty shells
  Sugar
- 1 cup milk
- 1 cup heavy cream
- 1 package (4 ounces) vanilla-flavor soft dessert mix
- 2 medium-size bananas
- 2 tablespoons lemon juice
- ⅓ cup apricot preserves
- 2 cups seedless green grapes, washed (¾ pound)
- 1 can (8¼ ounces) sliced pineapple, drained

1. Remove patty shells from package. Thaw at room temperature one half hour.

2. Place rounds of pastry, overlapping slightly, lengthwise on a lightly floured surface. Roll to a 16x4-inch rectangle. (If patties separate, moisten with a few drops of water.) Place on an ungreased large cooky sheet; trim edges evenly; prick well with fork; chill 30 minutes.

3. Reroll trimmings thinly; cut into ⅓-inch-wide strips about 4 inches long; brush with water; press ends together to make rings. Brush rings with water, then dip in sugar; place on cooky sheet along with rectangle of pastry. Bake pastry and pastry rings in hot oven (400°) 10 minutes. Remove rings to wire rack; reserve for decoration. Bake pastry rectangle 10 minutes longer, or until golden-brown. Remove to rack; cool.

4. Combine milk, ¼ cup of the cream and dessert mix in a small deep bowl; beat, following label directions. Chill 15 minutes. Peel and cut bananas into ¼-inch-thick slices. Sprinkle with half the lemon juice.

5. Split pastry into two layers. Place bottom layer on long serving dish or board; spread with about ⅔ of soft dessert; arrange banana slices on long side edges; spread with remaining dessert mix. Top with second pastry layer. Heat apricot preserves with remaining lemon juice until melted in small saucepan; cool slightly. Brush all over tart.

6. Beat remaining cream until stiff in a small bowl; spread over top of pastry. Arrange rows of grapes in cream, starting at outer edges. Cut pineapple slices in half and place in center. Complete the garnish with reserved pastry rings.

WALNUT PIE

Bake at 375° for 40 minutes.
Makes 6 servings.

½ cup butter or margarine, at room
    temperature
1 cup firmly packed dark brown sugar
1 cup dark corn syrup
4 eggs, lightly beaten
    Pinch of salt
1 teaspoon vanilla
1 unbaked eight-inch or nine-inch pie shell
1 cup coarsely chopped walnuts

1. Preheat the oven to 375°.
2. Cream together the butter or margarine and
brown sugar in a mixing bowl. Blend in the
syrup. Beat in the eggs.
3. Add the salt and vanilla to the mixture and
pour into the pie shell. Sprinkle walnuts over
the top.
4. Bake 40 minutes, or until filling is firm.

NECTARINE RASPBERRY TURNOVERS

Bake at 375° for 25 minutes.
Makes 12 turnovers.

Sour-Cream Pastry:
3 cups sifted all-purpose flour
2 tablespoons sugar
1 cup (2 sticks) butter or margarine
1 cup dairy sour cream
Filling:
¼ cup sugar
1 cup peeled, pitted and thinly sliced
    nectarines (about ½ pound)
1 package (10 ounces) quick thaw frozen
    raspberries, thawed and drained
    Water
    Sugar

1. Make Sour-Cream Pastry—Measure flour and
sugar into a medium-size bowl. Cut in butter or
margarine with a pastry blender until mixture is
crumbly; add sour cream. Mix lightly with a fork
until dough clings together and starts to leave
sides of bowl. Gather dough together with
hands and knead a few times. Wrap dough in
wax paper; chill several hours, or overnight.
2. Make Filling just before baking—Sprinkle
sugar over nectarines in a small bowl; toss with

a fork to mix well; add the well-drained raspberries. Preheat oven to hot (400°).
3. Divide dough in half. Keep one half refrigerated until ready to use. Roll out other half to
a 15x10-inch rectangle; trim edges even with
pastry wheel or sharp knife. Cut into six 5-inch
squares. Place about 2 tablespoons filling on
each square; moisten edges with water; fold
over to make a triangle. Crimp edges with a
fork to seal. Lift onto ungreased cooky sheet.
4. Reroll trimmings; cut into small leaves and
rounds with a truffle cutter or pastry wheel.
Brush tops of pastries with water; decorate with
pastry cutouts; make 1 or 2 small gashes in top
of each triangle to let steam escape. Sprinkle
each turnover with sugar.
5. Lower oven temperature to moderate (375°)
as soon as you put turnovers in. Bake 25 minutes, or until puffed and rich brown in color;
remove to wire rack to cool. Serve warm. Repeat with remaining pastry and filling.
NOTE: If you wish to bake only 6 turnovers,
shape and fill second half of pastry. Place in a
single layer on a cooky sheet; freeze. When
frozen, wrap in foil or transparent wrap. When
ready to use, bake as directed, increasing baking time by about 5 minutes. There is no need
to defrost.

GLAZED APPLE CHEESE PIE

Makes 6 servings.

1 three-ounce package cream cheese
1 tablespoon milk or dairy sour cream
1 baked nine-inch pie shell
6 large apples that hold their shape as they
    cook, such as Rome or Delicious
1½ cups plus two tablespoons water
1 cup sugar
1 three-inch piece stick cinnamon
1 teaspoon grated lemon rind
2 tablespoons lemon juice
2 tablespoons cornstarch
    Red food coloring

1. Soften the cream cheese with the milk or
sour cream and spread over the bottom of the
pie shell.
2. Peel the apples and cut into eighths. Place
1½ cups of the water and the sugar in a saucepan and bring to a boil. Drop in the apple

pieces and cinnamon stick and simmer until apples are barely tender but not broken.

3. With a slotted spoon, remove apple pieces. Drain and let cool. Discard cinnamon stick. Measure 1¼ cups of the apple syrup.

4. Add the lemon rind and lemon juice to apple syrup. Mix together the cornstarch and remaining water. Stir into apple syrup mixture. Bring to a boil, stirring, and cook two minutes over very low heat, stirring constantly. Color faintly pink with food coloring.

5. Fill the pie shell with the apple pieces, arranging the top layer in' an attractive pattern. Spoon glaze over the apples. Serve at room temperature. Garnish with whipped cream, if you wish.

(Pie will have formed a syrup.) With a baster or spoon, remove syrup to a 1-cup measure. (You should then have about ¾ cup, depending on the fruit.)

5. Melt remaining ¼ cup sugar in a small heavy saucepan. Heat very slowly until sugar melts into a colorless liquid, then turns golden-brown color and is caramelized. Stir in the reserved fruit syrup from the tart. Boil the syrup rapidly until it is reduced to about ½ cup. It will be slightly thickened. Take care it does not scorch as you are boiling.

6. Just before serving, spoon warm caramel sauce evenly over tart, reserving one tablespoon. Spoon whipped cream onto center; drizzle reserved caramel sauce over.

UPSIDE DOWN PEAR TART

Bake at 425° for 30 minutes.
Makes 8 servings.

    7 firm, ripe pears (about 3½ pounds)
    ¾ cup sugar
    ½ cup (1 stick) butter or margarine
    ½ package piecrust mix
    ½ cup heavy cream, whipped

1. Pare, halve and core pears. Slice 7 or 8 halves crosswise and on an angle, each into 4 or 5 slices, keeping slices intact. Arrange as whole halves in a 9-inch-deep pie plate, rounded side down and stem ends toward center; trim one pear half to a round to fit center. Slice remaining pears into ½-inch slices; arrange on top to fill plate.

2. Melt ½ cup of the sugar over medium-high heat in a small heavy skillet; continue heating until sugar caramelizes and turns golden-brown. Remove from heat; quickly stir in butter or margarine until almost melted, then pour over pears.

3. Prepare piecrust mix, following label directions or make pastry from your favorite single-crust recipe. Roll out to a 10-inch round on a lightly floured pastry board; place on top of pears. Do not attach to edge.

4. Bake in hot oven (425°) for 30 minutes, or until crust is golden and pears are done. (Place a piece of foil under pie in case juices should bubble out.) Cool on wire rack about 30 minutes. Invert onto a serving platter with a rim.

LEMON BLOSSOM TART

Bake shell at 400° for 20 minutes.
Makes 8 servings.

    1 package piecrust mix
    2 tablespoons sugar (for pastry)
    4 eggs
    ½ cup sugar (for filling)
    2 teaspoons grated lemon rind
    ¼ cup lemon juice
    4 tablespoons (½ stick) butter or margarine
    1 cup heavy cream

1. Combine piecrust mix, the 2 tablespoons sugar and 1 of the eggs in a medium-size bowl. Mix with a fork until well-blended.

2. Press evenly over bottom and up side of a 9x1½-inch layer-cake pan, making rim even with edge of pan. (Shell will be thicker than standard piecrust.) Prick well all over with a fork.

3. Bake in hot oven (400°) 20 minutes, or until golden. Cool completely in pan on a wire rack.

4. Beat remaining 3 eggs slightly in the top of a double boiler; stir in the ½ cup sugar, lemon rind and juice, and butter or margarine. Cook, stirring constantly, over hot (not boiling) water 10 minutes, or until very thick. Pour into a medium-size bowl; chill until completely cold.

5. Beat cream until stiff in a medium-size bowl; fold into lemon custard.

6. Remove pastry shell carefully from pan; place on a large serving plate; spoon lemon filling into shell. Garnish with additional whipped cream, if you wish. Chill 1 hour before serving.

BLACKBERRY PINEAPPLE TURNOVERS

Bake at 375° for 25 minutes.
Makes 12 turnovers.

  1 can (8 ounces) pineapple tidbits
  1 tablespoon cornstarch
  2 tablespoons sugar
    Dash ground nutmeg
    Dash ground cloves
  2 cups fresh or frozen blackberries
  1 recipe Sour-Cream Pastry

1. Drain pineapple into a 1-cup measure; add water to make ½ cup. Combine with cornstarch, sugar, nutmeg and cloves in a small saucepan; mix well.
2. Stir in blackberries. Bring to boiling, stirring constantly; bubble 1 minute. Remove from heat, stir in pineapple. Cool.
3. Make Sour-Cream Pastry; fill and bake turnovers, following directions for Nectarine Raspberry Turnovers (page 68).

CIDER APPLE PIE

Bake at 425° for 25 minutes.
Makes 6 servings.

  ½ pound dried apples
  3 cups cider
  ½ cup sugar
  ½ teaspoon ground cinnamon
  ¼ teaspoon ground nutmeg
    Pastry for a two-crust nine-inch pie
  2 tablespoons butter or margarine

1. Place the apples and cider in a saucepan. Bring to a boil and simmer until apples are tender and plump.
2. Combine the sugar, cinnamon and nutmeg; add to apples and cook 10 minutes longer. The apples should have absorbed most of the juice. Cool slightly.
3. Preheat the oven to 425°.
4. Line a 9-inch pie plate with half the pastry. Pour in the apple filling. Roll remaining pastry into a rectangle and cut into ½-inch strips. Dot apple mixture with butter or margarine and make a lattice of pastry.
5. Bake 25 minutes, or until filling is bubbly and pastry is golden brown. Remove from oven; serve warm. Or, let the pie cool completely.

DEVONSHIRE APPLE PIE

Bake at 350° for 40 minutes.
Makes 1 nine-inch pie.

  ¾ cup granulated sugar
  ¼ cup firmly packed brown sugar
  1 tablespoon flour
  ½ teaspoon ground cinnamon
  ¼ teaspoon ground nutmeg
  1 teaspoon lemon juice
  ⅛ teaspoon salt
  ½ cup dairy sour cream
  4 medium-size apples, pared, quartered, cored and sliced (4 cups)
  1 nine-inch unbaked pastry shell
    Streusel Topping (recipe follows)

1. Mix granulated and brown sugars, flour, spices, lemon juice and salt in a large bowl; stir in sour cream and apples. Spoon into pastry shell; sprinkle with Streusel Topping.
2. Bake in moderate oven (350°) 40 minutes, or until apples are tender and topping is golden. Cool.
3. Just before serving, garnish with Cheddar cheese slices, if you wish.

STREUSEL TOPPING: Mix ½ cup flour and ½ cup firmly packed brown sugar in a small bowl. Cut in 4 tablespoons (½ stick) butter or margarine with pastry blender until crumbly.

DOUBLE APPLE TURNOVERS

Bake at 375° for 25 minutes.
Makes 12 turnovers.

  2 cups chopped, pared apples (2 small)
  ¾ cup applesauce
  ¼ cup firmly packed light brown sugar
  ½ teaspoon ground cinnamon
  ¼ teaspoon ground mace
  2 tablespoons raisins
  1 recipe Sour-Cream Pastry (page 68)

1. Combine apples, applesauce, sugar, cinnamon, mace and raisins in a small bowl. Mix well with a fork.
2. Make Sour-Cream Pastry; fill and bake turnovers, following directions for Nectarine Raspberry Turnovers.

COCONUT CREAM PIE

Bake shell at 425° for 15 minutes.
Makes 1 nine-inch pie.

½ package piecrust mix
⅔ cup sugar
¼ cup cornstarch
3 tablespoons flour
½ teaspoon salt
2½ cups milk
2 eggs
2 tablespoons butter or margarine
1 teaspoon vanilla
1½ cups heavy cream
1 cup grated fresh coconut
OR: 1 can (about 4 ounces) flaked coconut
½ cup apricot preserves

1. Prepare piecrust mix, following label directions, or make pastry from your own single-crust recipe.
2. Roll out to 12-inch round on a lightly floured pastry board; fit into a 9-inch pie plate. Trim overhang to ½ inch; turn under, flush with rim; flute edge. Prick shell well with a fork.
3. Bake in hot oven (425°) 15 minutes, or until golden; cool.
4. Mix sugar, cornstarch, flour and salt in the top of a double boiler; stir in milk. Cook over simmering water, stirring constantly, until mixture thickens; cover. Cook 15 minutes longer; remove from heat.
5. Beat eggs slightly in a small bowl; slowly stir in about half of the hot mixture; stir back into remaining mixture in double boiler. Cook over simmering water, stirring constantly, 3 minutes; remove from heat. Stir in butter or margarine and the vanilla. Pour into a medium-size bowl; cover surface with wax paper or transparent wrap; chill.
6. Beat ½ cup of the cream until stiff in a small bowl. Fold the 1 cup grated (or 1 cup flaked) coconut into chilled pudding, then fold in whipped cream.
7. Whip ½ cup of the apricot preserves until soft in a small bowl; spread in cooled pastry shell; spoon cream filling on top. Chill at least 2 hours, or until firm enough to cut.
8. Just before serving, beat cream until stiff in a small bowl. Spread decoratively on top of pie; garnish with shredded coconut or rest of flaked coconut. Slice and serve.

LEMON TARTLETS VERONIQUE

Bake shells at 375° for 22 minutes.
Makes 1 dozen.

2 cups sifted all-purpose flour
3 tablespoons sugar
½ teaspoon salt
½ cup (1 stick) butter or margarine
¼ cup shortening
6 tablespoons water
Lemon Filling (recipe follows)
1 pound seedless green grapes, stemmed and halved
1 cup apple jelly, melted and cooled
1 cup heavy cream

1. Sift flour, sugar and salt into a medium-size bowl. Cut in butter or margarine and shortening with a pastry blender until mixture is crumbly.
2. Sprinkle water over top; mix lightly with a fork until pastry holds together and leaves side of bowl clean. Turn out onto a lightly floured pastry board; knead just until smooth; divide into 12 even pieces. Chill dough at least an hour for easier handling.
3. Press each piece of dough into a fluted 3-inch tart-shell pan to cover bottom and side evenly. Fit a small piece of wax paper over pastry in each pan; pour uncooked rice or beans on top to hold pastry in place during baking. Set tart-shell pans in a large shallow pan.
4. Bake in moderate oven (375°) 10 minutes; remove from oven. Lift out wax paper and rice or beans; return pans to oven. Bake 12 minutes longer, or until pastry is golden. Cool shells completely in pans on wire racks, then remove carefully from pans.
5. Spoon Lemon Filling into each shell; arrange grape halves, cut sides up, on top to form rosettes; brush grapes with apply jelly; chill.
6. Just before serving, beat cream until stiff in a medium-size bowl. Attach a fancy tip to a pastry bag; fill bag with whipped cream; decorate tops of tarts. Chill until serving time.

LEMON FILLING: Beat 6 eggs slightly in the top of a large double boiler; stir in 1 cup sugar, ½ cup (1 stick) butter or margarine, 2 teaspoons grated lemon rind and ⅓ cup lemon juice. Cook, stirring constantly, over hot, not boiling, water 15 minutes, or until very thick. Pour into a medium-size bowl; cover, chill. Makes 3 cups.

GATEAU DE POIRES HELENE

Preparation time: 12 minutes.
Makes 12 servings.

- 1 **eight to nine-inch baker's angel food cake**
- 1 **can (1 pound) pear halves**
- ¼ **cup creme de cacao**
- 2 **containers (6¾ ounces each) frozen whipped topping dessert, thawed**
- 1 **can (5 ounces) vanilla pudding**
- 1 **cup flaked coconut**
  Fudge topping (from an 11-ounce jar)
  Toasted coconut (optional)

1. Split cake horizontally into 3 layers. Drain pears. Combine 2 tablespoons of the juice with creme de cacao, drizzle over cake layers.
2. Press about 1 cup of the whipped topping into a medium-size bowl; stir in vanilla pudding and flaked coconut. Then spread this filling on two of the cake layers.
3. Stack filled layers with plain layer on top, on serving plate. Arrange pear halves with narrow ends to the center on top layer.
4. Pipe remaining whipped topping onto side of cake and between pears on top. Just before serving, spoon fudge topping over the pears. To top off the cake, just sprinkle with toasted coconut, if you wish.
NOTE: To toast coconut, spread 2 tablespoons coconut onto small cooky sheet; place in slow oven (325°) about 8 to 10 minutes.

CHOCO-RASPBERRY ICE BOX CAKE

Preparation time: 15 minutes.
Chilling time: Several hours.
Makes 8 servings.

- ½ **cup raspberry preserves**
- 2 **tablespoons orange-flavored liqueur**
- 2 **packages (two ounces each) whipped topping mix**
- 1 **cup cold milk**
- 2 **teaspoons vanilla**
- 1 **package (8½ ounces) chocolate wafers**

1. Combine raspberry preserves and orange flavor liqueur in a cup. Prepare topping mix with milk and vanilla, following label directions.
2. Spread raspberry mixture on one side of a chocolate wafer and whipped topping on second side. Make 10 cooky stacks of coated cookies until all cookies are coated.
3. Turn the first cooky stack on its side on serving tray; spread last cooky with whipped topping and press on the next stack. Repeat until all cookies are joined in a long roll.
4. Frost cake generously with whipped topping. Fit a pastry bag with a fancy tip. Fill bag with remaining whipped topping. Pipe a double row of swirls down the center of cake. Pipe remaining whipped topping around sides and bottom of cake. Spoon remaining raspberry preserves down the top of cake.
5. Chill at least 3 hours. To serve: Cut cake into thin diagonal slices.

BLACK-BOTTOM RUM PIE

Preparation time: 20 minutes.
Chilling time: Several hours.
Makes one eight-inch pie.

- 2 **cans (5 ounces each) vanilla pudding cup**
- 2 **cans (5 ounces each) chocolate pudding cup**
- 2 **tablespoons rum**
- 1 **envelope unflavored gelatin**
- ¼ **cup water**
- 1 **eight or nine-inch prepared graham cracker pie shell**
- 1 **container (9 ounces) non-dairy whipped topping**
  Chocolate curls

1. Place vanilla pudding in a small bowl; combine chocolate pudding and rum in another small bowl, reserve.
2. Soften gelatin in the water in a 1-cup measure. Place over hot, not boiling, water in a small saucepan until gelatin dissolves.
3. Stir 2 tablespoons of the dissolved gelatin into the vanilla pudding; add remaining gelatin mixture to chocolate-rum mixture. Place bowl containing chocolate-rum mixture in a pan of ice and water to speed-set. Chill, stirring often, until as thick as unbeaten egg white; pour into prepared graham cracker pie shell.
4. Add 1 cup non-dairy whipped topping into vanilla pudding mixture; fold in carefully; pile on top of chocolate mixture; chill until firm.
5. To serve: Decorate with remaining non-dairy whipped topping and chocolate curls.

JUBILEE CREAM

Makes 4 servings.

1 package vanilla-flavor whipped-dessert mix
1 teaspoon almond extract
½ cup toasted slivered almonds
1 cup cherry pie filling (from a 1-pound, 5-ounce can)

1. Prepare dessert mix with milk and water, following label directions; stir in almond extract. Chill at least an hour.
2. In a small bowl, mix almonds into cherry pie filling. Fill each of 4 parfait glasses this way: Holding glass on its side, spoon about ¼ cup of the cherry mixture into glass, then spoon chilled dessert mixture carefully into the other half of glass.

PEACH MELBA BAVARIAN

Preparation time: 10 minutes.
Chilling time: Several hours.
Makes 8 servings.

1 package (3 ounces) lemon-flavored gelatin
1 envelope unflavored gelatin
¼ cup cold milk
1 cup boiling water
2 egg yolks
⅓ cup sugar
Dash of salt
2 tablespoons peach brandy
1 package (10 ounces) frozen peach slices, cut into small pieces
1 cup heavy cream
Bottled raspberry sundae topping

1. Combine lemon-flavored gelatin and unflavored gelatin in the container of an electric blender; pour cold milk over and allow to stand 1 minute.
2. Pour boiling water into container; cover; whirl at low speed 2 minutes; remove cover. Add egg yolks, sugar, salt and peach brandy.
3. Replace blender cover and remove feeder cap. Whirl at high speed, gradually adding pieces of frozen peaches until mixture is smooth. Add cream if you have room in container; whirl until well-blended. (If you don't have room, stir with a rubber scraper until cream is well-blended.)

4. Pour mixture into a 5-cup ring mold. Chill at least 2 hours before serving.
5. To serve: Run a thin-bladed knife around edges of mold. Dip mold quickly in and out of a pan of hot water. Invert onto serving plate. Spoon bottled raspberry topping over.

QUICK CHERRY STRUDEL

Preparation time: 30 minutes.
Baking time: 25 minutes.
Makes 1 large strudel.

1 package (10 ounces) frozen ready-to-bake puff pastry shells
1 can (1 pound, 5 ounces) prepared cherry pie filling
2 teaspoons grated lemon rind
¼ cup packaged bread crumbs
1 tablespoon milk
¼ cup sliced unblanched almonds
2 tablespoons sugar

1. Preheat oven to 450°.
2. Let pastry shells soften at room temperature for 20 minutes.
3. Combine cherry pie filling and lemon rind in a small bowl; reserve.
4. On a cloth-lined, well-floured board, overlap pastry shells in a straight line. Using a floured stockinette-covered rolling pin, press down onto the pastry shells. (Note: You may use a floured rolling pin without the stockinette, but flour the rolling pin frequently to prevent the pastry shells from sticking.) Roll out from center of pastry shells to a 16x22-inch rectangle, being careful not to tear pastry.
5. Sprinkle pastry with bread crumbs.
6. Spoon cherry pie filling down length of pastry closest to you into a 2-inch strip and within 2 inches of edges. Fold in sides.
7. Using the pastry cloth, grasp at both ends and gently lift the cloth up and let the strudel roll itself up. Carefully slide onto a cooky sheet, keeping seam side down, and form into a horseshoe shape.
8. Brush top generously with milk; sprinkle on almond slices, pressing well in order to keep in place. Then sprinkle with sugar.
9. Lower oven heat to hot (400°), 25 minutes or until golden brown; let cool on baking sheet 10 minutes. Serve the strudel while still warm.

MOUSSE AU CHOCOLAT

Preparation time: 10 minutes.
Chilling time: 1 hour.
Makes 8 servings.

   1 package (8 ounces) semisweet chocolate
      pieces
   ⅓ cup hot, brewed coffee
   4 egg yolks
   2 tablespoons apricot brandy, or any fruit-
      flavored brandy
   4 egg whites
   3 tablespoons sugar

1. Combine chocolate pieces and hot coffee in the container of an electric blender; cover container. Whirl at high speed for 30 seconds, or until smooth.
2. Add egg yolks and brandy to container; cover. Whirl at high speed 30 seconds.
3. Beat egg whites until foamy and double in volume in a medium-size bowl; gradually beat in sugar until well-blended. Fold in chocolate mixture until no streaks of white remain. Spoon the prepared mousse into 8 parfait glasses or a serving bowl.
4. Chill at least 1 hour. To serve: Garnish with whipped cream and party candy-patties (from an 11-ounce package).

EASY CHEESE FRUIT TARTS

Preparation time: 5 minutes.
Chilling time: 30 minutes.
Makes 6 servings.

   2 packages (3 ounces each) cream cheese
   ½ cup milk
   1 can (9¾ ounces) raspberry or pineapple
      dessert mix
   1 package (5 ounces) pastry tart shells (6 to
      a package)
      Fresh or canned fruits for garnish
      Chopped pistachio nuts or almonds

1. Beat cream cheese until soft in a small bowl. Gradually beat in milk; continue beating until completely smooth. Add dessert mix; stir with a spoon 30 seconds, or until thickened.
2. Spoon into tart shells, dividing evenly. Decorate with fruits of your choice; sprinkle with nuts, if you wish. Chill until ready to serve.

QUICK SPICY RICE PUDDING

Makes 6 servings.

   1 cup packaged precooked rice
   2¾ cups milk
   1 package (about 3½ ounces) vanilla pudding
      and pie filling mix
   2 tablespoons raisins
   ⅛ teaspoon ground nutmeg
   1 tablespoon cinnamon-sugar

1. Combine rice and 2 cups of the milk in a medium-size saucepan; heat to boiling, stirring constantly; reduce heat; cover. Cook over low heat 5 minutes.
2. Add pudding mix to remaining milk; mix well. Stir into rice mixture. Bring to boiling, stirring constantly; stir in raisins and nutmeg. Turn into serving dish. Sprinkle with cinnamon-sugar. Chill 15 minutes, or until serving time.

RASPBERRY SNOW WITH CUSTARD SAUCE

Makes 6 servings.

   1 package (3 ounces) raspberry-flavor gelatin
   ¾ cup boiling water
   10 ice cubes
   2 egg whites
      Custard Sauce (recipe follows)

1. Dissolve gelatin in boiling water in container of electric blender; add ice cubes; blend at low speed until ice melts and gelatin starts to thicken. Add egg whites. (Save yolks for Custard Sauce.)
2. Blend at high speed until mixture triples in volume and starts to hold its shape.
3. Spoon into a 5-cup mold. Chill 1 hour, or until firm.
4. Just before serving, loosen around edge with a knife; dip mold very quickly in and out of a bowl of hot water. Cover with a plate; turn upside down; lift off mold. Serve with sauce.

CUSTARD SAUCE: Beat egg yolks with 2 tablespoons sugar and 1 teaspoon cornstarch in top of a double boiler; beat in 1 cup milk. Cook, stirring constantly, over hot, not boiling water 10 minutes, or until custard thickens slightly. Remove from heat; strain into a bowl; stir in 1 teaspoon vanilla. Cover; chill. Makes 1¼ cups.

COFFEE PARFAIT PIE

Preparation time: 10 minutes.
Chilling time: 1 hour.
Makes 8 to 10 servings.

3 pints coffee ice cream
3 envelopes unflavored gelatin
⅓ cup golden rum
1 tablespoon instant coffee
⅔ cup water
1 eight- or nine-inch prepared graham
  cracker pie shell
Chocolate syrup
Pecan halves

1. Remove ice cream from freezer to room temperature.
2. Sprinkle gelatin into rum in a 1-cup measure to soften, 5 minutes.
3. Combine instant coffee and water in a small saucepan, bring to boiling. Add softened gelatin; stir until completely dissolved.
4. Turn ice cream into a large bowl. Beat with electric mixer at high speed, until smooth. Pour gelatin in, all at once, while beating constantly and guiding mixture into beater with rubber spatula. (Mixture sets softly almost at once.)
5. Spoon into pie shell, mounding high in center, or pipe through a pastry bag fitted with a decorative tip. Chill until ready to serve. Just before serving, drizzle chocolate syrup over top and garnish with pecans, if you wish.

VIENNESE FRUIT TART

Makes 8 servings.

1 can (6 ounces) frozen orange juice
  concentrate
1 nine-and-a-half inch packaged sponge
  layer (6 ounces)
  OR: 1 nine-inch baked pastry shell
1 package (3 ounces) cream cheese
2 cans (5 ounces each) vanilla pudding
1 banana
1 can (1 pound) apricot halves
½ pint fresh raspberries
  OR: 1 package (10 ounces) frozen red
  raspberries, thawed and drained
½ pound (1 cup) seedless green grapes
½ cup apple jelly

1. Heat orange juice concentrate in a small saucepan just until hot.
2. Place cake on serving dish; brush generously with orange juice.
3. Stir cream cheese until very soft in a small bowl; stir in pudding. Spread mixture into bottom of cake layer.
4. Cut banana lengthwise into quarters; halve each quarter. Arrange 5 pieces of banana on pudding layer to form section dividers. Arrange apricot halves, raspberries and green grapes in a pattern in each section.
5. Heat apple jelly in a small saucepan until melted; brush over all fruits. Chill.

DIVIDENDS FOR DESSERTS

Tutti-frutti parfait: Drain a 1-pound can of fruit cocktail; combine fruit with a 6-ounce can of frozen concentrate for pineapple juice. Layer into parfait glasses with vanilla ice cream. Top each with a maraschino cherry.

Peanut cream: Blend ¼ cup cream-style or crunchy peanut butter with ¼ cup milk; stir in ½ cup prepared marshmallow cream. Spoon over plain custard.

Vermont cream mold: Line a 6-cup mold or bowl with waxed paper. Then fill with alternating layers of ladyfingers and butter-pecan ice cream, drizzling each layer with maple-flavor pancake syrup. Cover and freeze at least 4 hours. Serve with whipped cream and pecans.

Double butterscotch: Fix butterscotch pudding with a mix, following label directions; cool slightly. Fold in some butterscotch-flavor pieces. They'll give pudding a delightful crunch.

Sandwich stacks: Spread large thin chocolate wafers with chocolate-chip mint ice cream; stack three high; freeze.

Prune-whip topper: Beat 1 cup cream until stiff; fold in a 4-ounce jar of baby-pack strained prunes and 1 teaspoon grated orange rind. Spoon over squares of plain cake.

Jiffy Melba: Top plain vanilla pudding (made from a mix) with sliced fresh peaches and a dollop of red-raspberry preserves.

8-CALORIE CHOCOLATE KISSES

Bake at 275° for 20 minutes.
Makes 9 dozen kisses at 8 calories each.

3 egg whites
½ teaspoon cream of tartar
1 cup fine granulated sugar
2 tablespoons unsweetened cocoa powder

1. Beat the egg whites in small bowl of electric mixer until foamy. Add cream of tartar; beat until soft peaks form. Gradually beat in sugar. Fold in cocoa 1 tablespoon at a time.
2. Use a measuring teaspoon to drop level spoonfuls of meringue mixture on nonstick cooky sheets.
3. Bake in a slow oven (275°) 20 minutes. Let cool slightly on sheets before removing. Store in a very dry place.

LOW-CALORIE NESSELRODE PIE

Makes 10 servings at 147 calories each.

1 envelope unflavored gelatin
½ cup sugar
¼ teaspoon salt
3 tablespoons cornstarch
1¾ cups skim milk
3 egg yolks, beaten
3 egg whites, stiffly beaten
Sugar substitute to equal ¾ cup sugar
1 teaspoon vanilla
2 teaspoons brandy or rum extract
3 maraschino cherries, chopped
Low-Calorie Graham Cracker Pie Shell

1. Combine gelatin, sugar, salt and cornstarch in top of double boiler. Add skim milk slowly. Place over simmering water.
2. Cook, stirring constantly, until thickened. Blend half the hot mixture into the egg yolks in a small bowl. Stir back into remaining mixture. Cook 2 minutes.
3. Remove from heat; pour into a medium-size bowl; cool. Stir in sugar substitute, extracts and cherries. Chill over ice and water until mixture mounds slightly when spooned.
4. Fold in stiffly beaten egg whites until no streaks of white remain. Pour into pie shell. Refrigerate about 4 hours, or until set.

STRAWBERRY GLAZED CHEESE PIE

Makes 10 servings at 177 calories each.

Graham-Cracker Crust (recipe follows)
½ cup water
½ cup instant nonfat dry milk (powder)
½ cup sugar
4 eggs
¼ teaspoon salt
1 tablespoon lemon juice
1 teaspoon vanilla
¼ cup flour
1 pound cottage cheese (any kind)
Jeweled Fruit Glaze (recipe follows)

1. Prepare a 9-inch pie plate, using Graham-Cracker Crust.
2. Combine water, dry milk powder, sugar, eggs, salt, lemon juice, vanilla, flour and cottage cheese in container of an electric blender; whirl until smooth. (Or you may sieve cheese into a bowl, add remaining ingredients, then beat with a rotary beater until smooth.) Pour into prepared crust.
3. Bake in very slow oven (250°) for 1 hour. Turn oven off and leave pie in oven for 1 hour longer, then remove from oven; cool.
4. Top the cooled pie with Jeweled Fruit Glaze. Chill until glaze is set.

GRAHAM-CRACKER CRUST

Grease side and bottom of pan recommended in recipe with 1 tablespoon butter or margarine (or 2 tablespoons diet margarine). Sprinkle with ½ cup of graham-cracker crumbs; press firmly into place. Chill 1 hour, or until firm.

JEWELED FRUIT GLAZE

Wash and hull 1 pint of strawberries. Leave whole or cut in half lengthwise. Arrange on top of pie, cut side down. Blend 1 tablespoon cornstarch with 1 cup of water in a small saucepan. Cook over low heat, stirring constantly, until clear and thickened. Add enough liquid sweetener to equal ½ cup sugar. Stir in a few drops red food coloring. Cool slightly. Spoon over strawberries.
VARIATIONS: Canned waterpack pitted red cherries, frozen or fresh blueberries, or canned pineapple chunks may be glazed the same way.